¿Quienes son sus papas? For generations, this has been a question Laredoans boldly ask when meeting someone unfamiliar. It is meant to place the new acquaintance into a recognizable chain of Laredo's early families, who, over decades, have become extensive. This "short-cut" genealogy placed the individual within a matrix of history, religion, and social status. It didn't matter whether the name was European, Asian, or Native American. In some instances, the names would lead back to someone related in some way, or at least, recognizable and therefore, "placed" in the social fabric of the community.

In the twenty-first century, this "placing" exercise is becoming slightly more difficult, as Laredo's population has boomed and the original, early families have become more and more distant.

Jerry Thompson's ability to "short-cut" the colorful, centuries-old history of this community into a solid chronicle by means of photographs and short narratives is a feat of skillful research and writing prowess. We are impressed, educated, surprised, sometimes appalled, and always entertained by the narrative of this book. The new chapters added to this volume bring even more contextual contours to Laredo's long and fascinating history. And, as Laredoans, we are able to place our own lives in the historical fabric of this vibrant community. To know the city in the present era, we must comprehend and appreciate our historic past.

From the feel-good "Bill Batey and the Boys of '56" that traces the triumph of an amazing group of exceptional athletes from Martin High School, to "Aldo and the Fall of the Old Party" that carefully chronicles fascinating details of the watershed collapse of Laredo's powerful and legendary Independent Club, Thompson is at his best.

The Webb County Heritage Foundation is grateful, once again, to Jerry Thompson for this "gift of history" that helps us encounter the courage, tenacity, and vision of our ancestors.

We are especially grateful to Dr. Thompson, who is donating the profits from sales of this new edition of his *Pictorial History* to help fund the programs and services of the Webb County Heritage Foundation. It is through the generosity of this gift that the history of our community will be safeguarded for future generations to relish and enjoy.

Margarita Araiza
Executive Director,
Webb County Heritage Foundation

Laredo
A Pictorial History

Jerry Thompson

Design by
Paula Hennigan Phillips

THE
DONNING COMPANY
PUBLISHERS

The Donning Company Publishers
731 S. Brunswick
Brookfield, MO 64628

Lex Cavanah, *General Manager*
Nathan Stufflebean, *Production Supervisor*
Pamela Koch, *Senior Editor*
Stephanie Danko, *Graphic Designer*
Kathy Snowden Railey, *Project Research Coordinator*
Katie Gardner, *Marketing & Production Coordinator*

Jim Railey, *Project Director*

Library of Congress Cataloging-in-Publication Data

Names: Thompson, Jerry D.
Title: Laredo : a pictorial history / by Jerry Thompson ; design by Paula
  Hennigan Phillips.
Description: Brookfield, MO : Donning Company Publishers, 2017. | "Expanded
  third printing 2017." | Includes bibliographical references and index.
Identifiers: LCCN 2017002150| ISBN 9781681841045 (hard cover : alk. paper) |
  ISBN 9781681841052 (soft cover : alk. paper)
Subjects: LCSH: Laredo (Tex.)—History—Pictorial works. | Laredo
  (Tex.)—Pictorial works.
Classification: LCC F394.L2 T46 2017 | DDC 976.4/462—dc23
LC record available at https://lccn.loc.gov/2017002150

Printed in the United States of America at Walsworth

Contents

For Sara and Jeremy

Acknowledgments

Since this book was first published in 1986, a considerable amount of serious scholarship on the history of the city has been completed. Foremost among the scholars is Robert D. Wood, author of a wonderful book, *Life in Laredo: A Documentary History of the Laredo Archives* (Denton: University of North Texas Press, 2004). In addition, Wood has prepared a very helpful comprehensive index to the Laredo Archives. He has also translated and published hundreds of documents from this invaluable collection relating to death and taxes, genealogy, municipal correspondence, Native Americans, and numerous other subjects.

Anyone interested in the politics of Laredo will want to consult Roberto R. Calderon's lengthy dissertation at the University of California, Los Angeles (1993), "Mexican Politics in the American Era, 1846–1900, Laredo, Texas." A former student of mine and a native Laredoan, George T. Díaz, has written a wonderful book: *Border Contraband: A History of Smuggling across the Rio Grande* (Austin: University of Texas Press, 2015). A former resident of the border city and a scholar of all things Aggie, John A. Adams, has an equally appealing book entitled *Conflict and Commerce on the Rio Grande: Laredo, 1755–1953* (College Station: Texas A&M University Press, 2008). William F. Walsh II has written a marvelously illustrated book on the life of the colorful Hamilton Cobb Peterson, a former officer in the frontier army and lawyer in Laredo during the early days of Reconstruction (Privately published, 2012).

I am grateful to countless individuals for their invaluable assistance in the preparation of this new edition of *Laredo: A Pictorial History*. When I first came to Laredo fifty years ago, I had only a small inkling of the rich history and culture of Laredo and the South Texas border. Since that time, hundreds of individuals have opened their doors and their hearts. I am eternally grateful. It has been a long and joyous journey.

At the Laredo Public Library, Joe Moreno and then Rene La Perriere, special collections librarians, were most helpful. At Texas A&M International University, Jeanette Hatcher, special collections librarian, along with her fine professional staff, also went out of their way to be helpful. A number of individuals submitted to lengthy interviews that made possible some of the details in the two chapters on the Boys of '56 and the election of Aldo Tatangelo and the fall of the Old Party in 1978. Former *Laredo Morning Times* reporters and editors, Bill Bouldin and Carmini Dinini, who lived through the rough years of political transition, were not only helpful but also inspirational. María Eugenia "Meg" Guerra, daring former editor and publisher of *LareDOS: A Journal of the Borderlands,* was gracious enough to read and comment on the chapter on Aldo and the Old Party.

Before his passing in 2014, Bill Batey not only sat for hours to converse about his days on the hardwood at Texas A&M University, but also his spectacular coaching career at Martin and Nixon and high schools in Corpus Christi. The more I learned about Batey, the more I came to admire him and appreciate the game of basketball. Good friends John Valls and Andy Santos, both of whom were so valuable in bringing the '56 championship to Martin High School, were also gracious with their time. The same was true of Aldo Tatangelo, who not only agreed to several interviews, but also consequently donated his papers to TAMIU.

I am grateful to Irene Vidaurri Zubeck for sharing rare images she carefully and lovingly restored from the collection of James C. Kirkpatrick and Federico E. Vidaurri. Principal Guillermo Pro and Assistant Principal Elias Alonzo, as well as their staff at Martin High School, were always professional and went out of their way to be helpful. José E. Arredondo, a Marine Corps veteran of the horrors of Peleliu and Okinawa, not only agreed to come to my graduate class on the history of World War II, but also shared a striking image of young Laredoans on their way to war. Ricardo Alexander helped to locate a photo of a Laredo hero from World War II, Sgt. John B. Alexander. Richard Geissler went out of his way to locate a photo he took of Manuel "Chaca" Ramirez, a hell-raising Laredo reformer and agitator, if there ever was one. A colleague at TAMIU, Lila Canizales, was her usual gracious self in helping to put me in contact with boxing heroes Gaby and Orlando Canizales.

At TAMIU, I am thankful for the invaluable assistance of Rosanne Palacios, Vice President for Institutional Advancement, who took time to make inquiries and open doors that would otherwise have remained closed. Billy F. Coward, former president of Texas A&I at Laredo, took the time to dig out a couple of historic images from his photo album. Everyone at the Laredo Chamber of Commerce was eager to share albums and images. The staff at the Benson Latin American Library at the University of Texas at Austin never seemed to grow tired of answering email inquiries relating to the Manuel Ramirez collection of photographs. Freddie and Violeta Benavides took the time to locate a baseball card of Freddie when he was with the Cincinnati Reds.

Fellow historian Billy Hathorn was gracious in shared images he took of mayors Raul Salinas and Pete Saenz. Former mayor Saul Ramirez was also helpful in providing a photo of himself and President Bill Clinton. In particular, I would like to thank Mayor Betty Flores for sharing her large collection of images from the eight years she served as mayor. No one was more gracious and giving of her time than the former mayor. Will Kruger, information aide in the Austin office of Senator Judith Zaffirini, was helpful. Barrister Armando X. Lopez helped with the identification of individuals.

I owe a particularly large debt to Margarita Ariza, Executive Director at the Webb County Heritage Foundations, as well as Jim Moore, President of the Board of Directors, and Christina Saucedo, Archives Manager, not only for their valuable assistance, but also for their confidence and seemingly endless patience.

Miriam Queensen must also be mentioned and thanked for her editorial expertise. I would like to extend my heartfelt thanks to Steve Harmon, Director of Public Relations at TAMIU, not only for his courtesy and friendship over many years, but also for going out of his way to make recommendations and to be helpful. No one was more helpful and valuable in this new edition than Ana P. Clamont, whose expertise and endless assistance in imaging I could not have done without. I owe a large debt to my colleague at TAMIU for many years, Stanley Green, an authority on José de Escandon and Las Villas del Norte, and who was always eager and willing to share his latest archival discoveries. Green's book on the subject is eagerly awaited.

Lastly, I need to also thank my wife, Sara Amparo Cabello, for her support during the many years I have spent pleasantly mired and muddled in the complex and intriguing history of the Texas-Mexico borderlands.

Jerry Thompson
Regents Professor of History
Laredo, Texas
March 2017

For better or ill, it has been Laredo's destiny to be a gateway. As the pictures and text of this volume make plain, the citizens of Laredo have been touched by almost all of the historical developments of Spain and Mexico—and then Texas and the United States. At times they wished they had been left alone.

Dr. Thompson is a veteran at sifting through the documents of the South Texas past. Here he has drawn upon new sources—the memories of Laredoans and their photo albums. This book is a coming together of the craft of the scholar and those who are the conservers of their community's history.

The result is a chronicle of a town that is without category. Visitors have often puzzled over whether Laredo was American or Mexican. But in truth these are just two of the several forces that have shaped its life. There was a time, in 1840, when Laredoans reflected both sides and tried to create the Republic of the Rio Grande—incidentally giving Laredo a seventh flag, over and above the Six Flags claimed by Texas.

Some of Laredo's history is not to be duplicated elsewhere: a Spanish ranching town that had to contend not only with an inhospitable land and Indians, but with the Texas Revolution where troops from both sides either looted or called for mandatory hospitality, and then the Republic when dissident border rancheros fought against Centralist troops from Mexico, and then even stranger combinations during the Civil War when loyal Confederates from Laredo did battle against Union troops who found Republican allies in Mexico.

All the while, civilization was making measured progress here on the border. One of the benefits was the arrival of first-rate professional photographers—from Hamilton to Garcia to Serrano to Esquivel. They left a record, not only of the spectacular, but of citizens going about the daily business of living.

Their photographs, and the recollections of Laredo's inhabitants, have been put together by Dr. Thompson in a book that we will not just read but linger over. It is a rich visual experience. It is Laredo as it was.

Stan Green
Texas A&M International University

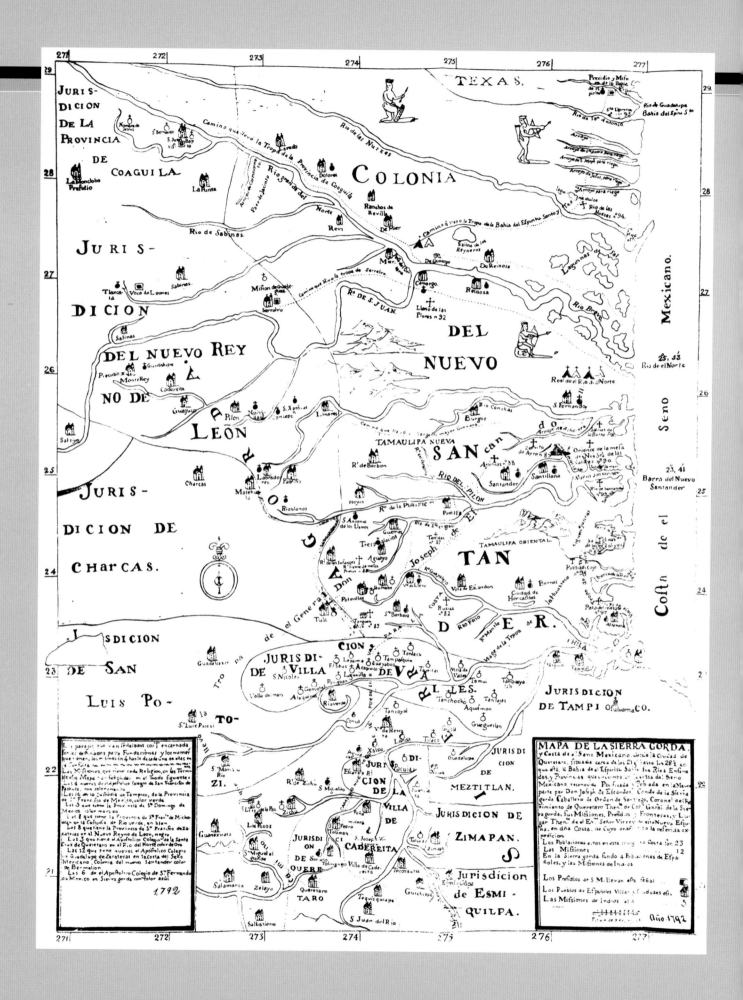

Chapter 1

Don Tomas Sanchez de la Barrera y Garza

Across the river and within sight of Dolores lived Don Tomas Sanchez de la Barrera y Garza. Little is known of the physical appearance of the man but Dona Encarnacion Garcia, who was born in Laredo in 1798, and married Bacilio Benavides, said that Sanchez was "un hombre guero," a man of fair complexion with blue eyes and blond hair.

Sanchez had been born at Valle de Carrizal in Nuevo Leon, near Monterrey in 1709, the son of Tomas Sanchez and Maria Josefa de la Garza. His baptismal date is listed in Monterrey as July 4. Sanchez's early career was in the military serving in the army of the King of Spain on the northern frontier. Later he managed a ranch in the Province of Coahuila. He was reported to have been "fond of his toddy and of the ladies."

While Sanchez was at his ranch near Dolores, he came to learn of a ford about ten leagues upriver near where he was pasturing livestock. The first Spaniard to make definite note of the ford was Jacinto de Leon when he led a detachment of soldiers downriver from the presidio at San Juan Bautista on a reconnaissance in 1745, and observed the easy crossing.

The ford, certainly one of the better ones of the Rio Grande, was called Paso de Jacinto in honor of Jacinto de Leon. The crossing was later called "Paso de los Indios," or Old Indian Crossing, and is located a few hundred yards upriver from Fort McIntosh. Sanchez decided to approach Jose de Escandon with a plan to establish a villa near the ford.

Hearing of Captain General Jose de Escandon's presence in Revilla in 1754, Sanchez journeyed downriver with his petition for the new villa. Escandon was receptive to the petition but had not given up hope of founding a settlement on the Nueces. Sanchez was therefore sent to reconnoiter the area and find a suitable location for a settlement and to report his findings to Jose Vasquez de Borrego at Dolores. Like the others before him, he failed to find an acceptable area to his liking on either side of the river. Sanchez reported this to Borrego who in turn was to contact Escandon. Sanchez's observations about the Nueces country were similar to those of Borrego. The Nueces, as far as the two men were concerned, was not practical for a settlement. Records indicate that Sanchez threatened to give up the entire enterprise if Escandon insisted on a villa on the Nueces.

Giving up his desires for a village on the Nueces, Escandon gave permission to Sanchez to establish his new settlement upriver at the proposed site. Sanchez, like his mentor Borrego, was given the title of captain and a grant consisting of fifteen leagues of land. Because he was able to persaude three other families, besides his own, as to the practicality of founding a new villa, preparations were soon underway.

Crossing his family and their belongings to the north side of the Rio Grande, the caravan assembled and began the trek upriver.

The party moved upriver winding its way through the virgin wilderness, crossing Becerro Creek, passing mesquite thickets and prickly pear patches, and across San Ildefonso Creek. Finally, after crossing Chacon and Zacate Creeks, the pioneers arrived at the location of their new village. The Laredo historian Seb Wilcox gave a beautiful description of the founding of the new villa almost two centuries later as the citizens of the city met in San Agustin Plaza to dedicate a monument to the founder. "As he left the village of Dolores and continued on his way up the north bank of the Rio Grande, he passed over what was then a prairie country, dotted only here and there with clumps of mesquite and huisache trees, and abounding in hills and valleys. When this little party reached the hill to the south of their destination, a beautiful panorama met their eyes. Before them they saw the broad green valley in the sharp bend of the Rio Grande—the location of their future homes."

"But they had little time to admire the beauties of nature. Homes had to be made. They brought the sound of the axe and broke the solitude of the prairie. The stone mason began his work. Adobe bricks were moulded and dried in the sun. Soon jacales were erected, the more fortunate enclosed by stone or adobe walls, others fenced with wooden stakes driven into the ground, and some merely surrounded by bullrushes—all for protection against the frequent raids of the barbarous Indians. Thus was Laredo founded, May 15, 1755."

The settlement was named by Escandon for Laredo, a coastal city in northern Spain on the Bay of Biscay. The new Laredo, however, bore little similarity to its sister city in Spain. Located on a crescent-shaped bay, the beautiful "Costa Esmeralda," Laredo, Spain, with its wide, sandy beaches, crystal-blue waters, and brownish-green mountains of the Cordillera Cantabrica which run to the sea, in no way resembled Laredo, Nuevo Santander.

One of the most important early dates in the history of the small community came on July 22, 1757. It was on this day that Don Jose Tienda de Cuervo, with a small caravan, came riding into town on his inspection tour of the settlements in Nuevo Santander. Jose Tienda de Cuervo went by the impressive title of "Knight of the Order of Santiago, Captain of Dragoons of the city of Vera Cruz, and Judge Inspector of the Gulf of Mexico." The inspector had been sent by Marques de las Amarillas, Viceroy of Mexico. He was assisted on his inspection tour by engineer Agustin Lopez de la Camara Alta and his assistants. Tienda de Cuervo informed Tomas Sanchez that on the following day, July 23, 1757, the inhabitants of the village should appear before him in a brush hut where he had set up headquarters for the purpose of taking depositions concerning the life and environment of this little settlement.

Juan Eusebio Trevino was the first to take the "oath before God and on a cross that he would speak the truth." He was

The map on page 10 of the province of Nuevo Santander was drawn by Alejandro Prieto during the colonial era. It has erroneously been attributed by a number of sources to a young officer in the United States Army during the Mexican War named Robert E. Lee. In reality, Captain Lee probably found a copy of the map in Mexico during the war and it somehow found its way into the Museum of the Confederacy in Richmond, Virginia. (Latin American Collection, University of Texas, Austin)

Jose de Escandon, the colonizer of the Province of Nuevo Santander, was born at Soto la Marina, Spain, in 1700. He came to the new world at the age of fifteen and enrolled in Los Caballeros Encomanderos, a cavalry company stationed in Yucatan. Later he was transferred to Queretaro where he was promoted to lieutenant and married into the noble family of Pedrajo. Largely because of his pacification of the Indians of the gulf coast and the Sierra Gorda of the Sierra Madre Oriental, he was promoted to colonel in 1740 and lieutenant-general a few years later. In 1746, the Audiencia de Mexico commissioned Escandon to establish several small villas in the Province of Nuevo Santander. Camargo, Reynosa, Revilla, Dolores, and Laredo were established between 1749 and 1755. (Laredo Public Library)

The signature of Tomas Sanchez de la Barrera y Garza (1709-1796), the founder of Laredo, is visible at the bottom of this document in the Laredo Archives at St. Mary's University, San Antonio, Texas. Sanchez was born at Valle de Carrizal (Fortin de las Flores) in Nuevo Leon near Monterrey in 1709. Sanchez founded Laredo, which he named after Laredo, Spain, on May 15, 1755. He died suddenly in the eighty-eighth year of his life, and his funeral took place at St. Augustine Church on January 21, 1796. His burial site has been lost with the passage of time, but it is generally thought that he was probably buried in the churchyard of St. Augustine. (St. Mary's University)

followed by Tomas Sanchez and Juan Bautista Sanchez. The questions asked these men and the others which followed were identical. The answers given by the respondents were also similar in nature. Sanchez told the commission that "...the breeding and the keeping of sheep, goats, and cattle" were the principal occupations of the settlers; that great droughts which are experienced between rains "were common and that the rains are so far apart that all crops wither and dry up." Sanchez stated that the settlement had no designated boundary. The settlers therefore pastured "their flocks and herds, each one according to his will, wherever it best suits his convenience."

The settlers had plowed enough land to sow about one hundred pounds of corn on half an acre. Some grain had also been planted. Although the crops had sprouted, they were found in such a "deplorable state, through lack of water," that they did not hope for any harvest.

Sanchez told Tienda de Cuervo that the settlement could subsist and maintain itself solely by the stock which it raised and "that if lands should be given them sufficient to extend the breeding of their stock, he is certain they could maintain themselves, because of the great amount of traffic which they have in them, some selling them here, and others taking them to other parts."

Trevino told of a discovery of a new ford across the Rio Grande "called the San Miguel de la Garza, three leagues downstream from this settlement, so easy that the sheep and goats cross it; by means of which a direct road is open from this settlement to Coahuila and Texas; and over which numerous travelers pass without any difficulty."

The question of Indians was explored in depth by the visiting inspectors. Trevino stated that "the nearest Barbarian Indians are the Borrados and Bocas Prietas, who are some fifty or sixty leagues distant," and whose number he could not estimate; but the common report was that they were many. Juan Bautista Sanchez contradicted Trevino somewhat, stating that the "Indians nearest are Borrados and Carrizos, who are some twenty leagues from this settlement." All who gave depositions agreed that the Indians had caused no trouble. The Apaches sometimes came within a few leagues of the settlement but had been peaceful, and none of the settlers had suffered from their presence. No attempt had been made to bring the Indians into the village since the settlers were having a most difficult time feeding themselves, much less the Apaches or various bands of the Coahuiltecans.

From those settlers who testified, Tienda de Cuervo was able to determine that the settlers possessed very little geographical knowledge concerning the country beyond them. When asked about distances from Laredo to other settlements on the frontier, the respondents gave varying answers. When asked about the Rio Grande, Tomas Sanchez stated that it was called "El Grande del Norte" but that he had no knowledge where its headwaters were "but that it empties into the sea."

A total of eleven families numbering eighty-five individuals had settled in Laredo by 1757. Out of the population, only four men were single. In comparison to the other settlements on the Rio Grande, Laredo was quite small. The population of Reynosa was 470, Camargo 638, Revilla 357, and Mier 400. Livestock were numerous, however. One hundred and one head of cattle were counted, 125 mules, 712 horses, and 9,080 sheep and goats were on the ranch.

Tomas Sanchez was to Laredo what Jose Vasquez Borrego was to Dolores. Herbert Eugene Bolton, the great historian of the Spanish frontier, evaluated Sanchez thus: "The superiority of Sanchez's position over that of his neighbors is manifest. He was a veritable medieval lord." There was little semblance of democracy in the early history of Laredo. The lack of such would deeply scar the community for many years to come and establish a dangerous precedent.

Sanchez owned a large percentage of the livestock: five hundred horses, all the mules, two oxen, fifty cattle, and two hundred sheep and goats. Sanchez, aged forty-eight, was married to Catarina Uribe and became the father of nine children. In the Sanchez household were seven servants who were listed by Tienda de Cuervo along with the donkeys and horses.

Other prominent individuals in the village were Juan Garcia Saldivar, Prudencio Garcia, Joseph Leonardo Trevino, Juan Francisco Garcia, Juan Bautista Sanchez, Agustin Sanchez, as well as Joseph Salinas, Joseph Flores, Pedro Salinas, and Joseph Ramon. The eligible bachelors in the community were Leonardo Garcia, Juan Diego, Joseph Diaz, and Leonardo Sanchez.

Attached to the main report of Tienda de Cuervo was a report by his assistant Agustin Lopez de la Camara Alta. This report gave valuable information concerning the distinctive geographical features of Laredo. "It is situated on the margin of the Rio Grande, or Bravo, on the North Bank, in a plain two leagues in extent, reaching to the hills of Santa Barbara, which meet it with two small arroyos, of which the upper, to the southwest, is called Arroyo de Lomas Altas, and that on the east side, Arroyo de Chacon." The assistant, Lopez de la Camara Alta, continued, "Roads lead out for the Presidio of San Antonio de Bexar, and in the other direction to the Capital of Coahuila, which is Santiago de la Monclova, distant 50 leagues. All the country between the Rio Grande and Nueces, which is wooded, low, with little water, and that which there [is] unhealthy. According to reports of those who have investigated, in some parts of this country they have been four days journeying without finding water, and the horses which have carried them have died."

Laredo, like Dolores, did not have suitable land for irrigation and planting. Corn, beans, and melons were planted in the vegas or the bottomlands along the river. Like the ancient Egyptians who depended on the Nile, the settlers of Laredo to a large extent were at the mercy of the river. Fed by the snows of Colorado and New Mexico, it could become a bestower of life or at other times, when the river flooded, it could become a destroyer, taking property and human life as it roared its way to the Gulf of Mexico. Chalanes, or flat boats, were constructed and provided transportation to the neighboring towns downriver. Salt was brought in from the lower valley and clothing and other necessities arrived from other towns in Nuevo Santander which possessed better transportation links to the civilized world than Laredo. Skins, hides, and tallow were exchanged for the manufactured goods. The waterfront thus became the marketplace of Laredo.

Laredo was also similar to Dolores in that the principal occupation of the settlers became that of raising sheep, goats, cattle, mules and horses. The villa was really the ranch headquarters for Tomas Sanchez. None of the land was privately owned. Escandon had given fifteen "sitios" of pasture land to the town, but not to the individual settlers. The social organization of Laredo in its conception and early history was therefore communal and bore a marked resemblance to the earlier English settlements at Jamestown and Plymouth on the eastern seaboard. Escandon thought that by having the settlers work the land in common, a closer bond of cooperation could be achieved and petty arguments and disputes avoided. Sanchez was, of course, placed in charge of not only the military, but also the civil administration of the village, with a commission and the title of Captain.

No priest was provided for Laredo. Formal religious ceremonies were held only when the priest from Revilla could make his way upriver to Dolores and then Laredo. A petition was sent to the viceroy requesting a permanent priest for the village and asking that funds to pay the priest be provided from the Royal Treasury. Six years later, the wishes of the inhabitants became a reality when a permanent priest arrived in the village.

The citizens of Laredo appear to have impressed Tienda de Cuervo. Months later, after returning to Mexico City, he filed his report to the viceroy stating that Laredo "... is important and it is expedient that it increase in size, for the sake of the crossing from the interior provinces to Texas."

The brush huts would become houses; the village would have its church; the eighty-five citizens would become thousands; the Paso de Jacinto would someday be bypassed by an international highway. Laredo, of all of Escandon's river settlements, would become the largest and most prosperous. The community which was then a gateway to Texas would become a gateway to Mexico. The many citizens of Laredo owe Tomas Sanchez much. He, with his handful of colonists, carved a settlement and a way of life from the wilderness. In the same year that Samuel Johnson published his famous *Dictionary of the English Language*, thirty-four years before the storming of the Bastille, Laredo was founded on that historic day in the summer of 1755.

Tomas Sanchez would continue, although intermittently, to be alcalde of Laredo. Sometime after the death of Dona Catarina, he married the young Teodora Yzaguirre to whom a boy and a girl were born. In the eighty-eighth year of his life, Don Tomas Sanchez died suddenly. His funeral took place on January 21, 1796, from San Agustin Church with high mass by the Reverend Bachiller Jose Manuel Perez. His blood would flow in the veins of hundreds of his descendants just as his memory would remain with others. His grave, unlike his memory however, has been lost in the passage of time.

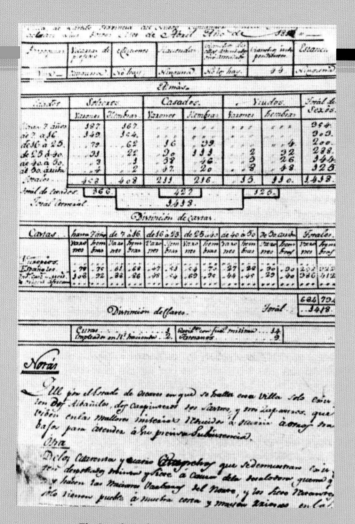

The Laredo Archives is a major source of information for historians desiring to study the first one-hundred years of Laredo history. Shown here is the census of Laredo from the Mexican period, 1819. (St. Mary's University)

In 1812 it appeared briefly as if Laredo would become part of Jose Bernardo Maximiliano Gutierrez de Lara's independent Republic of Texas. Gutierrez de Lara was born at Revilla (Guerrero) on August 20, 1774, and was one of the most important political leaders to emerge from the Rio Grande Frontier. Shown here is Gutierrez de Lara's seal for his independent republic which was doomed to fail. (Institute of Texan Cultures)

The Royal Visit of 1767

By 1767, many of the settlers of Laredo who did not own the land but held it in common, became excited about the possibility of obtaining individual grants. Some asked for an election of officers and the establishment of a municipal government.

Largely because of the reports of Jose de Escandon in 1755, and Tienda de Cuervo in 1757, the Spanish government took up the question of giving the citizens of Nuevo Santander individual land grants. In distant Madrid, Charles III sat on the throne of Spain. Charles, the third of the Spanish Bourbons, was well-schooled in the French concepts of administrative efficiency. Called by historians a model of an eighteenth-century ruler, he was a devoted administrator.

Orders, issued by Charles, came to change the political and administrative make-up of not only the Spanish Empire but the settlements on the remote and isolated northern frontiers. The king directed that certain "reforms in the colony of Nuevo Santander, and a partition of the lands of the established towns, with respect to the primitive settlers and other inhabitants," be implemented. On November 9, 1764, the Viceroy of New Spain received orders from Madrid to proceed with the desired reforms. However, bureaucratic delays in Mexico City slowed the desired changes.

The delay with the land reforms was largely the responsibility of Jose de Escandon. Escandon was quite hesitant about dividing the land until he had found a solution to the Indian problem. Authorities in Mexico City, feeling pressure from Madrid, had on various occasions, urged Escandon to make the desired reforms. Juan Fernando de Palacios, who became interim governor in 1767, had different ideas about land ownership than Escandon, and fearing the establishment of large latifundias, set out to partition the lands.

The viceroy, in hopes of speeding the reforms, appointed a Royal Commission in 1767, who in turn selected Palacios to head the "General Visit of the Royal Commission to the Colonies of Nuevo Santander." Palacios, "Knight of the Order of St. James and Field Marshal of the Royal Armies of his Majesty, Governor and Lieutenant of the Mexican Gulf, Sierra Gorda, their Missions, Garrisons, and Frontiers," was, as his title indicates, well-qualified for the position. On his trek to the frontier, he was accompanied by Secretary of the Royal Council Jose de Ossorio y Llamas, and numerous other minor officials.

Palacios and Ossorio were under orders to "appoint surveyors and experts to review the lands, to survey the town and its jurisdiction, to make necessary arrangements for granting possession of the tracts of land to individual colonists, and to have all transactions properly recorded in order that settlers and missionaries would have clearer titles from the Spanish crown."

The commission was not pleased with what they found in Laredo. Numerous problems had developed. Twelve years had passed since Tomas Sanchez led his little band of settlers through the wilderness to establish the villa, yet practically nothing had been done toward the establishment of a town or the building of a mission. In this, Sanchez had failed in his agreement with Escandon. The Commission was very critical of Sanchez's transgression. On the more favorable side, the Commission was impressed with Sanchez's selection of the location for the villa.

From existing records there is definite evidence to indicate that the authorities in Mexico City were somewhat confused by the status of the Laredo grant. The grants in the lower Rio Grande Valley were much different than the grant given Sanchez. This is the main reason the Commission entered the valley at Laredo. All distinguished visitors had previously entered the valley at Camargo.

Several of the ranchers living on the south bank of the river sent representatives to the Commission to request that the land where they had lived for oven ten years "be included in the jurisdiction surveys of Laredo and that the town commons be surveyed in the vicinity of their homes." Two ranchers inhabiting the south bank of the river, Jose Martinez and Tomas Cuellar, also testified about the impossibility of irrigation in the Laredo vicinity.

When the day came for the division of the land, they would be considered on the same basis as the other settlers. The Royal Commission reported that some of the original settlers, finding Laredo not to their liking, had decided to return to their original homes in Coahuila. Others were making preparations to leave the villa and notified the Commission that they were not interested in receiving land as they too planned to flee for the more civilized provinces of Mexico. For some reason, which was not made clear to Palacios and Ossorio, one man and his family had been expelled from Laredo.

The procedure by which the Royal Commission divided the land was similar in each of the villas on the frontier. At the completion of mass on a spring morning in May of 1767, all the citizens of Laredo were called together. The Commission then informed the citizens about the purpose of their visit to the village and about the procedure by which the land would be surveyed and divided.

The division of the land shows some semblance of democracy, altering the monolithic administrative system which had previously existed. From the citizens of the town, a surveyor, Jose Prudencio Garcia, and two experts, Juan Bautista Villarreal and Miguel Diaz, were chosen. The Commission then named an additional surveyor, Domingo Toboada, to represent the crown. Local officials who were chosen to assist in the division and surveying of the land were usually the older, more knowledgeable citizens of the town.

Once the experts and surveyors were sworn in as "agents of the Royal Commission," three kinds of land were designated: that which could be irrigated, that which would be used for the grazing of herds, and the land for the town commons.

Six leagues were marked off around the town in four directions. These became the jurisdictions, "political sub-division clearly resembling a county." Within each jurisdiction the land would be partitioned into individual plots, and these plots or *porciones* in turn were given to the individual settlers. The amount of land the settlers were to be given was determined by several factors. Included in the criteria was the number of years a person had served the crown either in a military or civilian capacity and seniority, or the number of years the person had lived in the village.

In most of the villas on the frontier, the procedure by which the town plots were surveyed was also similar. In Laredo, a site was selected for the public square or plaza. The plaza was one hundred varas in size (one vara equals 33.33 inches). Two streets were surveyed from each corner of the plaza. The streets were to be ten varas in width. On the streets facing the plaza, plots of land were surveyed for a municipal building, a town jail, and a church. The remaining plots of land facing the plaza were reserved for Tomas Sanchez and other prominent citizens of the villa. Town property was given to the citizens with the explicit understanding that they must build a house on the plot of land.

The next task facing the Royal Commission was the division of the land adjacent to the town. A certain point was selected on the Rio Grande as a place of origin. A cord, fifty varas in length, was then thrown from nineteen to twenty-five times to determine the width of each porcion. The porciones in the jurisdiction of Laredo were larger than in most other villas. This was because Laredo had a smaller number of citizens than the other river communities such as Camargo and Reynosa. Only eighty-nine porciones were laid out in Laredo as compared to 111 in Camargo. Furthermore, of the eighty-nine porciones of Laredo, twenty-three were unassigned due to the lack of settlers desiring land. However, Tomas Sanchez, captain and acknowledged leader of the villa, received two porciones. Other prominent members of the Sanchez family received an additional five porciones. An area north of the Laredo jurisdiction, stretching as far north as the Nueces River, was also placed under the authority of Laredo. The Sanchez family also received a grant of land here, sixty leagues north of Laredo.

The revenue collected from certain porciones was to be used in the building of the church which Sanchez had neglected. Revenues from the ferry service on the river were also to go for the church. A fee of two reales (twenty-five centavos) was charged each passenger, and for each package one real was added. The rates were set by the Commission. Local residents could travel free on the ferry.

The visit by the Royal Commission in 1767 marks the year that the official records of Laredo begin. It is from these records, many preserved as the Laredo Archives, that historians are able to learn of the early history of Laredo.

The recently organized Laredo Volunteer Fire Department gather on a barren St. Augustine Plaza for a fire drill sometime in the late 1880s. Fire hydrants visible on the north side of the plaza along Grant Street had only recently been installed. (Sam N. Johnson Collection, Nuevo Santander Museum)

Chapter 3

The Town

St. Augustine Church had only recently been
completed when this photograph was taken
in 1873. On the left is the original church
which faced south toward the river and was a
small structure only sixteen by one-hundred
and twenty feet in size. It was demolished
shortly after this photo was taken. Father
Alphonse Souchon was responsible for the
new church and had commenced collections
for such in 1866. (Ursuline Sisters)

This lithograph of Laredo showing the recently completed tower of St. Augustine Church
was made for Frank Leslie's Popular Monthly
in 1878, to accompany an article entitled,
"Our Southern Frontier: The East and West
Boundary Line Between the United States
and Mexico," by General Egbert L. Viele.
Viele was no stranger to Laredo as he had
been responsible for the establishment of Fort
McIntosh some thirty years earlier in 1848.
(Frank Leslie's Popular Monthly)

The Ursuline Convent can be seen on the left, and a recently completed St. Augustine Church on the right, in this rare 1873 photograph of Laredo taken from the Mexican side of the Rio Grande. The Convent, which was later demolished, was constructed of native stone and was three stories high. (Ursuline Sisters)

Barrileros gather water on the Mexican side of the Rio Grande in this 1888 photograph taken by Thomas J. Cockrell. The spire of St. Augustine Church rises in the background while the mercantile store of Raymond Martin can be seen just south of the church. (Mexican International Railway Views)

This photograph of Laredo was probably made in the late 1880s. The power plant of the Laredo Waterworks can be seen on the left while the cupola-domed Ursuline Con- vent is visible in the center as well as Flores Avenue leading to the river. The Casa Consis- torial on the south side of St. Augustine Plaza and St. Augustine Church, with its recently completed bell tower, are clearly visible. (Sam N. Johnson Collection, Nuevo Santander Museum)

This view of Laredo was probably taken in 1878 when artists and photographers for Frank Leslie's Popular Monthly *arrived on the border. Besides St. Augustine Church, a number of buildings along Zaragoza are clearly visible including the old Casa Consistorial which was used as a courthouse, city hall, and school. (Sam N. Johnson Collection, Nuevo Santander Museum)*

Before the establishment of the foot and wagon bridge across the Rio Grande in 1889, a ferry operated between Laredo and Nuevo Laredo. Although faded, this photograph is one of the few remaining images of the ferry which can be seen on the Mexican side of the river preparing for its run to the American side. The first ferry at Laredo was operated by Tomas Sanchez shortly after the establishment of the village in 1755. In 1848, when Laredo was temporarily part of Nueces County, a ferry was established under the jurisdiction of the county commissioners. Shortly thereafter, when Laredo became incorporated, control of the ferry passed to the jurisdiction of the community and in the

1880s was the subject of considerable litigation. For many years, public auctions were held on St. Augustine Plaza where bids were asked for the operation of the ferry.

Chalanes, such as the one in this photograph, were also common on the river well into the present century. (Sam N. Johnson Collection, Nuevo Santander Museum)

This faded 1882 photograph is one of the first views of the Laredo skyline from the north. The first Webb County Courthouse, visible in the background, had only recently been completed in May 1882. From 1880 to 1890 the city grew in population from 3,811 to 11,319. By April 1882, about the time this photograph was taken, one hundred buildings costing $120,000, were under way. So rapid was the growth of the town that two-hundred carloads of lumber arrived on the International and Great Northern only to be consumed within a single week. (Sam N. Johnson Collection, Nuevo Santander Museum)

This 1888 view of a "Fonda y Cafe," thought to have been in the eastern outskirts of Laredo near the banks of Zacate Creek, was taken by Thomas J. Cockrell for a small pamphlet published for the Mexican International Railway. (Mexican International Railway Views, Laredo Public Library)

*Citizens with milk containers pose for photographer Thomas J. Cockrell on a thoroughfare leading into Laredo in 1888. Such housing was typical of South Texas and northern Mexico at the time. (*Mexican International Railway Views, *Laredo Public Library)*

This street scene was taken around 1880. The store of S. F. Lamkin can be seen on the left. (Nick Sanchez Collection, Yolanda Parker, Institute of Texan Cultures)

Looking east from Salinas Avenue down Iturbide Street, this rare view of one-half of a stereograph was taken in 1875. Several individuals, probably city policemen, are heavily armed. A number of stereographs of Laredo were made by an unknown photographer in 1875. At least six survive, thus providing historians with a rare glimpse of the town more than one-hundred years ago. (Sam N. Johnson Collection, Nuevo Santander Museum)

The first Webb County Courthouse was completed in May 1882 at a cost of $40,000, despite a strike by brickmasons demanding wages of three dollars a day. It was built in the elegant high Victorian style. Unfortunately, it was consumed by fire in 1906. Fortunately, many of the records of the county, dating to 1848 were saved. (Sam N. Johnson Collection, Nuevo Santander Museum)

The Laredo Improvement Company was founded in 1888 by a number of prominent Laredoans. One of the first presidents was J. M. Hamilton. The company which promoted commerce, industry, and lured immigrants to the border, was also one of the largest land corporations in the nation. (Frank Leslie's Illustrated Newspaper, John Keck)

The Hamilton Hotel built in 1889-1890 was a three story masonry building with cast iron storefronts and elaborately bracketed cornices of pressed tin. After a hot day, businessmen and tourists would retire to the balcony and watch the activities in nearby Jarvis Plaza. A large part of the structure was later demolished. (Frank Leslie's Illustrated Newspaper, John Keck)

This sketch of Laredo's Masonic hall was made for Frank Leslie's Illustrated Newspaper in 1890. A delegation from the prominent newspaper, after traveling over a mesquite covered prairie "as far as the eye could see," was met at the International and Great Northern Depot by Mayor E. A. Atlee, Thomas Dodd, J. O. Nicholson, L. P. Bryant, Charles McLane, Rafael Vidaurri, Dario Sanchez, Eugene Yglesias, J. F. Flynn, C. C. Pierce, Dr. A. W. Wilcox, E. R. Tarver, J. J. Haynes, and Charles F. Yaeger. The delegation was later entertained with an elaborate banquet at the Hamilton Hotel. (Frank Leslie's Illustration Newspaper, John Keck)

During the last decade of the Gilded Age, the Laredo Opera House was a vital part of the Laredo social scene. The opera house, located at 2002 Matamoros, was under the direction of L. M. Valdez for many years. Valdez boasted the best in "High Class Vaudeville and Photoplays." (Frank Leslie's Illustrated Newspaper, John Keck)

Laredo Improvement Company's Building.

Opera House.

Masonic Hall.

The Commercial Hotel, at the intersection of Grant and Flores, was built by Raymond Martin in 1881, and was the first large hotel in Laredo. During the boom years of the 1880s, the hotel's register was filled with the names of traveling businessmen from all over the United States and Mexico. Joseph Christen acted as proprietor of the hotel for many years. (Frank Leslie's Illustrated Newspaper, John Keck)

In 1890, one of the largest stores in Laredo was that of the Deutz Brothers. J. Deutz, Sr., was born in Coblenz, Germany in 1827. He moved to New York in 1848, and after brief stays in San Antonio and Monterrey, Mexico, he came to Laredo in 1880 and opened a hardware store. The small store grew to become one of the largest and most complete hardware, crockery, and glassware businesses in the Southwest with business in eight states. At one time J. Deutz, Sr., served as president of the Laredo National Bank. After his death, the business was carried on by his sons Max, Henry, Joe, and Charley. Another son, Adolph, was in the plumbing and gas fitting business in Laredo. (George R. Page Papers, Webb County Clerk's Office)

Shortly after arriving in Laredo in 1877, Antonio Mateo Bruni opened a small store that grew into this large two story business in 1882. Bruni was able to open a second store in Nuevo Laredo and became one of the community's more prosperous businessmen. (George R. Page Papers, Webb County Clerk's Office)

The first Webb County Court House, built in 1882, was depicted on all county stationary during the decade of the 1890s. (George R. Page Papers, Webb County Clerk's Office)

This rare view taken in 1890 is the earliest known photograph of Market Hall. The building, complete with cupola, had been completed in 1885 at a cost of $60,000. (Charles G. Downing, Institute of Texan Cultures)

This view of the first Webb County Courthouse was taken shortly before the building was destroyed by fire in 1906. (Nick Sanchez Collection, Yolanda Parker, Institute of Texan Cultures)

This rare view of the Hamilton Hotel was taken in 1890 from Jarvis Plaza. The electric railway cars of the Laredo Improvement Company can be seen on both Matamoros and Salinas. Note the stagecoach operated by the hotel which sped overnight guests to and from the depots of the International and Great Northern, Texas-Mexican, and Mexican National Railways. Notice also the offices of the Rio Grande National Bank which occupied a large part of the first floor of the hotel. (Charles G. Downing, Institute of Texan Cultures)

The first Webb County Jail, a peculiar Roman-like building, was located at 1100 Farragut at the corner of Farragut and Flores. It was next to the first Webb County Courthouse and was damaged by the fire that destroyed the courthouse in 1906. It was demolished in 1931 during the Depression. (Sam N. Johnson Collection, Nuevo Santander Museum)

This excellent scene of Iturbide Street looking east was made shortly after the turn of the century. In the distance Eduardo Cruz's first dry goods store can be seen. On the right side of the street is the Deutz Brothers Store run by "H. Deutz, M. Deutz, J. Deutz, Jr., and C. Deutz," which advertised "Importadores y exportadores de ferreteria. Especialidad: herramienta para ferrocarriles y minas." John Herbeck's Laredo Steam Laundry, next to Deutz Brothers, can also be seen in this photograph. (John Keck)

El Precio Fijo, a Laredo institution, was first established in 1881 by the firm of Thomas and Withoff and was located on Zaragoza Street facing St. Augustine Plaza. The store was later purchased by August C. Richter and moved to another location. Richter was born in Cork, Ireland, November 13, 1863. Like millions of other Irish, he immigrated to the United States where he obtained a job as a shoeshine boy in New York. From that day forward, he would remember with great fondness the first cent he earned in his new country. He later worked his way to Indianapolis, Indiana, and eventually to San Antonio, Texas, by ox train. In Laredo in 1890, he joined with Louis D. Stumberg in selling "dry goods, boots, shoes, clothing, and hats." (Nick Sanchez Collection, Yolanda Parker, Institute of Texan Cultures)

Henry Stark, a traveling photographer, took this photograph of carriages and wagons on Flores Street in 1895. On the corner of Flores and Lincoln is the mercantile firm once owned by Santos Benavides. The Laredo Drug Store stood on the corner of Flores and Hidalgo. In the distance can be seen the cupola of the recently completed Webb County Court House. (View of Texas in 1895)

The two-and-one-half story Joaquin Villegas and Brother Dry Goods Store, which stood at Farragut and Flores, was built in Victorian style. The large building also served as a residence for the family. Villegas came to Laredo from the province of Santander, Spain, where he was born in 1844. He was first engaged in the mercantile business in Brownsville and later in Corpus Christi as a partner with Francisco Puig. In 1873, he came to Laredo and devoted himself to stock raising and opened a dry goods store. In 1874, he was joined by his younger brother, Quintin. The firm of J. Villegas and Brother, did an immense business not only in Laredo but also up and down the river and in northern Mexico where they sold chile, peppers, piloncillo, spices, coffee, and other items. The Villegas Building was later purchased by Central Power and Light Company and used as their main office. (Nuevo Santander Museum)

This excellent but unidentified Laredo street scene was taken around 1900. It is thought by several older citizens to be somewhere in the vicinity of the 900 block of Convent. (Institute of Texan Cultures)

This photograph, probably taken by Thomas J. Cockrell around 1890, is of the Yguana Mining and Smelting Works on the southeast outskirts of Laredo. (Charles G. Downing, Institute of Texan Cultures)

This view of the west entrance of Market Hall on Flores Avenue was taken about 1906. Notice the missing cupola. (Laredo Public Library)

Employees of the Laredo Times *gather for a group photograph around 1912. The* Laredo Times *was founded on June 14, 1881, by James S. Penn (1846-1901). The first newspaper was a four page weekly with all type set by hand. Two years later, Penn commenced publication of* The Laredo Daily Times *but continued to publish a weekly edition. When Penn died in 1901, his son Justo continued to act as editor and publisher. In 1928, the Penn Family sold the newspaper. (Nick Sanchez Collection, Yolanda Parker, Institute of Texan Cultures)*

This photograph of the first Webb County Courthouse was taken about 1905. The Court- house was located on the east side of the 700 block of Flores Avenue. The large American flag floating from the cupola was probably painted into the photograph. (Laredo Public Library)

This photograph of Market Hall was taken around 1910. The small horse taxis were for hire and were much like today's taxicabs. (Laredo Public Library)

This photograph of Market Hall, decorated for the George Washington Birthday Celebration, was taken sometime prior to 1905 when the cupola was destroyed by a tornado. (John Keck)

The east wing of Market Hall can be seen in this photograph taken around 1912. Carriages wait to speed citizens through the city's unpaved streets. (Laredo Public Library)

Well into the twentieth century, the Ross Hotel, owned by Charlie Ross, was one of Laredo's principal lodging establishments. Ross also owned a restaurant, fish hatchery, gas plant, chicken farm, saloon, lunch room, and billiard hall. (T. R. Esquivel, Jr.)

The Exchange Hotel, photographed about 1905, was located on West Farragut Street just across from the International and Great Northern Depot. The proprietor, Tomkins Jefferson Guernsey, on the right, came to Laredo in the 1880s as a railroad employee. Guernsey, a Welch immigrant, had first settled in Syracuse, New York, and had served in the Union Army before coming to Texas. Guernsey also owned a livery stable in Laredo. (Marge Hopson)

This view of Market Hall is from the corner of San Augustin and Hidalgo looking southwest. Food vendors, common at the time, can be seen plying their trade, and the New York Salvage Company is seen on the south side of Lincoln Street. This postcard view was taken around 1904. (Ernesto Dovalina)

The United States Post Office and Federal Building was completed in 1906 at a cost of $137,000 or thirty-eight cents per cubic foot. Built with a stone base and walls in the neo-classical revival style, the building was thought to be fireproof. (Laredo Public Library)

This postcard view of Jarvis Plaza, taken sometime around 1916, shows the Federal Building on the north side of the plaza and the recently completed Mercy Hospital on Juarez Avenue to the west. The plaza, developed in the first decade of the twentieth century, was a cool, green oasis in the downtown area which remains a scene for community gatherings and ceremonies. (Armengol Guerra III)

Surreys are parked on Flores Avenue opposite Market Hall in this postcard view taken sometime around 1900. (Laredo Public Library)

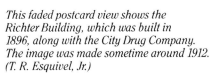

This faded postcard view shows the
Richter Building, which was built in
1896, along with the City Drug Company.
The image was made sometime around 1912.
(T. R. Esquivel, Jr.)

This postcard view of Iturbide Street was
taken around 1908. (Laredo Public Library)

D. H. Randolph, a South Carolinian, came to Laredo in 1880 to open a drug and stationery store. In 1904, Randolph's Botica del Rio Bravo was advertising "fresh drugs, medicine, toilet and fancy articles." Saddlery and harness shops, such as those of Antonio Magnon, who owned one of the largest in Laredo, were common in Laredo around the turn of the century and in the years before the appearance of the automobile. (Author's Collection)

Ike Alexander Men's Store, which occupied the central part of the Wilcox Building, is depicted in this old postcard. I. Alexander advertised "Men's furnishings, goods, shoes, hats, trunks, fine custom tailoring and custom made shirts a specialty." The Wilcox building stood at the intersection of Flores and Lincoln. (Mary Cook Collection, Nuevo Santander Museum)

This view of the Richter Building and City Drug Company was taken in the first decade of the twentieth century. (T. R. Esquivel, Jr.)

A surrey and a wagon can be seen in front of the Federal Building in this postcard view which was taken shortly after the building was completed in 1906. The Hamilton Hotel can be seen in the background. (Laredo Public Library)

In 1896, City Drug Store, also known as the Botica del Leon, was located at the intersection of Flores and Hidalgo opposite Market Hall. The store later changed locations several times. It was the first drug store in Laredo. Antonio Herrera is on the far right in this photograph. (Nick Sanchez Collection, Yolanda Parker, Institute of Texan Cultures)

John Colman poses in front of his store at 1120 Davis at the Texas-Mexican railroad tracks around 1910. Colman sold "staple and fine goods, hay, grain, and produce." (Laredo Public Library)

El Imparcial, next to Market Hall, was typical of a number of small vendimias which operated in the downtown area around the turn of the century. This photograph was taken around 1910. (Nick Sanchez Collection, Yolanda Parker, Institute of Texan Cultures)

J. M. Garza owned a dry cleaning and hat store on the northwest corner of Lincoln and Convent in 1901. Garza, in the white shirt, made, and cleaned hats. The Garza Family lived in the adjacent two-story house. Next door was the photography studio of Jose G. Garcia. (Bessie Gregg Rodarte)

Ox teams were common in Laredo's streets as late as World War I. (Armengol Guerra III)

In 1881, two-hundred men were employed in hauling water from the Rio Grande to the town. Their small carts, loaded with forty-gallon barrels and pulled by mules or donkeys, struggled up the steep riverbanks where the water was sold by the barrileros or aguadores to the towns people for a few cents a barrel. This photograph was taken by Thomas J. Cockrell in 1888. (Mexican International Railway Views)

Ox teams stop in front of El Mexicano Pawnshop as an unidentified photographer snapped this photograph. (Armengol Guerra III)

Even after the installment of the Laredo Waterworks in 1883, the barrileros continued to ply their business in the streets of Laredo. The Laredo Waterworks was contracted by the city to construct and maintain a waterworks system for $7,500. One-hundred hydrants were installed, and water was sold to the public at three cents a barrel. Still many citizens could not afford the new luxury. (Nick Sanchez Collection, Yolanda Parker, Institute of Texan Cultures)

A large number of the photographs taken by visitors to Laredo around the turn of the century were of the barrileros, members of Laredo's lower class. Although they were an oddity to the tourists, they were a common site in the streets of the city. (Laredo Public Library)

A barrilero is seen in a Laredo street in this postcard view. Such scenes were typical in Laredo in the latter part of the nineteenth century and the first decade of the twentieth. (Laredo Public Library)

Laredoans on their way to the Las Tiendas Ranch, thirty miles from Laredo and some nineteen miles west of Encinal, are seen in this photograph as they pause to water their mules during the all-day trip. This photograph was taken around 1907. (Ernesto Dovalina)

Two barrileros, or aguadores, are shown in this old postcard. By 1900, water from the river was being pumped to a central reservoir and then distributed to the citizenry. (Laredo Public Library)

The two-story Louis R. Ortiz residence was located at 905 Iturbide. From left to right, Joe Ortiz, Anita Ugarte Ortiz, L. R. Ortiz, and Paula Ortiz. The individual on the far right is unidentified. (Bruna Sutton)

Facing south, the photographer snapped this shot of Flores Avenue around the year 1910. Offices of the Laredo Times are on the left while the G. A. Stowers Furniture Company, J. M. Daniel Real Estate, City Drug Company, and Reed's Drug Store can be seen on the west side of Flores Avenue. (John Keck)

The west facade of Market Hall on Flores Avenue is shown in this photo around 1918. The City Drug Company advertising, "Cameras and Kodak Supplies," as well as Reed's Drug Store, can be seen on the west side of Flores Avenue. (Laredo Public Library)

Bartenders and citizens pose in front of Charles Ross's Office Saloon around 1904. The building was at the northeast corner of Flores and Hidalgo near Market Hall. (Ramiro Sanchez)

Two workers are seen at the office of the John Finnigan Company which was located in the 1000 block of Iturbide. The photograph was taken around 1900. (Laredo Public Library)

A crowd gathers on Flores Avenue near the old Webb County Courthouse sometime around 1905. On the left is the North American Fruit Exchange and J. M. Daniel Real Estate while the firm of J. Villegas and Brother is in the background. On the right is the G. A. Stowers Furniture Company. (Laredo Public Library)

Frederick Wilhelm Werner, on the right, was one of Laredo's best blacksmiths and wagon makers. Werner was born in Nuder Albm, near the city of Trier, in the Rhineland-Palantine region of Germany. At the age of sixteen he came to the United States and settled at Scranton, Pennsylvania, where he worked as a blacksmith for four years. In 1877, he moved to San Antonio where he was hired by the United States Army and sent to Fort McIntosh. He remained as the post blacksmith for nine years before going into business for himself. Werner eventually purchased considerable Laredo real estate including the two-story building at 514 Flores that contained the Masonic Hall, the Laredo Drug Company, and a barber shop. (Maria del Carmen Offer)

Two citizens around the turn of the century walk along what is today Water Street. The outline of Ursuline Convent and the tower of Laredo Waterworks and the power plant are visible. (St. Mary's University, Institute of Texan Cultures)

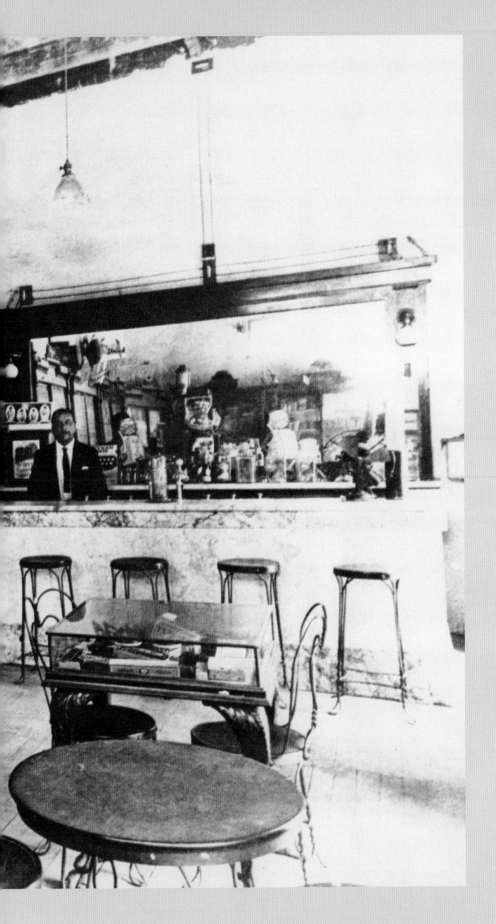

Dr. Isidoro Arturo Nava I, who came from Guerrero, Mexico, is shown on the right in his drug store and pharmacy about 1922. His son, Isidoro Arturo Nava II, is shown behind the counter on the left. Dr. Nava prepared all of his medicines in a separate room. (Arturo Nava)

The Botica Rio Bravo, in the late 1880s, contained D. H. Randolph's Drug Store and the United States Post Office which can be seen in the rear. The four citizens are unidentified. (Author's Collection)

The two-story Botica Zaragoza of Dr. Isidoro Arturo Nava stood at 710 Santa Ursula. The Nava family lived upstairs over the drug store and pharmacy. (Arturo Nava)

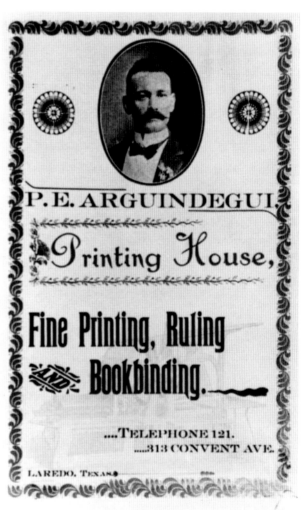

P. E. ARGUINDEGUI.

Printing House,

Fine Printing, Ruling AND Bookbinding.

....TELEPHONE 121.
.....313 CONVENT AVE.

LAREDO, TEXAS.

P. E. Arguindegui ran one of the largest printing houses on Convent Avenue in Laredo around the turn of the century. (Laredo City Directory, Laredo Public Library)

"LA CIUDAD DE MEXICO"

Oficina de Cambios

⚖ ⚖

LOS MEJORES TIPOS

⚖

Avenida Convento, 313.   Teléfono 566

Laredo, Texas

Manuel Linares

*Manuel Linares is seen in front of his "Oficina de Cambios" at 313 Convent Avenue in an advertisement around 1904. (*Laredo City Directory, *Laredo Public Library)*

Charlie Ross and his wife, the "Old Woman," owned a number of Laredo establishments as indicated by this rather chauvinistic ad in an old Laredo City Directory. *(Laredo City Directory, *Laredo Public Library)*

Ross'
Ross
Ross
Ross
Ross
Ross

HOTEL.
ANNEX.
SAMPLE ROOMS.
RESTAURANT.
FISH HATCHERY.
GAS PLANT.
CHICKEN FARM.
SALOON.
LUNCH ROOM.
BILLIARD HALL.

"Me-an'the-Old-Woman," Sole Proprietors.

Charlie Ross.

THIS IS "ME."   THIS IS THE

DROGUERIA Y BOTIGA
"HERRERA"

La mejor atendida y que se ha hecho popular por su activo servicio

MEDICINAS DE PATENTE

Perfumeria, Artículos de Tocador y Tabacos.

ACTIVO SERVICIO DE MENSAJEROS

Recuerde Ud. siempre el nombre:

"BOTICA HERRERA"

Sr. Arturo A. Herrera

EL NUEVO DEPARTAMENTO DE REFRESCOS

está perfectamente atendido

EXQUISITOS HELADOS
Y
CONFECCION
DE TODA CLASE DE
REFRESCOS AL GUSTO

*Arturo A. Herrera owned "Botica Herrera" which advertised "Perfumeria, Articulos de Tocador y Tabacos" in 1905. (*Laredo City Directory, *Laredo Public Library)*

*Antonio Magnon owned one of the largest "Harness and Saddlery" shops in Laredo in 1905. Rubber tires appeared to be the wave of the future in Magnon's advertisement. (*Laredo City Directory, *Laredo Public Library)*

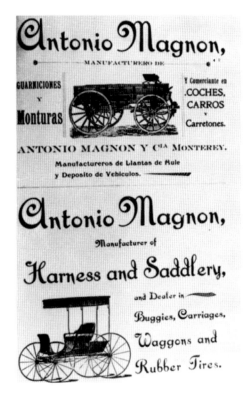

Antonio Magnon,

MANUFACTURERO DE

GUARNICIONES
Y
Monturas

Y Comerciante en
.COCHES,
CARROS
Y
Carretones.

ANTONIO MAGNON Y Cía MONTEREY.

Manufactureros de Llantas de Hule
y Deposito de Vehiculos.

Antonio Magnon,

Manufacturer of

Harness and Saddlery,

and Dealer in

Buggies, Carriages,

Waggons and

Rubber Tires.

In 1910 a new engine of the Mexican National Railways (using mesquite for fuel) with railroad executives, as well as a dog on the "cowcatcher," is ready at Laredo for the daily run to Monterrey. (Tom Goodwin)

Around 1910, unidentified American businessmen at Laredo pose with their "sobre-cargo" on the private car "Orizaba" of the Mexican National Railways. In 1881, the Mexico-Oriental-Interoceanic and International Narrow Gauge, commonly called the Mexican National, had commenced building south from Laredo. By November 1881, work crews had reached Lampazos, and by the summer of 1882, they had approached Monterrey. Including other construction crews that labored north from Mexico City, as many as 16,000 men were at work on the railroad at one time. (Tom Goodwin)

Employees of the "Boiler Depar[t]ment" of the Texas-Mexican Railway were photographed with engine No. 106 in the Depression year of 1935. On the extreme left is Elmer Phillips. Charles Kunz is fourth from left while Oscar Simpson is eighth from left. (Tom Goodwin)

An unidentified youngster poses atop an old engine of the Texas-Mexican Railroad similar to the one that first arrived at Laredo. The financially troubled railroad, earlier known as the Corpus Christi, San Diego, and Rio Grande Narrow Gauge, was the first to reach Laredo in November 1881. The completion of the Texas-Mexican diverted large amounts of freight bound for the Brownsville-Matamoros area and the interior of Mexico to Laredo and truly made Laredo the "Gateway to Mexico." (Texas A and I University Library)

This photograph of an engine of the Texas-Mexican was taken in 1915. The arrival of the Texas-Mexican in Laredo in 1881 signaled the beginning of the most important economic era in the history of the community. (Nick Sanchez Collection, Yolanda Parker, Institute of Texan Cultures)

The depot of the Texas-Mexican Railway was one of Laredo's main communication centers when this photograph was taken in the 1920s. In 1986, after a forty-year absence, the Texas-Mexican resumed passenger service to Corpus Christi and the depot once again took on a new importance. (Nick Sanchez Collection Yolanda Parker, Institute of Texan Cultures)

Passengers await the arrival of the Missouri-Pacific from San Antonio in this postcard view of the depot in the early 1930s. The depot remained one of Laredo's major communication centers well into the modern era. (John Keck)

Jay Gould's standard gauge International and Great Northern reached Laredo in December 1881, one month after the Texas-Mexican. The I and GN not only connected Laredo to San Antonio and points north, but also linked the town to the entire midwest. Los Dos Laredos celebrated the arrival of the railroads with a gigantic fiesta that commenced on Christmas Eve 1881, and continued past New Year's Day 1882. Bullfights, cockfights, horse and mule races, cheering crowds, as well as gala balls and celebrations of all kinds, characterized the festivities. (Laredo Public Library)

Laredoans unload freight at the International and Great Northern depot for delivery to the various business houses of Laredo in 1917.

From left to right are: Lindsey, Rios, Linares, and Lazaro Dovalina. The remaining men are unidentified. (Ernesto Dovalina)

The Rio Grande and Eagle Pass narrow gauge railroad was built from Laredo to the mines at Dolores, Minera, and Darwin in 1882. Construction on the line commenced in March of that year with one-hundred laborers hard at work. A. C. Hunt, ex-governor of Colorado and financier of the project, arrived in Laredo to supervise the work. The grandiose dreaming Hunt bragged of a day when the railroad would stretch along the banks of the Rio Grande from Brownsville to El Paso. A silver spike was driven into the first crosstie on May 24, 1882, to celebrate the laying of the first rail. By July 1882, dirt had already been broken south of town on the Brownsville line, but the railroad was never completed. Hunt had overextended his financial resources, and by 1885 he had declared bankruptcy. (T. S. Scibienski)

Part of the Santo Tomas coal mine near Minera is seen in this early 1890 photograph. The existence of coal in the vicinity of Laredo had been known since the colonial era. It was not until 1873, however, that

Charles Callaghan and Refugio Benavides, who had fought together in the Civil War, sent three large carts of coal to Corpus Christi for trial on the steamers running the coast. Before the completion of the Rio Grande and

Eagle Pass to the mines in 1882, the coal was brought overland in large mule drawn carts or sent downriver in barges. (Charles G. Downing, Institute of Texan Cultures)

The stationery of the Rio Grande Coal Company showed the loading of coal at the large Santo Tomas Mine in 1896. The Santo Tomas and nearby Black Diamond Mines, upriver from Laredo, were producing as much as one hundred tons daily at this time. (George R. Page Papers, Webb County Clerk's Office)

A group of young women from Laredo are seen on a picnic at the large Santo Tomas Coal Mine near Minera around the turn of the century. (T. S. Scibienski)

The large loading platform at the Santo Tomas Coal Mine can be seen in this photograph. (T. S. Scibienski)

The intricate workings of the Cannel Coal Mine upriver from Laredo can be seen in this photograph. The engine house, belching smoke into the sky, can be seen on the right while the elevator housing is left of center, and the loading of the coal onto the railroad is visible on the left. The small ore carts used in the mines can also be seen in the lower-center part of the photograph. (Haynes Collection, Barker Texas History Center)

The large tower at the San Jose Coal Mine at Dolores helped separate the refuse from the coal. The completion of the Rio Grande and Eagle Pass narrow gauge to the mines at Minera, Dolores, and Darwin made the mining of coal profitable. (T. S. Scibienski)

The water tower of the Rio Grande and Eagle Pass narrow gauge railroad can be seen in this photograph at one of the mines upriver from Laredo. (Sam N. Johnson Collection, Nuevo Santander Museum)

D. T. Roy, superintendent of the Santo Tomas Mine, watches as the Rio Grande and Eagle Pass takes on coal around 1905. Much of the coal was shipped to points as far away as Mexico City. (Sam N. Johnson Collection, Nuevo Santander Museum)

Many of the miners who worked the coal mines in the last two decades of the nineteenth century and the first two decades of the twentieth were recruited from the small villages and towns of northern Mexico. When the coal mines closed during the Depression, town lots were purchased for many of the miners in the northwestern outskirts of Laredo. (T. S. Scibienski)

Citizens gather in front of the San Jose Mine Store near Dolores in 1905. Three mines of the Cannel Coal Company, San Jose, Cannel, and the Dolores were in operation at Dolores at the time. (Sam N. Johnson Collection, Nuevo Santander Museum)

The small huts of the miners at Dolores, one of the largest mining camps, are seen in this photograph taken from the top of a slag heap. Dolores was first known as San Jose, but Charles B. Wright, president of the Cannel Coal Company, changed the name of the town to Dolores in honor of his daughter. In 1910, Dolores had a population of over one thousand. By 1930, with the closing of the mines, only twenty citizens could be counted. (T. S. Scibienski)

Workers at the John Armengol packing shed prepare Bermuda onions for shipment by rail to northern markets. After being harvested, the onions were brought to the sheds where they were trimmed and packed in ventilated crates. At the peak of the shipping season, more than two car loads a day were shipped. One-hundred plants were gathered into a bunch, and sixty bunches were packed in each crate. (Carmen Nelson)

Field workers prepare for a day of hoeing on the John Armengol San Rafael Farm, which by 1926, was the largest Bermuda onion farm in the world. In 1926 alone, the Armengol firm shipped 200 million Bermuda onion plants to northern markets. During the growing season, more than five thousand gallons of water were pumped from the Rio Grande every minute for the sprawling San Rafael Farm. The Armengol firm was established in 1881 by Joseph Armengol, a Spanish immigrant uncle of John Armengol. In 1883, James Armengol, John's brother, joined his uncle in the enterprise. Following the death of the elder Armengol, and the failing health of his brother, John Armengol came from his large ranch in Chihuahua to take charge of the firm. (Carmen Nelson)

GATHERING ONIONS
LAREDO. TEXAS

From the time Thomas Carter Nye introduced onion growing to the Laredo area until well into the twentieth century, onion production remained a vital part of the Laredo economy. Most of the onion fields were along the river, north and south of the city. The individuals depicted in this postcard are probably the owners of the property. (Laredo Public Library)

At the packing sheds on the San Rafael Farm, the onions were graded before being shipped. Many plants were discarded. Usually the Bermuda onions from the Laredo area reached the northern market before onions from any other area of the country. (Carmen Nelson)

This postcard view, made around 1908, shows oxen-pulled wagons of onions arriving at the yards of the International and Great Northern where the crates were shipped to northern consumers. *(Laredo Public Library)*

Prosperous onion growers gather for a convention at the Hamilton Hotel in 1912. By 1915, the Laredo area produced 75 percent of all the early Bermuda onions grown in the United States. The professional baseball team from Laredo at the time was even known as the "Bermudas." *(Laredo Public Library)*

This view of Laredo looking northwest over the city was taken around 1915. Salinas Avenue is clearly visible as is the Federal Building in the distance. (John Keck)

This photograph of Laredo looking east-northeast over the city was taken about 1915 from atop the water tower near the river bank. Ursuline Convent and St. Augustine Church are seen on the left as the Rio Grande flows on the right. (John Keck)

This view of Houston Street looking east was made around 1930. On the left can be seen the second Webb County Courthouse and Jail. (Martin High School)

This photograph was taken from St. Augustine Church looking northwest over the city in the 1920s. Note the homes, many of which have been demolished, along Grant Street on the north side of St. Augustine Plaza. Notice also the Federal Building and the Hamilton Hotel in the distance. (Martin High School)

Laredo High School, on the south side of St. Augustine Plaza, as well as Ursuline Convent and the International Bridge are seen in this view which was made in the 1920s. (Martin High School)

This view of Laredo in the late 1920s shows much of the central business district. On the far left is the spire of St. Augustine church, and on the far right is the water tower of the city's waterworks. (Martin High School)

COURT HOUSE AND JAIL
LAREDO, TEXAS

The Second Webb County Courthouse was constructed in 1909. It was designed by Alfred Giles, a San Antonio architect noted for designing courthouse and public buildings throughout the Southwest and Mexico. H. Sparbert was the contractor. The building is characterized by its graceful archways on all four sides. In 1986 the building remained in a serious state of deterioration. (John Keck)

Iturbide Street has remained throughout the years as one of Laredo's main thoroughfares. The downtown streets of the city were named by Mayor Samuel M. Jarvis in the early 1870s for Mexican and American military and political heroes. (Anita and J. C. Martin)

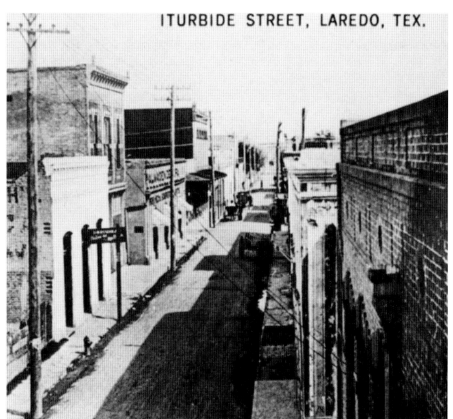

ITURBIDE STREET, LAREDO, TEX.

Mercy Hospital was located on the west side of Jarvis Plaza from 1899 to 1957. From a central building facing the plaza, the hospital expanded with three wings. When the hospital moved to its present site in the heights, the former structure was demolished. (Laredo Public Library)

A delivery truck sits in front of the Wolf and Reuthinger Bakery at Lincoln and Santa Maria around 1927. George Ernest Reuthinger had purchased the bakery from the Borchers Family. (Johnnie Reuthinger)

A mixture of carriages and automobiles is shown in this postcard view of Flores Avenue around World War I. (T. R. Esquivel, Jr.)

The Strand Theater on Flores Avenue opposite Market Hall remained for several decades as a major source of entertainment for a large percentage of the city's populace. In this photograph the theatre is decorated for the George Washington Birthday Celebration. (T. R. Esquivel, Jr.)

The Elks Club is photographed in preparation for the George Washington Birthday Celebration. (Laredo Public Library)

This view of automobiles and wagons parked near the northwest corner of Market Hall along Flores and Hidalgo was made in the late 1920s. Notice the billiard hall, panaderia and cafe on the north side of Hidalgo. (John Keck)

Traffic on Convent Avenue near the new International Bridge was very different from what it would be in the decades to come. Note the money exchange houses and the Ursuline Convent on the left. (Laredo Public Library)

This image of taxicabs waiting outside of Market Hall in the early 1920s was made by J. G. Garcia and is one of the best photographs ever made of the building. Notice the small portico, which was later removed, over the western entrance to the building. (Meli Coleman)

Eduardo Cruz erected his second Las Dos Republicas department store at 1115 Iturbide in 1913. Cruz, one of Laredo's more prosperous businessmen, was born in Cadereyta, Nuevo Leon, in 1860. At the age of fifteen, he went to Matamoros where he worked in a dry goods store. In 1881, he came to Laredo where he married Margarita Vidaurri. After a brief stay in Corpus Christi, he came to Laredo and opened his own business in 1894. (Nick Sanchez Collection, Yolanda Parker, Institute of Texan Cultures)

A small child gazes out the rear window of J. T. Halsell's new automobile around 1915. The automobile, perhaps more than any other invention, brought tremendous change to Laredo in the early decades of the Twentieth Century. Like many older cities, Laredo's streets were narrow and were made for horses and buggies, not automobiles. (Mary Cook Collection, Nuevo Santander Museum)

This postcard view of Hidalgo Street was taken near the intersection of Convent Avenue in the 1930s. On the left is Sulaks Men's Store and Kress Department Store. On the right was the large Valdez Building and furniture store. (Laredo Public Library)

The three-story brick Bender Hotel was built in 1905 by M. Little. The hotel has undergone few alterations and retains much of its original appearance. The hotel was bought in 1940 by A. J. Condren from Floyd Billings. Condren sold the hotel in 1953. Little, the original contractor, was responsible for building many of the business structures in downtown Laredo. (John Keck)

Sames, Moore, and Company began with W. J. Sames and J. R. Moore, the former a native of Hartford, Connecticut, and the latter from Greenwood, Missouri. They both came to Laredo in 1889 and secured employment in the office of B. F. Nicholson with whom they remained until 1893 when they bought out his business and organized their own company. From left to right in this photo are: Reed Puster, J. R. Moore, W. J. Sames, and son Harry Sames. In 1910, Sames and Moore opened the first Ford dealership in Texas with three automobiles. By the late 1920s, they were selling over one-thousand a year. In 1925, Sames and Moore dissolved their partnership with Sames taking the Ford dealership and Moore the wholesale business. (Sames Motor Company)

Mechanics for Sames, Moore, and Company are seen at work in 1917. The automobile on the left is owned by the Webb County Sheriff's Department as indicated by the emblem on the radiator. (Sames Motor Company)

The Pena Hotel, which stood on the south side of the 100 block of Farragut Street, was built around 1890. The building was demolished during World War II. (John Keck)

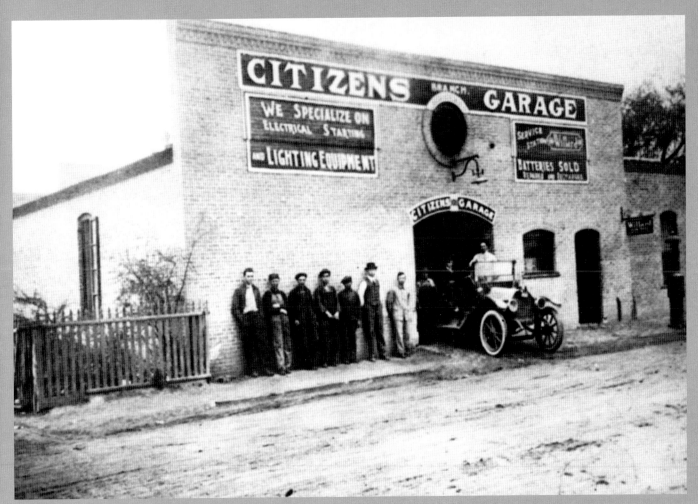

Workers pose in front of the Citizen's Garage at 1011 Matamoros in 1914. Sitting in the car is Houston Marney. Tom Musset is standing in the car while Jacobo Cavazos is in the doorway. Second from left is A. M. Yeary. The building was still standing in 1986. (Amber Yeary)

Alfredo Santos's grocery store was built at 1901 Santa Maria in 1926. The Santos Family came from Candela, Mexico, in 1920. The business is still in operation at the same location and is owned by Arnulfo (Fito) Santos. (Nuevo Santander Museum)

Casso, Guerra, and Company was located at 1301 Iturbide in 1919. From left to right are two unidentified employees; Juan Perez; Eliseo Pruneda; Andres Ramos, Jr.; Dario Garza; Raul Casso, Jr.; Matias Guerra; unidentified; Alberto Barbosa; Juan Villarreal; Benicio Sepulveda; Macedonio Guerra; Raul Casso; and Alfonso Casso. Raul Casso (1880-1981) came to Laredo with his wife and three children during the Mexican Revolution and the burning of the firm of M. Guerra Hermanos in Nuevo Laredo in 1914. By World War I, the company was distributing goods not only in Laredo but to the small towns and ranches all over South Texas. Besides his brothers-in-law, sons Raul, Jr., and Alfonso joined the firm in the early 1920s. Shortly before World War II, the company moved to a new location at 310 Guadalupe. A few years before the war, the Guerra brothers sold their interest and the Raul Casso family became the sole owners. In 1969, Raul Casso sold his interest to his three children. In 1982, Raul Casso, Jr., and Angelina Casso de San Martin sold their interest leaving Alfonso Casso the sole stockholder. (Alfonso Casso)

Much of the iron work and balconies had been removed when this photo was taken of the Hamilton Hotel in the 1920s. The hotel was badly damaged by the tornado of 1905. (Laredo Public Library)

This excellent view of Flores Avenue was made sometime in the 1920s. On the west side of Flores is the Werner Building, the Strand Theatre, the old Santos Benavides Mercantile Firm, Herrera Drug Store, and the Western Union. (John Keck)

This excellent view of the Laredo National Bank at the intersection of Lincoln and Flores was made by J. G. Garcia in the early 1920s. (Meli Coleman)

"Business center"
Laredo, Tex.

Samuel Serrano took this excellent photo-graph of the "Business center" of Laredo in the early 1930s. (Author's Collection)

With bootlegging, rum running, and tequila smuggling, prohibition brought considerable lawlessness to Laredo and the Mexican Border as it did to other communities in the decade of the 1920s. This photograph of an arrest by prohibition agents in Laredo was published in a national magazine and was entitled, "Wet Top." (Mary Cook Collection, Nuevo Santander Museum)

Willis D. Leyendecker Foreman   Edward D. Leyendecker Secretary   Peter P. Leyendecker Prest. and Mgr.   Peter P. Leyendecker Vice-Prest.   Miss M. Leyendecker Treasurer

CITY LUMBER COMPANY

ESTABLISHED IN 1899

27 Years of Faithful Service by the Leyendeckers Rendered in Building the Gateway Cities · · · Laredo, Texas, and Nuevo Laredo, Mexico.

PHONES 128 and 617   WASHINGTON ST. AT SANTA MARIA AVE.

The City Lumber Company, at Washington and Santa Maria, was run by the Leyendecker Family for seven decades. All descendants of John Z. Leyendecker, the family remains one of the largest in Laredo. (Webb County Heritage Foundation)

An International Truck for International Hauling on an International Bridge was the advertisement of the Salinas Motor Company in 1926. The International Truck was that of the Roberto Zuniga Company. (Martin High School)

Hidalgo Street, as evidenced by this postcard view taken in the early 1930s, was one of Laredo's main thoroughfares. The Royal Theatre, a major source of entertainment for many decades, is visible on the right. (Laredo Public Library)

This photograph of a Richter's Ford delivery van was taken in 1930. From humble beginnings in 1881, the firm continued to grow in the following decades. By the 1930s, Richter's El Precio Fijo had moved into a large new building at Flores and Iturbide. (Laredo Public Library)

Jose G. Garcia took this photo of the Merchant's State Bank and Trust Company in the 1920s. The bank stood at the intersection of Convent and Lincoln and was owned by Henry B. Zachary. (Meli Coleman)

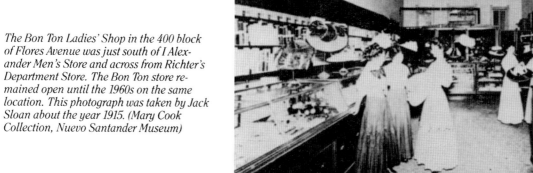

The Bon Ton Ladies' Shop in the 400 block of Flores Avenue was just south of I Alexander Men's Store and across from Richter's Department Store. The Bon Ton store remained open until the 1960s on the same location. This photograph was taken by Jack Sloan about the year 1915. (Mary Cook Collection, Nuevo Santander Museum)

A streetcar makes its way up Flores Avenue in this photograph taken by J. G. Garcia in the 1920s. Reed's Drug Store and the Strand Theatre are visible on the west side of Flores. (Meli Coleman)

This view of street cars on Flores Avenue and taxicabs lining the west side of Market Hall was taken in the late 1920s. (T. R. Esquivel, Jr.)

Street cars on Flores Avenue can be seen in this postcard view of the southwest corner of Market Hall around 1925. The small portico on the west of the building was later removed. (John Keck)

Commencing in 1889, streetcars were an important part of transportation in Laredo. In fact, Laredo had the first electric streetcars west of the Mississippi. Because the streetcars also ran across the bridge to Nuevo Laredo, it was also the first international electric street railway. The company was first organized by the Laredo Improvement Company in 1889. In 1892, the Laredo Electric and Street Railway Company took over from the Laredo Improvement Company. (Nick Sanchez Collection, Yolanda Parker, Institute of Texan Cultures)

In the early 1920s the first airmail plane arrived in Laredo. Such rapid communications were a welcome addition to the once isolated frontier village. (Mary Cook Collection, Nuevo Santander Museum)

A streetcar can be seen crossing Zacate Creek in this photograph. When the rails were first laid, the line ran from the International and Great Northern Depot east along Farragut Street to Santa Rita where it turned north to Matamoros and east along Matamoros in front of the Federal Building to Salinas. Rails led south on Salinas to Farragut and east on Farragut to Flores where the lines turned south in front of Market Hall to Lincoln and east along Lincoln across Zacate Creek to the Heights. Later the lines were straightened to take passengers down Farragut without the detour by way of Matamoros. (Nick Sanchez Collection, Yolanda Parker, Institute of Texan Cultures)

A driver poses in front of a Laredo streetcar in this damaged photograph. (T. R. Esquivel, Jr.)

When the electric lines ended in Nuevo Laredo, the street cars were sometimes pulled with mule power. (Laredo Public Library)

Streetcars were relegated to history in 1935. Although buses took their place, many citizens preferred the more traditional mode of transportation. (Laredo Public Library)

Four members of the Laredo Fire Department are prepared for action in this 1916 photograph. Notice the chemical extinguishers on the rear and side of the vehicle. Only recently had motorized vehicles replaced horse-drawn equipment. By today's standards, however, the fire fighting equipment and techniques of the time were primitive. (Mike Perez)

89

By 1916, the Laredo Fire Department had purchased motorized vehicles and were better prepared to fight fires which had plagued the business district of the city ever since the large multi-storied buildings had become part of the landscape in the 1880s. Notice that horse-drawn equipment, however, was still part of the department in 1916. (Mike Perez)

These seven firefighters were the first paid force to comprise the Laredo Fire Department. They pose in front of the fire station at 900 Matamoros. (Mike Perez)

The men and equipment of the Laredo Fire Department are ready to roll from the Central Fire Station at 912 Matamoros. George Renken was fire chief at the time. Photo by Samuel Serrano. (Mike Perez)

Workers at the quaint Bluebird Mobile Station and Gateway Tire Store are photographed around 1932. The station was located at 904 Juarez and was owned by A. M. Yeary. Note the sign, "It Pays to Pay Cash." (Amber Yeary)

Jarvis Plaza from the corner of Farragut and Salinas appeared as a tranquil oasis in this photograph taken around 1930. Cars line the curb next to the plaza, and the Federal Building looms in the background. (Nick Sanchez Collection, Yolanda Parker, Institute of Texan Cultures)

The San Eduardo Farm, on the east side of Lobo Creek on Highway 358, sixteen and one-half miles from Laredo and sixteen and one-half miles from Mirando City, advertised Coca Cola for sale in this photo taken in the 1930s. (Chris and Gil Trevino)

An oil well already appeared on the horizon when this photograph was taken of Mirando City in the early 1920s. Within a year, five thousand people would be receiving their mail at the community. (Radcliffe Killam)

Mirando City, which was a little over a year old when this photograph was taken on March 17, 1923, was already a boom town. The oil industry has come to South Texas in a big way. (Radcliffe Killam)

As this neatly painted automobile indicates, the Depression election of 1932 was one of the hottest contested elections in the twentieth century as a "New Party" or Progressive Party took on the "Old Party," the dominant Independent Club. When all the votes were cast, the "New Party" had fallen four hundred votes short, and the Independent Club would remain in power for another forty-six years. (Laredo Public Library)

Because of good weather and flat terrain, the Laredo Air Field became an ever increasing part of Laredo's economic life in the 1930s. (Webb County Heritage Foundation)

Hollywood came to Laredo in March of 1938 when Paramount Pictures filmed "The Texan" on location near Dolores, upriver from Laredo. (Webb County Heritage Foundation)

During World War II, citizens and dignitaries from Laredo and Nuevo Laredo met to pledge their unity in the defeat of totalitarian Japan and Germany. (Sam N. Johnson Collection, Nuevo Santander Museum)

Samuel Serrano framed this photograph of the New Hamilton Hotel beautifully in the late 1930s. When the Depression began to wane, many felt the building to be symbolic of a bright economic future for the city. (Esparanza Serrano Maldonado)

Bacilio Benavides was one of the most important political leaders during the early history of Laredo. Born on April 15, 1800, he was said to have been a man of liberal education. At the age of sixteen in 1816, he became postmaster in Laredo and served in that capacity for eleven years. From 1827 to 1848, during some of the most difficult times in the history of the village due to numerous Comanche raids and revolutions, he either served as alcalde or military commandant. During the brief period of the Republic of the Rio Grande, he sympathized with the Federalist forces and may have even fought in their ranks. In 1859, he was elected state representative, being the only Mexican American in the Eighth Legislature. He died in 1863. (Author's Collection)

The Republic of the Rio

By 1837, northern Mexico had become the center of opposition to the authoritarian centralist government in Mexico City. Numerous individuals in the states of Nuevo León, Coahuila, Chihuahua, Sonora, and Tamaulipas hoped for the day when the restoration of the Mexican Constitution of 1824 might become a reality. Resistance to the Centralist regimes of Presidents Anastasio Bustamante and Santa Anna was particularly strong in Tamaulipas.

The settlers on the northern frontier of Tamaulipas had always felt isolated from the Mexican government. The geographical isolation of the communities along the Rio Grande had also produced an economic independence from Mexico. This was partly due to a closer proximity to Texas trading centers such as San Antonio. The inability or lack of desire on the part of the central government to protect the settlers in northern Tamaulipas from marauding Indian parties had produced a mood of desperation and hostility among the citizens there.

By no means was Federalist resistance to the central government restricted to the northern states. Periodically revolts also flared in Yucatan, Jalisco, Oaxaca, and Chiapas.

Revolution flared in the north in December of 1837 when Gen. Jose Urrea, recently appointed commander of the Department of Sonora, led a rebellion at Arizpe in northern Sonora. Most of the army commanders and their garrisons did not waver in their support of the central government and although the government exerted considerable effort at breaking the back of the Federalist movement, revolts continued. In October of 1838, insurrectionists seized the port of Tampico and forced the Centralist commander to flee on board a ship bound for Matamoros.

Downriver from Laredo on November 5, 1838, Antonio Canales issued a "pronunciamiento" at Guerrero which called for opposition to the central government. This was the spark that was to spread the revolution across the Rio Grande frontier. Small in stature, Canales was said to have been a cultured and well educated gentleman. As a prominent lawyer, Canales, in the early 1830s, served in the state legislature of Tamaulipas where he was elected president of the Chamber of Deputies.

As the leader of a revolutionary movement, his lack of military training, inability to command troops and reluctance to make military decisions, was to constantly hinder the Federalist cause. During the Federalist-Centralist wars which swept like a wildfire across northern Mexico, he would often, at the most critical moments, resort to astrology in determining the next move of the Federalist Army.

Canales's righthand man, on whose shoulders the strength of the Federalist cause rested, was Antonio Zapata, after whom Zapata County is named. Born into poverty in Guerrero, Zapata became a sheepherder in his youth. He acquired a small ranch, married an orphan girl and began acquiring more land and

Chapter 4

Grande

additional herds of sheep. By the mid 1830s, Zapata had accumulated a fortune in sheep and land. He owned much of the land on the north bank of the river near the town which today bears his name. It is thought that at one time he may have driven as many as ninety thousand sheep to Mexico City. From his tremendous sheep profit, Zapata had also bought into the mercantile business in Guerrero.

Following the Mexican War against Texas, in which the Mexican government seized thousands of his sheep, Zapata became heavily indebted to foreign merchants. Unable to pay $70,000 in debts, Zapata was forced to sacrifice most of his property and even "the clothes of his wife and children."

Zapata had also received considerable prominence in the Guerrero area as an Indian fighter. He was known to the Indians as "Sombrero de Manteca" because his hat usually "shone with perspiration and oil from his hair mixed with the dirt which settled upon it." Like Canales, Zapata strongly supported the Mexican Constitution of 1824. The two men's desire for the restoration of republicanism to Mexico is perhaps one of the few traits which Canales and Zapata had in common.

Second in command, Zapata was the real inspiration of the revolution. Few men could match his daring. He was determined that federalism would triumph, or he would die in the struggle. Many Anglo-Texans who fought with the Federalist armies, felt Zapata to be one of the "bravest men of his time." He was deeply admired by those who came in contact with him. Santos Benavides, a Laredo teenager at the time of the Federalist wars, recalled years later that Zapata always wanted to fight regardless of the odds. On the other hand, Canales would do everything to avoid combat even when the Federalists were at an advantage. Many, especially the Anglo-Texans, thought Canales to be a coward.

Joseph M. Nance, historian of the Texas-Mexican frontier, who has interpreted the Federalist-Centralist Wars from An Anglo-Texan perspective, feels undeniably that Canales was a coward. Zapata's daring, matched with Canales' overcaution and obsession with astrology, often led to bitter arguments between the two. Years later, Santos Benavides told Mirabeau B. Lamar that on at least one occasion Zapata had threatened to kill Canales when Canales began to talk of surrendering or compromising with the Centralists. "If you dare to do either whilst I am living I will surely kill you. Death shall be certain—my vengeance shall be more speedy and terrible than that which you apprehend from the foe, and drives you into treachery. You know very well that it is my spirit that holds our soldiers together, that it is to me that you yourself, as well as the army, look for victory. At the first signal of betrayal or desertion, the force now under your command shall be turned upon you as a foe, more hateful than the central despots," Zapata proclaimed. According to Benavides, Canales was always "overawed in the presence of Zapata."

Exactly two months after Canales issued his "pronunciamiento" at Guerrero, the citizens of Laredo followed suit. Prominent individuals in the community gathered in the Justice of the Peace Court on San Agustin Plaza to discuss the receipt of various communications relative to the Federalist uprising. From the beginning, there was never any doubt as to the actions Laredo would take. Speaking strongly for the Federalist cause were Alcalde Jose Maria Ramon, Francisco de la Garza, Agustin Soto, and Tomas Flores. The men passed a resolution to the effect that "this town will continue in the future to act under the Constitution of the year 1824." The time for celebration was at hand. Despotic centralism, on which many of the community blamed their problems, had been, at least for the moment, cast aside and the heady exhilaration of freedom with the promise of political liberty burst forth.

For over eight hours the streets of Laredo were alive with the sounds of excitement. Bells rang and people cheered. To a city neglected by the Mexican government and often besieged by Commanche warriors, it was one of the few happy moments in the long history of the community. In their jubilation, men fired their guns into the air. The pistol shots echoed across the rippling waters of the Rio Grande and were clearly audible for miles south of the village on the south bank. Principle among the Federalist leaders of Laredo was Bacilio Benavides, uncle of Santos Benavides and alcalde of Laredo in 1836-1837. The elder Benavides and his sixteen-year-old nephew were to assist Canales and the Federalists in the months to come by launching a relentless guerrilla war against the Centralists. Santos later testified that he and his uncle "harassed the enemy on their march, waylaid them in the defiles, and fired on them at night."

As before, the Centralist government moved quickly to quell the Federalist uprising. Gen. Martin Perfecto de Cos of Texas Revolution fame was appointed commander of the government forces in Coahuila, Nuevo Leon, and Tamaulipas. Late in November of 1838, the Centralist cause was dealt a crushing setback with the defeat of a large army at Tampico. Inspired by Federalist causes, Canales moved to drive the Mexican government from Matamoros. With France at war with the Mexican government, the French successfully blockaded most Mexican ports. The Federalists were most anxious to develop a trade through Matamoros. With no artillery available, Canales was unable to take the city. A boost to the Federalist cause came from upriver with Antonio Zapata's defeat of the Centralist Army at Mier.

From the winter of 1838 to the summer of 1839, the tide of battle swung to and fro across the deserts and mountains of northern Mexico. The Federalists would gain momentum only to lose it again as numerous towns and cities were taken and retaken. Saltillo and Monterrey fell to the Federalists, and the tide of battle seemed to be shifting. In March, however, the French lifted their blockade of the Mexican ports and concluded peace. This was a definite psychological boost to the Centralist forces in the field as they could now turn their full attention to the Federalists. President Bustamante, leaving Santa Anna in command of the government, took the field himself against the Federalist insurgents.

Zapata was forced from Soto la Marina on the east coast, plundering the town and countryside as he evacuated the area. So severe were his actions that one Texas newspaper accused him of "barbarity." In August, Zapata was disastrously defeated and managed to escape death only by fleeing the scene of the battle in great haste.

In late May, Federalist forces in Saltillo surrendered. In June, Tampico and Tuxpan fell to the Centralists. Liberal terms were extended to the defeated Federalists. Prisoners were allowed to reenlist in the Centralist Army with the same rank they had previously held. If they so desired, they could withdraw from the war altogether without any punishment. Such action on the part of the Mexican government served to weaken the Federalist cause severely. In August, Monclova fell to the Centralists and hundreds of defeated and deserting Federalists struck northward for the safety of the Republic of Texas. Many ragged, starving, and defeated soldiers passed through Laredo and the other river villages.

Forty Federalists were captured in August as they fled across the Rio Grande at Guerrero. One of those fleeing northward was the Federalist lawyer, Juan Pablo Anaya, who arrived at Laredo in August of 1839. Departing for San Antonio, Anaya left four hundred men in Laredo under the command of Col. Macedonio Capistran. As Federalist resistance collapsed all across northern Mexico, Capistran too was forced to evacuate the town. A few weeks later, a Centralist force under the command of Manuel de la Fuente occupied Laredo. The new commander was under orders to range north and east from Laredo to prevent, if possible, any Federalist forces, whether Mexican or Texan, from entering Mexico.

Never again would the Federalists achieve the success they had in the first year of the war. With the Centralists in possession of all of northern Mexico, the chances for success on the part of the Federalists were very dim as the winter of 1838 approached. Canales and Zapata moved northward to rest and regroup at Lipantitlan on the Nueces. With the Centralist garrison concerned with a possible Federalist invasion of the area, little time and effort were devoted to providing security from the awesome Comanches. A Mexican newspaper at Matamoros reported Casimiro, a leading Comanche chief, to be devastating and ravaging the Laredo vicinity in the early summer of 1840.

From Lipantitlan, Canales set out not only to win the support of Mirabeau B. Lamar, newly elected president of the Republic of Texas, but also to recruit Texans for the Federalist cause. Canales was assisted in his attempt at winning support in Texas by Anaya and Jose Maria Carbajal. Anaya, who entered Texas first via Laredo, went to San Antonio, Austin, and finally to Houston where he conferred with President Lamar in hopes of concluding an alliance between the Federalists and Texas. Lamar told Anaya that Texas could in no way contribute materially to the Federalist cause and had no intention of participating in the conflict. Lamar was willing only to undertake offensive operations against the Centralists if they continued to refuse to recognize the Republic of Texas. Anaya did receive encouragement from several prominent individuals in Texas, however. Even by its neutrality, the Lamar administration

seemed to have encouraged the Federalist cause.

From his headquarters at Lipantitlan, Canales also issued a proclamation inviting Texans to join the Federalists. Canales offered the Texans twenty-five dollars a month and a half league of land if they would serve for the war. The Texans could also have their share of the spoils. More than two hundred Texans traveled to join Canales at Lipantitlan. Some came for adventure. Others joined Canales in hopes of crushing the Mexican government and thus insuring the military security of Texas. Some traveled south, seeing in the war a chance to benefit themselves materially. The men were a strange-looking lot. Many in ragged and tattered clothing had no shoes. Most had rifles and horses, although some had neither.

The Texans chose as their commander Reuben Ross whose nephew by the same name had served with the Gutierrez-Magee expedition before being murdered in Tamaulipus. The younger Ross, actually a lawyer by profession, had served previously in the army during the Texas break from Mexico in 1836.

A handful of poorly equipped Carrizo Indians from the Reynosa vicinity traveled northward to join Canales's army. The Indians, many of whom had previously been imprisoned at Matamoros, had been brutally treated by the Centralists. Equipped with only a few primitive weapons, the Indians were anxious for revenge. Numerous Mexicans from the Rio Grande Valley traveled to Lipantitlan to join Canales. The Federalist cause had been born anew from the adventurous appetites of Texans and the revenge sought by abused Indians.

With an army numbering more than a thousand men, Canales set out from the Neuces for the Rio Grande. He chose as his first objective the Centralist garrison in his hometown of Guerrero. Uniting with Zapata and his handful of volunteers, the army crossed the Rio Grande in boats at Carrizo (Old Zapata) on the night of September 30. Most of the Carrizo Indians swam across the river to the south bank. The army was slowed by the lack of boats and rafts, but by the morning of October 1, just as the sun began to make its appearance on the eastern horizon toward the gulf, the army was in position before Guerrero. As the Federalists advanced on the town, the Centralist garrison of two hundred attempted to defend the town.

In command of the Centralists was the old warrior Jose Bernardo Maximiliano Gutierrez de Lara. Ironically, Gutierrez de Lara had two sons in the opposing Federalist Army. Upon seeing his men overrun and surrendering, Gutierrez attempted to flee Guerrero by crossing the river to the north bank. No sooner had the old man entered the water than he realized his escape would be hopeless and capture inevitable. He turned back. One of the Texan Federalists saw Gutierrez and proclaimed: "Look! There is the priest! Seize him!" "I am no priest; I am Bernardo Gutierrez. I desire to see the American commander," the old warrior replied. One of the Texans went to find Ross who appeared before the prisoner. "Are you related to the Major Reuben Ross who was my compatriot in 1812 and 1813?" the warrior asked. "I am his nephew," Ross responded. "I am Bernardo Gutierrez. Knowing the character of the uncle, I doubt not that I will be treated with humanity by the nephew," Gutierrez proclaimed.

Gutierrez was taken to the Texan camp as a prisoner. He had just taken a seat on a pile of baggage when Canales's force of Mexicans and Indians came into the Texan camp. Sighting

Gutierrez, Canales strode toward the sixty-five-year-old veteran exclaiming, "Ha! I see the traitor! You shall not escape your deserts!" Canales lunged at Gutierrez with his sword as others set upon the old man, tearing his clothes and ripping off his buttons. Gutierrez's two sons pleaded with Ross to save their father's life. Ross appeared, stopped the attack, and rebuked Canales for his actions. Although Gutierrez was later set free, he refused to support the Federalist cause. He even wrote Zapata severely criticizing what he called the use of "foreign auxiliaries."

On the same day Guerrero fell, Canales ordered the Federalist Army downriver toward Mier. The Federalists entered Mier to find the Centralist garrison gone. Francisco Gonzales Pavon had ordered his troops southward along the road to Monterrey. With Ross and his Texans as the advance guard, Canales did not hesitate in his pursuit of Pavon. About twelve miles south of Mier, Ross found Pavon's men deployed in battle formation. Pavon had placed his four artillery pieces on a hill to protect his infantry and cavalry. Ross, accompanied by the Carrizo Indian auxiliaries, ordered his men into a ravine, and dismounted and took up a position behind several large boulders expecting to be supported by the army's main body as it came up.

Many of the Federalists, largely due to Canales's lack of leadership, chose this most inopportune time to mutiny. Zapata, as usual, did everything possible to exhort the Federalists forward. His effort was met with continued defiance. Pavon, seeing that the Indians and Texans were not being supported by the remaining Federalists, ordered his artillery to commence firing on the Texan position. Time and again the Centralist guns pounded the Texans. After four hours, the battlefield suddenly fell silent. No sound or shot came from the ravine. Pavon, feeling his cannonade had surely slaughtered the Texans, ordered his infantry and cavalry forward to attack the Texan position.

No sooner was the Centralist Army within rifle range than the entire Texan force poured a deadly fire into the Centralist line. Part of the Federalist force, encouraged by the turn of events, came up to attack the Centralist right flank. Twice again Pavon ordered his Centralists to charge the Texans, and twice again they were driven off with heavy casualties. Canales refused to order his Federalists forward. Zapata, cursing Canales with every breath, rode forward with twenty-five Mexicans.

No sooner was the final Centralist charge repulsed than Ross and Zapata charged the Centralist line. Both sides became desperate with much of the fighting hand to hand. The Texan officers lost control of the charging Texans, and the attack became every man for himself. The Texans drew off as nightfall was approaching. Before sunrise the following morning, the Federalist camp was aroused with a report that Pavon was in full retreat.

The Centralists had been without water since early the previous morning, so Pavon sent a rider forward with a white flag in hopes of stalling the Federalist pursuit long enough to allow his men to reach water. The Texans, reinforced by a battalion of Mexican Federalists, were able to maneuver into a position between Pavon and the precious water supply. Pavon hoisted a white flag and surrendered, not to Canales, whom Pavon accused of being a coward, but to the Texans.

The battle of Alcantro Creek had cost the Centralists eighty-five killed and as many wounded. The Texans lost seven men, two of whom died on the battlefield and five others from wounds later.

For many years, Laredo was part of the Mexican state of Coahuila y Texas. After the independence of Texas in 1836, both Mexico and Texas sought to control the area between the Rio Grande and the Nueces Rivers. (Texas State Historical Survey Committee)

The Texans hoped to bury their dead in the churchyard at Mier but were refused permission to do so by the local priest. Although he claimed to be a Federalist, the priest said the Texans were "heretics," not Roman Catholics, and must bury their dead elsewhere.

While the Federalists rested and regrouped at Mier for more than a month, word spread up and down the river of their victory on Alcantro Creek. Many others, believing the Federalists now to have the advantage, hastened to join their ranks.

Canales next moved against the Centralists at Matamoros. By the second week in December 1839, Canales was in position before the town with seventeen hundred men. Several skirmishes resulted when Zapata and the Texans began to attack the Centralist outposts. The Centralist commander, with fifteen hundred men and eighteen cannon, wisely refused to come out of the town to do battle. For four days Canales continued to hold his men in line before Matamoros while Zapata rode around the town hoping to draw the Centralists out.

Canales next moved to take Monterrey. Here, he also failed as he had in taking Matamoros for many of the same reasons—his unfounded suspicions, over-cautiousness, and possible cowardice. Gen. Mariano Arista had been rushed northward by the Centralist government to organize and command the Auxiliary Division of the North. Arista arrived in Monterrey the day before Christmas 1839, after issuing a proclamation to the inhabitants of Nuevo Leon, Coahuila, and Tamaulipas in which he called Canales a "traitor."

Six days after Arista arrived in Monterrey, the two armies clashed outside of town. After an artillery duel in which the Federalists used the cannon they had captured at the battle on Alcantro Creek, Arista was forced to retreat into Monterrey. He was closely pursued by the Federalists who succeeded in occupying a position on a hill on the western edge of the town. Some of the men took refuge in an unfinished church, later to be known as the Bishop's Palace and become the center of another battle in an even larger war. Zapata, with his usual daring, was successful in several skirmishes with the Centralists, but Canales refused to reinforce Zapata, claiming that Arista was attempting to trick his army into

A signature from the Laredo Archives familiar to students of Texas and Mexican history is that of Martin Perfecto de Cos. Cos, Santa Anna's brother-in-law, surrendered San Antonio to a Texan army under Edward Burleson on December 11, 1835. Cos's defeated army reached Laredo on Christmas Day 1835. In 1838, Cos returned to the frontier again, this time to command the Centralists forces. (Laredo Archives, St. Mary's University)

the open and then attack.

Much against the desires of Zapata, who wanted to attack the town, Canales ordered a retreat. According to one observer, Canales in the ensuing retreat, "not knowing what to do, permitted his men to fall into the utmost disorder and confusion. . . . Men were strewn in confusion for ten or twelve miles, with their ammunition stampeded by mules." The entire Federalist Army probably would have been destroyed by Arista if it had not been for Zapata. Zapata, acting as the rear guard on numerous occasions, turned upon the pursuing army and held them in check. Arista finally broke off his pursuit and returned to Monterrey.

Early in January of 1840, Zapata, Canales, and the Texans, their ranks reduced by desertion, reached the Rio Grande. Zapata went to his home opposite Guerrero, while Canales made for the river at Mier.

The Federalist Army was deserving of a better fate. It began with the victory of Guerrero, forced the evacuation of Mier, and then overcame mutiny and treachery to win victory at Alcantro Creek. Only the timidity of Canales avoided an engagement at Matamoros and later prevented the army from following up its advantage at Monterrey. Finally, the incompetence of Canales's disorderly retreat threatened the army's destruction.

After Crossing the Rio Grande on January 7, 1840, Canales issued a call for a convention to meet for organizing a government for the "Republic of the Rio Grande." The new Republic was to comprise the states of Nuevo Leon, Coahuila, and Tamaulipas. On the east bank of the Rio Grande, opposite Guerrero, at the Orevena Ranch near present-day Zapata, the delegates organized a government for the new Republic based on the Mexican Constitution of 1824. Jesus Cardenas, a lawyer from Reynosa, was chosen president. Francisco Vidaurri y Villasenor, one-time governor of Coahuila and Texas, was selected vice-president. Antonio Canales, instigator of the new Republic, was chosen commander in chief of the Republic's army. Juan Francisco Farias was chosen secretary and Manuel Nina quarter-master general.

The new government was also to consist of a legislative council of eight members. Five were to be regular members, and the additional three were to be supplementary members. The president and vice president were to hold regular seats in the council. Each state comprising the new Republic was also to send a representative. Juan Nepomuceno Molano, with considerable political experience in Matamoros and Ciudad Victoria, was chosen to represent Tamaulipas. Manuel Maria de Llano, who had at one time been governor of Nuevo Leon, was to represent that state. Francisco Vidaurri was to represent Coahuila. Jose Maria Carbajal, Canales, and Anaya were chosen as the supplementary members of the council.

Laredo was chosen the capital of the Republic of the Rio Grande. It was decided that the new government should remain at Guerrero for the present where a printing press was available. By early February, the Guerrero press was already turning out the official Federalist newspaper, the *Correo Del Rio Bravo Del Norte,* under the auspices of Jose Maria Gonzales Cuellar.

The convention also enlarged the boundaries of the new Republic to include the Mexican states of Zacatecas, Durango, Nuevo Mexico, and Chihuahua. To recruit new volunteers, the leaders promised to appropriate not only church and convent property but all large estates as well.

After completing their work on January 28, the elected officials crossed the river to Guerrero where the individuals were officially inaugurated. Before crossing the Rio Grande, the Federalist soldiers had been given plenty of mescal to boost their spirits for the upcoming ceremony. By the time the men had reached Guerrero, many were dead drunk. To celebrate the occasion, Zapata agreed to host a ball at his house on the plaza in Guerrero. Anyone, regardless of status or rank, who wished to attend the function was welcomed. Many of the soldiers were almost naked, however, and were unable to attend the ceremony for lack of clothing.

On the same day the new officials of the newly-created Republic finished their work, Canales appealed to Arista in a letter for a halt to hostilities. "I am disposed to end a war; the longer it lasts, the more terrible are the symptoms it presents," Canales wrote. Arista replied that he had no intentions of offering an armistice and that Canales's letter was "an insult to a legitimate government which . . . I respect and defend." Arista was particularly perturbed about Canales's use of Texans in the Federalist Army.

Canales remained at Guerrero for three weeks but, upon receiving word that Arista was advancing, led his army upriver through Laredo to Presidio del Rio Grande where he arrived on March 3, 1840. Canales was hoping that from a position upriver from Laredo, he might more easily recruit men from Coahuila and Durango, but his hopes for large numbers of new recruits failed to materialize. Many Texans attempted to persuade Canales to move his headquarters to a point on the Nueces where the Federalists could more readily recruit Texans. As many as sixty of the Texans under Colonel Jordan returned home to Texas when Canales refused this request.

When word reached Zapata and Cardenas at Guerrero of Arista's advance up the south bank of the river, the men hastily moved the government to Laredo. Cardenas was escorted by a "life guard" consisting of sixty Texans under the command of Capt. Jack Palmer, whom Bacilio Benavides called "a good natured man, but no great fighter." From Laredo, Zapata went to Santa Rita de Morelos in hopes of gathering supplies and possibly money for the new Republic. Cardenas, remaining in Laredo, chose as his capital a small rock building on San Agustin Plaza between the square and the riverbank. The building, constructed of native stone and adobe, has endured until modern times.

Cardenas appointed Jose Antonio Navarro to represent the Republic of the Rio Grande in Texas. Navarro, influential and well-respected in Texas, would make an excellent representative, Cardenas felt. As a resident of Texas, Navarro refused the nomination, however, feeling that Cardenas was attempting to use him to influence the Republic of Texas to enter the conflict. Navarro did not wish to be used to influence the Republic of Texas to enter the conflict and felt he could not "intermeddle officially with the domestic quarrels of the Mexicans." Cardenas next appointed Jose Maria Jesus Carbajal to represent his new government.

From Laredo, President Cardenas sent Capt. John T. Prince northward into Texas for the purpose of enlisting volunteers. Men were to be enlisted for six months unless discharged earlier. Privates were to receive twenty-five dollars a month. The men were to be paid from the time they left Texas for the war. From Laredo, Prince went to Victoria where he was able to enlist one hundred volunteers. Before the men could reach Laredo, however, a dramatic change of events had changed the status of the new capital.

From Guerrero, Arista continued to advance upriver toward Laredo. Arista's vanguard army alone was more than four times the size of Laredo's meager defenses. Laredo's status as the capital of the Republic of the Rio Grande was short lived, lasting only a few weeks. President Cardenas had no choice. He fled northward into the chaparral of the Nueces Country reaching Lake Espantosa on the Nueces where he moved downstream and set up his temporary headquarters.

The march from Guerrero to Laredo had taken Arista four days. His army marched into the Federalist capital on the evening of March 19, 1840. As Arista forded the river at Laredo and stepped from his horse on the north bank for the first time, he reportedly remarked, "O famous Rio Bravo del Norte, God only knows whether after this campaign in Texas, I shall recross you." At Laredo he was joined by Capt. Juan Jose Galin with 150 presidials.

In Laredo Arista learned that Zapata was at Santa Rita de Morelos upriver from Laredo. He hurriedly ordered eighty-eight of his crack cavalry to apprehend Zapata. Jesus Barrera, a soldier with Zapata, recalled several years later that Zapata was preparing to leave Morelos to join Canales when the prominent citizens of Morelos persuaded him to remain another day and "proposed to kill a beef for him." Zapata "yielded to their kindness and ordered his men to dismount, saying that he would spend the day in Morelos."

The Morelos citizens even offered to care for the Federalists' horses. Unknown to Zapata and his men was the fact that the obvious gratitude was a ruse and the residents of Morelos were really ardent Centralists plotting his murder. No sooner had the Federalists' horses been taken away than the Centralist sympathizers opened fire on Zapata and his men. Zapata managed to escape the hail of bullets and with his men took refuge in a large white house on the plaza. As many as two hundred Centralist soldiers, who had been secretly concealed by the Morelos citizenry, now joined in the fray.

For three hours the struggle continued. Zapata and his men began to run dangerously low on ammunition. Their only hope was to be reinforced by Canales. Canales never came. Of the thirty men Zapata had with him, seven died in the battle. Only one man, Martin K. Snell, managed to escape.

A large Centralist force arrived in town just in time to witness the final few minutes of the battle. Zapata and his handful of gallant defenders were out of ammunition, and no alternative remained. Zapata strode from the house into the street and surrendered, "breaking his sword in the face of the victors."

The rebels were bound by the Centralists and held prisoners. Arista, who arrived the following day, told Zapata that if he would join the Centralists, a pardon could be arranged. Zapata refused. Arista next told Zapata his life could be spared if he would promise "to lay down his arms and cooperate no further with the Federalists." It was the final concession, but again, Zapata refused, telling Arista that he wished to be treated as a prisoner of war. Arista replied that he must either abandon his cause or die. "I have taken up arms against the tyranny of the gov't and I will never lay them [down] except in death, until the wrongs of my people are redressed, and their rights secured," Zapata replied.

Zapata and the survivors of the Morelos encounter were tried before a hastily summoned court-martial, found guilty of treason, and ordered shot. Zapata was accused in particular of "enlisting Texans to fight his own country." As Zapata stood before the Centralist firing squad, a "tear was seen to roll from his eye about the time his eyes were bandaged."

Arista ordered Zapata's head cut off and preserved in a cask of brandy. Ampudia was ordered to take the head to Guerrero. Ampudia, with a large army, came through Laredo with the gruesome trophy which was taken out of the cask and put on display for anyone to see, especially potential Federalists who might have ideas similar to those of Zapata. Such was Zapata's destiny in questioning the authority of the Centralist government. In Guerrero, Zapata's head was placed on a pole opposite his house on the plaza, where it remained for days in plain view of Zapata's wife and children as a warning "to the people who worshipped him" and others who might have the least inclination of rebelling against the government.

As Zapata and his handful of gallant defenders attempted to stave off capture in Morelos, Canales, with a force of four hundred, advanced on the town. Waiting for Canales was Arista with a force more than three times the size of that of the Federalists. On the outskirts of Morelos, the Federalists made their stand but after more than two hours of bitter fighting, were overrun and severely defeated. Canales lost more than one-half of his army. Almost all of those who were not killed were captured. Hardest hit were Canales's Carrizo Indians who fought to the bitter end and were almost annihilated. Although they were pursued closely for several miles, Canales and a few of his men were able to escape.

Fleeing across the Rio Grande, Canales moved his defeated army once again to familiar recruiting grounds on the Nueces River where he set up his government at Espantosa Lake. With the evacuation of the Federalists from the Rio Grande, all trade and commerce between the river and the Republic of Texas was cut. Many of the citizens of Laredo were now forced to look southward for their economic dependence. It was reported in Texas that the Centralists had settled "down along the Rio Grande" and were in the process of "taking civil, military, and domestic possession of the whole country."

With the strengthening of Centralist forces on the river, Mexican cavalry began to operate freely north of the Rio Grande, and in some instances, they were reported to have reached the Nueces. President Lamar, alarmed at the report of Mexican cavalry in the vicinity of the Nueces, ordered Edwin Morehouse into the Nueces country and contemplated ordering troops "to occupy a position near or upon the banks of the Rio Grande." One Texas editor, having delusions of Manifest Destiny and grandeur for Texas, purportedly stated that he preferred "the mountains beyond Monterrey" as a boundary for the Texas Republic.

Canales never gave up hope of persuading the Republic of Texas to form an alliance with the Rio Grande Republic. Rumors never officially substantiated, reported that the two republics had signed an alliance as early as December of 1839 at Laredo in which Texas pledged "to aid the Federalists of the Rio Grande in their struggle for independence."

From his Nueces base, Canales once again saw rejuvenation in Texas. Traveling to Austin, Canales again consulted with Lamar, who sympathized with the Federalist cause but refused to support officially or in any way contribute materially to the movement. Canales next journeyed to Houston and Galveston where he procured clothing, provisions, and supplies for another expedition. As usual, the Federalist cause met with great success in Texas. In some instances individuals left civil positions to take up arms with the Federalists.

By August of 1840, more than three hundred Texans were in camp at Canales' new headquarters at Lipantitlan. No sooner did Canales return to camp than he began preparations for an offensive operation against the Centralists. Canales would strike first at Laredo. He chose Col. Samuel W. Jordan, the veteran, and Col. Luis Lopez for the mission. The expedition was under orders to drive the Centralists from the north bank of the river. Canales was specifically interested in procuring several thousand pounds of lead which the Federalists had previously hidden at Laredo.

The expedition, consisting of fifty Anglo-Texans and one hundred Mexicans, left the Nueces for Laredo the second week in July 1840. By the late evening of the twenty-fourth, the men were within thirty miles of Laredo. A forced night march brought the men to the river. Precautions were taken to avoid Centralist sentinels known to be stationed some distance outside of Laredo, probably on the San Antonio Road. Some time on the twenty-fourth before reaching Laredo, the entire expedition had taken to the chaparral. Such tactics had slowed the column as the men were forced to travel through chaparral so thick that the men could scarcely make their way. Finding a corral about one-half mile outside of town, the men decided to leave their horses there and continue on foot.

By moving at night, the men were able to position themselves close to the town in the tall grass and brush between San Agustin Plaza and the river. There was no doubt in the men's minds that the town could be taken. Their only fear was that the Centralists might escape. To avoid this, Lopez was left to the north of town.

Scouts had brought the expedition vital information concerning the town's defenses. Jordan and Lopez had learned that Laredo was commanded by Captain Rodriguez, a man Lopez called a "vile prostitute" and a "Chicharron."

Jordan, Capt. John T. Price, and their men were able to get a few hours of sleep on the early morning of the twenty-fifth as they lay in wait less than one hundred yards from San Agustin Plaza. The Texans felt they could take the local garrison before the Centralists would have time to defend themselves. Their secrecy was revealed an hour before daybreak when "an old woman making her way to the river for water discovered them." With the alarm given in the town, the men rushed for the plaza. Jordan entered the plaza from one direction and Price from another. "The garrison was taken [by] surprise and became panic stricken and fled," according to one report. Only a few of the Centralists resisted the Texans. Many were caught in the military barracks on the plaza and were taken completely by surprise. Others fled the town by swimming the Rio Grande.

Three of the Centralists were killed in the battle, six were wounded, and seventeen were taken prisoners. The remainder managed to escape, including Rodriguez who fled "naked" and "severely wounded." Two of the enemy spies, Matias Zertuche and Ramon Botello, were caught the following day, tried as spies, and executed by the Federalists. Many official documents as well as horses, mules, saddles, muskets, and lances were also seized in the raid on the town. No Federalists had fallen in the battle although "one life was lost by the accidental firing of a pistol."

Matters had just become quiet when Lopez and the remainder of the Federalists came riding hurriedly into the plaza from the north. Lopez had overrun the sentries who had attempted unsuccessfully to bar their entrance into the town. Most of the fleeing Centralists, however, had crossed the river to the south while Lopez had entered the town from the north.

Although rumors reached Texas that Laredo had been sacked by the Federalists, the conquerors and the Laredo citizens appear to have gotten along quite well. "The people of the place evidenced no unfriendly disposition; but on the contrary gave such assurances of their attachment to the cause of Federalism, that the alcaldes were suffered to remain in office," one man reported. Lopez, in his official report, told Canales that the citizens of Laredo were "in perfect liberty and security, for the volunteers [Texans], as well as the Mexican soldiers have deported themselves during the fight in the town in such a manner as will always reflect honor upon them."

The men remained on the river for a few days to rest before their long trek back to the Nueces. Reaching camp at Lipantitlan a few weeks later, the men found the Federalist Army continuing to grow in strength with the addition of numerous Texans recruited by Juan N. Seguin. "The success of Jordan at Laredo inspired the army, and even gave some seeming valor to the cowardly Canales," it was later recalled.

Although large numbers of Centralist cavalry continued to

roam at will north of the Rio Grande, it was now the Federalists who were on the offensive. About 260 Federalists under Lopez, Jordan, and Juan Nepomuceno Molano crossed the Rio Grande near present day Rio Grande City in early September of 1840. After capturing Guerrero, Mier, and Camargo, the small army turned south into the Mexican interior.

Although some of the Texans questioned the decision, it was decided that Ciudad Victoria would be their major objective. As the small towns and villages fell to the advancing Federalists, a dispute developed between the Mexicans and the Anglo-Texans over whether the Texans had the right to plunder the Mexican villages. Molano felt that the Texans were entitled to the "spoils of war" only in those places where the inhabitants had taken up arms against the Federalists. The Texans disagreed.

With the Federalists continuing to feud among themselves, the army entered Victoria on September 29. Although the citizens of Victoria, especially the merchants, welcomed the Federalists with open arms, the army, particularly the Texans, proceeded to plunder the town, even raping women whom they threatened "with dagger and pistol to force them to succumb to their brutal desires."

From Victoria the army turned westward into the Sierra Madre de Oriental toward Saltillo. Unknown to Jordan and the Texans was the fact that Molano and Lopez had treacherously agreed to lead the Texans into a death trap. A Centralist agent had offered the two as much as 100,000 pesos to desert the Federalist cause and come over to the Centralist, and in the process lead the Texans into a massacre. Repeatedly Jordan received rumors and reports that Molano and Lopez were marching him and his men to their death. Confronting the Mexican officers with the news, Jordan was assured that such a plot was absurd.

Later as he faced a large Centralist army outside of Saltillo, on October 23, Jordan urged an immediate attack but was turned down. After Molano had gone into the Centralist camp ostensibly to discuss peace terms with the Centralists commander, Lopez suggested that he and Jordan separate into two groups for an attack upon the Centralists. Jordan was to attack the Centralists' left, while Lopez was to attack their right. The attack went as ordered until it was suddenly discovered that the Texans were marching straight into a gorge. Jordan, now suspecting a plot, immediately changed directions and proceeded to follow Lopez.

As the Texans disappeared around a hill, Lopez told his men that they were hopelessly outnumbered and should surrender. Only Col. Jose Maria Gonzales of Laredo objected and urged his men to "stick to their integrity." Within a short distance of the Centralists lines, Lopez halted, fired his gun into the air, and supposedly shouted: "Long live the Republic of Mexico, kill the Texans." Most of his men, including a Captain Garcia from Mier, followed Lopez into the Centralist lines.

Colonel Gonzales refused to follow, however, telling his handful of followers that he would never go over to the Centralists and that they must somehow escape the Centralists' trap. By fleeing through the mountains, Gonzales and a few of his men were able to escape and eventually to make their way back to Laredo.

All that remained of the Federalist forces were the Texans and a few Carrizo Indians. The Centralist Army now outnumbered the Texans more than fifteen to one. Several times the Centralists charged the Texans but were driven off, each time with a deadly rifle fire which killed hundreds. Virtually surrounded, Jordan, his men, and the Carrizo Indians courageously fought their way out of the Centralist trap, a deed which defies belief. More than four hundred of the Centralists had been killed, while the Texans had lost five.

Making their way over the mountains, the Texans became lost in the darkness. After several hours of endless wandering, the men finally found their bearings and headed north for the Rio Grande. Often, they were attacked by the Centralist cavalry which had been sent in pursuit. From the rugged mountains some of the Centralists and their sympathizers even rolled huge boulders down on the Texans.

Finally reaching the road leading to Monclova, the men came across three of Gonzales' men who had been left there to assist any of the men Gonzales thought might escape the tragedy of Saltillo. From the Monclova road the Texans, fleeing for their lives, turned eastward to Candela. Here they were joined by Gonzales who accompanied the men northeast toward Laredo. About thirty miles south of town, the men were met by J. M. Menchaca and Antonio Perez who had been dispatched from Laredo by Seguin who had arrived there with reinforcements for the Federalists. The fatigued army finally reached the river on October 31, 1840.

For two days the army rested at Laredo, during which time a trunk was opened which contained several letters from the Centralist commander at Saltillo to Molano, letters which revealed beyond any doubt that Molano and Lopez had been planning for sometime to lead the Texans into a death trap. Jordan and Seguin combined their small forces and began a march downriver to receive their pay for the past months.

At San Ygnacio they met President Cardenas who reported he was going to Laredo on important business. Further downriver they came across a messenger and, upon searching him, found a message in the man's shoe. The message was from Canales to Molano revealing Canales's desires for surrendering his army. Jordan dispatched Leandro Arreola and J. M. Menchaca to Camargo to prevent Canales from leaving town and "to apprehend and hang him" if he attempted to flee.

Most of the Texans, now realizing that Federalism was dead in northern Mexico, tired of endless marches, battles, and skirmishes fought over a vast expanse against overwhelming odds, took what few belongings they had and struck out northward for the Nueces and home.

On the north bank of the Rio Grande opposite Camargo on November 6, 1840, surrender terms were completed between Canales and the Centralists. Arista hailed the event as a "day of glory." Four days later Canales met "El Tigre del Norte" at Cadereyta to receive a twenty-one gun salute and be embraced by his former adversary. A few days later Cardenas and the last of the Federalists stacked their rifles and arms in Laredo. The Republic of the Rio Grande was dead, never again to be revived. It had lasted for 283 violent, tumultuous days.

The Mier Expedition

On a cool winter morning early in December of 1842, the citizens of Laredo were awakened to learn that more than seven hundred Texans were secretly deployed around the town. The Texans were part of the Somervell Expedition, the most written-about body of men ever to descend upon the Rio Grande during the entire history of the Republic of Texas. Before the last of the expedition had been heard of, Laredo had been plundered, many of the Texans had been captured at Mier—some to be later executed, England had broken diplomatic relations with Mexico, and the United States had become diplomatically involved in the historical events of the area.

Late in November the "Southwestern Army of Operations," determined to get revenge for two Mexican raids on San Antonio, broke camp at San Antonio and took up the line of march for what the men thought was Presidio del Rio Grande. The army, comprised of militiamen and hastily enlisted ragged and undisciplined volunteers, was a heterogenous collection of frontiersmen as indicated by one of the soldiers, John Henry Brown, who wrote that the army "embraced more than one preacher, many church members, a full array of Texas farm boys and every variety of the genus homo." "Buckskin breeches" covered with grease and dirt were the closest thing the men had to a uniform. Some had shoes, but many of the men wore moccasins. Water was carried in gourds since canteens were unheard of. Horses were of different breeds, colors, and sizes. A few of the men rode mules. Each "soldier" was equipped with a rifle, pistol and one hundred rounds of ammunition. Because no wagons were available, two hundred mules were loaded with the army's meager supplies. Three hundred beef cattle were driven along for meat. A spy company, which was sent in advance of the main body, carried a banner made by one of the ladies of San Antonio bearing the words: "We give but ask no quarter." One of the Texans recorded in his diary that the purpose of the expedition was "to meet our country's foe, and hurl his haughty insolence back to his teeth." Another volunteer reported the army to be "composed of volunteers burning with anxiety to meet the enemy and exchange at least a few shots."

Somervell was under orders from President Sam Houston to "proceed to the most eligible point on the western frontier of Texas and concentrate with the men now under your command, all troops who may submit to your orders, and if you can advance with a prospect of success into the enemy territory you will do so forthwith. You will receive no troops unto your command, but such as will march across the Rio Grande under your orders if required by you to do so. If you cross the Rio Grande, you must suffer no surprise."

Alexander Somervell had no intentions of marching for Presidio del Rio Grande as previously planned. The Texas high command had chosen Laredo instead, and the feint toward the central Rio Grande was only to mislead any possible Mexican spies.

After crossing the Medina River, the expedition turned toward the Laredo Road. Guides became lost and misled the men near the Atascosa River, and the entire army wound up in a huge bog or quagmire. For three days, the men "floundered through that sort of country." The horses and pack animals sunk into the mud to their bellies and were difficult to pull out. Only by "extraordinary effort" did the men reach the Laredo road.

After fording the Frio River, the men reached the Nueces River to find the entire valley flooded. The river had overflowed its banks for a distance of two miles along the north shore. The water in the main channel was so deep that the Texans felt there was no alternative but to build a bridge across the muddy river. The men were ordered to cut as many trees as possible and float the logs into position. Once the trees had been placed into position, smaller branches were also cut and used, over which cane was placed. The crudely constructed bridge was said to have been so sturdy that the men were able to ride their horses across the river. The labor in building the bridge and the trek from San Antonio had so exhausted the men that Somervell ordered a halt to the march so the men might get some rest and recuperation. With the march to the Rio Grande already behind schedule, many of the men began to run low on provisions and go hungry. Hunters were sent out from camp into the brush country and were able to kill several deer. The venison provided a most welcome feast.

No sooner were the men and their animals across the Nueces than a severe "norther" hit. A driving rain accompanied by high winds drenched the men in a downpour. Lightning burst forth from the heavens and began to dance about upon the desert floor. The roll of thunder which followed stampeded the men's horses and mules. More than a thousand of the frightened animals raced around and through the Texas camp. One soldier, attempting to avoid the frightened beasts, fell backwards into a prickly pear patch. For several days one of the army's doctors spent his spare time carefully removing the needle-like thorns from the poor man's backside.

For two days, Somervell and his army remained camped on the south bank of the Nueces River. The general ordered all the remaining cattle to be slaughtered and the meat cooked and dried in preparation for the descent upon Laredo.

In the early hours of December 6, 1842, the army began the march from the Nueces. A few soldiers were left behind to round up all the missing animals. The route from the Nueces to Laredo was nothing more than a narrow cart road frequently passing through dense thickets of chaparral and wide-open prairies. About twelve miles from Laredo the Texans halted and made a temporary camp. The prairie around the camp was so barren that no firewood could be found. A severe north wind arose, and squalls of rain swept through the camp. Not one single tent was available to shelter the men. It was all the men could do to keep warm around a smoldering fire made from a few sticks. Wolves howled on the prairies, and panthers, which were plentiful in the area at the time, screamed in the distance. The entire atmosphere was eerie, perhaps a prophecy of what awaited the men on the banks of the Rio Grande, some thought.

The citizens of Laredo were once again to become victims of the warring republics of Mexico and Texas. Invading armies were something the citizens of Laredo had grown accustomed to through the years. Florencio Villarreal was alcalde of Laredo, and Reyes Ortiz and Miguel Dovalina were aldermen while Faustino Ramirez held the office of justice of the peace. The military commander in Laredo was Calixto Bravo.

Bravo, upon learning of the approach of the Texans, realized it was senseless to attempt to defend the town with eighty men. He, therefore, decided to evacuate Laredo and move his force to Guerrero. More than one hundred citizens of Laredo fled with Bravo, some going only as far as the south bank to stay with relatives or friends. As many as a thousand head of horses, mules, and cattle were driven across the Paso de Jacinto at high water to the south bank of the river. Other animals were herded into the chaparral around the town. Supplies, which had not been taken across the river, were hidden in the brush outside of town, the authorities fearing the Texans might plunder Laredo.

At sunset on the evening of December 7, after halting briefly outside of Laredo on the San Antonio Road, the Texan Army began its final descent on Laredo. As usual, Hays and his spies were sent in advance of the main force. "The skies became clear and the stars shone forth in the glory of a beautiful night," one of the soldiers recalled. As before, the road was nothing more than a narrow path through the dense chaparral but became wider as the army neared the river. The moon went down, and the night became uncommonly dark. Various groups of the army fell into confusion, and some of the "soldiers" became separated from the main group. One man strayed from the main column, got lost in the chaparral and the darkness, and was never heard of again. About two miles outside of town, the army halted to await word from Hays.

General Somervell had also ordered six of his best mounted companies, under command of Col. James R. Cook, to march in advance of the main column and cross the river to cut off the contemplated retreat of the Mexican garrison. Cook and his men were to cross at either Paso de Jacinto above the town or Paso de Miguel de la Garza below Laredo and take a position on the south bank of the river, opposite the town. Once this maneuver had been completed, Somervell, with the main body of Texans, would march on Laredo from the north. If Cook found it impossible to cross the river, he was to place his army between San Agustin Plaza and the river.

About three miles from Laredo, Cook ordered his men to take to the chaparral to prevent being discovered. The men moved along the Chacon Creek for a mile or two and then rode into the creek bed itself reaching the Rio Grande below Laredo. John C. Hays and a company of spies, in advance of Cook, had hoped to find boats in which to transport the men and their weapons to the south bank. Finding nothing on the north bank, Hays and several of his men swam across the river, but could find only a single canoe on the south shore. The river was almost at flood stage, and the current was strong. Hays sent word that the river could not be crossed. Cook reached the river at about three o'clock in the morning and continued the search for a suitable location for a crossing. After several attempts to cross the river, he too gave up and reported to Somervell that a crossing was impossible.

Leaving four men from each company to guard their horses, which were left at the junction of Chacon Creek and the Rio Grande, the Texans began to move on foot along the sandy river bank to a position between the plaza and the river, just as Somervell had ordered.

Well before daylight the Texans were in a position between the plaza and the river bank. Their ranks were extended up and down the river to form a "half moon" around the town. It was cold, and the men, wrapped in blankets, hovered together in small groups. Not a sound could be heard as the men were ordered to keep quiet for fear of waking the sleeping populace. As the sun began to come up, the sound of dogs barking on the south bank of the river could be heard. People from across the river began to come down to the river for water, but the Texans remained motionless on the far bank and were not discovered. Once a woman in a canoe started to cross the river to the north bank but discovered the Texans and quickly paddled back to the opposite shore. The Texans were surprised that she showed no alarm but calmly dragged the canoe up on the river bank and was soon out of sight in the dim, early morning light. Later a small boy from the north bank came down to the river to water a mule. Captured, the boy appeared frightened, telling the Texans that the Mexican military was gone. A few minutes later two women suddenly appeared at the water's edge and discovered the Texans. Screaming, they fled up the steep river banks into the town. Their position discovered, the Texans released the boy and began preparations to enter the town. Hurriedly, the men scrambled up the embankment and formed at the head of several streets.

As they entered the town, no resistance was offered. Not a rifle was fired either in conquest or defiance. For some time the citizens of the community had been expecting the Texans. Only minutes after the Texans entry into town, the Lone Star flag could be seen waving in the early morning light from the small steeple of San Agustin Church. About thirty minutes later the vanguard of the main army entered Laredo from the north. By this time, most of the citizens, especially women, children, and elderly men, had gathered on the streets. One soldier recorded that the cry of

"Buenos dias caballeros! Nosotros [somos] amigos de los Americanos!" was common. What the Texans did not know was that the jubilation on the part of the Laredoans was not sincere. The pan dulce and piloncillos held out to the Texans by the Laredo populace came not out of gratitude but out of fear. Alcalde Villarreal officially surrendered the town to General Somervell. Cooperation with the Texans, the alcalde hoped, might save Laredo from pillage. He went from Texan to Texan shaking hands and greeting the men. The entire Texan Army of more than seven hundred men was paraded through the town and then led by Villarreal to a campsite near the river on a sand bar about one mile above the town.

The march from San Antonio to the river had lasted for seventeen days instead of the planned seven. The entire army had run out of food. Somervell thus wasted no time in levying a requistion on Laredo for food and clothing. Many of the citizens thought the levy outrageous but complied out of fear. At about noon, several head of cattle were driven into the Texan camp and slaughtered. The meat, however, lasted the army for little more than a few meals. With their bellies full for the first time in days, the men rested and slept. From their position upriver from Laredo, the men could easily observe the village across the river to the south. Numerous white flags were visible waving from the dwellings there.

Some of the Texans became angered when it was learned that valuable supplies had secretly been hidden by the fearful Laredoans. Several sacks of flour were found cached in the brush outside of town. Noticing the tracks of numerous carts and wagons leading downriver from Laredo, the Texans concluded that more supplies were hidden elsewhere.

By afternoon, scouts began to arrive with rumors that a large Mexican force, equal in size to the Texan Army, was approaching Laredo. Somervell thought it advisable to move the Texan camp to a location downriver from Laredo to a point where Chacon Creek merged with the Rio Grande. At the new location the Texans were protected from attack by the high banks of the Rio Grande to the south and Chacon Creek to the east. The campsite became known as Camp Chacon. Here a young man was accidentally shot in the heart, the first casualty of the Somervell Expedition. At Camp Chacon, many of the Texans began to drink some mescal which they had purchased or stolen in Laredo. Others seemed overjoyed with smoking marijuana which they had also "found" in town.

Although Somervell had strict orders prohibiting any of the Texans from leaving camp, more than one-third of the entire army, having little respect for Somervell or military rules and regulations, left camp on the morning of December 9 for the purpose of "visiting" Laredo. What the Texans did in Laredo in the next few hours would be debated by leading diplomats in Austin, Mexico City, London, and other world capitals for years to come. Many of the men were drunk. All were without military leadership. Some wanted revenge for the Mexican raids on San Antonio.

The pillage started when several of the rambunctious Texan ruffians rode up to the town jail on the south side of San Agustin Plaza and demanded that the jailer free his prisoners. The jailer, not intimidated, refused and was immediately set upon by the Texans who forced him to open the cell doors. About twenty prisoners were freed.

Other Texans found Alcalde Villarreal and threatened to hang him if he did not reveal where he had hidden his silver. The Texans were about to go through with their threat, having the noose already around the alcalde's neck, when several of the more sane Texans rode up and set Villarreal free.

Many of the Texans, angry at finding only a few horses on their entry into town, now began to seize any mount in sight. Others, who had little or no clothing and blankets began to steal every piece of cloth they could find. Stores were broken into and sacked of every item which the Texans could lay their hands on. Groups of men were seen going up and down the streets with huge battering rams. The men would get a running start and were able to batter down any door regardless of size or thickness. For several hours, the pillage of the town continued. Many of the victims of the hooligans were helpless women.

Trinidad Garcia lost "one good horse and another not so good, a pacing mare and a good breeding jack, seventy-five pounds of tobacco and nine pairs of patent leather shoes, one large and one small telescope and a walking cane with silk tassels, the sail, mast and a set of cordage for a sailboat." From Reyes Ortiz the Texans stole "two gentle horses, seven work animals, one gentle mare and a pair of pistols, along with one hundred pounds of sugar." Maria del Carmen Gamboa lost "a new bedspread, one new sheet, a blanket, one chair and a new musket." Taken from Paula de la Garza were "a hat, three good sheets, three large and three small pillow slips, a colored blanket, a linen jacket and a bedspread." Maria Garcia lost "a hat, saber, four chemises and four underskirts," besides "an assortment of goods of a more personal nature."

Lorenza Gil came up missing "a set of jewelry, one fine quilt, three fine blankets, two hundred pounds of sugar, two bedspreads, three embroidered sheets, two new napkins and twenty-five pounds of coffee." Bacilio Benavides, ex-alcalde and later state representative, lost "one hundred and fifty pounds of flour, nine wool rugs, a pistol and a gentle horse." Ex-alcalde and Indian fighter Ildefonso Ramon lost "four loads of flour, one hundred and fifty pounds of sugar, ten pounds of chocolate, a silk shawl, eighteen pairs of shoes, one set of silverware, a musket, a silver decorated powder box, a saber and one gentle horse." From Maria Guadalupe Garcia the thieves stole a "short fat hog and a horse," while Andrea Trevino lost "a good mule and a mare." "Women's apparel, two pairs of silk stockings, a fine linen dress, one ladies jacket, three silk umbrellas and an embroidered sidesaddle" were taken from Vivian Diaz.

Narciso Martinez lost "two pounds of candles and a fine hat." Santos Benavides, later mayor, county judge, Confederate hero, and state representative, lost "a silver mounted saddle valued at one hundred pesos." Ex-alcalde Jose Maria Gonzales lost "four hundred pounds of pepper, six pairs of shoes, a carbine, three silk umbrellas, two silk crepe dresses and two dozen sets of harnesses," all from his mercantile business. The Texans stole from Agustin Dovalina "one fully equipped saddle, a change of clothes, and a fine rope." In the pillage, Bartolome Garcia lost "two new saddles, a new quilt, two good shawls and two blankets."

A few of the terrified citizens lost their life savings. One of the Texans later boasted that he had stolen from one of the Laredo families, one hundred doubloons as well as four of the finest blankets he had ever seen. One of the blankets "had the rising sun in the center and its rays terminated to its outer parts with brilliant colors of the rainbow." The Laredoan from whom the covering was stolen is said to have wept as the blanket was taken, claiming that it had taken his sister in Monclova three years to make the blanket and that it was the pride of his family.

Somervell, upon learning what his men had done in Laredo, immediately called a council of war. It was agreed that the stolen property should be restored to the inhabitants of Laredo. With a good two-thirds of his men still in camp, Somervell ordered that a guard company in the shape of a huge *V* be placed before the camp. The open ends of the *V* pointed toward Laredo so that every man could be apprehended. Some of the thieves were able to avoid the trap, however, as indicated by the diary of one of the soldiers: "Once arrived [at] camp every man was ordered to come forward and deposit whatever he had taken. There was no other alternative. But some who smelt the rat in time, who had valuable things, got outside the lines and hid their ill-gotten gains in the schapparall [sic]...and some staid out until the army moved on, and then followed in the wake of it."

Another soldier recorded the entrance of the pillagers into camp: "...they came loaded with as various and motley an assortment of pillage, as was ever brought within the lines of a civilized force. Blankets, beds and bed-clothes, cooking utensils of various design; horses, mules, and asses; beeves, veals and muttons; poultry of every genus of ornithology; honey, bred, flour, sugar, and coffee; saddles and bridles; coats, hats, and every other specimen of male apparel known amongst the gentler sex that our blushing muse forbids us to catalogue."

Most of the Texans did not approve of what had happened in Laredo. Some who participated in the plunder later came to realize the dastardliness of their action: "Here was a town, on the soil claimed by Texas; its inhabitants, claiming to be Texans, and opened their doors to us, as to friends—had received the soldiers of Texas as deliverers, and yet, those inhabitants, were not safe in the possession of their private property."

Once the loot had been collected, it was placed in a pile which was said to have been the size of a large house. Many of the Texans asserted that they had purchased the goods while others claimed the items in their possession had been given freely by the citizens of Laredo. Somervell and his officers were not listening to any such excuses. The General hastily wrote a letter to Alcalde Villarreal attempting to apologize for the actions of his men, "I regret to learn that some bad men belonging to the army under my command have committed acts of outrage in your town. The army is composed of volunteers and is difficult to control. But I am to state to you that these acts have excited the indignation of a large portion of the army and are utterly reprobated by myself and officers under my command. We will make you all the reparation in our power, by returning all such articles as are not essential to the army." Villarreal was asked to come downriver with several carts and take the stolen items and restore the loot to the proper owners. However, much of the plunder, such as foodstuffs, was kept by the hungry army.

Chief spokesman and defender of the plunder of Laredo was Thomas Jefferson Green who later wrote a book on the expedition. Green wrote: "did not the Texans have a clear right by the lex talionis [law of retaliation] of war...to lay every Mexican town

Florencio Villarreal was alcalde of Laredo when the Mier Expedition descended on the town with devastating force in 1842. Villarreal, a prosperous rancher with lands on both sides of the river, had previously served three times as village alcalde. After the sacking of Laredo, Somervell wrote a letter of apology to Villarreal expressing his regrets for the conduct of his men and promising to return the items stolen from the townspeople (Maria del Carmen Offer)

upon the border in ashes? Did not the burning of our towns in 1836, and the subsequent plunder of Refugio and San Antonio, give them this right? It clearly did! A greater interest was manifested...for the 'poor Mexicans,' which was sung morning, noon and night, throughout the camp, than for our own men."

Principal critic of the actions of the Texans who sacked Laredo was the very man who authorized the expedition, Sam Houston, president of the Republic of Texas. Houston placed most of the blame on Green and did not forget the sacking of Laredo for many years. In a speech before the United States Senate in 1854, Houston referred to Green as a dog, a loafer, and a dastardly coward. "Laredo was inhabited by Mexicans," Houston wrote, "but they were Texan citizens, and as such, entitled to its protection. They were citizens of Texas, and none but an enemy of Texas could raise his hand against them or molest one of them."

Eight years after that terrible day in 1842 when the town was sacked, the people of Laredo, now citizens of the United States, who had suffered at the hands of the irresponsible Texans, formed a committee under the guidance of Mayor Bacilio Benavides, one of the victims, and Estanislao Escamilla, city secretary. They hoped to be repaid for the damages they had suffered. Other members of the committee were Anastacio Gonzales, Pablo Ramirez, and Margarito Sanchez. The group estimated the value of the stolen items to be "twelve thousand six hundred and eighty-one pesos and thirty-seven and one-half centavos." A bill, setting forth the claims of the victims of the "sack of Laredo" was drafted and presented to the Senate by Hamilton P. Bee who was representing Laredo in the Texas House of Representatives. No compensation was ever granted by the legislature.

107

The Texans who sacked Laredo in 1842, are shown in this old sketch as they sailed down the Rio Grande. They were badly beaten at Mier, and 248 of the men were marched off to prison in Mexico. (New York Public Library)

In the same year that the Mier Expedition raided Laredo, Santos Benavides was married to Augustina de Villarreal in St. Augustine Church. The exact date was Thursday, October 27, 1842, and the priest was Father Jose Trinidad Garcia. The marriage, as was the tradition, had been announced the three previous Sundays. (Matrimonios, Libro I, 1790-1858, St. Augustine Parish Archives)

In a heavily retouched photograph, the Mier prisoners pose with their Mexican guards. After surrender at Mier, the Texans were marched to Monterrey and Saltillo. At Salado, 110 miles south of Saltillo, the Texans made a daring break. Most of those who escaped were recaptured and marched back to Salado where the famous "Lottery of Death" or "Black Bean Incident" commenced. Seventeen black beans were placed in an earthen jar along with 159 white beans. A white bean meant life, a black bean meant death. Those who survived the Salado executions were first imprisoned near Mexico City and later at Perote Prison, 160 miles east of Mexico City on the road to Vera Cruz. Although some escaped, the remaining Texans were held until September 14, 1844. (Library of the Daughters of the Republic of Texas, the Alamo)

In this exaggerated sketch made in 1850, wagons are seen crossing the mouth of Zacate Creek before entering the village of Laredo. With the establishment of a permanent military post at Laredo in 1848, commerce increased. (United States and Mexican Boundary Survey)

Chapter 6

The People

Citizens of Laredo gather on a cold winter morning in 1888 for the camera of Tomas J. Cockrell. (Mexican International Railway Views)

One of the oldest Laredo photographs is this glass plate of Francisco Gutierrez de Lara, brother of the famous Jose Bernardo Gutierrez de Lara, and his twin daughters, Maria Juliana de la Trinidad Gutierrez de Lara Trevino, on the left and Maria Dolores Juliana Gutierrez de Lara Trevino, on the right. Francisco was born on December 3, 1788, and his daughters on June 29, 1818. (Sandra Garza)

This tintype of Antonio Pena, an early settler of Laredo, is one of the few such photographs even taken of a Laredoan. Most early portraits of Laredo citizens were either taken by itinerant photographers or by studios in such places as Galveston, San Antonio, and Monterrey, where citizens of the border community were traveling. (Author's Collection)

112

This rare tintype is of Encarnacion Garcia de Benavides, wife of Bacilio Benavides and aunt of Santos Benavides. Her recollections of the physical appearance and demeanor of Tomas Sanchez, the founder of Laredo, has proven valuable to historians. (Author's Collection)

Besides his heroic military career, Santos Benavides (1823-1891), shown here with his wife, Augustina de Villarreal, also served as mayor from 1856 to 1857, county judge from 1859 to 1860, and as state representative from 1879 to 1885. (Hector Farias)

Refugio Benavides (1821-1899), shown here in the latter part of his life in the 1880's, was one of the most important mayors in Laredo history. The older brother of Santos, Refugio's political career began as an alderman in 1852, and in 1859 he was elected mayor. During the Civil War, he rose to the rank of captain and served with distinction in Benavide's Regiment. He returned as mayor in 1873 and was reelected in 1874 and 1875. He also served briefly as a Texas Ranger. (Miguel Benavides Family)

Tirza Garcia (1853-1920), daughter of Bartolo Garcia, married Raymond Martin on January 10, 1870. Ten children, five sons and five daughters, were born of this marriage. The sons included Raymond V., Marcelino G., Jean M., Joseph Claude, and Albert. The daughters were Antonia M., Herlinda M., Magdalena M., Marie, and Louise. (Anita and J. C. Martin)

Raymond Martin (1828-1900), the son of Maria Antonetta Chanfrean and Juan Maria Martin, was born at Auzas Haute, France. In 1845, at the age of seventeen, like brothers Paul and Joseph before him, Martin set sail for America. Other brothers and sisters included, Marie, Marcellin, Marion, Pauline, Magdalaine, and Jeane. Landing in New Orleans, he hoped to become a merchant like his father, but soon moved to Pensacola, Florida. He later caught the stage to San Antonio and, in 1856, rode south to Laredo. With meager financial resources, he opened a store one block south of St. Augustine Church. In 1858, he became an American citizen and was elected alderman in 1859. By 1860, he was the wealthiest man in Webb County. The following year he purchased several hundred head of sheep, commencing an industry that would dominate the economy of the Rio Grande Plain within two decades. By 1882, Martin was said to have owned ninety thousand head of the wooly creatures. Although he was defeated for county treasurer in 1873, Martin, within three years, had come to dominate Laredo politics, a position he would hold, with minor interruptions, until his death on March 2, 1900. (A Twentieth Century History of Southwest Texas)

Francisca Benavides Farias (1842-1909), the sister of Eulalio, Juliana, Cristobal, Andrea, and half-sister of Santos, Refugio, and Ricarda, was married to Francisco Farias (1833-1915). Farias Elementary School honors his memory today. (Author's Collection)

John Leonard Haynes was born in Liberty, Bedford County, Virginia on July 3, 1821. As a young man, he moved to Mississippi where he briefly edited the Lexington Advertiser. During the Mexican War, he served in Zachary Taylor's army on the Rio Grande and in northern Mexico. After the war, he settled at Davis' Ranch or what is now Rio Grande City. He was elected county clerk of Starr County, and in 1857, he was chosen state representative. He was reelected in 1859 and was one of the few members of the Eighth Legislature to attempt to explain the actions of Juan Cortina following Cortina's Brownsville Raid. During the Civil War, Haynes helped raise a regiment of Tejanos for the Union Army and rose to the rank of Colonel. Great-grandchildren of John L. Haynes included: Anita Haynes Villarreal; Maria Luisa Haynes; Consuelo Haynes Novoa; Jorge B. Haynes; Roberto H. Haynes; Mauricio Haynes; James Haynes, Jr.; Robert J. Haynes; Richard Haynes; Nora Lee Haynes Notzon; Mabel Haynes Vidaurri; and Lilian Haynes Ramirez. (The Texas Album of the Eighth Legislature)

John Z. Leyendecker was born on September 10, 1827, at Mallmerod in the Dutchy of Nassau, Germany. At age eighteen, he came to the United States on the Riga out of Antwerp. After fifty-eight days on the cold Atlantic, he arrived at Galveston. After a brief stay in the Texas hill country, he came to Laredo in 1847. He married Andrea Benavides, a sister of Santos Benavides, on June 1, 1857. When Andrea died, he married Juliana, sister of his first wife, on August 1, 1865. Ten children would be born of the second marriage; they were Bonifacio Juvenal, Pedro Pablo, Paula Inez, Jose Patricio, Petronila Maria Magdalena, Miguel Tomas Mauricio, Tomas de Aquino Leandro, Clara Maria de la Nieves, Juan de Jesus Inocente, and Alfonso Maria de Ligorio Santa Ana. Leyendecker served as assistant quartermaster under Santos Benavides during the Civil War and became postmaster in Laredo during Reconstruction. (Ursuline Sisters)

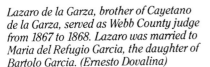

Lazaro de la Garza, brother of Cayetano de la Garza, served as Webb County judge from 1867 to 1868. Lazaro was married to Maria del Refugio Garcia, the daughter of Bartolo Garcia. (Ernesto Dovalina)

Cristobal Benavides (1838-1904), younger half-brother of Refugio and Santos Benavides, was a gallant Confederate officer, prominent rancher, and astute merchant. After the Civil War, Cristobal joined with brother Santos to form the firm of S. Benavides and Brother. He became sole proprietor of the firm at 815 Grant in 1875. In 1867, he married Lamar Bee, the daughter of the distinguished Civil War general, Hamilton P. Bee. Six daughters and four sons were born of the marriage. The sons were all educated at St. Edwards College in Austin, and the daughters attended St. Mary's College in San Antonio. (A Twentieth Century History of Southwest Texas)

Two of the most powerful men in Webb and Zapata counties were Antonio Mateo Bruni and Blas Maria Uribe. Uribe, born on February 3, 1811, was the patriarch of the Uribe Family of Zapata and Webb Counties. He built much of the old fort that still stands at San Ignacio. A. M. Bruni (1856-1931) was born in the small village of Bedonia in the province of Parma in the Apennine Mountains of northern Italy. Bruni, who was orphaned at the age of twelve, left home at the age of sixteen making his way to the United States where he lived with an uncle in San Antonio until 1877 when he made his way to Laredo by stage. Bruni first established a general mercantile store, invested in city property, and expanded into the sheep business. By the time of his death in 1931, he owned 13,042 cattle, 468 horses and mules and had accumulated $495,000 in depression-valued land that was selling for a few dollars an acre. (Fred Bruni)

schools in the city. He left home at an early age, however, to join an unsuccessful filibustering expedition in Nicaragua. Captured, he spent several torturous months in prison. Released, he joined Gen. Zachary Taylor's invasion of northern Mexico during the Mexican War and later participated in Gen. Winfield Scott's capture of Mexico City. With the termination of the war, Jarvis decided to return overland to Texas but stopped in Vallecitos, Nuevo Leon, Mexico, where he took a job as a manager of a silver mining company. Here he learned to speak fluent Spanish, married a Mexican lady, and raised a large family. At the conclusion of the Civil War in 1865, he moved to Brownsville and then came upriver to Laredo. He was appointed mayor during Radical Reconstruction and set out to improve the physical conditions of the town. He also served as county judge and collector of customs and wielded considerable political clout along the border. He named many of the streets in Laredo and donated land to the city for parks. With the end of Reconstruction, Jarvis, stepped down as mayor but remained active in Republican and reform politics until his death. (Elizabeth and Jack Foster)

Samuel Matthias Jarvis (1822-1893) was the father of the Laredo Republican party. Born in New York City to wealthy, socialite parents, Jarvis attended some of the best

James Saunders Penn (1846-1901) was born at Clinton, Mississippi, but at the age of nine, came to Rutersville, Fayette County, Texas, with his parents. He attended college briefly, but enlisted in Tom Green's Texas Regiment during the Civil War where he rose to the rank of major. After the war, he fled to Brazil where he became a merchant at Rio de Janeiro. He returned to the United States after five years and went into the stationery business. He then came to Laredo on May 1, 1881, and started a printing business. Six weeks later, he established the Laredo Times. Penn took his own life on May 17, 1901. (Esther Stewart)

James J. Haynes, son of John L. Haynes and Angelica Wells Haynes, served for many years as Chairman of the Webb County Republican party and as collector of customs. He was born at Rio Grande City in 1853 and, at the age of nine, was left in Texas with his mother when his Unionist father fled to Mexico during the Civil War. (A Twentieth Century History of Southwest Texas)

Honore Ligarde, born at Bordeaux, France, in 1855, served eight years as county commissioner, six years as alderman, six years as tax assessor, and six years as tax collector. In his native France, he served for one year in the army and married Elizabeth Martin, a niece of Raymond Martin. In 1881, he came to Laredo where he went to work for Elizabeth's uncle as chief bookkeeper. After Martin's death in 1900, Ligarde continued to manage the Martin's vast estate. The Ligardes were parents of four children: Hermance, Fred, Amedee, and Antoinette. (A Twentieth Century History of Southwest Texas)

Dario Gonzales (1840–1896), shown here with his wife, Celedonia de la Garza, served as sheriff and tax assessor-collector from 1883 to 1885. As a respected member of one of Laredo's oldest families, he was one of the leaders of the Guaraches during the Election Riot of 1886. (Ernesto Dovalina)

Jose Benavides (1855–1918), shown here with his wife Delfina Vidaurri Farias (1862–1936), was inspector of customs for twenty-three years. A pioneer citizen and rancher, Benavides was the son of Refugio Benavides and Teresa Pizana. (Sanchez Collection, Webb County Heritage Foundation)

Leonard Haynes, son of John L. Haynes and Angelica Wells Haynes, was a prominent Zapata County rancher and surveyor. Here he posed for the camera of T. K. Hamilton in Laredo in 1886. Note the rifle, pistol, knife, and ammunition. A graduate of Cornell, Leonard ran a fur and hide business in Puebla, Mexico for a number of years. He had three wives, Edith Camden, Maria Luisa Meza, and Alice Doran. He died in Los Angeles, California in November 1926. (Barker Texas History Center)

Probably the most famous inmate ever to be lodged in the Webb County Jail was King Fisher. Fisher, shown here with his wife, Sarah, was arrested in 1881 after a gunbattle with Webb County Sheriff Dario Gonzales and his deputies. Fisher was wounded in the gunfight by Alex Trimble. Accused of horse stealing, Fisher was later released and sent this photograph to Sheriff Sanchez. Fisher, along with Ben Thompson, died in a hail of bullets at the Vaudeville Theatre in San Antonio in 1884. (Ernesto Dovalina)

The Leyendecker Family shown here around 1910 are from left to right, Juliana Leyendecker (wife of John Z. Leyendecker); Juvenal Leyendecker; Cecilia Leyendecker; Claude Claflin, Sr., holding Claude Jr.; Pauline Leyendecker Claflin; Lawrence Leyendecker; Margaret Leyendecker; John A. Leyendecker; Henry Leyendecker; and Ernest A. Leyendecker. In front holding the doll is Agnes Leyendecker. The photo was taken at 1512 Convent. (Dave Leyendecker)

Four young women from Laredo, dressed in their finest, posed for this photograph in 1894. From left to right are Bruna Ortiz, Manuela Vidaurri, Nieves Vidaurri, and Emilia Ortiz. Bruna Ortiz later married Valentine Puig; Manuela Vidaurri married Adolfo Farias; Nieves Vidaurri married Jose Mogas; and Emilia Ortiz married Baldomero Puig. (Bruna Sutton)

Another influential family in Laredo history was that of Abraham Kazen, Sr. Kazen was born at K'nat, Lebanon, about 1868 and came to the United States in the late 1880s. With his brothers, Anthony and Joe, Kazen peddled dry goods in the small towns and ranches between Laredo and San Antonio. By 1890, they had established residence in Laredo and were operating up and down the Rio Grande. Kazen returned to Lebanon in 1902 and married Anne Reston. They raised a family of four sons and a daughter. From 1912 to 1914, he operated a store in San Marcos and Benavides. Kazen lived to be ninety-seven years of age. Left to right in this photograph, taken in 1923, are, E. James; Abraham, Jr. (standing in front); Charles; Philip; and Carmen. Charles Henry served in the army during World War II as a captain and was appointed the first Allied judge in Naples after the liberation of that city. He served as Webb County clerk from 1946 to 1958 and was later customs collector. Philip was district attorney in Laredo from 1938 to 1942 and served in various government capacities during World War II. E. James Kazen was appointed district attorney when his brother resigned in 1942. He served until becoming District Judge in 1958. Judge Kazen's children included three lawyers and two teachers. One son, George, is federal judge in Laredo. Abraham, Jr., commonly known as "Chick," was elected to the state legislature and served in the Unted States House of Representatives from 1967 to 1985. Carmen Kazen Ferris, only daughter of Abraham and Anne Kazen, was a home economics teacher in the public schools for a number of years. (Abraham Kazen, Jr.)

Members of the Floyd Family pose over a chess board. From left to right, an adopted son, Alejandro Marulanda, and their parents Guadalupe Marulanda de Floyd, and Priciliano Floyd. For many years Priciliano Floyd was active in the Guarache party and was elected to the city council in the 1890s. He was the son of Horace Hamilton Floyd and Ynocensia Salas. After serving in the Mexican War, his father, H. H. Floyd, had settled at Roma where Priciliano was born in 1853. Priciliano worked for a short time as a clerk in Corpus Christi but came to Laredo in 1875 and entered into a partnership with the Villegas Brothers. Two years later, he established a mercantile firm of his own. He sold his store in 1887 and purchased a four thousand acre farm a few miles below Laredo. He also purchased a sixty thousand acre ranch in Coahuila and served as vice-president of the Durango Milling and Mining Company. (Ricardo Floyd)

The Penn Family sat for this formal portrait around 1888. Standing, left to right, are Albert M., Virginia, Justo S., Viola, and Amar. Seated are Virginia Josephine Muller Penn and James Saunders Penn. James S. Penn commenced publication of the Laredo Times *on June 14, 1881. After James Penn died in 1901, Justo continued to publish and edit the newspaper. (Ernest Leyendecker)*

Members of the Laredo Mistletoe Club, a blue blood social club, were photographed around 1898. In the back row, standing from left to right, are Minnie Pace Derby, George Derby, Judge A. Winslow, Clarence G. Jackson, Lizzie Mann Jackson, and Justo Penn and his wife. In the front row, left to right, are Galbraith, Lottie Pierce Gatewood, Romayne Galbraith, and an unidentified person (possibly A. C. Hamilton). (Mike Perez)

The Bruni Family, one of the most influential in Laredo's history, posed for this formal photograph. From left to right are Maria, Fred, Adela, Consolacion Henry Bruni, Minnie (Herminia), A. M. Bruni, and A. H. One child, Louis H., was not present. Leopoldo E. and Herlinda were later born of the marriage. One other child, Mateo Angel, died in childhood. Antonio M. was married to Consolacion at San Fernando Cathedral in San Antonio on March 5, 1879. Consolacion was a great-granddaughter of Parick Henry. (Fred Bruni)

Amador Sanchez, son of Santiago Sanchez, was mayor of Laredo from 1900-1910. Sanchez, who had previously served three terms as district clerk, became Webb County sheriff upon resigning as mayor in 1910. Educated at St. Mary's University at Galveston, and a civil engineer and surveyor by profession, he ran a 100,000 acre ranch in Tamaulipas, Mexico, and had considerable Mexican mining interests. Shortly after being elected sheriff during the Mexican Revolution, Sanchez was indicted for conspiring to overthrow President Francisco Madero. Sanchez pled guilty in a Brownsville Federal Court to selling horses to Mexican revolutionaries. He was sentenced to pay a fine of twelve hundred dollars and was placed on probation for two years. Sanchez was married to Marie Benavides, daughter of Cristobal Benavides. (A Twentieth Century History of Southwest Texas)

The office of Louis R. Ortiz was located at 1905 Iturbide. Jitney Jungle now stands on that location. From left to right standing, are L. R. Ortiz, Joe Ortiz, and Anita Ugarte Puig. Ortiz was born in Laredo in 1858 and attended school in San Antonio, Monterrey, and New York. He spent several years in the mercantile business before being elected county and district clerk in the 1880s. Ortiz was also one of the area's leading stock raisers. He was married to Anita Ugarte in 1885. (Bruna Sutton)

Victorino Juarez II (1860-1933), shown here, was the son of Victorino Juarez (1814-1889). The Juarez family were descended from Felix Juarez and Guadalupe Garcia who came from Palafox to settle in Laredo in the 1790s. The older Juarez was married to Eustaquia Mendiola and was one of the leaders in the Bota party. He served as county commissioner of Precinct One from 1884 until his death in 1889. Besides Victorino, six children were born of the marriage: Ildefonso, Julian, Antonio, Francisca, Severiana, and Florentina. The younger Victorino married Lucrecia Serna. They were parents to six children: Guadalupe (the late Mrs. Valentin Bernal); Manuel Jesus, Sr. (1896-1981), who is survived by his wife Juanita de Leon; Sofia (who died at the age of 2); a third Victorino (married to Manuela Guajardo); Julian (married to the late Maria Hernandez); and Enriqueta (the deceased Mrs. Rumaldo Vasquez). Victorino and Lucrecia also adopted a daughter, Nazaria. (Juanita L. Juarez)

Citizens of Laredo gather as a cattle drive enters the outskirts of the city in the late 1890s. (Laredo Public Library)

This badly damaged photograph is the only known image of the public hanging of Celedonia Chivarria in 1885. Sheriff Dario Gonzales, assisted by Eugenio Yglesias as deputy, was in charge of the hanging. Ezequiel Gonzales was the executioner. Chivarria was convicted of the brutal murder of Guadalupe Trevino and Antonio—whose last name was never known—on May 3, 1879, in Encinal County east of Laredo. (St. Mary's University, Institute of Texan Cultures)

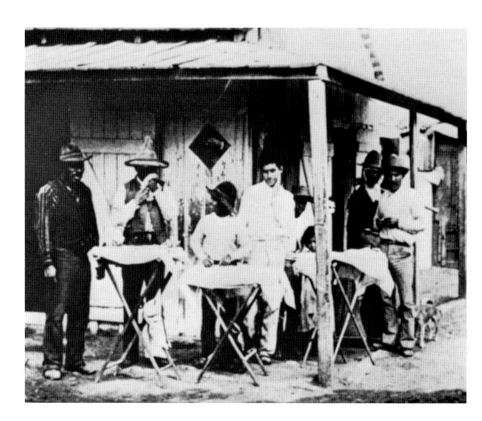

Candy sellers near Market Hall, were the subject of Henry Stark's camera in 1896. (Views in Texas)

The seven calendars on the wall of The Laredo Times *office on Flores Avenue indicate this photograph was taken on March 20, 1913. Jim Falvella, a reporter at the* Times, *is on the left. Willard W. Gregg, managing editor, is in the center, and Justo S. Penn, owner and publisher, is on the right. Penn also served as Webb County judge from 1928 until 1939. (Bessie Gregg Rodarte)*

On the left rear of this photograph, taken about 1910, is Pedro Armengol Guerra. Transportation in Laredo before the appearance of the motor car was very different. (Armengol Guerra III)

J. Fensterner shows off his new buggy for the camera. Fensterner, one of a large number of German immigrants to settle in Laredo in the 1880s, ran a tailor and dry cleaning business. He was also an amateur photographer. (St. Mary's University, Institute of Texan Cultures)

The Laredo Fire Department Hose Racing Team, which won the state championship in 1915, is photographed in front of the Federal Building. The Fire Department, after a disastrous downtown fire on the night of January 1, 1914, had been reorganized. Officers were August C. Richter, president; George R. Page, vice president; C. C. Biggio, chief; J. W. Falvella, assistant chief; J. R. Fasnacht, secretary; and Sam W. Brown, treasurer. (Mike Perez)

The Lone Star Hook and Ladder team of the Laredo Fire Department posed for this group photograph in 1910. Motorized vehicles had not yet become part of the department's equipment, but the first horse-drawn engine had been purchased by the department in the 1880s and was driven by Mauricio Didieu. (Mike Perez)

The entire Laredo Police Department consisted of seventeen men in 1917. Seated on the far left is Candelario Mendiola. Seated, second from left is Ponciano Vasquez, and in the center-front is M. G. Benavides. Standing, eleventh from left is Jacobo Salazar. (Miguel Benavides Family)

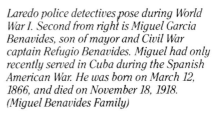

Laredo police detectives pose during World War I. Second from right is Miguel Garcia Benavides, son of mayor and Civil War captain Refugio Benavides. Miguel had only recently served in Cuba during the Spanish American War. He was born on March 12, 1866, and died on November 18, 1918. (Miguel Benavides Family)

Mike Brennan served as chief of police in Laredo for over twenty years. Brennan's career commenced when policemen either walked or rode horses; by the time he retired, automobile accidents and traffic tickets had become a major part of a policeman's duties. (Laredo Police Department)

The V. L. Puig Family was the first in Laredo to own a Rambler touring car. In the front seat are V. L. Puig and John R. Puig. Behind, left to right, are Baldomero Puig; V. L. Puig, Jr.; Luis Puig; and Joe Puig. In the back are Amelia Puig, Bruna Ortiz Puig, and Mrs. Bruna Puig. (Joseph Puig, Laredo Public Library)

The children of Cristobal Beñavides gather around their fallen father in September 1904. The children include, Carlota, who was married to Z. Valdez; Maria, wife of Amador Sanchez; Santos M., city treasurer for many years; Lamar, wife of Dr. H. J. Hamilton; Aurelia, the wife of Francisco Garza Benavides of Monterrey, Mexico; Cristobal; Eulalio; Luis, Melitona; and Elvira. (Cristobal Valdez)

Four Laredoans joyfully pose for an unidentified photographer during the first decade of the twentieth century. Standing, left to right, are Candelario Mendiola and M. G. Benavides. The two men seated are unidentified. (Miguel Benavides Family)

A number of Laredoans enjoy a weekend at the Mowry Ranch about 1901. Standing, left to right, are Oscar Perron, Edgar Perron, Will Roy, Robert Alexander, an unidentified cowboy, and Henry Spohn. Sitting, left to right, are Alice Mowry, Lillian Bolliter, Maria Mowry, Estella Burbank, Eliza Herrera, and Julia Schultz. In front is baby Mowry and the daughter of Mr. and Mrs. Robert Anderson. (Mary Cook Collection, Neuvo Santander Museum)

Mary Mullen Wright and her favorite grandson, Harry E. Sames, are shown in front of the Wright boarding house at the corner of Santa Maria and Victoria in 1901. Harry was the son of William J. Sames who came to Laredo in 1890. (Mrs. H. E. Sames)

Judge Andrew Winslow (1848-1928) came to Texas from Florida in 1877. He arrived in Laredo on Christmas Day 1881 on the first passenger train to enter the city over the tracks of the International and Great Northern. He presided as master in chancery in the receivership of the Laredo Improvement Company and arbitrated more than a half million dollars in claims against the company. Winslow served as Webb County judge from 1920 to 1928. He was married to Julia A. Ferrel and they were the parents of four children. Their eldest son, Julius Melligan Winslow died in 1906. Other children included John J., who served in the Spanish American War; E. Blaine; Margaret J.; and Walter W. (A Twentieth Century History of Southwest Texas)

Bessie Barnett posed with the American flag during a patriotic ceremony at Ursuline Academy in 1919. (Sister Gerard Langord)

Beginning with the decade of the 1880s, theatre became a major form of entertainment in Laredo. On the far right seated in the front row, in what appears to be a 1920 production of Gilbert and Sullivan's Mikado, is Josephine Didieu who later married John Robert Haynes. (Mauricio Haynes)

Around 1915, four prominent Laredoans, Amador Sanchez, George R. Page, D. Quintana, and Justo Penn, attempted a serious pose for an unidentified photographer with a slightly tattered canvas. (Author's Collection)

Thomas Carter Nye was a pioneer in onion farming in South Texas. In 1898, Nye bought acreage in North Laredo along what is today Mann Road, and imported onion plants from the Canary Islands. He also planted a small vineyard and experimented with growing olives. Nye was born on May 17, 1844, in Matagorda, Texas, and was raised by an English lady, Elizabeth Harvey. His father died when one of his ships went down in a storm. His mother had died during child-birth. During the Civil War, Nye fought at Sabine Pass, was captured at the Battle of Chickamagua, and was held prisoner on Rock Island where he contracted smallpox. Nye Elementary School honors his memory today. (Elizabeth Sorrell)

The Married Ladies' Social Club in 1917 included, from left to right, seated, Mrs. Albert Martin, Mrs. George Derby, Mabel C. Wall, Margaret Barlow Tish, Agnes Duetz Huberick, Mrs. Miles T. Cogley, Mrs. T. A. Austin, Mrs. Harry W. Johnston, and Rae Westbrook Weber. Standing, left to right, are Mrs. Joe Vidales, Mrs. Burbank, Mrs. L. J. Christen, Mrs. John Davis, Fannie Brewster, Mrs. Horace C. Hall, Mrs. Charles Dietz, Kerran Young, Mrs. George Woodman, Mrs. W. W. MacGregor, Mrs. A. E. Younkin, Mrs. C. M. Fish, and Mrs. Alex MacDonald. (Margaret Tish)

W. R. Pace, center, and Charles C. Pierce, right, gather with an unidentified friend, on the left, in Pierce's law office. (Sam N. Johnson Collection, Nuevo Santander Museum)

Workers display a variety of animal skins at the John Finnigan Company Warehouse at 119 Market around 1900. (Laredo Public Library)

The offices of United States Customs were located in the Federal Building around 1915. On the extreme left is Mary Devine. (Devine Collection, Jennie L. Reed)

George Reuthinger, (1858-1926) left, owned one of the finest saddlery shops in South Texas. Reuthinger's saddles were known far and wide for their quality. In 1904, Reuthinger advertised, "saddles, harnesses, leggings, carriage trimmings, phaetons, buggies, spring wagons, buckboards, and anything on wheels at rock bottom prices." Born in Neunkirch, Schaffhausen, Switzerland, he served in the Swiss army as a young man but came to America shortly thereafter. He married Hortense Robin in 1891, and the couple would eventually raise five children. The children included, Elizabeth, Minnie, Tillie, George, and Steve. (Johnnie Reuthinger)

On the far left, behind the typewriter, is Matias DeLlano. Third from left is Antonio Valls. Both are shown here in the offices of the Armengol Company around 1910. (Carmen Nelson)

Directors pose for the opening of the
First State Bank and Trust on April 9, 1928.
Seated from left to right are Pat Stanford, Ike
Hirsch, Ed S. Russell, A. M. Bruni. Standing
are Joe Moser and J. O. Walker. The First
State Bank and Trust later became the Union
National Bank. (John Keck)

Employees of the Laredo National Bank on
January 16, 1936, included Ramiro Sanchez,
general bookkeeper; Albert R. Vela, teller;
James Haynes, note teller; and Refugio J.
Benavides, note teller. The books of the bank
were carried in the large "Boston Ledger,"
shown on the right. (Ramiro Sanchez)

In 1928, the Laredo Fire Department poses in new uniforms in front of Central Fire Station. George Renken, from San Antonio, had recently been hired by Mayor Albert Martin to reshape the department. Laredo fire chiefs have included, O. P. Reid, Eugene Christen, Chester Biggio, Renken, Mike Perez, Sr., and since 1966, Mike Perez, Jr. (Mike Perez)

Basilio Guerra, seventh from left, is shown here by the soda fountain at City Drug around the year 1928. (Ramiro Sanchez)

Employees of Western Union, on Flores Avenue, are at work in this scene around 1907. (Nick Sanchez Collection, Yolanda Parker, Institute of Texan Cultures)

Employees of the City Drug Store are photographed here around 1918. Arturo Herrera is in the striped shirt and Antonio Herrera is on the far right. (Nick Sanchez Collection, Yolanda Parker, Institute of Texan Cultures)

A number of prominent Laredoans gathered on November 9, 1916, to honor the family of Venustiano Carranza of Mexico. Standing, left to right, are Higinio Valdez, Jr.; Alcala Flores; Roberto F. Alexander; Pepito Mogas; Samuel C. Alexander; Manuel Lozano; and Jose Riestra—the Mexican Consul. Seated, left to right, are Panchita Garcia, Maria Flores, Oralia Salinas, Guadalupe Salinas, Virginia Carranza—the daughter of President Venustiano Carranza, and Elisa Guerra. Seated on the floor are Lilia Withoff and Delfina Alexander. (Ricardo Floyd)

Laredo citizens gather around the car carrying the family of Mexican President Venustiano Carranza. During a visit to Nuevo Laredo in 1916 by the famous Mexican revolutionary, Carranza's family spent time visiting relatives and friends in Laredo. (Laura Floyd)

140

Graforms of Naranjo's Business College in 1926 gather for a group photograph. Dr. Naranjo is in the center of the photograph. T. R. Esquivel, Sr., is in the back row. (T. R. Esquivel, Jr.)

This innovative "Three-wheeled Star Car" was one of the feature attractions in the 1924 Washington Birthday Parade. Behind the car is B. G. Salinas. Rosita Gonzales is in the front seat while Francisca Leal is in the rear. Raquel del Valle and Fidel Gonzales, Jr., pose on the running board. (1924 La Pitahaya)

Oliver W. Killam, champion of the South Texas wildcatters, poses on the running board with an unidentified friend during the oil boom that hit South Texas during the 1920s. Killam, on the right in this photograph, was born in Lincoln County, Missouri, on April 27, 1874, the son of D. T. Killam and Julia Magruder Killam. Killam was educated in the public schools of Missouri and the University of Missouri, where he took his LL.B. degree in 1898. In 1902, he married Hattie G. Smith. Three children, Winfield, Radcliffe, and Louise were born of this marriage. Killam moved to Oklahoma where he served in the Oklahoma legislature from 1910 to 1916, first as representative and then as senator. In 1920, he came to Laredo and commenced to drill a test well on the Mirando lease, forty-five miles southeast of Laredo. In April 1921, he brought in the first well. By December of the same year, he had brought in a second well. Killam continued his operations in the Laredo field, drilling some 150 wells within five years. In 1926, he sold most of his production to the Magnolia Petroleum Company but retained his gas wells. (Radcliffe Killam)

Jose G. Garcia's excellent photography is exemplified in this photograph of an unidentified couple. (Meli Coleman)

John Nance (Cactus Jack) Garner, the soon to be elected vice president of the United States, and John Valls, district attorney, pose during the Washington Birthday Celebration in 1932. On the extreme left is Tom Connally. (Sam N. Johnson Collection, Nuevo Santander Museum)

142

John A. Valls, a powerful district attorney in Laredo for three decades, delivers a speech at a 1932 Independent Club rally. Note the elaborate decorations and the fact that the speech was being broadcast. (Texas A and I University Library)

In 1956, Senators Lyndon B. Johnson and John F. Kennedy came to Laredo while campaigning for Adlai E. Stevenson. They are joined in this photograph by Mayor J. C. (Pepe) Martin and Governor Price Daniel. Photo by T. R. Esquivel, Sr. (T. R. Esquivel, Jr.)

The influence of Mayor J. C. (Pepe) Martin is evident at the Democratic Convention in Los Angeles in 1960 as O. P. Carrillo of Duval County, Governor John Connally, Jack Skaggs from Hidalgo County, and Philip Kazen from Laredo gather for an impromptu caucus. Governor Connally was Chairman of the Texas delegation. (Anita and J. C. Martin)

Nixon meets Nixon in 1972. While campaigning for reelection, President Richard Nixon visited Laredo. While inspecting customs facilities on Convent Avenue, he is greeted by J. W. Nixon, Laredo Independent School District Superintendent. Two secret service agents look on. Although he lost traditionally Democratic Laredo, Nixon received a higher percentage of votes in Webb County than any Republican president since the Progressive Era. J. W. Nixon served as superintendent of the Laredo Independent School District from 1945 to 1973. (Estevan Reyes, Jr.)

143

One of the most creative photographers in Laredo history was Jose G. Garcia (1875-1939). As a young man, Garcia studied under T. K. Hamilton, another well-known Laredo photographer. He later purchased Hamilton's studio. A large number of Garcia's photographs of some of Laredo's early floods survive today in a number of collections. Many remember Garcia for his excellent portraits. He posed his subjects at his studio at 1210 Lincoln as few others could. His photographs of Laredo's historical landmarks also demonstrate a skill rarely seen among Laredo's photographers. (Meli Coleman)

Samuel Serrano Cabrera (1895-1951), shown here with his three daughters, Leonor, Rosa Maria, and Olga Ortencia, was one of the best photographers in Laredo history. Serrano's portrait and group photos still grace many Laredo homes and photo albums today. In 1934, Serrano left Laredo to work for the Kodak Company in Mexico City. When he returned to Laredo during World War II in 1943, photography materials were difficult to obtain and he did not resume his professional practice. Sometime after the death of his first wife, Ortencia Garcia, Serrano married Esparanza Maldonado in 1928. Four children, Francisco Samuel, Emilio Fernando, Arturo Virgilio, and Martha Esparanza, were born of the second marriage. (Esparanza Serrano Maldonado)

One of the earliest and best Laredo photographers was Henry White Stevenson, a descendant of James White, the founder of Knoxville, Tennessee. Stevenson sat for this jolly and innovative self-portrait around 1900. Stevenson not only photographed many prominent Laredoans, but also managed to maintain studios in San Antonio and Hidalgo del Parral, Chihuahua. Probably his most famous photographs were those taken south of the border during the Mexican Revolution. (Chris and Gil Trevino)

Sebastian S. Wilcox, pioneer Laredo historian, was born on December 9, 1884, at Burnett, Texas. He studied at Southwestern University at Georgetown and came to Laredo in 1911 where he became court reporter for the Forty-ninth District Court. Wilcox is best remembered as the man who saved the Laredo Archives from destruction. He wrote articles for the Southwestern Historical Quarterly on local history entitled: "Laredo During the Texas Republic" (1938), "Laredo City Election and Riot of 1886" (1941), and "The Spanish Archives of Laredo" (1946). Seb, as he was affectionately known, gave numerous speeches on Laredo history and, based on the exhaustive genealogical work of Father Florencio Andres at St. Augustine Church, helped to compile a number of family histories of prominent citizens. (Author's Collection)

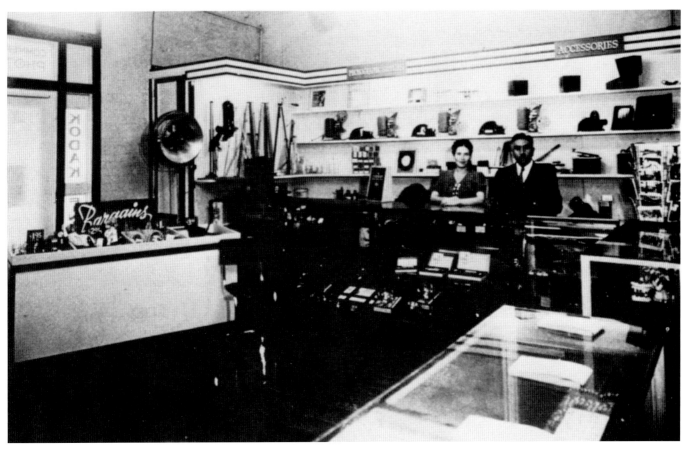

T. R. Esquivel, Sr., one of Laredo's most gifted photographers, was to the flood of 1954 what Garcia had been to the flood of 1922. Esquivel is shown here at work in his downtown shop and studio. Esquivel's fine photographs run the gamut from Mexican and American dignitaries at the annual Washington Birthday Celebration to amateur baseball and softball leagues, and from social and civic functions to historic churches and public buildings. Esquivel's son, T. R. Esquivel, Jr., continues his father's work today. (T. R. Esquivel, Jr.)

Mayor Hugh Cluck is welcomed home by a number of prominent Laredoans in the late 1930s. Left to right, are unidentified, Jimmy Richter, George Spence, Alvin Hansen, Joe Valle, Frank Hill, Gonzalo Farias, Emmie Cluck, Mayor Hugh Cluck, Police Chief Dave Gallagher, Robert Rosenbaum, unidentified, Bill Hall, and Jimmy Haynes. (Mary Cook Collection, Nuevo Santander Museum)

The *Major Brown* Com

Andres Martines was alcalde of Laredo from 1833 to 1834 and during the Mexican War. Although Martines was born in 1788, his place of birth is unknown. Family tradition holds that his biological parents were of Anglo descent who were killed by Indians near Laredo. The orphan was raised by Juan Jose Martines and Isabel Salinas Martines. On October 8, 1811, Martines was married in St. Augustine Church to Maria Francisca de la Garza. The couple eventually had eight children: Andres, Jr.; Bernardina; Teresa; Leonardo; Nicolas; Tomasa; Andrea; and Juana. Andrea married Lieutenant Hamilton P. Bee who came with Mirabeau B. Lamar and the American army during the war. With the conclusion of the war and the signing of the Treaty of Guadalupe-Hidalgo which divided Laredo, Martines agreed to become alcalde of the settlers living on the south bank. He thus held the distinction of being the last alcalde of Laredo under Mexican rule and the first alcalde of Nuevo Laredo. (Maria del Carmen Offer)

I t was during the war with Mexico that the citizens of Laredo watched as a strange object appeared on the Rio Grande. On October 24, 1846, the steamboat *Major Brown* arrived in Laredo and anchored near the town on the north bank of the river. The citizens of Laredo were astonished at the size of the craft and the fact that it was able to come so far upriver. The *Major Brown* was a 125-ton sidewheeler, 150 feet long with a draft of 3 feet, loaded.

In June of 1846, while Gen. Zachary Taylor's army was still on the lower Rio Grande, Maj. John Saunders, an engineer in the Army, had been directed by Taylor to employ Mifflin Kenedy, an experienced seaman, to select suitable boats for use on the Rio Grande. Saunders purchased the *Corvette, Colonel Cross, White-ville,* and the *Major Brown*. With General Taylor preparing to march on Monterrey, all of the boats were first used in transporting supplies to Camargo. With a lull in the fighting after the battle for Monterrey, Gen. Robert Patterson thought it feasible to explore the possibilities of navigation on the Rio Grande.

It was thus that the *Major Brown* was ordered to proceed as far upriver as practical and if possible, establish military communication with Presidio del Rio Grande. To ascertain if the river was navigable to any high point, the *Major Brown* was chosen specifically for the voyage, since it drew only two feet of water when empty while the other steamboats drew four and five feet. The trip would be made in the fall during which time the river would be at low ebb. Captain of the vessel was Mark Sterling from Pittsburgh, Pennsylvania. Lt. Bryant P. Tilden, Jr., of the Third Regiment of Infantry was in command of the twenty privates and non-commissioned officers assigned to the *Major Brown.*

A large part of the country between Camargo and Presidio del Rio Grande was still controlled by Mexican guerillas under Antonio Canales. Muskets for every individual and plenty of ammunition, as well as one month's provisions, were provided for the voyage and the uncertainty that lay ahead.

On October 1, 1846, the steamer left Camargo bound for Presidio del Rio Grande. From Camargo to Mier the voyage went as expected. Large herds of sheep, cattle, and goats grazing near the river banks were noted by the travelers. Beyond Mier the nature of the country began to change. The bluffs along the river bank became higher. An occasional white cypress tree as well as the ever-present willow and mesquite were observed.

Early on the morning of October 4, a short distance above Mier, several mounted and armed Mexicans appeared on the east bank of the river. The *Major Brown* slowed, and the Mexicans were signaled to appear at the boat and identify themselves. Instead, they wheeled their horses and fled toward a small stone house on a hill overlooking the river. Several of the men on board, apparently for no reason, fired at the fleeing Mexicans. One of the vaqueros was reported wounded. The boat was stopped, and by flying a white flag, two of the men were persuaded to come on board. The vaqueros had been gathering cattle which were being sold to an American in Mier. Their arms were for defense against the Indians, not for making war against the Americans, they reported. After being given something to eat and drink, the men were allowed to depart in peace.

Reaching the junction of the Salado, the *Major Brown* changed course slightly and steamed up the tributary for some distance. Hills rose abruptly on both sides of the river exposing the various outcroppings of rock. Blackened igneous rocks appeared on the surface of the sterile and austere landscape. Scrubby mesquite and prickly pears were the only visible vegetation.

Just below the town of Guerrero a beautiful sight, the "Guerrero Falls," halted the progress of the expedition. The falls, over twenty feet high, stretched from the center of the river to the right bank. On the other side of the river were large and extended rapids over which the water roared, plunging headlong into the main stream.

As the *Major Brown* anchored below the falls a short distance from Guerrero, vaqueros carried the news into town that "the Americans were coming in a thing that split the rocks right in two, forcing a passage for itself." Large numbers of Guerrero's citizens, including the town alcalde and priest, came to the riverbank to greet the Americans. Lieutenant Tilden reported that the "boat was literally thronged, day and night, during the three days that she lay at Guerrero. A second and third table was required at almost every meal . . . for the accommodation of visitors, who ate either from hunger or curiosity. The citizens' "astonishment and wonderment at everything connected with the machinery of the boat was truly amusing."

Relations between the Americans and the citizens of Guerrero were extremely warm. Many of the citizens expressed a desire that "peace might be soon established on a permanent footing between Mexico and the United States." The Americans in return were impressed with "the beauty and courtesy of the women" as well as the "cordiality of the men." While the *Major Brown* was anchored below Guerrero, a party of Lipan Indians raided several ranches in the vicinity. Five small boys were carried off in the raid, and several men were either killed or wounded. Two of those wounded were brought to the *Major Brown* where their wounds were dressed. After spending the night on board, the men were carried on litters to the town the following morning. The citizens, fearful of continued Indian raids, asked the Americans to "send troops for their protection."

The Mexicans took the Americans to a coal deposit near town. The coal was reported to be hard, bituminous, and of a first-rate quality. At Captain Sterling's request, six to eight tons of coal were brought on board the ship. Lieutenant Tilden also reported the existence of a small "quantity of silver ore . . . in the neighborhood of the coal."

Early on the morning of October 8, the men continued their trip. An "immense crowd of all ages and sexes . . . thronged the shore, to take a farewell of the *Major Brown*." Tilden reported that the "waving of scarfs, handkershiefs, shawls, and blankets," as well as "wishes for a prosperous voyage and a speedy return," were common.

After leaving Guerrero, the river continued to drop. Rapids and shoals became common, and the current became stronger. Huge rocks jutting forth from the rapidly receding waters were encountered. Every foot of the rough waters was carefully sounded before the *Major Brown* was allowed to proceed. With the river at low ebb, Captain Sterling and his men became apprehensive of continuing.

The progress of the *Major Brown* became very erratic. One day, twenty-five miles were made, and the next day—only three. Passage through some of the rapids became frightening.

Frequently the *Major Brown* would put into shore near the numerous ranches along the river, and mesquite was cut to fire the boiler. Mexican vaqueros, who appeared friendly, always told the same story. News of the *Major Brown* had spread upriver from Mier and Guerrero. They had been expecting the steamboat for sometime. Some of the vaqueros were anxious to show the Americans some papers which they took from their hat bands. One was the Mexican version of the Battle of Monterrey.

Numerous Carrizo Indians were also spotted on shore. The Indians were armed with bows and arrows. Many were peons in the service of the Mexican ranchers along the river.

Below Laredo, the river continued to narrow. The hills were now rocky, and passages over the reefs became more dangerous than before. The *Major Brown* would navigate one rapid only to encounter another.

On October 24, 1846, the *Major Brown* reached Laredo. The citizens, like the vaqueros downriver, had been expecting the boat for sometime but were just as "astonished" at the sight of such a large vessel as the citizens of Guerrero had been. "This town lies on both sides of the river [and] contains about fifteen hundred inhabitants, and its buildings are for the most part stone," Tilden reported. On the south bank, "the buildings are mostly of cane and of wood and mud, and it numbers not far from five hundred inhabitants," the lieutenant continued.

"This town is important in a commercial point of view, being on the direct route from San Antonio de Bexar, in Texas, to Monterrey," but "has few points of attraction for the agriculturist or the manufacturer," Tilden reported. Tilden predicted that if a hundred thousand dollars would be spent in improving the river above Mier, boats "drawing four feet can readily ply between the mouth of the Rio Grande and Laredo." Laredo was destined without doubt, he felt, to become "the head of navigation on the Rio Grande."

With the river continuing to fall, Captain Sterling considered it impossible for the *Major Brown* to continue upriver. The boat was anchored under the high banks of the river near San Agustin Plaza where, due to the low water, it remained throughout the Mexican War.

Lieutenant Tilden's prophecy that Laredo would become the head of navigation on the Rio Grande remained unfulfilled. Never again would a steamboat or other vessel the size of the *Major Brown* reach Laredo. The many rapids and narrow passages as well as the erratic rise and fall of the water level, varying from dry to rampaging floods, made navigation of the river impracticable.

Today, modern dams block the passage of the river in several places, and cities and towns have grown up where vaqueros and shepherds once pastured their flocks. The anchorage of the *Major Brown* at Laredo is now the site of an international bridge which serves as the link between two cities, two nations, and two civilizations.

Mirabeau Buonaparte Lamar, a Georgia painter, poet, and publisher, commanded the American army in Laredo during much of the Mexican War. Because of recent flooding, Lamar reported Laredo to be "very little more than a heap of ruins." Lamar had served as a cavalry colonel at San Jacinto, and in 1838, succeeded Sam Houston as president of the Republic of Texas. Lamar's company was not the first American army to reach Laredo, however. In July 1846, Captain Richard Gillespie, in command of a company of Texas Rangers, has raised the American flag over Laredo. (Texas State Archives)

Chapter 8

Lt. Egbert L. Viele Establishes Fort McIntosh

Shortly after the termination of the war with Mexico, the United States Army moved to establish a military post at Laredo. Orders dated February 3, 1849, which came from the headquarters of the Eighth Military Department in San Antonio, were simple: "Company G., 1st Infy., now at Camp Ringgold, on the Rio Grande, will as soon as practicable after the receipt of this order march to Laredo, and occupy that point." The order was signed by Capt. George Deas, assistant adjutant general, at the request of Maj. Gen. William Worth.

Commander of Company G of the First United States Infantry was Egbert Ludovickus Viele, who for sometime had been stationed at Ringgold Barracks near Davis's Ranch or what is today Rio Grande City. Lieutenant Viele, from New York, had graduated thirtieth in a class of fifty-six from the United States Military Academy in 1842. The young lieutenant, along with thirty-three men of the mounted infantry, left Ringgold Barracks late in February 1849. Viele's wife, Teresa, remained behind at Rio Grande City. She would later recall her experiences on the Texas Frontier in a classic entitled *Follow the Drum*. Winding their way northwesterly along the Rio Grande, Viele, after several days march, led his men across the mouth of Chacon Creek, and a few minutes later entered the town of Laredo.

After parading his men through town and presenting himself to the community's political leaders, Viele moved west of town and set up a makeshift camp. The date was March 3, 1849, and for the next one hundred years, with two brief exceptions, the United States Army would be present in Laredo.

The lieutenant chose a high, relatively flat area on the east bank of the river just north of where the Rio Grande makes its turn eastward and passes below the town, to set up camp. The camp, just below the Paso de los Indios, was called Camp Crawford in honor of George W. Crawford, who was secretary of war.

Living in tents and frequently exposed to the elements, the health of the company deteriorated quickly. Within one month after the soldiers had ridden into the plaza on that March morning in 1849, Viele was faced with several desertions and had five of his men, two corporals and three privates, die of cholera.

Lieutenant Viele continued to command Camp Crawford through the hot summer of 1849. On the last day of the year, he surrendered command to Capt. John H. King, a native of Michigan.

One week later the name of the post was officially changed to Fort McIntosh in honor of Lt. Col. James S. McIntosh who had died on September 26, 1847, of wounds received two weeks earlier in the Battle of Molino del Rey during the Mexican War.

Fort McIntosh was one of a series of forts established across the Texas frontier in the period following the Mexican War. Forts Worth, Graham, Gates, Croghan, Scott, Lincoln, Duncan, and McIntosh, all named after Mexican War heroes and established in 1849, stretched from the Trinity River in the north to the Rio Grande in the south. McIntosh was the southern terminus of the defense line and was also part of another chain of forts protecting the Mexican frontier.

The line of fortifications stretched from Fort Brown at the mouth of the Rio Grande to Fort Bliss at El Paso in far West Texas with McIntosh anchoring the center of the line. Forts in the Laredo area were Ringgold Barracks, established downriver at what is today Rio Grande City in October of 1848, and Fort Duncan at Eagle Pass, established in 1849. Most of the forts were relatively small with garrisons of two, three, usually no more than four companies.

Life at Fort McIntosh was not pleasant. The fort was probably one of the least desirable of any post in the Department of Texas. The soil near the fort was of such a sandy nature that crops were almost impossible without extensive irrigation. Furthermore, irrigation was impractical because the plain on which the fort was located was at least fifty feet above the waters of the Rio Grande. Even in places where a crop seemed likely, the soil contained small portions of clay. The sand and clay, fifteen to thirty feet thick in places, rested on a bed of cretaceous limestone.

Almost no trees, except for a few scrawny mesquite, were present. Along the river banks, an occasional willow, ash, or mulberry could be found.

Many of the soldiers from eastern and northern states were astounded to discover that Laredo had only two seasons—summer and winter. An assistant surgeon was surprised to find that the Laredo summer "usually commences in March and ends in November" and that the "thermometer sometimes reached 107 degrees in the shade." The soldiers found the winters very mild, except "northers" which swept down on the post and continued "from three to eight days accompanied usually by rain." The mean annual rainfall in 1852 was reported to be 16.63 inches based on the three previous years.

Lumber could not be found in the Laredo vicinity at any price. Some lumber was brought from Ringgold Barracks but at a very high cost. Wood was purchased from whomever brought it to the post, usually at about three dollars a cord.

Forage was difficult to find. Because of the "sterility of the soil, no good grazing can be found near the post," one of the soldiers recorded. Furthermore, the crops in 1852 were reported to be entirely destroyed by a prolonged drought. It was thought that there was not sufficient grass within thirty miles of the post on which the post animals could graze and live. The drought had destroyed the corn crop although small quantities of the precious grain, which had been raised in the bottomlands along the river, could be bought. The post was dependent on hay which had been purchased the previous year at thirty dollars a ton.

Food for the soldiers had to be brought in from Fort Brown,

Ringgold Barracks, and Corpus Christi. Beef was purchased from Victoriano Salinas, Esteban Rodriguez, Agustin Soto, and numerous other local ranchers in the vicinity at seven cents per pound. The quality of the meat was reported to be "miserably bad." However, "a wild beef was occasionally lassoed 15 to 25 miles from the post and brought in and tied to a stake and fed on prickly pear for 5 to 10 days and killed."

Most of the soldier's mail, anxiously awaited each week, came by way of New Orleans by ship to Fort Brown, overland to Ringgold Barracks, and finally to Laredo.

Most of the duty at the post consisted of escorting supplies and mail and scouting for Comanche and Lipan Indians. Early in 1850, Indians stole about fifty horses in the Laredo vicinity. A detachment of troops commanded by Lt. Walter W. Hudson was sent in pursuit. The trail of the stolen animals led in a northeasterly direction. The detachment of troopers, after a close pursuit of the Indians for several miles, were able to recover about thirty of the animals. On April 7, 1850, however, while driving the horses back to Laredo, the column was ambushed by the same Indians.

The soldiers, outnumbered by the Lipan, took cover in a mesquite thicket, the usual means of defense in the brush country. The Indians, instead of being driven off with superior firepower as the Laredo troops had hoped, successfully attacked the thicket. The Indians killed a private and wounded four others, including Lieutenant Hudson, a native of Kentucky. Wounded four times and in serious condition, he died twelve days later on April 18, 1850. Seven years later a fort on the Devil's River was named in honor of the young officer. Lieutenant Hudson holds the distinction of being the only officer in the United States Army to die in combat while stationed at Fort McIntosh.

In December of 1853, with the Fifth Infantry at the fort, work was begun on a star-shaped earthen fort. In charge of the construction was Maj. Richard Delafield of the Corps of Engineers. Delafield, a veteran officer, had graduated first in his class from the United States Military Academy in 1814. Questions arose in Delafield's mind about the building of the earthen fort since the United States Government had never formally purchased the land on which the fort was to be built. Work, nevertheless, went on.

Construction lasted for more than five months.

The earthworks was located on high level ground overlooking the Paso de los Indios and was ideally located. Attack from the west in the direction of the river would have been impossible due to the steep river banks. The two longest points of the star fort jutted out to the northeast and southwest. Here and elsewhere in the fort, artillery pieces were located. A magazine constructed of stone, with descending steps, arched roof, iron doors, and overlaid with earth, for which Delafield was forced to hire a mason, was built in the southeastern part of the fort. A traverse the same size as the magazine was located in the southwestern part of the fort. The works, located fifty feet above the waters of the Rio Grande, was approximately one hundred by one hundred feet in size. Most of the construction work was completed by the Fifth Infantry.

Nineteen men commanded Fort McIntosh during the decade following the establishment of the post in 1849. Of the nineteen, five—Viele, Richard King, Sidney Burbank, Gustavus Loomis, and Randolph B. Marcy—became brigadier generals in the Union Army. One, Charles R. Woods, rose to the rank of major general. King was decorated for bravery at the Battle of Chickamauga; Burbank was decorated for valor at Gettysburg; Woods for bravery at Vicksburg, Chattanooga, Atlanta, and Bentonville. Henry Clay Wood, who as a second lieutenant had briefly commanded Fort McIntosh in 1858, was awarded the Medal of Honor for courage at Wilson's Creek, Missouri, in August 1861.

Three men who commanded Fort McIntosh—William W. Loring, Daniel Ruggles, and James E. Slaughter—cast their futures with the "stars and bars" of the Confederate States. Ruggles became famous as commander of the Confederate artillery which pounded Union forces at the bloody battle of Shiloh. Loring, who rose to the rank of major general in the Confederate Army, later became a general in the Egyptian Army.

Egbert L. Viele wrote handbooks for the U. S. Army before becoming a prominent New York politician and chief architect for Central Park in New York City. In the twilight of his life, Viele could still recall with pleasure that otherwise uneventful day on March 3, 1849, when he had led a small band of troopers into the frontier village of Laredo to establish a fort.

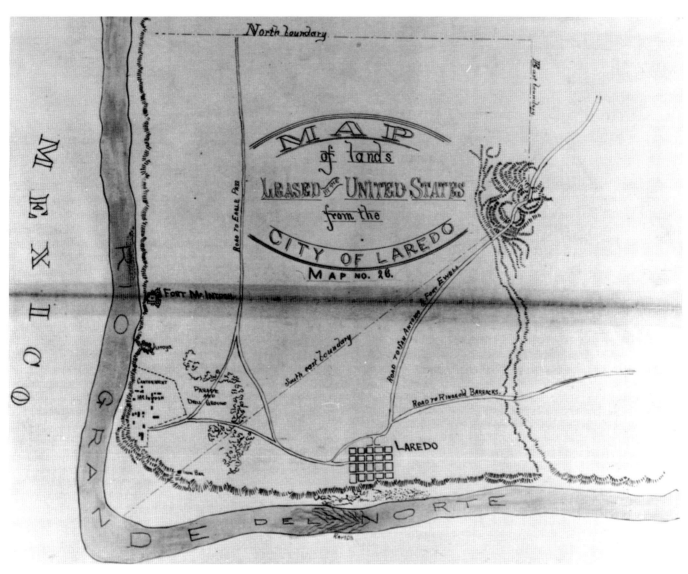

On March 3, 1849, Lt. Egbert Ludovickus Viele, shown here as a Union general during the Civil War, founded Camp Crawford less than a mile west of the small village of Laredo. The name of the post was later changed to Fort McIntosh in honor of Lt. Col. James S. McIntosh who had died in the Mexican War at the Battle of Molino del Rey. (National Archives)

This early "map of lands leased by the United States from the City of Laredo," is dated 1855 and was found in the National Archives. Note the distance from the fort to the town and the fact that by 1854, "Cantonment McIntosh" was distinguished from "Fort McIntosh." The latter fort was constructed by Major Richard Delafield of the Corps of Engineers in 1853 just below the Paso de los Indios, a well-known ford on the Rio Grande. (National Archives)

Chapter 9

When Robert E. Lee Came to Laredo

Late on the evening of March 25, 1860, soldiers at Fort McIntosh looked up to see a guidon flapping in the wind and a company of the Second United States Cavalry approaching from the north. The well-groomed troopers astride excellent, sleek horses had ridden hard from Fort Duncan at Eagle Pass. They were followed by two supply wagons. The horse soldiers were commanded by Bvt. Col. Robert E. Lee.

It was not Lee's first visit to Laredo. Four years earlier on a hot afternoon in August of 1856, Lee, accompanied by Maj. George H. Thomas, later known as the "Rock of Chickamauga," had passed through Laredo on his way to Ringgold Barracks at Rio Grande City. At Fort McIntosh, Lee and Thomas were joined by Maj. Randolph B. Marcy for the journey downriver. The three officers were to become part of the court-martial of Maj. Giles Porter. Porter was accused by the army of habitual drunkeness.

But in March of 1860, Lee was on more serious business. Juan Nepomuceno Cortina had laid waste to the Rio Grande Valley from Brownsville to Rio Grande City for a distance of 120 miles and as far north as the Arroyo Colorado. Rio Grande City was depopulated and only one family was left in Edinburg. Cortina's raiders had burned the ranchos belonging to individuals whom Cortina thought were in sympathy with the Anglo land barons of the lower valley. Texas folklorist J. Frank Dobie wrote that Cortina was, "The most striking, the most powerful, the most insolent, and the most daring as well as the most elusive Mexican bandit, not even excepting Pancho Villa, that ever wet his horse in the muddy waters of the Rio Bravo."

During his brief stay in Laredo, Lee spoke briefly to several citizens. "I have come," Lee said, "with full power to put down the outlaws and will do it if it takes all of the soldiers on the frontier." Lee was determined to crush Cortina, if necessary.

Although Lee was offered the warmth of one of the houses at the fort, he chose to camp on the open ground with his men near the river. While the men were in camp, a cold norther blew in, and the temperature plummeted. With the men freezing in their exposed camp, Lee gave the orders to break camp early. The men were not surprised. It was Lee's habit to begin the day's march at 5:30 A.M. after reveille at 4:00 A.M. The men would halt at around 2:00 P.M. so that the horses could graze until dark.

Wanting to load their wagons with corn for their mounts, Lee's troopers lingered in Laredo until 1:00 P.M. By this time a hard driving rain, accompanied by sleet, had hit the town, and Lee was anxious to depart. Lee ordered his troopers on ahead but waited outside of town for the supply wagons. Unable to locate the troopers' camp in the evening, Lee was forced to make an uneasy camp in the chaparral. Early the next morning he was in the saddle before daylight in hopes of locating his men. What he found was shocking. The men had suffered terribly in the cold, and at least two were dead from exposure. Some of the bluecoats had bought whiskey in Laredo and at least one of the dead men had been so drunk that he had not taken proper precautions against the weather.

By noon the storm had lifted, the South Texas sun was out and the men resumed their journey. Within five days, Lee's troopers were at Ringgold Barracks. In less than a year, Lee would leave Texas forever. Civil War had engulfed Texas and his native Virginia. The Old Dominion had beckoned, and Lee responded. As gallant a soldier as America would ever produce, his name, like a gray messiah, would become a rallying cry in thousands of Confederate military camps and bivouacs far from the vast expanses of South Texas.

Robert E. Lee, shown here as a colonel in the United States Army, came to Laredo twice during his ante-bellum career. In 1856, Lee, accompanied by George H. Thomas, passed through Laredo on his way to Ringgold Barracks at Rio Grande City. In March 1860, Lee was back in Laredo. This time he was on a more important mission. Juan N. Cortina had raided Brownsville and had laid waste to the Lower Rio Grande Valley; therefore, Colonel Lee was ordered to take action. (John Keck)

Chapter 10

The Battle of Carrizo

With the approach of Civil War in 1861, and the abandonment of the frontier forts by the United States Army, the small towns and villas along the Rio Grande became particularly vulnerable to raiding bands of Mexican guerillas and revolutionaries. Fearing a possible Union attack on the coast, Confederate forces along the upper Rio Grande were few in number.

Hearing rumors of a possible attack on Carrizo by the Mexican revolutionary Juan Cortina, Santos Benavides left Laredo on May 11 with a small detachment of troops for the river village.

What further angered the Confederate authorities along the Rio Grande were rumors, passed by Cortina himself that Tejanos, or Mexican Texans, who were resisting Confederate officials in Zapata County, had formed an alliance with Federal authorities in the North as well as with Unionists in Texas. With money furnished by the Unionists, Cortina was reported to be buying arms and horses. In reference to Cortina's impending raid, John S. "Rip" Ford, Confederate commander on the Rio Grande wrote Governor Edward Clark, "the scoundrels who set the Zapata rebellion . . . have aided in organizing a foreign force to invade Texas. I cannot tell where the storm may burst. I shall endeavor to meet the bandit and drive him across the Rio Grande."

As the numerous rumors spread up and down the Rio Grande Valley, many ranchers and sheepmen, especially those living in close proximity to the border, fled their homes for the more secure environs of the larger towns. From Roma northward to Laredo, the only villages which remained occupied were Carrizo and the small settlement of San Ygnacio.

Benavides, along with thirty men, took up quarters at Redmond's Ranch near Carrizo. Benavides wrote Ford of his arrival: "In consequence of the various reports that Cortina was going to cross the Rio Grande in this neighborhood, I came down here and have 30 men protecting this place, and intend to remain here until I hear positively of his whereabouts, and the number of his force." Within hours of his arrival at Carrizo, County Judge Ysidro Vela reported to Benavides that Cortina was in camp at Malabucco, sixteen miles from Mier on the road to Agualeguas. According to Vela, Antonio Ochoa, a Cortina partisan who had led an uprising in Zapata County the previous month, had "collected all the thieves, murderers, and assassins of Guerrero, and gone to Cortina." Vela felt Cortina's intentions were to attack Carrizo.

Noah Cox, a leading secessionist from Roma, agreed with Vela, feeling that Ochoa and Cortina were organizing men in Mexico for the purpose of crossing into Zapata County "with the avowed intention of plundering and burning the small frontier towns."

Cox organized a home guard for the protection of Roma and Starr County. "We . . . will defend ourselves as long as we can. Cortina and Ochoa are together, and they have possibly over one hundred men by this time," Cox reported. Cox's small company consisted of forty residents of Roma, thirty-four of whom were Tejanos. The company was hastily organized, poorly armed, and helpless against Cortina's veteran raiders.

Fearing Cortina, H. Clay Davis at Rio Grande City, was also on the verge of panic. "I have just received an express from Juan Villarreal of Camargo," Davis wrote, "who says there is no doubt that Cortina with a considerable force is marching up the country, with the intention of crossing the Rio Grande near Guerrero."

Upriver at Carrizo, Henry Redmond wrote Ford pleading for help. Redmond, convinced that Cortina would cross into Zapata County at any moment, wanted Benavides to station more troops at Carrizo. According to Redmond, Cortina had also joined forces with Octavio Zapata and a man named Serna, one of Guerrero's leading political figures. Cortina, according to Redmond, was telling his partisans he would kill every gringo in Zapata County. Redmond blamed most of Zapata County's problems on the residents of Guerrero, who Redmond felt were all followers of Cortina. A correspondent for the *Corpus Christi Ranchero* echoed feelings similar to those of Redmond: "I will tell you that hell hole of iniquity, Guerrero, has got to be wiped out before perfect security will be obtained for our Rio Grande settlements. It is the nucleus around which Mexican bandits . . . gather."

Mexican authorities in Matamoros had previously assured Ford they would do everything possible to stop Cortina, but Judge Vela was skeptical. "The authorities of Mexico may insinuate that they will zeaously [sic] endeavor to prevent him from organizing an armed force to invade our soil, but it is vice versa. They would more zeaously [sic] encourage the scheme than use prompt measures to prevent it," the judge wrote. According to Vela, "Actions speak louder than words." The judge had been forced to abandon his home and seek refuge at Redmond's Ranch. A band of Cortina's men had gone to Vela's ranch where they shot his cattle, stole his horses and destroyed the cornfields; thus forcing the judge to flee to Carrizo for fear of his life.

From Carrizo, Benavides sent scouts to locate, if possible, the whereabouts of the wily Cortina. With most of the residents of Zapata County in sympathy with Cortina, it was impossible for Benavides to make a move without Cortina's hearing of it. Others, especially the large landowners and the handful of small merchants in Carrizo, as well as the county office holders, were in sympathy with Vela and Redmond, and were reporting Cortina's movements to Benavides. "There is no doubt that he is organizing a force and that he intends to cross the Rio Grande near this place. I am constantly on the alert, and verily believe that I can repel his attack," Benavides wrote Ford.

On May 19, Cortina with his raiders splashed across the Rio Grande about four miles below Carrizo and went into camp. The following day ten of Cortina's advance guard ran into three of Benavides's pickets, and a brief skirmish ensued. The three

Confederates reported to Benavides that Cortina, with the bulk of his raiders, was safely on the Texas side of the river and that his force was growing hourly, being augmented by residents of Guerrero as well as citizens from Zapata County. Many of the Zapata County Tejanos were doubtlessly hoping to revenge the death of the men killed at the Clareno Ranch the previous month.

By the morning of the twenty-first, Cortina, by stationing various squads around Carrizo, had Benavides and the Laredo force surrounded and shut up in Redmond's Ranch. The bandit king had also succeeded in capturing two dispatch riders on the road from Roma to Carrizo.

All sorts of rumors reached the besieged Confederates. Cortina was reported to have between fifteen hundred and two thousand men. Roma and Rio Grande City were purported to have fallen. Two residents of Carrizo, Anselmo Flores and Pedro Reyna, attempted to persuade Benavides to leave and let the gringos defend themselves. Benavides, however, was determined to stand and fight.

Benavides had no doubt that Redmond's Ranch could easily be defended, especially the largest of the buildings which was made of stone and had been used before the war by the United States Army as a fort. Furthermore, enough water and food were available to last several weeks. Morale was also heightened by the possession of a small cannon along with plenty of ammunition.

Several of Cortina's pickets were able to get within a few hundred yards of the ranch and fire a volley of shots at the defenders. Other than alert Benavides's green troops, the shots did little damage. Several of Cortina's men were easily visible on the small cactus-covered hills surrounding the ranch complex and the village of Carrizo. However, Cortina's men did little more than ride around on their horses, a tactic Benavides felt was being used to confuse the besieged Confederates.

In the evening just as the sun began to set on the western horizon across the muddy waters of the Rio Grande, Benavides, Mussett, Vela, and Redmond positioned themselves on the large porch of Redmond's Ranch and took turns gazing through a spy glass at Cortina's men. Late into the evening, with a full moon out, the men could be seen marching about and deploying before the ranch complex.

On May 21, as nerves began to wear thin, the Laredo captain attempted to push an express through to Laredo for help. Private Angel Jimenez volunteered and set out for Laredo but was overtaken and captured a few miles outside of town. Within an hour another rider, mounted on Benavides's horse, with pistol in hand set out for Laredo at a full gallop. After a terrifying ride through Cortina's lines, the private reached Laredo safely.

As the young private raced upriver to Laredo, Cortina's partisans continued to fire intermittently into the ranch complex.

No casualties were reported, yet the Confederates spent an uneasy night.

The next morning, just as daylight broke across the South Texas desert, a lone rider came racing up to the ranch and almost collapsed from exhaustion. He was Refugio Benavides, Santos's brother, who had raced his horse down the Mexican side of the river and had managed to avoid Cortina's pickets at the river crossing near Carrizo. Refugio brought word that the remainder of the Laredo Confederates were on their way from Laredo.

Less than three hours later, a force of thirty-six men arrived at Carrizo. The force was headed by Bacilio Benavides, Santos's uncle, and Lt. Charles Callaghan. With no rest the Laredoans had made the sixty-five mile ride from Laredo in thirteen hours. The men as well as horses were completely fatigued. The Confederates had been stopped briefly by the villagers at San Ygnacio who told the Laredoans that Cortina had fifteen hundred men deployed around Redmond's Ranch, and any attempt to break through his lines would be senseless. Believing the residents of San Ygnacio to be in sympathy with Cortina, the men had continued downriver. Just outside of Carrizo, within sight of Redmond's Ranch, the Laredoans ran through a squad of Cortina's men who were stationed on the Laredo Road.

At the very moment the Laredo force reached Carrizo, Cortina and his men had entered the village and were in the process of breaking into the customs house and the court house. Believing Benavides to have surrendered, many residents of Zapata County joined Cortina and his men in the pillage.

Although exhausted from the long ride downriver from Laredo, Benavides asked for volunteers to join him in an all out attack against the bandit chief and his men. Benavides, along with forty men, caught Cortina and seventy of his followers a short distance from Carrizo, and a bitter fight ensued. The Laredoans charged Cortina on horse and were successful in completely overrunning the partisans. With several of Cortina's men killed in the initial charge, the remainder broke for the Rio Grande. With swords in hand, the Confederates pursued the bandits to the river bank. Seven of Cortina's men were killed, fifteen wounded and eleven captured. It was later learned that two of the bandits drowned while attempting to swim the Rio Grande to safety in Mexico. None of the Confederates were injured in the fight although Lt. Juan Garcia Soto and Private Dario Aresola lost their horses in the battle. Pvt. Angel Jimenez, who had been captured by the bandits the previous day, was recaptured. The entire battle had lasted only a few minutes.

In his report of the battle to Ford, Benavides wrote: "Before attacking Cortina, I particularly ordered my men not to arrest any of the bandits, but to kill all that fell into their hands. Consequently, I have no prisoners." In a preceding paragraph of the same report, Benavides stated plainly that eleven prisoners had been taken in the fray. What happened to the captives can only be pondered. It is assumed that they were either shot or hanged as such was the custom along the Rio Grande frontier.

On the morning following the battle, Cortina was reported to be a short distance from Guerrero with a handful of men and to be moving down the country in full retreat. Benavides, who remained at Carizo for several days, reported Cortina's force to be composed of the citizens of Guerrero and Zapata County, many of whom had been involved in the April uprising.

In Orders No. 21, Ford wrote of the battle at Carrizo: "Thanks are due to Captain Benavides and his men for their gallantry in expelling a foe from our territory. Their conduct merits the highest praise. Thanks are also due to the Hon. Basilio Benavides, Refugio Benavides and the citizens of Webb County for their promptitude in going to the rescue of their fellow citizens of Zapata County when threatened by imminent danger. They have shown themselves to be loyal to the government of the Confederate States under trying circumstances and deserve the commendation of every true friend of the South." In a personal letter to Benavides, Ford wrote: "Your judgement, ability, and gallantry in the affair receive encouragement from every quarter. I sincerely congratulate you upon your success. You and the people of Webb County have furnished indisputable evidence to the world of your devotion to the cause of Constitutional liberty."

Ford did not hesitate in reporting Cortina's defeat to Governor Clark in Austin. Clark, who appears to have had some doubt about Benavides's loyalty prior to the battle at Carrizo, wrote the Laredo captain: "Whenever our enemies have appeared on our soil, you and your brave men have been present and driven them back, with great honor to yourselves and the gratification of your state." Clark even went as far as to send an elegantly engraved pistol to Benavides along with a letter which read, "I am happy to believe in your hands it will always be used in the defense of your country and prove an instrument of terror and destruction to her enemies." Wallace E. Oaks, a friend of the governor, took the pistol to Benavides personally, and although detained in San Antonio for some time, arrived on the border in November 1861. To Ford and Governor Clark, Benavides' continued loyalty to the Southern cause was critical. It is safe to speculate that had Benavides refused to serve the Confederacy and remained neutral or joined with the Federals, the war on the Rio Grande would have taken a much different course. Benavides, especially in late 1863 and early 1864, was the Confederacy on the Rio Grande, and without the loyalty of that element of the Mexican-Texan population which the Laredo captain represented, the entire southwestern flank of the Confederacy might have been exposed, and the Stars and Stripes might have waved over Austin long before the summer of 1865.

At the time of the Battle of Carrizo, the most powerful and influential man in Zapata County was Henry Redmond who owned a large store at Carrizo which was also called Redmond's Ranch. Redmond, a cunning Englishman, had come to the border as a young man in 1839 shortly after Texas gained its independence. He acquired land on the river, married into the local population and made friends with Antonio Zapata, the fiery Mexican revolutionary hero who was executed in 1840 while attempting to create the ill-fated Republic of the Rio Grande. Redmond was instrumental in establishing Zapata County which he had named after his revolutionary friend Zapata. He became postmaster at Carrizo, justice of the peace, the first county judge, and collector of customs as well.
(Kingdom of Zapata)

In May 1861, Juan N. Cortina led a band of
Tejano and Mexicano revolutionaries across
the Rio Grande and commenced sacking the
small village of Carrizo (Zapata). One of the
targets of Cortina's raiders was the small
two-story Zapata County Courthouse, shown
here. On the afternoon of May 22, 1861,
Captain Santos Benavides attacked Cortina's
raiders and a furious fight developed. After
losing seven men killed, fifteen wounded and
eleven captured, Cortina limped back into
Mexico to safety. (Arturo C. Gutierrez)

Juan Nepomuceno Cortina, shown here as
a general in the Mexican Army, was one of
the most controversial figures on the Rio
Grande Frontier. Cortina, best remembered
for his raid on Brownsville in 1859, actively
fought Confederate forces along the Rio
Grande at the commencement of the Civil
War. (Texas Southmost Library)

Santos Benavides, after his defeat of Cortina
at Carrizo, went on to become the highest
ranking Mexican-American to serve the
Confederacy. Benavides was born on
November 1, 1823, the son of Jose Jesus
Benavides and Margarita Ramon, and great-
great-grandson of Tomas Sanchez. Benavides
would live under five flags: those of the
Republic of Mexico, the Republic of the Rio
Grande, the Republic of Texas, the United
States, and the Confederacy. He died on
November 1, 1891. (Texas State Archives)

Chapter 11

The Benavides Incident

It was during the Civil War in March of 1862 that an event involving Santos Benavides at Laredo almost became a serious international incident. Santos Benavides, in preparation for a march to Carrizo, had allowed two of his men to cross the river to visit relatives living on the south bank. In Nuevo Laredo, the Tejanos were bluntly told by the town alcalde "that if they wished to pass about the town, they must leave their pistols which they had in their belts with him until they were ready to return." According to Benavides, the men complied with the request but were fired upon and one of the men, Encarnacion Garcia, was killed in the confusion.

According to the Mexicans, the men "committed some disturbances" at which time the Nuevo Laredo authorities had attempted to arrest the pair, but the Laredoans resisted by drawing their pistols, and fighting broke out. One of the soldiers escaped the fracas, fled across the river, and immediately reported the incident and the shooting of Garcia to Santos Benavides.

Benavides immediately crossed the river and went to the alcalde. While the captain was in Nuevo Laredo, word that Garcia had been killed spread to the Confederate Tejanos on the north bank. Within minutes forty of Benavides's men were in the saddle and splashing across the muddy waters of the Rio Grande ready to take revenge for the death of their comrade. Captain Benavides met the force at the river bank and ordered the men not to enter Nuevo Laredo until he had completed his consultation with the alcalde.

In blunt language Benavides demanded that the alcalde arrest those responsible for the death of Garcia. The alcalde replied that he had no force to make the arrest, which irked Benavides to reply that he would help the alcalde make the necessary arrests and was authorized by treaty to use force if necessary. The alcalde, obviously intimidated by Benavides's threats, issued an order for the arrest of those responsible for the shooting. By this time, according to Benavides, the "assassins had all fled." For several hours Benavides searched the town and surrounding countryside, but no sign of those involved in the shooting could be found. The alcalde agreed to give Benavides additional time to look for the assailants, but after three days of frantic searching, Benavides was forced to admit that he had no "clue of the direction they had taken."

Downriver at Matamoros, Governor Albino Lopez of Tamaulipas saw the entire incident in a different light than the Laredo Captain. To Lopez, Benavides was trampling on the civil and military authorities of Mexico.

By this time the situation on the Rio Grande Frontier had become explosive. On March 15, 1863, several of General Hamilton P. Bee's Confederates crossed the Rio Grande into Mexico below Brownsville and captured Edmund J. Davis and four other Texas Unionists who were recruiting Tejanos and Confederate deserters into the Union Army. On the north bank one of the Texas Unionists, William W. Montgomery, was brutally hanged. Although Bee disavowed any knowledge of the incident, Governor Lopez was furious. "Mexico is a neutral territory," the Governor warned in terse language. To Lopez the invasion of Mexican soil at Boca del Rio and Nuevo Laredo were "one of the most serious crimes against international law. Attacks like those made by Santos Benavides will produce bitter feelings; the slightest motive may render fruitless all efforts of the chief authorities to settle the existing differences."

Bee, in an apologetic mood, promised Lopez that "the conduct of Capt. Santos Benavides at Nuevo Laredo will be officially inquired into as soon as I receive his report." Bee also assured the governor that Davis would be released and "sent to the right bank of the river." Four days later, with Benavides's official report of the Neuvo Laredo disturbance arriving in Brownsville, Bee forwarded the report to Governor Lopez. "From my long acquaintance with Captain Benavides," Bee wrote , "and high appreciation of him as a man of prudence and discretion, I am satisfied that the authorities on both sides of the line may equally confide in him as not likely to do any act to compromise the relation which should exist." Still diplomats in Mexico and in Richmond watched the border with a growing uneasiness.

Within months Benavides, Bee, and Lopez had more serious events to worry about and the incident at Nuevo Laredo was all but forgotten. In more tranquil times, the seizure of Nuevo Laredo by Captain Benavides might well have become a major international incident.

As a young man, Col. Santos Benavides first tasted the sting of combat when he served under his prominent uncle Bacilio Benavides, during the Federalist Wars and the abortive struggle to create the Republic of the Rio Grande. In March 1863, Benavides seized control of Nuevo Laredo in reprisal for the shooting of one of his men in the town. In the process, Colonel Benavides provoked a serious international incident. His account of the seizure of Nuevo Laredo was only recently discovered in the National Archives. (Institute of Texan Cultures)

Hamilton P. Bee came to Laredo as a young man with Mirabeau B. Lamar during the Mexican War. He became the first county clerk of Webb County in 1849 and served in the Texas House of Representatives from 1849 to 1859. In Laredo, he married Andrea Martines. Their daughter, Lamar, married Cristobal Benavides in 1867. During the Civil War, Bee rose to the rank of brigadier-general, first commanding Confederate forces on the Rio Grande and later in Louisiana. His brother, Barnard, was killed at First Bull Run. (Texas State Archives)

The Battle of Laredo

It was March 19, 1864, and east of Laredo forty-two men waited behind a large corral and watched the face of Federal vengeance materialize in the distance. Three years in the saddle had brought them and their colonel, Santos Benavides, to this place along Zacate Creek. The last four months of the war and the Yankees in front of them were about to dictate the fate of Rebel Texas.

The crisis began on November 2, 1863, in the Lower Rio Grande Valley when Confederate Brig. Gen. Hamilton P. Bee, a Laredo native, who represented Laredo in the state legislature, confronted the greatest dilemma of his military career. "The enemy are in force. Brazos Island is covered with tents; six regimental flags were counted; twenty-six vessels, some of them very large," Bee wrote from Brownsville. With fewer than 100 men to defend the town, Bee knew his days on the Rio Grande were limited. He was up against some 6,998 black, white, and Mexican-Texan troops from Illinois, Iowa, Missouri, Texas itself, and distant Maine; all elements of the Union's Thirteenth Corps. They had come down the coast from New Orleans through a terrible storm to participate in Maj. Gen. Nathaniel P. Banks' plan to cut the Texas cotton trade and strangle the Confederacy.

Three days after raising the Stars and Stripes over Brazos Island, the invasion force hit the Confederate coastline at the mouth of the Rio Grande River and began a thirty-mile march to Brownsville. Reporting their arrival on Rebel soil, expedition leader Banks wrote President Abraham Lincoln, "the flag of the Union floats over Texas today."

While this news may have been welcomed in Washington, in Brownsville it meant disaster. As Union troops approached the town, a long train of forty-five wagons carrying valuable Confederate supplies raced north for the Nueces River. Acting on orders, Confederates set fire to Fort Brown and "all cotton which was liable to fall into the hands of the enemy." The blaze soon surged out of control, spreading from the fort to Brownsville itself, and within hours an entire block of buildings along the river front and ferry landing were afire. Flames increased the Rebels' sense of urgency; several hundred bales of cotton that had not yet been consumed by the fire were thrown into the Rio Grande. "Peril was around me on all sides," Bee wrote as the destruction fever peaked. Eight thousand pounds of powder exploded at Fort Brown, driving the frightened townspeople into terror.

At ten o'clock the next morning, the Union Army marched into the battered streets of Brownsville, meeting little resistance. The Ninety-Fourth Illinois Volunteers, advance guard of their Union corps, led the way. Their force was augmented five hours later when the First Missouri Light Artillery and the Thirteenth Maine Volunteers marched up Elizabeth Street.

With their mainland base secure and their confidence still running high, the Federals decided to push inland later that month. With a force of fifteen hundred men, Unionist Texas refugee Edmund Jackson Davis led the movement upriver. Davis had just been promoted brigadier general on the tenth of that month, so with his new commission in his pocket, his infantry loaded on the river steamer *Mustang,* and the First Texas Union Cavalry to follow along the shore, the force pressed on to its first objective, Ringgold Barracks. The fort fell with no resistance. From there a smaller detachment of Union cavalry pushed upriver to the village of Roma, but again found no Confederates. This began a regular pattern; the First Texas Union Cavalry, the only mounted regiment brought from New Orleans, and elements of the hastily recruited Second Texas, a Tejano and Mexicano cavalry unit, would continue to operate upriver along the Rio Grande. Using Brownsville as a base, they would also drive north into the Nueces country searching for the enemy.

In many ways, by 1863 the war in South Texas had become a civil war within a civil war. It was now Texan against Texan, and Tejano against Tejano. It was a nasty guerrilla war that ravaged the already desolate land and left hundreds dead and thousands starving. And with the hasty retreat of General Bee's Confederate forces from the lower Rio Grande Valley, the only sizable Rebel unit remaining on the river was the small force commanded by Col. Santos Benavides at Laredo.

Benavides was born on November 1, 1823, the son of Jose Jesus Benavides and Margarita Ramon, and great-great-grandson of Tomas Sanchez, the founder of Laredo. Santos would live his life under five flags; those of the Republic of Mexico, the Republic of the Rio Grande, the Republic of Texas, the United States, and the Confederacy. As a young man he had seen political upheaval and first felt the sting of battle during the Federalist-Centralist Wars which ravaged the Rio Grande Valley from 1838 to 1840. These internecine quarrels made him familiar with civil war and taught him how to rise above it.

During the filibustering Somervell Expedition of 1842, a motley band of rowdy and drunk Texans sacked a small store Benavides operated in Laredo. Being Tejano, Santos was considered fair game by the rules of Anglo-Texans. He resisted taking up arms against the Republic of Texas, or later, the American Army when it occupied Laredo during the Mexican War. Instead, Benavides openly cooperated with the Anglo-Americans, and by 1856 he had been elected mayor of Laredo and three years later Webb County Judge. In fact, by the time of the Civil War, Santos had become a leading political and financial figure along the central Rio Grande. Some even called him the "Merchant Prince of the Rio Grande." Along with his brother Refugio, who had also served terms as Laredo's mayor in 1857 and 1859, and his younger half-brother Cristobal, Santos favored the Secessionist cause. John "Rip" Ford, a famous Texas Ranger and a leading Texas Confederate, later wrote that "the Benavides family broke ground in favor of secession [and] did the Confederacy an immense favor by

declaring for her."

In the midst of the labyrinthine and often anarchic political situation that had existed in the Texas-Mexican border region for decades, Santos and his family stood among the few who had managed to keep abreast of the situation.

Benavides and the Confederate Tejano population he represented were the Confederacy on the Rio Grande in 1863-64. Had Benavides refused to serve the Confederacy, remaining neutral, or joined with the Federals, the war in that part of Texas might have taken a very different turn. Rebel department commander Maj. Gen. John Bankhead Magruder knew this as well as anyone else. With the implied promise of a brigadier generalship—should he recruit enough Rebel Tejanos to the cause—dangled in front of him by Magruder, Ford, Bee, and others, Santos performed valuable diplomatic as well as military service, utilizing his revolutionary ties in Mexico to expedite the shipment of Confederate cotton through Laredo to the neutral port of Bagdad at the mouth of the Rio Grande.

Early in 1864 Benavides became worried about a possible Union attack on Laredo from farther down the Rio Grande Valley. In February of 1864, Martin Gonzales led a twenty-five man reconnaisance that rode two hundred miles into the lower valley and was able to monitor all Union troop movements. This led Benavides to believe that the enemy could not make a move without his knowledge.

In San Antonio, Rip Ford had become more than an ex-Texas Ranger and Confederate politician; he was now Col. John Ford with a plan for a "Rio Grande Expedition" to push the Federals back down the valley and out to sea. Benavides and his men were to be a part of it, joining the old Ranger as he moved from San Antonio through Laredo and on to victory. But on March 17, 1864, as Ford proudly marched out of San Antonio with his ragged Confederate army of conquest, he heard news that could mean trouble.

Ford's advance units, commanded by Capt. Mat Nolan, had been attacked by Union guerrillas, all Tejanos, commanded by Cecilio Valerio at Los Patricios some fifty miles southwest of Banquete. "An active officer; well acquainted with the country; brave and vigilant," Valerio knew the land of South Texas as few others did. At the head of his band of 125 men, loosely attached to the Second Texas Union Cavalry, he gave Ford's Rebels a fight that "could only be repulsed after a desperate fight and at the cost of much blood and property."

In Laredo, Benavides, under orders from Ford, was in the process of collecting supplies for the Rio Grande Expedition. But the winter of 1863-1864 proved to be one of the coldest and driest in memory. "You cannot imagine how desolate, barren, and desert-like this country is; not a spear of grass, nor a green shrub... nothing but moving clouds of sand to be seen on these once green prairies," a Rebel wrote.

Benavides was so ill from exhaustion that for days he had been unable to rise from his bed. "For three years he had been in the field constantly without a tent or bed and often without blankets, without food...without water and almost all the time riding through the country," a Rebel recalled. From his bed he listened to scouts' reports, and remained confident a surprise Union advance against Laredo or nearby Eagle Pass was not possible. Then came word from a Rebel sympathizer in Matamoros that a sizeable Federal cavalry force had left the lower valley for Corpus Christi. Another force was also reported to be marching for the Nueces country to recruit men for a move westward against Eagle Pass. And still other rumors reached the colonel that a Union force was advancing up the Rio Grande for an attack on Laredo or, again, possibly on Eagle Pass. As Benavides waited at Laredo, Confederate cotton continued to move through the town to be stockpiled in St. Augustine Plaza.

Galloping out of those "moving clouds of sand" on March 19, came an excited vaquero named Cayetano de la Garza. A relative of the colonel, he would one day be known as the Paul Revere of Laredo. Garza reported a large Union cavalry force approaching the town from downriver. Benavides at first questioned how a force, reported to number one thousand, could get by his scouts, but De la Garza insisted his story was true, and Benavides sounded the alarm. The Federals had managed to avoid Benavides' guards by leaving the river road and advancing through the chaparral.

As men raced through the sun-baked streets and St. Augustine Plaza preparing for the impending attack, Benavides rose from his bed to meet the Union onslaught. He immediately deployed a small cavalry force along the river road southeast of the town to delay the Federals. Then he put in an urgent call to have more than one hundred men, grazing their horses in a camp twenty-five miles north of town, sent in on the double. Next, he dispatched an express upriver to Eagle Pass to bring down all available Confederates from there. The presence of those scattered troops was vital; Benavides had to defend Laredo with forty-two men from the companies of his brothers Refugio and Cristobal, and thirty men from a company of Texas militia who, by sheer luck, arrived on the river just a few days before the Union attack. The only other defenders were several citizens who volunteered to deploy as sharpshooters on top of adobe buildings around the plaza. If Rip Ford's force was ever coming, it would never get there in time to be of any use to Benavides.

Although the Yankee column was reported to outnumber Benavides's command more than ten to one, the colonel told a fellow Rebel: "This would not have happened had I not been confined to bed for some days. I would have known all about their advance and would have gone below and attacked them. As it is I have to fight to the last; though hardly able to stand I shall die fighting. I won't retreat, no matter what force the Yankees have—I know I can depend on my boys." Santos then gave specific orders to brother Cristobal: "There are five thousand bales of cotton in the plaza. It belongs to the Confederacy. If the day goes against us, fire it. Be sure to do the work properly so that not a bale of it shall fall into the hands of the Yankees. Then you will set my new house on

fire, so that nothing of mine shall pass to the enemy. Let their victory be a barren one."

With the streets leading into Laredo barricaded with cotton bales and the plaza rooftops covered with volunteer snipers, the ailing colonel rode out of Laredo to meet the foe.

Under the afternoon sun, in the "desolate, barren, and desert-like...country," old friend Edmund Davis's revenge approached. Armed with "Burnside carbines, revolvers, and sabers," the Federal force, really numbering only about two hundred men, attacked.

For many years, historians have been uncertain as to who commanded the Union "cotton raid" against Laredo. Extensive research into Union Army records reveals that the Union expedition was led by Maj. Alfred E. Holt whom Davis called a "competent and attentive officer." The attacking Union force, with Capt. James Speed as second in command, had progressed slowly upriver from the lower valley. The terrible drought had dried up watering holes, parched the earth and left little trail grass. The column was also slowed by a train of supply wagons escorted by Lt. Clarendon Gray and Company E of the Tejano Second Cavalry. Horses and mules were forced to survive on half-rations of oats. During the expedition many of the valuable mounts gave out and had to be left by the roadside to die.

It was two Union spies operating out of Nuevo Laredo that reported to Brownsville of Benavides' bad health and of the thousands of dollars in Confederate cotton piled neatly row on row in St. Augustine Plaza.

Unsteady in the saddle, Santos brought his brothers' forty-two men out to a large corral on the eastern outskirts of Laredo along Zacate Creek, a spot where his men would have the most cover and clearest field of fire on the advancing Yankees. The remaining force stayed in town for a final defense. As a ruse, Benavides sent Third Sgt. Dario Gonzales, bugle in hand, riding up and down Zacate Creek blowing the bugle as he raced about. Benavides was hoping to give the impression that far more men were prepared to defend the town than were really present. The colonel's men waited and watched the enemy force dismount, form into groups of forty each, and prepare to charge the Rebels. With the first wild Union rush forward, a three hour battle was on.

"Benavides and his men fought with the coolest bravery," an eyewitness said. This was proven by Rebels Juan Ibarra and Major J. S. Swope, singled out for their heroism in the records of the Laredo fight. While the colonel's men opened fire on the rushing Federals, Swope, mounted on a "magnificent sorrel," charged the Yankees and emptied his pistol into their ranks before retreating, his horse hit three times. Ibarra, not to be outdone, also charged the Federals, fighting bravely until his horse was shot out from under him. Benavides's men, after three hours of combat, did not sustain one Rebel fatality.

For the Union forces, the battle was a disaster without a postscript; they left no written record of the fight. Despite superior numbers and reputation, and after three assaults, they were driven into the chaparral, carrying their casualties with them. Then as sniping slackened and the South Texas sun set, they picked up the pace of the retreat, not stopping until they were three miles below Laredo. Back in the barren wastes that had spawned the attack, they went into camp for the night and tried to assess the damage.

The darkness did not bring any peace to Laredo's civilian and soldier defenders. They remained on constant alert. Benavides expected another attack, if not during the night, then certainly the next day. The eerie stillness was cracked at two o'clock in the morning when pickets north of town reported a sizable cavalry force advancing rapidly. As blackness and the threat of death gathered about, the men quickly prepared themselves for a last stand. "A general rejoicing took place among our little force," the colonel wrote. The ominous horsemen were Confederates arriving from their camp north of town. Bugles sounded, and soldiers and citizens screamed with joy. The bell atop St. Augustine Church pealed the sound of the town's happiness and relief into the crisp March night. There is little doubt it was heard in the Yankee camp to the southeast.

But with the coming of daylight, Benavides decided it was best to take the initiative. Brother Refugio was sent out with sixty men to find the enemy.

Captain Benavides crossed Zacate Creek, near the battle-scarred corral, and found a number of bloody trails in the sand along the dry stream-bed. A grisly track of blood-soaked rags ran on out into the tall grass and scrubby mesquite, leading three miles downriver to the Federal camp, now abandoned. The small Union force had retreated in haste, probably encouraged in their departure by the noisy and timely arrival of Rebel reinforcements the night before. The only evidence of Union occupation was some clothing found strewn about the camp; the only booty was five horses, all branded "U.S."

Again, on the brighter morning of the twenty-first, Refugio Benavides was sent out as a scout. This time the blood trail extended farther downriver, where the captain reported the Yankees had broken up into small squads retreating at a dead run.

On the third day after the battle, a report reached the Laredo colonel that a large force of Federals was again approaching the eastern outskirts of town. "Benavides...being very much exhausted...again got into his saddle and galloped out at the head of a body of his men determined to fight," a Rebel said. Benavides, however, was so weak he fell from his horse and received an ugly head wound. His nervous energy had played out, and according to W. W. Camp, the regimental surgeon, he was "wholly exhausted and very unwell."

Benavides was confined to his room because of "fatigue and exposure," and could only rise from his bed "at the hazard of his life," the surgeon reported. Rip Ford kept moving on toward Laredo, and hearing of the colonel's condition, wrote Benavides urging him to allow some "officer in rank...to take charge of the troops." Confined to his sickbed, but with Laredo secure, Santos Benavides had ended his gallant role in the Battle of Laredo.

In the months to come Benavides would never be honored with a Confederate brigadier generalship; Rebel ally Rip Ford would turn against him in a dispute over the recruitment and disposition of troops along the Rio Grande. And strangest of all, Edmund J. Davis, pilloried and driven from Texas, would return to become Reconstruction governor and once again, one of Benavides's personal and political friends.

John L. Haynes (1821-1888) shown here with his wife Angelica in 1864 at Baton Rouge, Louisiana, came to South Texas during the Mexican War. In 1850, he became county clerk of Starr County and was elected to the Texas legislature in 1857 and again in 1859. During the Cortina War which ravaged the Lower Rio Grande Valley, Haynes, although not a Cortina partisan, vigorously rejected the bitter anti-Tejano feelings of the state legislature and the Anglo establishment in Brownsville. With the coming of secession, Haynes fled into Mexico in early March 1862, leaving his wife and four children in Texas. Davis, along with E. J. Davis, went to New Orleans, New York, and Washington. Returning to Texas, Haynes raised a regiment of Tejanos and Mexicanos for the Union Army. After the war, Haynes became a leader in Texas Republican politics and ran unsuccessfully for Congress and for lieutenant-governor. He served as collector of customs at Galveston and later at Brownsville and Brazos Santiago. Children of John and Angelica included, John L., James, Henry, Robert, Leonard and Mary. This carte de visite was taken by A. A. Turner. (Lawrence T. Jones III, Austin)

Edmund J. Davis (1827–1883), Radical Reconstruction governor of Texas, got his political start as a city alderman in Laredo in 1852. The Florida born barrister became district attorney for the Twelfth Judicial District in 1853 and district judge in 1855. In the ensuing years, Davis spent considerable time riding the circuit between Laredo, Corpus Christi, and Brownsville. During the Civil War, Davis fled to Mexico and later to New York and Washington, where he helped convince President Abraham Lincoln of a plan to send an army to occupy the Rio Grande Frontier and cut the flow of Confederate cotton into Mexico. Davis helped to raise a regiment of Texans for the Union Army and rose to the rank of brigadier-general. He was forced out of the governor's office in 1872, ending Reconstruction in Texas. (Photographic History of the Civil War)

Probably taken in Brownsville in 1864, this photograph depicts four Laredo Confederates who include, left to right, Refugio Benavides, Atanacio Vidaurri, Cristobal Benavides, and John Z. Leyendecker. (Ursuline Sisters)

John Z. Leyendecker, brother-in-law of Col. Santos Benavides, was an assistant-quarter-master under Benavides during the Civil War. Leyendecker was ostracized by family members who lived near Fredericksburg, Texas and who remained loyal to the Union. (Edward Leyendecker)

This carte de viste of Cristobal Benavides is one of the rare images of a Tejano in a Confederate uniform. Cristobal, half-brother of Santos and Refugio, married Lamar Bee, daughter of Gen. Hamilton P. Bee, after the war in 1867. The exceptional gallantry by the Benavides brothers during the Civil War has brought considerable praise by Civil War historians. (Cristobal Sanchez)

Col. Santos Benavides (1823–1891) was the highest ranking Mexican-American to serve the Confederacy. Benavides defeated Juan N. Cortina in the Battle of Carrizo in May 1861, attacked Mexican revolutionaries under Octaviano Zapata near Mier in September 1863, and drove off Union soldiers from Laredo in March 1864. Benavides, along with brothers Refugio and Cristobal, both captains, was praised by a joint resolution of the Texas legislature. Colonel Benavides was even given an elegantly engraved pistol by Gov. Edward Clark. By the end of the war, Benavides had come to command the Thirty-third Texas Cavalry. (Author's Collection)

Chapter 13

The Military

The Robert Haynes family entertain soldiers from Fort McIntosh in 1883. Seated behind the table in civilian clothes is Robert Haynes. On the right, his wife, Margarita Ramirez, holds the banjo. Leonard Haynes sits on the grass with his bride, Edith Camden. On the grass in front of the table is Mary Haynes, a famous actress who took the name Van Buren. (Consuelo Novoa)

Not all Tejanos who fought in the Civil War enlisted to serve the Confederacy. Shown here is Sgt. Patricio Perez of the Union Second Texas Cavalry. Perez, who was thirty-two when he joined the Union Army in South Texas, was born at Rancherias, Tamaulipas. Five other Tejanos who fought in the Union Army listed their place of birth as Laredo. (Courtesy of Delia Alaniz)

Santos Benavides, Jr., the adoptive son of Santos and Augustina Benavides, is shown here as a sergeant in the United States Army. Santos, Jr., has often been misidentified as Col. Santos Benavides, his more famous father. Notice the US on the beltbuckle and the sergeant's stripes. Sergeant Benavides actually bore little resemblance to his father, Colonel Benavides. (Mary Cook Collection, Nuevo Santander Museum)

Three of the original four barracks buildings are seen in this view of Fort McIntosh. The brick for the barracks was procured locally, but the timber for the roofs, ceilings, and floors was brought overland in wagons from Corpus Christi. Only one of the buildings remains, and is used today for administration purposes by Laredo Junior College. A number of the remaining historic structures at the fort are on the National Register of Historic Places. The other three buildings were demolished. (National Archives)

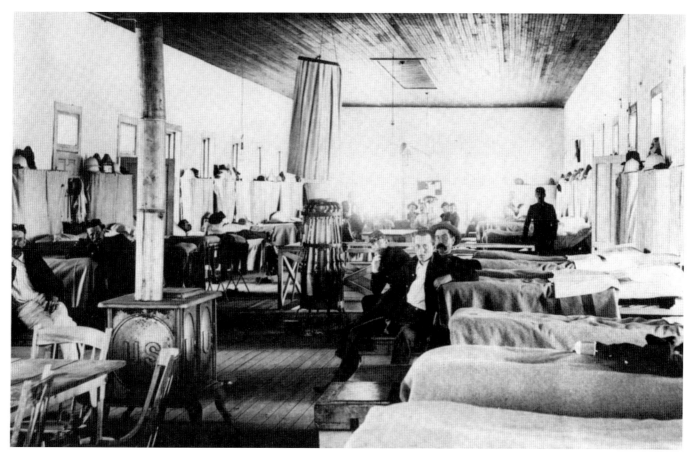

Soldiers at Fort McIntosh are caught in this informal setting on the second story of their barracks by a visiting military photographer. Despite sometimes harsh conditions, cleanliness usually took a top priority at frontier posts such as Fort McIntosh. Notice the gun rack at the head of the stairwell and the suspended covering to keep the ever-present dust out of the rifles. Prussian inspired pith helments can be seen above the men's cots. (National Archives)

The original two-story Fort McIntosh Hospital remains in use by Laredo Junior College. The west wing of the post hospital was a later addition. (National Archives)

A number of two-story homes used for officer's housing at Fort McIntosh lined the north perimeter of the parade ground. Today college classrooms and parking lots fill the area. (National Archives)

The Guardhouse at Fort McIntosh has been completely restored and is used today by the Nuevo Santander Museum for military exhibits. (National Archives)

An officer in a pith helmet poses near the water plant at Fort McIntosh. Water from the Rio Grande was gathered in a settlement basin and then pumped to the various buildings at the post. Previously, the water was hauled from the river in barrels. This photograph of Fort McIntosh was found in the files of the National Archives in 1974. (National Archives)

The Commissary Building, right, is thought to be the only building still standing which dates to the antebellum era of Fort McIntosh. The Commissary Building on the left is used today by the Nuevo Santander Museum as an exhibit hall. The older building is used jointly by Laredo Junior College and the Laredo Art League. Both buildings have been completely restored. (National Archives)

A motley-looking group of Laredo volunteers pose upon arriving at Camp Mabry in Austin, Texas, for basic training during the Spanish-American War in 1898. Laredo, like most American cities, was swept with a mood of patriotism following the sinking of the Maine in Havana Harbor on the night of February 15, 1898. A number of Laredo volunteers fought in Cuba and in the Philippines during the war. (Miguel Benavides Family)

A soldier and a dog are seen in the entrances to the Bakery at Fort McIntosh. The building, only partially restored in 1986, still stands on the southwest part of the campus of Laredo Junior College. (National Archives)

Civilian volunteers have become Company K of the First Texas Volunteers. This photograph was taken at Camp Mabry, Austin, Texas, shortly after the men completed their basic training in 1898. (Miguel Benavides Family)

Eight Laredo Spanish-American War veterans strike a patriotic pose in this photograph taken around 1900. On the extreme left, standing is Candelario Mendiola, and on the far right, standing, is Miguel G. Benavides. In April 1929, Laredo veterans formed the Frank Earnest Chapter of United Spanish War Veterans, Camp No. 44. Members who were still living at the time included: Jesse E. Applewhite, Erwin E. Atlee, Joseph W. Brewster, Wilber C. Greenstreet, Willard W. Gregg, William B. Hamilton, John D. Honeyman, Daniel Trazivuk, Neil Trumbull, John C. Twiss, John J. Winslow, Thomas Devine, John Halsell, William W. Allen, George C. McCanley, Frederick E. Mershon, Royle X. Mims, George J. Monahan, Justo S. Penn. J. A. Simpson, and Sterling J. Sorrell. (Miguel Benavides Family)

Mounted, with sabers ready, Company K, First Texas Volunteer Cavalry, is ready for war in this photograph at Camp Mabry, Austin, Texas, in 1898. (Miguel Benavides Family)

From the time Fort McIntosh was founded in 1848, many Laredoans found employment with the military. Shown here in 1909 are five civilian teamsters and ambulance drivers. At top left is Lazaro V. Dovalina. (Ernesto Dovalina)

Miguel Benavides, son of Refugio Benavides, a volunteer in Company K, First Texas Cavalry, is seen after the Spanish-American War. After his service in Cuba, Benavides joined the Laredo Police Department. (Miguel Benavides Family)

Company K of the Black Twenty-Fifth United States Infantry sat for a group photograph in front of the barracks at Fort McIntosh in 1906. Their white company commander can be seen in the front-center. From the time the Sixty-second Wisconsin Colored Infantry occupied Laredo at the conclusion of the Civil War, a number of all Black units, including the famous Buffalo Soldiers or Tenth Cavalry, were stationed at Fort McIntosh. (National Archives)

During the Mexican Revolution, a number of National Guard units from Missouri, New Hampshire, and Maine were sent to Laredo. Here a group of guardsmen pose in front of their Sibley-shaped tents. (Nuevo Santander Museum)

A unit of National Guardsmen are camped while on maneuvers near Laredo during the Mexican Revolution. (Nuevo Santander Museum)

Son of Tirza Garcia and Raymond Martin, Albert Martin (1889-1972) was one of many Laredoans to enlist in the United States Army for action in France during World War I. Martin would later serve as mayor of Laredo for fourteen years (1926-1940). Twenty-four young men from Laredo did not return from the war. They included: Maurice Akabass, George Bigden, Adam Bold, Moises Carrejo, Jack Correu, Alfred J. Cousineau, Leonardo Diaz, Louis F. Folsom, William Ford, Francisco Garcia, Benjamin Hastings, William H. Lake, Milus Little, Edmundo Lopez, Lake W. Loftus, Lorenzo Rendon, J. P. Rossi, Gustin K. Smith, Harold Smith, Dewey Tillman, Percy R. Winch, Charles E. Woodul, Jose Ybarra, and Jose Zamora. One Laredoan, David Barkley, was posthumously awarded the Medal of Honor for bravery during the Meuse-Argonne Offensive. Barkely drowned while attempting to swim the Meuse River with important dispatches. (Anita and J. C. Martin)

Manuel M. Tellez holds the distinction of having served in both World War I and World War II. In 1918, Tellez first enlisted in San Antonio at the age of eighteen and was assigned to the Ninth Infantry Division. He was in the trenches near Verdun on Armistice Day, November 11, 1918, and returned home with the Thirty-sixth Division. At the age of forty-three, in 1942, Tellez attempted to enlist again but was told, "you old people go home and work around the house." Tellez persisted and eventually served in a motor transportation company at Kelley Field in San Antonio. His grandfather, Luis Martines Tellez, served under Col. Santos Benavides in the Civil War. (Manuel Tellez)

Headquarters Battery of the Fifth Field Artillery was stationed at Fort McIntosh in January 1926. The photo was taken on the south side of the fort. On the left can be seen what would become the San Francisco Javier Neighborhood. On the far right are the tops of the large barracks. During the Depression, a stone wall was built completely around the fort. (Nuevo Santander Museum)

The Fourth Missouri Infantry, a National Guard regiment sent to Laredo during the Mexican Revolution, poses for the camera of E. Moore north of Laredo around 1916. On the right is the regiment's supply train. Most of the regiment was housed in Sibley-shaped tents shown in the right background. (Devine Collection, Jennie L. Reed)

In December 1926, another unit of the Eighth Engineering Batallion gathered for this photograph. The Engineers were still not using motorized transportation as indicated by the seventeen mule-drawn wagons in the rear. The caption on the photograph indicates that Major F. Williams was in command. (Nuevo Santander Museum)

As they face southwest at Fort McIntosh, B Troop of the Eighth Engineers are captured on file here in Feburary 1933. First Lietuenant A. B. Shattuck was in command while First Lieutenant McDonald D. Weinert was in charge of the First Platoon, and First Lieutenant Walter W. Hodge was in command of the Second Platoon. The older age of the enlisted men was perhaps indicative of the depth of the Depression by 1933. (Nuevo Santander Museum)

This panoramic view of Fort McIntosh was made around 1930. Only one of the large barracks buildings (the one on the far left) remains. Most of the large commissary buildings on the left of the photo have been demolished. A number of the officers' spacious two-story homes on the north side of the parade ground remain. Note the railroad spur, in the center of the photograph, that ran directly to the fort. (Nuevo Santander Museum)

Pvt. Luis D. Guerra, Sixtieth Coastal Artillery, was in the Philippines when the Japanese bombed Pearl Harbor and World War II engulfed the Pacific. After four months of bitter fighting on Bataan, Guerra was able to escape to Corregidor in Manila Harbor where the Americans later surrendered on May 7, 1942. After three years of brutal and inhuman treatment in a number of Japanese prison camps, the six-foot two-inch Guerra died near Osaka, Japan, on September 18, 1944. Luis was one of five brothers who fought in World War II. Four others survived. They included, Capt. Rafael A. Guerra, veteran of the Battle of the Bulge; Carlos Guerra, a naval veteran of the Battle of Okinawa; Sgt. Refugio Guerra, Jr., who saw action in Central Burma, India, and Sumatra; and Guadalupe J. Guerra, who served in the Air Force. (Mr. and Mrs. Lino Mendiola)

Cpl. Carmen Guerra, Jr., joined the Army in March 1941 and was sent to help bolster American forces in the Philippines. He was stationed at Manila when the Japanese attacked Pearl Harbor on December 7, 1941. Guerra fought with other gallant Americans to defend the Bataan Peninsula. Although captured, he managed to survive the infamous Bataan Death March and a number of inhuman prison camps in Japan. He was finally liberated by American forces when they entered Osaka on September 2, 1945. (Carmen Guerra, Jr.)

Roy M. (Max) Offerle was only sixteen when he enlisted in D Battery, Second Battalion, 131st Field Artillery, of the Thirty-Sixth Division, prior to World War II. He was captured by Japanese forces on Java in March 1942. Sergeant Offerle was sent to work on the famous Railroad of Death in Burma which included the Bridge on the River Kwai. Savagely treated and suffering from a number of tropical diseases, Offerle managed to survive, despite forty-two months of Japanese cruelty. Perhaps his greatest loss was watching his older brother, who had also been captured on Java, die in his arms. Max Offerle was liberated on August 15, 1945. (Max Offerle)

Manuel Vidaurri, Jr., joined the United States Army in 1941 at the age of twenty-nine. After basic training, he was sent to Clark Field in the Philippines as part of the 200th Coast Artillery. He was having lunch at Clark Field when the Japanese attacked on December 7, 1941, destroying all the American aircraft on the ground. He fought the Japanese at Lingayen Gulf and for four long months became part of American history as one of the heroic "battling bastards of Bataan." With other Americans, he surrendered on April 9, 1942. On the infamous death march that followed, Vidaurri watched as his friends were bayoneted and tortured. At Camp O'Donnell, he worked in the rice paddies and on a Japanese airfield, surviving mostly on rice balls and grasshoppers. He suffered from malnutrition, dysentery, beriberi, and tropical ulcers. Vidaurri was later sent to Cabanatuan Prison Camp, and eventually Japan, where he remained throughout the war, unloading ships at a steel factory. After forty months in prison, he was liberated on August 16, 1945. (Manuel Vidaurri, Jr.)

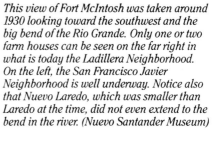

This view of Fort McIntosh was taken around 1930 looking toward the southwest and the big bend of the Rio Grande. Only one or two farm houses can be seen on the far right in what is today the Ladillera Neighborhood. On the left, the San Francisco Javier Neighborhood is well underway. Notice also that Nuevo Laredo, which was smaller than Laredo at the time, did not even extend to the bend in the river. (Nuevo Santander Museum)

Sgt. Homero L. Martinez, a member of the famous "Lost Battalion," joined the Army on February 22, 1941, and went overseas as a member of the 131st Field Artillery, Sixty-First Brigade, Thirty-Sixth Infantry Division in November 1941, one month before Pearl Harbor. After four months of fighting he was captured on Java and spent forty-two torturous months in a number of Japanese prison camps in Burma where prisoners labored in the jungle on the Railroad of Death that included the Bridge on the River Kwai. Martinez experienced beatings, brandings, and the infamous Japanese water torture. After the war, Martinez became one of the leaders in the local Reform party and in 1986, he was elected Webb County Republican Chairman. (Homero Martinez)

The history of Laredo Air Force Base goes back to World War II when the Army established an airfield which included some 1,550 acres and a gunnery range that stretched along the Rio Grande between Laredo and Eagle Pass which included 600,000 acres. A Gunnery Instructor School was moved from Florida to the base in 1944. By the end of the war, the Laredo Air Force Base included 14,000 personnel and listed 250 aircraft in its possession. (Richard Newbury)

Three jet aircraft of the United States Air Force are superimposed over Laredo Air Force Base. For over two decades, until the base closed in 1973, Laredo Air Force Base turned out hundreds of pilots for the Air Force. Note the area to the northwest of the base that now comprises the Hillside subdivision. (Richard Newbury)

The Guarache Party Is

William Hovey Mowry (1845-1903) served as County Clerk of Webb County from 1879 to 1884. As a reformer, he was one of the organizers of the Guarache party. He was married to Margarita Benavides (1857-1931), the daughter of Refugio Benavides. (Webb County Courthouse Annex)

By early September of 1884, a group of men, some inspired by the provocative and never ending editorials in the *The Laredo Times,* others with long held grudges against the dominant Raymond Martin Democrats, and some wanting a share of the political power, had commenced to meet weekly in an attempt to run a full slate of candidates against the regular Democrats at the upcoming election to be held on November 4. Two of the organizers of what would come to be called the Reform Club were Santos Benavides and his son Juan. They were joined by C. C. Pierce and W. H. Mowry.

The informal gatherings at Santos Benavides's home on St. Augustine Plaza had, by late September, become large meetings open to anyone desiring to help defeat the Martin Democrats at the upcoming election. The sympathetic Daniel Milmo, who along with his brother Patricio, owned the Milmo National Bank, placed a large room in the bank at the disposal of the reformers for their weekly meetings.

Within a week, an executive committee had been formed. Prominent members included councilmen John Grant and H. Douglass, local attorneys J. O. Nicholson and Juan Benavides and the aging warrior Refugio Benavides.

From the very beginning, several crucial coalitions were necessary for the success of the reformers. The question of what the local Blaine and Logan Republican Club would do was settled when J. J. Haynes was recruited to become secretary of the Reform Club. Success at the polls also meant that reformers must gain the loyalty of a large part of the lower class of the town, many of whom were economically dependent on the city, county, or machine-owned businesses and ranches.

One of the most responsible and influential groups representing the interests of the lower class was the Club Azul Independiente Mejico-Tejano. The club, however, was headed by Jose Maria Vela who happened to be city tax assessor and collector and a Martin Loyalist. Another organization which also represented a large percentage of the lower class was the Sociedad Mutualista Union Mexicano. They refused, however, to make any promises.

El Laredense, a Spanish language newspaper in Nuevo Laredo, was no help whatsoever. In fact, *El Laredense* was in a war of words with James Penn of the *Times,* accusing Penn of ambivalence toward the Mexican-American community. Penn, on the defensive for one of the few times, asserted that he was indeed "a friend of the Mexican People." *La Voz de la Pueblo,* a Laredo newspaper, had traditionally been supportive of the Martin machine and could not be counted on. What the reformers had badly needed was a sympathetic Spanish language newspaper to get their message across to the Mexican-American population of the city.

The Reform Club was also hoping for support from Encinal County which was still unorganized and attached to Webb County for administrative purposes. There was also hope that the miners at the large Santo Tomas Mine would support the reform efforts. Although the miners were subject to the whims of the mine owners, party leaders were dispatched to Carbon to meet with the miners. Other reformers were sent into Encinal County to spread the word that the Reform Club would support any efforts on the part of the people there to permanently separate from Webb County.

From the beginning of the campaign, the reformers were forced to answer accusations that the club was really a front for the local Republican Party. Penn, in the pages of the *Times,* responded by referring to Santos Benavides, the leader of the reform movement, as "a life-long Democrat...already well-known for his democracy when many of his loud-mouthed detractors were yet in their swaddling clothes." Another accusation, frequently made by both sides, was that the other party intended to vote hundreds of aliens.

Perhaps the most persistent rumor on the streets of Laredo was that Isidro Salinas, a prominent citizen from La Jarita, Mexico, had been hired by the Reform Club and was hard at work preparing to import voters from Mexico.

Chapter 14

Born

By mid-October, the two parties had a full slate of candidates signed up and were preparing for battle. As expected, one of the races which attracted the most attention was that for county judge. The Martin Democrats ran the incumbent, Jose Maria Rodriguez, who was also doubling as chairman of the Webb County Democratic party. The reformers put up Juan V. Benavides. Both men were well-educated, articulate and eloquent, and were good campaigners.

By the first week in October, a month before the election, political emotions in Laredo had already reached an all time high. The Reform Club had commenced to meet twice a week at the Milmo Bank, usually on Wednesdays and Saturdays, to hear speakers denounce the "ring" for every conceivable crime committed in the county. One of the most eloquent speakers was C. C. Pierce who always spoke to the gathering in Spanish. Juan Benavides was equally eloquent in English.

Part of the Reform party's popularity was due to the fact that Santos Benavides always treated those assembled to beer at a local saloon after the meeting. For example, on October 13, the Reform Club met to hear an "excellent brass band" from Nuevo Laredo after which they listened to several speakers and then retired to a saloon "to pledge success to the ticket in schooners of foaming beer." Only three days later, "Don Santos treated the Reform crowd to 1,000 schooners of foaming beer." "Politics enjoys a monopoly in Laredo at the present," a local correspondent wrote. "Bands are playing, speeches [are] marching about," he recalled.

By mid-October, the campaign had reached a fever pitch. On Saturday, October 15, the reformers met at Milmo Hall for their usual firey meeting after which 350 partisans paraded the streets for almost an hour before assembling again at Market Plaza where they formed a large circle to hear a stirring appeal by Santos Benavides. Afterward, they retired for their usual beer. Benavides's weekly beer bills would have bankrupt a less financially secure citizen.

Although there is little documented proof as to the kind of campaign the Martin Democrats conducted in 1884, it appears from the few surviving newspapers of the time that their methods were amazingly similar to those of the Reform Club. Martin partisans would assemble for a political speech, followed by a parade through the streets after which they would retire to a local saloon for beer.

Several violent confrontations between marchers from both camps helped to intensify the already emotional campaign. One fight broke out when a number of Martin Democrats stationed themselves on a street corner and commenced to shout "foul epithets" at the passing Reform Club. During the early weeks of the campaign, the leaders from both political parties, usually the well-to-do, left the parading to their lower class followers. This was a reflection on the oligarchical nature of Laredo politics. As the campaign intensified, however, men like Santos Benavides were frequently seen on horseback at the head of the semi-weekly

processions. Large bandwagons, with political signs attached, followed. Next came several hundred men on foot carrying banners and flags.

The dramatic climax of the Reform Club campaign came on Saturday, October 26. Despite the recent heavy rains that had turned the streets into a quagmire, three hundred reformers met at Milmo Hall promptly at 8:00 P.M. and although disappointed that a delegation from Encinal County did not arrive, they listened to the usual music from the Nuevo Laredo Brass Band after which they retired to hear the usual encouragement from party leaders.

C. C. Pierce, the principal speaker for the evening, strode forward and produced a guarache strapped to a long pole, stating in Spanish that the guarache, symbol of the lower class, had been buried under the corruption of the "ring" for eight long years, but that it was now being unearthed by the Reform Club. "Deafening acclamations of applause" thereafter greeted his every word as a chorus of "viva los guaraches" rang throughout the hall and into the darkened streets. The Reform party had unofficially become the Guarache party. But still Pierce was not through. He called forth two poor reform followers, one of whom was a one-legged cripple who hobbled forth on crutches while the other was a gray haired old man. Pierce told of how the two men had been dismissed by their employer, a prominent Martin Democrat, because of the two men's intentions of voting the reform ticket.

With emotions aroused, 250 "Guaraches" filed out of Milmo Hall, marching through the mud and water up to their ankles, as they carried their new banner aloft—"the ever glorious guarache." The men made their way through the darkened streets to the I and GN depot where they were treated to beer. They then marched back to Milmo Hall. By this time, however, a number of the reform followers were too drunk and fell out along the way. Juan Benavides, who was on horseback, tried to halt the parade, asking the men to retire for the evening, but an excited "Guarache" seized the reigns of his horse, and the march continued.

A serious confrontation developed between the two rival factions late the following Wednesday evening. Both the Guaraches and the Martin Democrats, who were now being called the Botas, were in the streets in force. No sooner had the Guarache parade commenced than a large group of Botas gathered to taunt their rivals. Not content with this, the Botas then commenced to follow the Guaraches, shouting foul epithets at Santos Benavides. A number of Guaraches turned on the Botas, and a brawl broke out. The Botas later argued that many of the Guaraches were drunk and that it was the reformers who had started the fight.

As the election neared, many citizens were fearful that the two parties would commence to arm themselves and that the fist fights would become gun fights. On Saturday before the election, both the Botas and Guaraches were in the streets in large numbers, but the expected confrontation never developed. The Guaraches, who were said to outnumber the Botas 680 to 440, were content to gather at the home of Santos Benavides on Flores Street and serenade the old warrior on the occasion of his sixty-fourth birthday.

As the campaign reached a climax, the local press became even bolder than before. "The old leprous conglomeration of mephitic garbage and reeking corruption which has for decades clung like eating cancer to the body politics of Laredo," Penn editorialized, must be eliminated at all costs. Penn even tried to ridicule the Botas with his poetry:

Soon will be known the people's choice
Against the Barnacles they shout;
And all Laredo will rejoice
To turn the mugwumps out.

A few days before the election, the wildest of rumors were circulating in the saloons and on the streets. In response to claims that the Guaraches had plans to vote several hundred Mexican aliens, the reformers claimed the Botas were planning to run a special train from Saltillo for the same purpose.

The biggest political demonstrations by the two parties came on the night before the election. Santos Benavides, as he had done previously, led a large contingent of Guaraches through the streets. Just as the reformers had retired to one of the saloons for "eatables and drinkables," word came that a special train had just arrived from Carbon with 250 more Guaraches.

Within minutes, the Guaraches, now joined by the miners, were in the streets again. In front rode Colonel Benavides, followed by the Guarache flag protected by Jose Maria Herrera, Rafael Cardenas, and Pedro Gonzalez. Next came two large wagons drawn by several teams of horses. A number of colorful and clever signs designed by W. H. Mowry were attached to the wagons. One showed a Bota and a Guarache see-sawing with the Bota high up in the air and about to lose his equilibrium. Behind the wagon came more than two hundred reformers carrying more signs. One read, "Down with the Ring," while another asked for "An International Bridge."

Less than two blocks away, the Botas could be heard as they too paraded the darkened streets. The dye had been cast. Both the Botas and the Guaraches were determined to prevail at the polls.

At dawn on election day, November 4, 1884, the weather in Laredo appeared damp and overcast as a light mist clung to the town. The weather was perhaps a bad omen for the Guaraches. Many of the veteran Guaraches had known all along that they were struggling against difficult odds. The attitude of "if we don't beat them this time we will beat them next time" was common at party headquarters. Still, the Guaraches had generated considerable enthusiasm for reform in Laredo, and on election day many partisans were confident. The presence of federal marshals in town only served to heighten their spirits.

As the polls opened, hacks, surreys, and wagons of all kinds, sped through the dampened streets carrying Bota and Guarache voters to their precinct voting places. Men on horseback were seen to gallop about carrying messages from party leaders to political workers in the streets at the polls.

Within hours it was evident that the Botas were in complete control of the election process. Determined to win the election, the Botas had set out to deliberately intimidate as many Guarache voters as possible. The local press, perhaps exaggerating the conduct of the Bota election officials, reported that the polls were "surrounded by individuals, presumably deputy sheriffs, who display murderous looking six-shooters." Only one man at a time was allowed to approach the ballot box and "in some instances ballots were snatched from the hands of voters, and their contents scanned." A few Guarache partisans were even stoned as they approached the polls.

About noon, a potentially violent incident occurred when a number of Botas commenced throwing rocks at the Guarache bandwagon. Bota deputies and city policemen were either too busy at the polls or chose to do nothing.

During the day, there was a large number of arrests by deputy federal marshals, of illegal voters. Most were the poor from Nuevo Laredo who stated that they had been paid to vote by prominent citizens of Laredo. The partisan Guarache press blamed the illegal voting on the Botas and demanded that those caught be severely punished but admitted that the "poor devils" were not as guilty as the men who hired them.

By late afternoon, it was evident that the entire Guarache party had gone down to a crushing defeat. By early evening, the Botas were already celebrating their victory with stewed chickens and kegs of beer. In a victorious and feisty mood, the Botas also held a festive parade through the streets complete with a marching band. Insultingly, they also brought forth a guarache, proud symbol of the reformers, and buried it in effigy to the lively shrieks and cheers of several hundred partisans.

Although the Bota election officials refused to give the elections results to the local press, by sundown the vote totals were well known on the streets, at Bota and Guarache headquarters, and at the local saloons. Out of five county precincts, the Guaraches had managed to carry only one. Even then their plurality was by only a few votes. With most voters casting the straight party ticket, the totals for the various candidates rarely varied more than a few votes. Out of almost eighteen hundred voters, the largest in Webb County history, the Botas had prevailed quite easily. Only in the business district had the Guaraches done well. Disappointingly, the Guaraches had been easily beaten in Carbon and in Encinal County.

The election victory was a great personal triumph for Raymond Martin and other prominent Bota leaders. With their victory at the polls in Webb County, their prestige in regional and state political circles was at an all time high. Commencing in 1885, the Bota machine would control practically all county offices from that of county judge down to the constables. Furthermore, E. F. Hall, a Bota, had been elected state senator and E. A Atlee, another Bota, was chosen as state representative from the Eighty-third District.

Many political observers were certain the reform movement in Laredo was dead. The Guarache press, determined to have the last word, offered an ominous warning: "But the guarache is not dead; he only sleepeth; and it requires neither the ken of a prophet, or the son of a prophet, to say that he will yet rise in the vehemence of his indestructible soul." Although the election of 1884 was the most exciting and hardest fought in Laredo history, it was in reality, little more than a dress rehearsal for 1886. As some predicted, the Guarache would indeed rise again.

Chapter 15

The Election Riot of 1886

Although the Botas had swept the general election of 1884, the city council, elected the previous April, remained deeply divided. J. J. Haynes, supported by H. Douglass, John Grant and Peter Steffian represented the Guarache interests while L. E. Puster, Eloy Arguindegui, Antonio Salinas, and Julian Garcia were strong Botas. Only on a few rare issues, such as the serious smallpox epidemic which engulfed the city, were the councilmen able to lay their political alliances aside. Dr. McKnight, the city physician, reported a number of cases at the April 10, 1884, council meeting. Yellow flags, indicating the homes of the sick, were common throughout the city. The smell of disinfecting sulphur hung low over the city, and newly whitewashed homes were common. Two large tents were obtained from the army at Fort McIntosh for a field hospital. Other issues which appeared bipartisan easily became politicized.

One of the biggest problems facing the city council was what to do with the Bota city attorney, J. P. C. Whitehead. For over six months, until the issue finally came to a head, Whitehead was found to be in a constant state of inebriation. At a meeting of the council on October 3, 1884, for example, Whitehead appeared in what Haynes called "a beastly condition of intoxication" and "behaved in a highly boisterous and improper manner." Six weeks later he had to be carried from a session of the mayor's court because of his inebriated condition. In early December he failed to appear at a council meeting and was found "lying on the floor of his office" in a drunken stupor. Haynes led the Guarache councilmen in drawing up charges of incompetence and misconduct and asked for Whitehead's dismissal. Whitehead retained Judge E. F. Hall, a leading Bota, to represent him, and the fight was on. After a special committee came up with inconclusive evidence as to the charges leveled against Whitehead, the Bota councilmen gave up, and the city attorney was fired.

Another issue which became highly political was the conduct of several city policemen. City Marshal Stephen Boyard was particularly incensed that policemen were frequently observed to be drunk while on duty and were seen frequenting the saloons and houses of prostitution. A special police committee ruled that the pay of city policemen, which was forty-five pesos a month, was pitifully inadequate. Regulations were drawn up stating that only men of "good moral character" would be eligible to become policemen. Furthermore "no policemen, while on duty, shall be permitted to visit any saloon, gambling house or public resort, unless in the discharge of his official duty."

Another devisive issue was the contract to build the street railway and the international bridge. The International Bridge and Tramway Company, and the Laredo Bridge and Street Railway Company had originally competed for the contracts. The latter, owned by Raymond Martin and several colleagues, had been given the contract to build both, but in September 1884, a petition containing the name of fifty-one citizens, almost all of whom were Guaraches, was presented to the council asking for a reconsideration of the projects. Bota aldermen argued that the Martin owned company "was composed of our own people" and that the work was being done with "Laredo money, by Laredo people, and for the benefit of the city of Laredo." When a vote to accept the Guarache petition resulted in a tie vote, the Bota mayor, Dario Sanchez, voted to reject the petition. Serious disagreements also developed over the quality of workmanship of the new market and city hall. Although the Guaraches insisted on an investigation, the Botas once again dominated and the investigation never took place.

Exhausted by the bitter general election of November 1884, the municipal election the following spring did not generate the interest some had expected. The lack of excitement was indicated by the fact that only twelve "special policemen" were hired to keep order on election day. In the race for mayor, the Bota incumbent, Dario Sanchez, more than doubled the vote of his Guarache opponent, Pricilliano Floyd. With the new city charter in effect, only four councilmen were up for reelection. Tomas Villastrigo, Rosendo Garcia, and James A. Kirkpatrick, all Botas, were easily elected. Only J. J. Haynes was able to hold on to his seat from the Guarache controlled Fourth Ward but only by a narrow two votes over E. A. Atlee. Whereas the old city council had pitted four Botas against four Guaraches, the new council consisted of six Botas and only two Guaraches. As expected, the two Guaraches, Haynes and Douglass, lost what little influence they had. Still they conceded little. As 1886 approached, events in the county courthouse would come to have a profound effect on city politics. Dario Gonzales, a Bota and respected member of one of Laredo's oldest families, doubled not only as sheriff but also as tax assessor and collector. When Gonzales took office in 1883, he had posted a bond of $7,000 with Raymond Martin acting as one of the major bondsmen. As tax collector in Encinal County, Gonzales had collected more than $2,000 in taxes in that county for 1882 and 1883, but had never put the money into the county coffers. When the discrepancy became known, the county not only sued Gonzales but removed him from office. The case was eventually decided in Gonzales's favor by the Texas Supreme Court two years later. In the meantime, however, Gonzales never forgave the Botas for the public embarassment of having been removed from office. Imbittered, he joined the Guaraches taking a small band of loyal followers with him. By April 1886, he had become one of the major leaders in the party.

The Botas replaced Gonzales with Dario Sanchez, who was serving as mayor at the time. In one of the few times they were able to agree, Bota and Guarache councilmen were able to settle on E. A. Atlee as mayor although he was known to be sympathetic to the Botas. As one of the town's leading attorneys, Atlee had somehow managed to garner the support of the Guarache aldermen.

Jose Maria Rodriguez (1828-1912), shown here as a young man in 1860, was one of the most powerful political figures in Laredo history. Born in San Antonio, Rodriguez was an Isleno, a proud descendant of the Canary Islanders who had helped to settle the town. Rodriguez was educated in the finest schools of New Orleans and spoke fluent Spanish, French, and English. In 1855, he fought with Jose Maria Jesus Carvajal in a short-lived revolution against the Mexican dictator, Antonio Lopez de Santa Anna. He came to Laredo in 1859 where he taught school for a short time. When Bacilio Benavides was elected to the state legislature in 1860, Rodriguez rode north to Austin as Benavides's official interpreter. He would eventually marry Benavides's daughter, Feliz. Rodriguez served thirty-five years (1878-1913) as Webb County judge. (Barker Texas History Center)

Another issue contributing to the violence and killing in 1886 centered around the controversial city marshal, Stephen Boyard. From the time Boyard had become city marshall in 1884, he had been under fire from several leading Botas. Definitely a reformist, Boyard had been more and more drawn into the Guarache camp. As early as July of 1885, Boyard had removed T. J. Moore from the city police force charging him with "neglect of duty, drunkenness and conduct unbecoming an officer." A month later, Boyard removed Teodoro Trevino and Octaviano G. Garcia. By March of 1886, Boyard had become such a Guarache loyalist that the Bota dominated city council attempted to remove him from office. At a stormy meeting of the city council on March 4, 1886, Boyard was charged with "misconduct, corruption and malfeasance" in office by "knowingly permitting gaming against the laws of the state and city." As expected, the vote to remove Boyard was along strict party lines, the four Bota aldermen voting in the affirmative and the two Guaraches, Haynes and Douglass, voting nay. Many of the leading Guaraches saw the attack on Boyard as an attempt to control all city offices and position the Botas for the approaching municipal elections on April 6, 1886.

At a second meeting of the council which was called one week later to hear the evidence in the case, so many angry Guaraches and determined Botas showed up that the council was forced to meet in the city hall. Boyard pled not guilty before the tense council and the city attorney proceeded to present the case for the city. By late afternoon, witnesses were still being called and the council adjourned until three o'clock the next afternoon. The next day, March 12, a Friday, the case dragged on into the evening and the council was forced to adjourn and agreed to meet the next morning at ten o'clock for a rare Saturday session. With the defense concluding its testimony, the case came to an emotional end. Attempting to forestall the inevitable, Haynes attempted a series of parliamentary maneuvers to confuse the Bota councilmen and by some miracle obtain Boyard's acquittal. After a series of motions to dismiss the charges, Haynes moved that J. Garcia be disqualified "since he did not read nor write the English language" and since the proceedings had been conducted in English, he could not make an intelligent decision. He was overruled but attempted the same tactic with Villastrigo only to be overruled again. After what appeared to many Botas as a fillibuster, the crucial vote for removal was finally called, and Boyard was ousted by a vote of five to two with alderman Grant absent. Three days later, a large and angry crowd of Guaraches met at Adams' Hall to denounce the Botas and sign a petition of protest asking the council to reconsider their decision of removing Boyard. In a surprise move that must have shocked several Botas, the Mayor vetoed the resolution to remove the marshal, and another special meeting of the council was called. With the Guarache councilmen boycotting the meeting, the Botas overrode the veto by a vote of five to zero.

A few days later, Guarache leaders were able to persuade Judge J. C. Russell, a friend of Santos Benavides and sometime sympathizer of the Guaraches, to issue an injunction against the city preventing the removal of Boyard. The Botas pleaded with Russell to lift the injunction before his departure for Brownsville, and when the judge refused, Bota leaders attempted to argue that Rice had been appointed prior to the issuance of the injunction and could therefore not be removed. With Russell refusing to make a final decision in the case and the election approaching within a week, Laredo was in the unique position of having two city marshals although it was Boyard who was the more conspicuous of the two.

The fight between the Botas and Guaraches for control of city government in 1886 was in many ways similar to their fight two years earlier. The campaign had opened in February with the usual speeches, torchlight parades, and excessive consumption of alcohol. J. S. Penn of the *Times,* who by 1886 had become bipartisan and certainly more objective, recorded that, "Laredo gets smashed on the Anheuser-Busch beers every election and the demand is so great as never was. Election bums are pouring in from the country, and stand in lively expectation just in front of every bar in town." Perhaps the race which attracted the most attention was that between Boyard and Higinio Garcia for city marshal although the race between Juan V. Benavides and Charles A. McLane for city attorney was also hotly contested. Although the Guaraches were fighting an uphill battle, they had traditionally done well in the Fourth Ward where Guarache J. L. Bartlett was running against Paul Sauvignet, and especially in the Third Ward where L. J. Christen was expected to win over A. E. Krempkan. In the First Ward C. C. Pierce was pitted against the incumbent Eloy Arguindegui, and in the Second Ward Melchor G. Trevino faced an uphill battle against the Bota incumbent, Julian Garcia.

One major difference between the campaigns of 1884 and 1886, however, was that by 1886 many of the party leaders and street marchers had begun to arm themselves. The effectiveness of the campaign seemed to be determined by which party could make the most noise. The Botas, for example, took great pleasure in shooting their pistols at anvils. The Guaraches were even better. They obtained an old cannon dating back to the period before the Civil War that had been brought to Laredo to help protect the town from the Indians. When John Z. Leyendecker was postmaster, he had taken the cannon and placed it in front of the post office as a convenient hitching post with the barrel in the ground. The Guaraches had taken the cannon, cleaned it, placed it on wheels, and painted it a nice yellow to simulate brass. During their torchlight parades, they would frequently fill the cannon with powder and fire it off to frighten the Botas. A Guarache named Moran even acted as the official cannoneer of the party, always dressed in a bright red shirt and frequently riding astride the cannon as it was pulled through the dusty streets. During their parades the two parties frequently came within shouting distance of one another, and there were the usual jeers and touts, but violence was avoided until the night of Sunday, March 28, 1886.

After a pool game at the Commercial Saloon at the corner of Grant Street and Flores Avenue, Alexander Meuly, an immigrant from Switzerland who owned a ranch in Nueces County, had involved himself in a political argument with Douglass, the Guarache councilman. Meuly drew a pistol and killed Douglass. The Guaraches were furious, and there was even talk of lynching Meuly. To help ease tensions, Judge Russell had Meuly temporarily transferred to Brownsville. The city council was scheduled to meet the next day but did little more than adopt a resolution of respect and condolence, agree to pay the funeral bill of seventy-four dollars and recess to attend the funeral at four o'clock in the afternoon. Fearing further violence and honoring the age-old Laredo tradition

of attempting to intimidate the opposition party, Sheriff Sanchez appointed fifty "special deputies" to help keep the peace. The decision to do so brought angry protests from the Guaraches. In response, Boyard, who was still acting as city marshal, commenced to appoint city policemen, using the same excuse as Sanchez.

By election day, April 6, the campaign had easily become the most bitter in Laredo history, even surpassing the general election of 1884. Election day dawned bright and clear and the two parties scurried to and fro seeing that their supporters voted. There were the usual complaints of illegal voters and a few arrests for drunkeness, but generally the election passed without the violence that some had expected. Tensions were heightened when word came from the four polling places, all homes of leading Botas, that the election was indeed close.

As all Laredo had expected, the election of 1886 was extremely close. Much to the Guaraches' chagrin, Stephen Boyard was defeated in the race for marshal by Higinio Garcia by a mere 11 votes, 629 to 618. With almost everyone voting the straight party ticket, as was the Laredo tradition, Bota Charles A. McLane narrowly edged Guarache Juan V. Benavides in the race for city attorney. Other Bota candidates won by similar margins. In the First Ward the Bota incumbent, Eloy Arguindegui, easily defeated his Guarache challenger, Charles C. Pierce, by 100 votes. In the Second Ward, Bota Julian Garcia, beat out his Guarache opponent, Melchor G. Trevino, 122 to 112.

Although it was evident that the Botas had won the day, the Guaraches had carried both the Third and Fourth Wards. In the Third, L. J. Christen, a bright new face on the political scene, defeated A. E. Krempkan, 174 to 143, and in the Fourth Ward, J. L. Bartlett beat out Paul Sauvignet, 127 to 110.

Both parties were determined to celebrate their victories at the polls. By 5:00 P.M., with the usual beer flowing freely, party loyalists were already parading the streets. Bands played throughout the night, and the partisans marched. Only now and then were brief recesses called as men made their way to the nearest saloon. In the excitement, the Guaraches were said to have fired off their cannon every five minutes. Some of the town's more responsible citizens had retired early but spent a sleepless night because of the noise.

Even as the first rays of a new day crept into the streets, the yells of the "half drunken mob" could clearly be heard. One observer recalled that party captains, those who were able to get some rest, awakened "ugly and pining for a scrap." In the streets Botas and Guaraches alike were said to have been "thicker than the hair on a dog's back." The Guaraches pulled their cannon down by St. Augustine Plaza and continued to fire salvos at regular intervals. Children in the high school were so frightened by the noise that teachers dismissed classes for the day. Hoping to put a stop to all the noise, J. J. Haynes sought out Sheriff Sanchez. Although Sanchez was having lunch with his family, the sheriff agreed to try and halt the noise but only if Haynes would accompany him since he was a Guarache and was certain to be more influential. In an obvious compromise, it was decided that the Guaraches could continue to fire their cannon if they would only relocate it.

By mid-morning, a number of Botas had already commenced to congregate in their meeting hall which was upstairs over Las

On the day of the Election Riot, April 7, 1886, Sheriff Dario Sanchez led the Bota victory parade through the streets of Laredo. In 1885, Sanchez had resigned as mayor to become sheriff. In the lengthy litigation that followed the riot, Guaraches accused Sheriff Sanchez of precipitating the violence by appointing sixty-two Bota deputies. (Sanchez Collection, Nuevo Santander Museum)

Father Alphonse Souchon, who was standing on the east side of St. Augustine Plaza near the church, was an eye witness to the gun-battle between the Guaraches and the Botas on April 7, 1886. Father Souchon was one of the most respected leaders in the long history of St. Augustine Church. In the 1860s, he began the process of collecting funds for the building of a new church. In 1873, his dream became reality with the completion of the church which still stands on the east side of the plaza and is today one of the city's most important religious and historic landmarks. (Ursuline Sisters)

Dos Republicas, a department store owned by Eduardo Cruz. All expressed a desire to hold a gala procession to celebrate their victory at the polls. Some of the younger, more aggressive Botas, suggested that a mock funeral be held to symbolically bury a guarache in effigy just as they had done in 1884. It was agreed that a good place to carry out the ritual would be in front of Dario Gonzales's house.

An unknown Bota hastily sketched a funeral notice in Spanish, rushed it to a nearby printer and within hours the official looking announcement was being distributed on both sides of the river. Some of the "funeral invitations" were even posted on buildings around St. Augustine Plaza. The flyers bore a weeping willow tree, and in a sarcastic and mocking text, announced the death of the Guarache party. The "funeral cortege" was to gather at the Bota Hall at three in the afternoon for the procession. "All Botas, all Bota sympathizers, all Bota indifferents, in fact every man that ever saw or heard of a boot were invited to attend," one correspondent recalled.

The "funeral invitations" were soon in the hands of the Guaraches. Talk of retaliation became rampant, especially among the younger, hot-headed party supporters, some of whom were still drunk from the night before.

Dario Gonzales told a group of Guaraches that he would not attempt to prevent the Botas from "celebrating or parading the streets," but he would never allow them "to bury the Guarache." "If you are on my side," Gonzales said, "I want you to help me protect my home."

At a hastily called meeting at the Guarache headquarters, several party members agreed that they would do all in their power to prevent the Botas from marching. In fact, if the Botas tried to march, they would spend the next few days "buying cemetery lots and improving them," one Guarache threatened. We will "bury some of them," another Guarache bragged. Gonzales was quoted as saying that "someone else," besides the Guaraches, was "going to be buried."

Realizing that a bloody confrontation was in the offing leaders from both parties agreed that something must be done. About 2:30 p.m., Priciliano Floyd met with Mayor Atlee to plea that the mayor do everything in his power to stop the Bota procession. Atlee agreed to try, but upon arriving at the Bota Hall, he could do little more than persuade the Bota band to stop playing for a few minutes. Floyd next approached Sheriff Sanchez with the same request. Sanchez and Floyd walked to Adolph Deutz and Brother's store where several angry Guaraches had gathered. All agreed to meet in the office of Senator E. F. Hall as soon as possible. Porfirio Benavides, Judge J. M. Rodriguez, and Sanchez represented the Botas, while Floyd, Gaspar Maus, Theo. Sanders, Juan Ramos, Cecimo Garcia, Sr., and Boniface Leyendecker represented the Guaraches. Sheriff Sanchez opened the meeting by suggesting that if the Guaraches would allow the Botas to march in peace, they would not bury the Guarache party in effigy as their "funeral invitation" had promised. The Botas could march down one street; the Guaraches could parade on another, if they so desired, Sanchez said. One of the reform leaders warned Sanchez that the Guaraches were greatly agitated by the funeral invitations." If the Botas marched, there was certain to be trouble, he cautioned. Sanders was heard to tell C. M. MacDonnell that he and Martin could stop the march if they really wanted to, and if they didn't they would be the ones responsible for the blood that would be shed, not the Guaraches.

Unwilling to compromise, Porfirio Benavides, MacDonnell, and Rodriguez walked out of the meeting, arguing that they were within their rights to march anytime they so desired. Sheriff Sanchez was left to negotiate alone. After several minutes of raised voices, threats and counter-threats, Sanchez agreed to try and persuade the Botas not to bury the Guarache party in effigy, and he left for the Bota Hall. The sheriff found Martin, MacDonnell, and Juan Ortiz assembled before a large crowd. All were determined to carry through with the march. Furthermore, they demanded that they be protected. The Guaraches had already celebrated with a parade, and now the Botas were determined to do the same. A correspondent to the *San Antonio Express*, calling himself "a Bota and a Life Long Democrat," admitted that the Bota leaders could have prevented the impending violence by calling off the procession. To have done so, however, "they would have had to surrender their manhood."

Rumors from Guarache "scouts" that the Botas were determined to proceed with their funeral procession reached Guarache headquarters within minutes. Some of the calmer members of the party suggested that no harm would be done by allowing the Botas a bit of fun. A majority, however, remained quite adamant over the "funeral invitations." They were determined to defend their honor. The Guaraches were further excited when word arrived that the Bota band had plans to insult several young ladies who had presented the Guaraches with a handsome banner a few days before the election. Runners were sent to the Bota Hall demanding that the Botas disarm and call off their parade. Sheriff Sanchez responded that the procession must proceed as previously planned. MacDonnell was heard to say that the procession must go on, "no matter what the consequences were."

Fearing they might be attacked, Botas who were not already armed, proceeded to arm themselves. Most of their new Winchester rifles came from the stores of Martin and MacDonnell. In response, the Guaraches also began to gather arms. Marshal Boyard was said to have given a number of Guaraches rifles and passed out a considerable quantity of ammunition.

In the excitement a Guarache, Tomas Herrera, was seen to spur his horse up to the Milmo National Bank where A. Brune (not to be confused with A. M. Bruni) and Daniel Milmo were standing on the balcony. "Give us carabines [sic]," Herrera was heard to say, "the Botas will beat us, they are arming themselfs [sic]." Brune replied, "you go and attack them with sticks, rocks or the best you can."

Other Guaraches, accompanied by cannoneer Moran in his red shirt and riding astride his cannon, assembled on Iturbide Street. With their primed yellow cannon pointing directly at the Bota Hall, and their red and black flag defiantly waving, the Guaraches appeared to be challenging the Botas to mortal combat, as was the medieval tradition. Other groups of Guaraches, numbering from three to as many as twenty, had begun to assemble on street corners near the plaza. Many were armed with six-shooters and Winchesters. Several of the Guaraches were deputy marshals and appeared to be little more than walking arsenals.

All of the business houses in the vicinity of the Bota and Guaraches headquarters and the plaza were hastily closed, some

even being barricaded. Promplty at 5:30, trumpets sounded, and the Bota band commenced to play. One witness recalled hearing a hundred voices, all in Spanish, as the procession assembled in front of the Bota Hall. In front came W. H. Adams carrying the party banner accompanied by Sheriff Sanchez and Judge Rodriguez. Next came a procession of four men abreast, many of whom were deputy sheriffs. The Bota band followed. Behind the band came a long line of men, two abreast and about sixty deep, all armed with their new Winchesters. Thirty horsemen, also carrying Winchesters and brandishing pistols, brought up the rear.

One of the few Botas who refused to march was Raymond Martin. Later when he was asked why, he replied that he "was not a damn fool."

The procession, more than a block long, moved slowly east along Iturbide Street to Flores Avenue where they turned south two blocks to Zaragoza Street. Here they turned east along the south side of St. Augustine Plaza. As they neared the two-story residence of Raymond Martin, several of Martin's daughters assembled on the balcony to cheer the marchers and shower the Botas with flowers.

A large band of angry Guaraches followed closely behind, hurriedly pushing their cannon and ammunition box. The Guarache musicians followed, merrily playing "El Torito." The group with the cannon broke off from the main body, however, and continued down Iturbide Street to the intersection of St. Augustine Avenue, where Moran planted his cannon in the middle of the dusty street.

Due to conflicting evidence, it may never be known who fired the first shot. Even many of the participants were not certain how the violence started. Dario Gonzales claimed that as the Botas marched along the south side of the plaza, Francisco Garcia, single handedly, rode forward and attempted to stop them. Sheriff Sanchez was heard to say, "Quico, go away, we don't want to fight, we are peacefully celebrating." According to Gonzales, Garcia turned to go, but Plutarco Ortiz took aim and shot him off his horse.

Others claimed that the shooting was started by Concepcion "Chono" Herrera, who was hurrying to join the Bota procession and fired two shots in the air, screaming that he was "going to kill [the] cabron Guaraches." A few reported that Theo. Sanders, who was following the Bota procession, fired a pistol shot in the air to frighten the Botas.

Father A. M. Souchon was standing in front of St. Augustine Church on the east side of the plaza at the time the fighting started. He later testified that he saw two shots fired at the Bota procession from the north side of the plaza. According to the French priest, "the men who did the shooting were on horseback, and they were running. They shot and ran up the street from the river."

Regardless of who fired the first shot, within minutes a general crescendo of rifle, pistol, and cannon fire echoed throughout the city. The Guaraches attacked the Botas from the front and rear, "breaking their ranks and scattering them in confusion." The Botas, however, had contemplated the Guarache attack and had cleverly positioned several riflemen on the roofs of a number of homes and businesses in the vicinity of the plaza. The snipers were said to have done the "most deadly work."

What had been feared by so many for so long had at last

AYER
a las seis de la tarde fallecieron
en està ciudad y en la FLOR de su edad
El Club Gonzalez-Guarache
y sus organos La Voz del Pueblo y La Geringa.

[Q. E. P. D.]

Sus denodados partidarios, al participar al Gran Circu
Demócrata LA BOTA y la Sociedad "Union Mexicana," ta
triste, prematuro y previsto acontecimiento, suplican a s
miembros y correligionarios, se dignen elevar al Sér Supr
no las preces que su piedad les dicte, por el eterno descar
o de los finados, y concurrir á los funerales y entierro qu
endrán lugar hoy á las tres de la tarde.

El cortejo fúnebre se reunirá en el salon de LAS Dos R
PUBLICAS.

One of the events that precipitated the Election Riot of 1886 was the printing of a funeral notice by the Botas announcing the death of the Guarache party. Translated the notice reads:

YESTERDAY
at six in the evening died
in this city, and in the Flower of their age,
THE CLUB GONZALES-GUARACHE
May They Rest in Peace

Their devoted supporters, in announcing to the Grand Democratic Society, La Bota and the Society "Union Mexicana," such a sad, premature and unforseen occurrence, beg their members and associates to have the goodness to raise to the Supreme Being the prayers that their piety teaches them, for the eternal rest of the deceased, and to attend the funeral services and burial which will take place at three in the afternoon.
The funeral procession will assemble in the hall of Las Dos Republicas.
Laredo, Texas, April 7, 1886

(St. Mary's University, Institute of Texan Cultures)

become reality. April 6, 1886, would long be remembered as the day the streets of Laredo ran red with the blood of Botas and Guaraches alike.

In less than five minutes, late in the afternoon of April 7, 1886, more than five thousand rounds of gunfire were exchanged between the Botas and Guaraches in and around St. Augustine Plaza in what is certain to have been one of the biggest gun battles in the entire history of the American West. Those who walked over the scene of the fighting later reported that the plaza and adjoining streets resembled a Civil War battlefield. Bullets were said to have "whistled from all directions, from windows and from behind street corners." "The fight must have been a furious one from the appearance of the walls and woodwork of the hotels and other buildings about the plaza, which were filled with lead," wrote Charles M. Barnes of the *San Antonio Express*. During the heaviest of the fighting, many of the buildings in the vicinity of the plaza were turned into miniature fortresses. St. Augustine Church, as well as the Wilson House, and all the stores and homes in the vicinity were badly damaged. Hundreds of shell casings littered the plaza, and the bodies of the dead and wounded lay scattered about.

With his cannon filled with nails, scrap iron, and rocks, Moran, the Guarache cannoneer, was said to have fired several salvos at the Botas on the south side of the plaza. Fortunately, Moran's aim was inaccurate, and the cannon shots did little more than damage several buildings. A considerable amount of shrapnel was reported to have landed harmlessly in the Rio Grande. The roar of the Guarache cannon, however, gave the Guaraches a psychological advantage just as it had during the campaign. At regular intervals, the echoing boom of the fieldpiece could be heard throughout the city. During the heaviest of the fighting, a band of charging Botas attempted to capture the cannon. A gallant unnamed Guarache rode forward in a shower of gunfire, lassoed the cannon, and pulled it to safety.

When the fighting first started, an eye witness recalled that "men shouted, women screamed, and. . .regular pandemonium reigned." As many as 250 men were said to have been involved in the fighting at one time or another.

When they were first attacked, the Botas had scattered in all directions, but their leaders were quick to gain control. Like seasoned war veterans, Sheriff Sanchez, MacDonnell, Adams, Judge Rodriguez and Robert Sanchez, brother of the sheriff, acted "like regular military officers, always in the thickest of the fight . . . leading on their men." The Guarache leaders too were reported to have been "bold and determined."

The initial fighting lasted for several minutes. Slowly the gunfire subsided as the combatants ran out of ammunition. At this juncture, a number of men on horseback were seen to excitedly spur their horses away from the plaza at a full gallop. It was later discovered that the men had done so not to escape the blood letting but to secure more ammunition. Upon obtaining the ammunition, they were seen to rein their horses toward the plaza and once again join the fighting which lasted intermittently for over an hour.

Laredoans would never forget where they were and what they were doing when the battle commenced. Feliz Rodriguez, the forty-four-year-old wife of the county judge, was in the upstairs section of her home on the north side of the plaza playing with her children and those of her neighbor when the shooting started. She watched anxiously as the Botas came down Iturbide Street and then turned abruptly east along Zaragosa Street. When the fighting commenced, she realized one of her children had been left on the first floor. Running to open a door on the balcony leading to the head of the staircase, she was met by a volley of rifle fire and was almost killed. "Everytime I attempted to get out, they fired at me," she recalled. "The last time I looked out the door I saw a crowd surround a young man, a Guarache on horseback, and they riddled him with bullets. He fell, and the smoke so suffocated me that I fell upon the floor. The shock produced by that terrible spectacle has made me ill ever since, and the horrible scene will haunt my memory all the balance of my life."

Like all the other merchants in town, Cristobal Benavides, a Guarache sympathizer, had closed his store as soon as the Bota parade started. A relative and Civil War comrade, Natividad Herrera, as well as several other men, were in the store at the time. Against Benavides's warnings, Herrera ran up the back stairs of the store to get a closer look at the fighting. Just as he leaned over a fence, a number of Botas took aim and fired at him. Recognizing one of the Botas, Herrera was heard to shout, "Jose Mariano Garcia: What are you shooting at me for, you idiot?" No sooner had Herrera spoken than his hat was shot off. "He then raised his Winchester and emptied it into the crowd," Benavides recalled. Nearby, a number of Botas indiscriminately fired several shots into Benavides' residence down the street, narrowly missing his wife, Lamar, and their seven children. Three days later, Benavides, still unable to control his anger, told a San Antonio reporter, "We picked up a number of bullets in the house. Here is one which struck within a few inches of her head. I am keeping it and will remould it and return it, through my pistol, to the man who fired it at her."

Sheriff Sanchez later testified how he had been at the head of the Bota procession when the Guaraches had opened fire on the marchers. Sanchez recalled seeing a Guarache crouched in a doorway blazing away at him. He returned the fire but later went to his brother's house to see one of the wounded Botas.

One of the men killed in the initial attack was a young Bota named Estevan Hernandez. On horseback and unarmed, Hernandez was shot in front of the residence of Dario Gonzales, only a stone's throw away from St. Augustine Church. Mortally wounded, Hernandez fell from his horse but managed to drag himself to the residence of Augustina Vasquez, who was so frightened by the bloody appearance of the wounded man that she fled the premises. In the Vasquez home, Hernandez was nursed and comforted by his mother, Jesusa Hernandez, and a married sister, Juana Cortes, while Juana Nuncio and Catarina Piña stood by his side. Before he died, Hernandez was able to reveal that he had been shot by Caseno Garcia Gonzales, who was known as "El Flojo." He had yet to reach his twenty-first birthday.

Another victim was Sharp Whitley, a young American who had only recently been released from the county jail. A Bota leader, Antonio Salinas, was said to have shot Whitley behind the customhouse near the river. Salinas was said to have continued to fire into the victim's body long after he was dead. He later boasted to several people, including his grandfather, that "he had killed the American." Witnesses said Salinas, who had a grudge against Whitley, walked up to the young man, drew his pistol, placed it to the head of the victim and blew his brains out. Salinas also bragged to Eugenio Yglesias of the dastardly deed.

During a break in the fighting, three young Botas, Gregorio Sanchez, Teofilo Dovalina, and Valentin Perez, were on horseback on their way home. A Guarache named Rosendo Guerra, they later testified, took aim from a nearby house and shot Sanchez. Badly wounded, Sanchez fell from his horse. His friends carried him home where he died the next day. Sanchez was twenty-five years old. Another young Bota, Ramon Rodriguez, one year older than Sanchez, was said to have been shot by Juan Ramos, Victor Duran and Andres Torres Sandoval. According to several witnesses, Juan Garcia and Santos P. Benavides were responsible for the death of fifty-two-year-old Ricardo Gonzales, another Bota.

Other known dead included Camp Burdette, age twenty-two; Librado Guerrero, age forty-five; Thomas Donovan; Francisco Garcia; Romano Rodriguez; Encarnacion Vargas; Benito Lopez; Refugia Garza; and Henry Baker, a Guarache policeman. Another victim, Pancho G. Gonzales, was so badly wounded in the face and ribs that he later died of his wounds. One unnamed man was found dead near the I and GN depot in the northwestern part of town, several blocks from the center of the heaviest fighting. Cayetano de la Garza and Plutarco Ortiz, both prominent Botas, were wounded in the fighting. Manuel Zuniga, who was shot twice, once in the foot and once in the thigh, was said to have survived his wounds as did Jose Sanchez who lost an ear in the battle. Boniface J. "Bonnie" Leyendecker, the son of John Z. Leyendecker, was also wounded, but recovered.

One of the saddest deaths was that of Herman Poggenpohl, a leading Bota. Poggenpohl and his wife, Lena, had immigrated to the United States from Czechoslovakia. In 1870, Poggenpohl had made his way to Laredo where he found work as a tinner. From a few meager savings he had bought a parcel of land and had become one of the areas more prominent sheep ranchers. When the fighting erupted, Poggenpohl had run into the office of attorney H. G. Dickinson where he waited until the fighting had subsided. At about 7:00 p.m., a group of Botas were returning to their headquarters when they were fired on by a band of Guarache snipers. Several shots were exchanged, one of which struck Poggenpohl who was standing down the street in front of Dickinson's office. Poggenpohl had remarked to Dickinson and several friends that the fighting "was getting too hot" and had turned to go inside again when he was struck in the chest, the bullet ranging downward and lodging in his back. He was carried to his home where Dr. A. W. Wilcox was summoned. Wilcox was able to remove the bullet, and for the next two days Poggenpohl appeared to rally. Five days later, however, at four o'clock in the afternoon of April 12, he died, leaving a grieving wife and three children. With a gentle rain falling, his funeral took place the next day from the Episcopal church.

For two days following the fight, the bells of St. Augustine mournfully tolled as a number of funeral processions wound through the city carrying the victims of the riot to their final resting place. On April 8, eight funerals took place at St. Augustine Church. Days after the fighting, several of the badly wounded continued to die at the rate of two or three each day. One of those who died of wounds was a woman in Nuevo Laredo who was said to have walked out on her balcony to get a better view of the fighting and was shot in the abdomen. Two others, one of whom was probably Refugia Garza, were wounded in the fighting and later died.

A page from the burial records of St. Augustine Church reveals the terrible death toll of the Laredo Election Riot. On April 8, 1886, eight funerals took place at the church. (St. Augustine Parish Archives)

The exact number of casualties in the election riot will probably never be known. Dr. Wilcox, who presided over the inquests of many of the dead, stated that three of those killed died within fifty feet of his house while another fell in his yard. Newspaper reports initially listed the number of dead at nine with about twenty wounded.

The names of sixteen of the victims are known. A number of the dead were said to have been residents of Neuvo Laredo and were carried across the river and buried there. It was reported that several of the victims were quietly taken away and secretly buried, each group not wanting the other to realize the real extent of their losses. Almost everyone in town admitted that the officially reported number of dead was perhaps only one-half of those who actually died. "Bonnie" Leyendecker, a leading Guarache who witnessed much of the fighting, estimated the number of dead at sixty with many more wounded. From surviving records, both official and unofficial, it is probably that as many as thirty died in the riot with perhaps forty-five or more wounded.

Out at Fort McIntosh, less than a mile west of town, Bvt. Col. Ruben F. Bernard of the Eighth Cavalry, had been closely observing the tumultuous politics of Laredo for over a month. Colonel Bernard, a crusty Civil War veteran of Yellow Tavern, Cold Harbor, Winchester, and Appomattox Court House, had under his command eighty-four men of Companies D and E of the Sixteenth Infantry and fifty-three men from Company A of the Eighth Cavalry.

Bernard felt his men were more than sufficient to stop any trouble in town, but he did not have the authority to intervene in any civil disturbance. If absolutely necessary, however, there was one possible way that he might be able to send troops into Laredo. "Expecting...trouble for some time," Bernard had observed what he called "a horde of cutthroats and outlaws, both in Mexico and about Laredo" who were awaiting for any opportunity to "cross to either side of the river...to pillage either of the Laredos." For several uneasy nights preceeding the election, Bernard had received reports that large numbers of men were gathering at various points on the Mexican side of the river. The colonel felt they were only awaiting the proper moment to cross the river. On election day and the morning of the riot, many of the same men appeared along the river banks for the first time during daylight. "I determined upon the first outbreak of hostilities to march my forces out and disarm every man I saw and guard the river bank and stop any incursion," Bernard admitted. On the day of the riot, Bernard noticed that the ferry boats, heavily loaded with men, were making many more trips than was normal. Bernard called out the two companies of the Sixteenth Infantry and ordered them to prepare for action.

By late afternoon, as the Botas were commencing their victory parade, Bernard became further alarmed at the large number of Mexicans who were crossing the river.

With the crack of gunfire and the boom of the Guarache cannon, Bernard knew there was trouble. A staff officer was hurriedly sent into town to report on the extent of the violence. The officer returned to report that Bernard's fears had become reality. The violence was worse than anything he had suspected. Twenty men were already reported dead. Other reports confirmed that hundreds were continuing to cross from Mexico. "That's what I have been waiting for," the colonel was heard to say. "Now we'll go and stop it." Leaving the cavalry on guard at the fort, the two companies of infantry, with Captains H. A. Theaker and H. C. Ward in command, were quickly assembled, formed in columns of fours, and double-timed into town. Heavily armed, neatly dressed, and with their rolled blankets and full field marching packs on their backs, it was obvious the soldiers were not to be deterred. Greatly relieved that the town had escaped further violence, a number of townsmen came forth to cheer the soldiers. Several volleys of rifle fire passed very close to the soldiers, but without looking to the right or left, they did not hesitate until they had reached Market Hall.

Squads of soldiers were sent to patrol the streets around the plaza. Anyone seen with a rifle or pistol was quickly disarmed. An army ambulance was soon filled with rifles, pistols, shotguns, and other arms. Saloons were ordered closed. Martial law was declared with no one permitted to appear on the streets after dark unless they obtained a pass. Bernard sent for Sheriff Sanchez and Marshal Boyard. Boyard's men were to help guard several of the public buildings while Sanchez's deputies were to patrol the river banks to halt the incursion of ruffians from Nuevo Laredo. Bernard had noticed that with the cessation of hostilities, the ferry boats were more crowded than ever, and some of the Mexicans in their eagerness to get across were not even waiting for the ferry but were swimming.

As night settled in heavy and dark, Bernard sent squads of men to guard the post office, customhouse and Milmo National Bank. The company of cavalry was ordered to assist the deputies in patrolling the river banks. Throughout the night the army continued to patrol the quiet streets which only hours before had echoed to the sounds of rifle fire and the cries of the dead and dying. Many homes remained barricaded.

With the army in control of the town, a number of county and city officials appeared at the telegraph office on the plaza. Mayor Boyard wired Governor John Ireland to send troops at once. Sheriff Sanchez pleaded with the governor for "assistance to enforce the law." Bota Senator E. F. Hall, while blaming the Guaraches for the bloodshed, nevertheless, asked for an "unbiased force" to "aid the civil authorities." Santos Benavides, growing old but still influential in state politics, also telegraphed the governor for help.

Although preoccupied with labor violence in North Texas, Governor Ireland realized the situation in Laredo was beyond the control of the local authorities. Brother-in-law of J. S. Penn of the local press, the governor was well aware of the rough nature of Laredo politics. The state militia would have to be sent in. At one o'clock in the afternoon on the day after the riot, Captain H. P. Howard of the San Antonio Belknap Rifles, received an urgent telegram from the governor ordering him to take twenty-five men and board the next train for Laredo. "Preserve and enforce the law. Use great precaution," Ireland wired. Later in the day, the governor decided to send in a second twenty-five man company, the San Antonio Rifles, under the command of Captain J. F. Badger. Both militia companies were placed under Brigadier General A. S. Roberts. In addition, a company of Rangers under Capt. George H. Schmitt, which was being sent from Pearsall to help quell the labor violence in North Texas, was diverted to Laredo instead.

At 3:20 on the morning of April 9, a special train pulled out of San Antonio with the militia, Rangers, and "war" correspondents from the *San Antonio Express*—all bound for Laredo. Speeding

Herman Poggenpohl, a leading Bota, was one of the unfortunate victims of the Laredo Election Riot. A non-combatant, Poggenpohl was accidentally struck in the chest by a stray bullet and died five days later. Poggenpohl, along with his wife Lena, had immigrated to the United States from Czech- slovakia. He had made his way to Laredo in 1870, where he found work as a tinner. By 1886, he had become one of the area's leading sheep ranchers. Today a street in Laredo honors his memory. (Ursuline Sisters)

Dr. A. W. Wilcox reported that three of the riot victims died within fifty feet of his house. It was Wilcox who attempted to remove the bullet from Herman Poggenpohl. Dr. Wilcox was himself a candidate for political office on a number of occasions. (Albert Muller)

across the South Texas prairies at an unbelievable twenty-seven miles an hour, the men had already reached Cotulla by sunup, and by 9:50 A.M. they were at Laredo. Only a few dignitaries and townsmen were at the depot to meet them. One of those who met General Roberts and his aids was Lt. Beaumont B. Buck, who on behalf of Colonel Bernard, placed the facilities of Fort McIntosh at the disposal of the militia and the Rangers. Roberts declined, saying he preferred a more central location, so his men could more easily patrol the town. In tight military formation, the troops marched into Laredo and were given breakfast at the Wilson House and the Commercial Hotel. Next, they reassembled and marched to the courthouse which was to serve as a barracks and headquarters. Here General Roberts met for more than an hour with a number of city and county officials. Marshal Boyard emerged from the courthouse to say that he did not expect further violence as long as Sheriff Sanchez did not attempt to arrest any Guaraches involved in the riot. Feelings were still running too high, Boyard warned. Sheriff Sanchez agreed but warned that Boyard had better not try to arrest any Botas. Leading Botas and Guaraches all felt that matters should be left to a grand jury. Roberts agreed. No arrests were to be made.

With the arrival of the Rangers and militia, Laredo attempted to return to normal. Groups of men could be seen on street corners and in the business houses quietly discussing the sad events of April 7. By late afternoon, the militia assembled on St. Augustine Plaza to drill. More than one thousand Laredo citizens were said to have watched. It was obvious that law and order had returned to the town. Within two days, the Belknap and San Antonio Rifles were back on the special train that had brought them to the border, this time heading home to San Antonio. Laredo was to be left in the hands of the Rangers. The militia arrived "home...from a foreign shore" to be showered with flowers and kisses from mothers, sisters, and sweethearts. Many said they were willing to return again to the "front" if necessary.

In Laredo, Captain Schmitt reported to Austin that "considerable excitement" continued to prevail in the town. Nevertheless, "the citizens was [sic] awful glad we came" Schmitt wrote. Sleeping at the courthouse and taking their meals at the Commercial Hotel, the Rangers continued to patrol the town, day and night. By April 16, the Rangers who were now mounted for the first time, were able to provide an even closer surveillance of the town. Schmitt wrote: "Things is [sic] in a bad state of affairs here, but my presents [sic] assure order and everybody are so far well pleased with me." "Things is worse here than published in the papers" and "I am satisfied that a new fight would be most unavoidable if I would leave here," he continued.

Fifty-nine citizens, almost all of whom were prominent Guaraches, including Dario Gonzales, A. Brune, Santos Benavides, Daniel Milmo, Councilmen James J. Haynes and L. J. Christen, Juan V. Benavides, Charles C. Pierce, and John Z. Leyendecker, sent a petition to Governor Ireland asking that the Rangers be left in Laredo indefinitely. Wishing to take no chances, they even asked that the number of Rangers be increased.

Three weeks after the riot, the Rangers were still in the streets of Laredo, and Schmitt reported that he was not expecting to leave for six months. "Trouble are liable to be up any day," he wrote. "The feelins of the two parties are very bitter." Indeed, it would be several months before the Rangers were to depart Laredo.

Reaction to the Laredo Election Riot throughout Texas was one of dismay and disbelief. Governor John Ireland found the riot embarassing and vowed to prevent any repetition of the events of April 7, 1886. Without mentioning anyone in particular, Ireland told the press that any Laredo public official who was guilty of any wrongdoing should be ousted from office. Many Laredoans, including Santos Benavides, were also embarassed. Benavides, in a letter to the *Galveston Daily News,* referred to the riot as a "great disorder." He reminded readers, however, that such violence was not a regular occurrence in Laredo. Besides, the aging colonel argued, everyone knows "the devil takes advantage of a weak spot."

The Texas press had a field day with the bloodshed on the border. The *Corpus Christi Caller,* reflecting the sentiment of a number of other Texas newspapers, stated that the riot was "a disgrace" and "regretted by every good citizen in Texas." The *Caller* went on to question whether the citizens of Laredo "belong to an enlightened age." The *San Antonio Express* could not understand why men "would indulge in riot and bloodshed over such a trivial question." The guilty parties in Laredo "deserve only the severest condemnation and all the punishment their acts can bring upon them," the *Express* continued.

Several leading Texas newspapers such as the *Galveston Daily News* and the *San Antonio Express* covered the bloodshed in Laredo quite extensively. Laredo newspapers *El Horizonte, La Voz Del Pueblo, El Laredense,* and the *Laredo Times,* were certain to have done the same.

At least two correspondents observed the fighting firsthand. Unfortunately for the historian, no copies of any Laredo newspaper survived for the entire month of April 1886.

The *Galveston Daily News* headlined the riot for several successive days. "Battle on the Border," "Bloody Border Battle" and "The Great Laredo Riot," were typical of the *Galveston News* coverage. The *San Antonio Express* rushed "war correspondents" to the "front" to write of "Blood Lust," "The Woeful War on the Rolling Rio Bravo," "The Charge of the Light Brigade" and "Bloody Streets." Sensational banner headlines in the *Austin Daily Statesman* and a number of other Texas dailies were common.

The legal ramifications resulting from the riot would keep a host of Laredo and Texas attorneys busy for years to come. The most widely publicized court battle came when the Guaraches set out to remove Sheriff Sanchez from office. Labeled "The State of Texas Ex Rel. Daniel Milmo, Santos Benavides, et al vs. Dario Sanchez," the case proved to be the biggest show in town since the city council had removed Marshal Boyard. Sixteen Guaraches, including L. J. and Joseph Christen, J. J. Haynes, W. H. Mowry and Martin Ramon, joined in the legal action against Sanchez. The trial opened in early June in the Twenty-eighth District Court before Judge John C. Russell, a heavy drinker and Guarache sympathizer. Local attorneys W. W. Showalter and J. O. Nicholson represented the Guaraches, while Thomas W. Dodd, Charles A. McLane, Mayor E. A. Atlee and Stanley Welch represented Sanchez. The Guarache attorneys were successful in getting Sanchez suspended from office until the case could be decided. In his place Judge Russell appointed G. B. Broadwater. Broadwater, however, notified the judge that he had no intentions of serving in such a volatile position. Russell then appointed A. Brune, a

Guarache. In response, the Bota controlled commissioners court, refused to accept Brune, arguing that they were "perfectly satisfied that Dario Sanchez has committed no crime." Bota County Attorney H. G. Dickinson attempted to persuade the state attorney general that the law by which Judge Russell had removed Sanchez from office was unconstitutional. Failing to do so, Brune was reluctantly accepted by the commissioners. The Bota attorneys next tried to get the case dismissed, but Russell ruled that the charges were "too grave."

Selecting an impartial jury in politically polarized Laredo was virtually impossible. After calling several hundred potential jurymen, nine Anglos and three Blacks were eventually chosen. Thirty-six witnesses were subpoenaed including prominent Botas C. M. MacDonnell, Raymond Martin, Cayetano de la Garza, and Judge J. M. Rodriguez as well as Guaraches Priciliano Floyd and Stephen Boyard. Sanchez was accused of "incompetency and official misconduct." Specifically, he was charged with "prostituting his office" by appointing sixty-two deputies, forty-nine of whom were ignorant of the English language." Furthermore, he had led the deputies through the streets on the day of the riot knowing that to do so would lead to violence. It was further asserted that Sanchez, by acting as a presiding officer at the election, had vacated his office. Sanchez was also charged with instructing the jailer not to receive any Botas who were arrested for illegal voting.

By mid-June, the temperature in Laredo had soared to over one hundred degrees, and partisan politics responded accordingly. Witnesses, sporting "palm fans," were said to be "squirming under cross examination."

By late June, the case had gone to the jury. Hundreds gathered in groups around the courthouse anxiously awaiting the verdict. Within hours, wild rumors had reached the streets that the jury stood eleven to one for acquittal. A verdict of not guilty was expected momentarily. The next day, however, the jury reported that they were hopelessly deadlocked, and Judge Russell declared a mistrial. The jury had stood eight to four for acquittal. The Guarache attorneys responded by asking Russell to move the case to Nueces County, but before the judge could rule on the motion, the Bota county commissioners met, declared the office of sheriff vacant, and at the same meeting, reinstated Sanchez. After several more days of legal wrangling and maneuvering, Russell ruled their action legal, and Sanchez resumed his duties as sheriff.

Another case attracting considerable attention was that of *Stephen Boyard vs. Higinio Garcia.* Boyard alleged that Garcia had been elected by fraud and should be removed as city marshal. Judge Russell had the case transferred to Cotulla in LaSalle County where it was later dismissed.

On July 4, partisan politics took a brief respite as over one hundred of the town's more prominent citizens caught the Eagle Pass and Rio Grande to San Pedro Park, a green oasis four miles upriver from the Santo Tomas coal mines. Here they heard patriotic speeches and a reading of the Declaration of Independence. They also listened to music, ate barbecue, and danced into the night.

Back in Laredo, Judge Russell continued to hear the endless cases resulting from the riot. A grand jury had been convened which surprisingly contained partisan politicians like Porfirio Benavides and Priscilliano Floyd. The judge "delivered a long and emphatic charge" to the jurors asking that they give no quarter.

Bvt. Col. Ruben F. Bernard of the Eighth Cavalry was in command of Fort McIntosh at the time of the Laredo Election Riot. As a Civil War veteran of several major battles, Bernard was no stranger to violence. Bernard double-timed two companies of infantry into Laredo to halt the disastrous confrontation. Relieved that further bloodshed was avoided, Botas and Guaraches alike praised the military intervention. (National Archives)

Andrew Hans Thaison defeated Miles T. Cogley for mayor of Laredo in 1895 to become the first Guarache mayor in the city's history. Thaison was born on February 12, 1849, in the city of Haderslew in the Danish province of Sleswig. He immigrated to the United States when he was nineteen and made his way to Chicago where he found employment in a brickyard. Although Thaison later moved to Iowa and Nebraska, he came south to Texas in 1875. After a brief attempt at farming, he went into the brick business in Austin, and in the fall of 1881, along with an older brother, he came to the Border. In Laredo, he established himself as one of the most respected businessmen in the brick and construction industry. Despite his heavy Danish accent, he was elected Guarache alderman in 1892, and from that point on, his rise in the Guarache party was quite rapid. (Etta Russell)

Indictments were to be handed down against "all who took part in the late riot, all who supplied arms and all who encouraged the riot by word or gesture." Russell in particular, asked that the illegal voting, which he felt was the major contributing factor to the riot, be looked into carefully. The time-honored custom on the Rio Grande to "import voters" meant, the judge said, "that the party with the most money got the most votes." Such was a disgrace, and it must be stopped, he went on to say. The conduct of the county judge, county commissioners, sheriff, mayor, and marshal, were to be closely scrutinized to see of there was any effort to prevent the riot. To indict all those mentioned in Russell's instructions would undoubtedly have resulted in the arrest of half the town, including almost all the prominent leaders of both parties.

Working over a period of several weeks, the jury heard an endless line of witnesses, both Botas and Guaraches. Lists of armed Bota marchers and the Guaraches who attacked the parade were compiled, checked, and checked again. Finding men from both parties who could agree on many of the events of the riot proved impossible. In the end, much of the evidence was contradictory. As a result, few indictments were handed down. Indictments were returned, however, against Boyard, Judge Rodriguez, Mayor Atlee, and Sheriff Sanchez, all for malfeasance of office. The Bota leaders were also charged with unlawful assembly and failure to prevent a riot. Yet the cases were eventually dismissed.

One of the few murder indictments was that of Antonio Salinas for the execution style shooting of Sharp Whitley. Most of the witnesses who had heard Salinas brag of the shooting, however, were either Bota colleagues or relatives. One of the few who did agree to testify against Salinas was Boniface J. Leyendecker who stated that he saw Salinas point a pistol at Whitley, and although he had turned his head and was unable to watch the shooting, he had heard the report from the pistol. Leyendecker was present when Salinas came up from the riverbank and told several men, "I killed that 'bolillo.' He is lying up there in the bushes." There is no evidence of Salinas ever being convicted.

As Judge Russell has directed, much of the work of the grand jury consisted of an investigation of the large number of people who were said to have voted illegally. Eventually seventy-seven indictments were returned by the grand jury. Most of those accused were poor citizens of Nuevo Laredo and the outlying ranches of Webb County. Some had not been in the city the necessary six months. Others were arrested for voting twice. One man, Juan Olvera, had gone even farther and was charged with "willfully and knowingly voted again and again and again." A few of the cases were dismissed for lack of evidence. A large number of those indicted either lived in Mexico or had fled there. Some had gone to other parts of Texas and could not be located. Few were ever convicted.

The numerous court cases had settled little between the Botas and Guaraches. By July, it was time for the selection of delegates to the congressional, senatorial, representative, and state conventions, and the Guaraches were willing to concede little. Politics in Laredo, despite the lessons of April 7, 1886, became confrontational and dangerously tense once again.

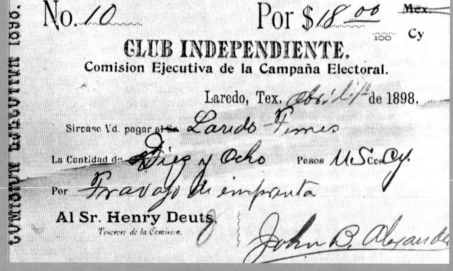

The bitter feelings that resulted from the Election Riot dominated Laredo social and political life for decades. Late in January 1890, Juan Antonio Garcia, shown here, shot and killed Plutarco Ortiz in a duel near the old City Cemetery. Garcia accused Ortiz of killing his brother, Francisco, on the day of the riot. Although Garcia allegedly fled to

Mexico after the shooting, it was a well-kept family secret that he was at Las Tiendas Ranch in northwestern Webb County. In the Spring of 1891, Garcia surrendered to the authorities, thus commencing one of the most emotional trials in Webb County history. More than two hundred potential jurors were disqualified before a jury was finally selected. Although Garcia was acquitted, it would be well into the twentieth century before the bloodshed of April 7, 1886, would be largely forgotten. In 1901, Garcia died in an accident in Louisiana. (Petra Idrogo)

In November 1894, eight years after the Election Riot, the Independent Club was founded. The founders were all Republicans, many of whom had been with the Guaraches in 1886. In the years that followed, a large number of Bota Democrats would also join the party. Except for twelve years during the Progressive Era, the Independent Club was predominantly Democratic. As one of the most powerful political machines on the Border, the Independent Club would dominate Laredo politics until 1978. (George R. Page Papers, Web County Clerk's Office)

Chapter 16

George Washington on the Rio Grande

The origins of Laredo's George Washington's Birthday Celebration can be traced back to July 4, 1869, and a man named Samuel M. Jarvis. Jarvis, who was serving as Radical Reconstruction mayor of Laredo, was anxious to see "American" holidays celebrated on the border. Only "Diez y Seis de Septiembre" and "Cinco de Mayo" were major holidays in Laredo at the time.

Born in New York City to wealthy, socialite parents on October 9, 1822, Jarvis attended some of the city's best schools but left home at an early age to join an unsuccessful filibustering expedition in Nicaragua. Captured, he spent several torturous months in prison. Released, he joined Gen. Zachary Taylor's invasion of northern Mexico during the Mexican War and later participated in Gen. Winfield Scott's capture of Mexico City.

At the termination of the conflict, Jarvis decided to return overland to Texas but stopped in Lampazos, Mexico, where he took a job as a clerk with a mining company. Here he learned to speak fluent Spanish, married a Mexican lady and raised a large family. At the conclusion of the Civil War in 1865, he moved to Brownsville and then came upriver to Laredo.

On February 22, 1870, Jarvis had handbills distributed announcing a Washington's Birthday Celebration "in honor of the Birthday of the first President of the United States." Although this is the first indication of such a celebration in Laredo, it cannot be determined how long the ceremony continued thereafter. In 1872, Jarvis, the father of the Laredo Republican party, stepped down as mayor, and the celebration appears to have been discontinued.

It was not until 1898 that Jarvis's idea of a Washington's Birthday Celebration was revived with the Yaqui Tribe No. 59 of the Improved Order of Red Men responsible for the event. The Laredo lodge, which was chartered in May of 1897, was a highly patriotic group of some of the town's most prominent and prosperous individuals.

Sometime in late 1897, the Yaqui Tribe started preparations for a celebration the following year. The Red Men named an executive committee to map out plans for the event. Joseph Netzer was named general chairman and was the moving force behind the organization. He was assisted by I. Alexander, Eugene Christen, John Gilligan, A. C. Hamilton, S. N. Johnson, Charles Moser, L. R. Ortiz, J. S. Penn, and Charles Ross. J. F. Mullally acted as executive secretary.

The night before the celebration, the Yaqui Tribe put on a burlesque play at Market Hall entitled *One Night With the Red Men*. A large crowd gathered to hear Mayor Louis J. Christen deliver a short patriotic address and welcome visitors. Then the hilarity commenced with Miguel Benavides, who would enlist within months for the war with Spain, as "Hot-Booze, Man Afraid of Fire Water," and Justo S. Penn, who would also enlist in the army, as "Spotted-Tail, the Dude." Future mayor Robert McComb was "Painted Plover," Henry Deutz played the role of "Little

Wounded Knee" while Thomas Dodd was "Joseph Weasel Bear." County Clerk and future County Judge George R. Page, who in real life had all kinds of marital problems, was "Man-Afraid-of-his-Squaw." Francisco Fierros was "Walking-Cloud," Reverand J. Ward was the "Great Prophet" while Sam Howard was "Hail-Stones-in-his-Stomach." Charlie Ross was "C. Capias, of Brief & Capias." Will C. Long played the role of "John Timmid, a Pale Face, who wishes to become a Red Man," and Johnny Thompson served as "Samuel Brief, Esq., Attorney at Law with an Eye to Business."

The local press said of the celebration: "The Indian Chiefs and their many braves. . .were realistic warriors with their truly Indian costumes, wild war whoops and lively dances. Their drill work and march was much appreciated as also the six beautiful tableaux in which they posed so advantageously. The red lights casting their lurid rays over gay feathers, many colored costumes, fierce eyes gazing over drawn bows and extended spears, altogether made a grand picture which held the fixed attention of the audience." At intermission and in conclusion, Lottie and Annie Pierce sang a number of patriotic songs.

At dawn on February 22, the festivities continued. At Market Hall, City Marshal Barthelow drew up the entire police force heavily armed and ready for action. He was joined by Mayor Christen and other city officials.

Several thousand spectators had gathered. Some climbed onto rooftops while others crowded balconies. All had their eyes on Market Hall. Within minutes "a tramp of feet, a rattle of sabers, a grinding of wheels on the macadamised street, and the blare of a bugle" could be heard. Cavalry and infantry from Fort McIntosh complete with a Gatling gun appeared in front of Market Hall. Suddenly from three directions, "Indians all painted and bedaubled, with tomahawks aloft, bows strung, quivers filled with arrows, with savage yells, swarmed upon the plaza and charged with a dare devil spirit right into the muzzles of the guns that were in readiness to defend the city and its honors." For ten minutes the fierce battle raged. Intermittently between the boom of a cannon, the shrieks of the Yaqui Indians could be heard. Soon the defenders were driven from the field.

Minutes later Mayor Christen hoisted a white flag and agreed to an unconditional surrender. Chief A. C. Hamilton received the keys to the gates of the city which he delivered to Pocahontas who was portrayed by Nettie Matherne.

Next came a gala parade through the streets of Laredo, "a pageant, which in size, gorgeousness, variety and dazzling grandeur, as compared with all other parades, processions, or pageants ever witnessed in this city, was a colossal height to a yawning chasm," *The Laredo Times* reported.

In the afternoon there were various band concerts on the various plazas which were followed with a reenactment of the Boston Tea Party. A replica of a British merchant ship, one

Soldiers parade north along Flores Avenue in 1898 during the George Washington's Birthday Celebration in what is thought to be the earliest surviving photograph of the annual event. Two months later the United States and Spain were at war. (Nick Sanchez Collection, Yolanda Parker, Institute of Texan Cultures)

hundred feet in length, with full rigging, had been constructed for the occasion. At precisely 8:30, there was "a flash of light, and the big ship in Boston harbor stood outlined from stem to stern, from top mast to water line, with various colored electric bulbs." Within minutes there was a rush on the ship and William C. Chamberlain, as captain in the British Navy, surrendered to A. C. Hamilton, disguised as an Indian but leader of the Sons of Liberty. Thousands gathered in the growing darkness as tea chests containing candy were smashed, and the candy was thrown overboard to the spectators. Simultaneously, two thousand small American flags were distributed to the spectators. Next, S.D. Moore of the Red Men boarded the ship and delivered a patriotic speech.

Next came one of the biggest fireworks displays ever seen on the border. "At 9:20 a frame twenty feet high and twenty feet wide began to sizzle and spit fire and sparks. Brighter and brighter it grew, its colors changing to all the rays of the rainbow." A great shout went up, bands played and citizens cheered "as the immortal feature of George Washington burst forth in a blaze of light, surrounded by a halo, bearing these words, *The Father of His Country.* As the letters faded into the darkness, *Good Night* in flaming letters lit up, and the band struck up Dixie as the crowd commenced to disperse. It had all been the biggest and grandest celebration in Laredo history.

In the years that followed the Washington's Birthday Celebration would continue to grow. Within twenty years, as many as fifty to one-hundred thousand spectators would line the city's streets to watch the gala annual parade. On February 2, 1923, the Washington's Birthday Association of Laredo, Inc., received a charter from the state of Texas.

But the gala celebration which continued to attract visitors from all over the United States and Mexico had its beginnings in the mind of men like Samuel M. Jarvis and Joseph Netzer long ago in another century.

Festivities during the first years of the George Washington's Birthday Celebration consisted of the Yaqui Tribe of Red Men, a fraternal organization of Laredo blue bloods, attacking Market Hall and forcing the mayor to relinquish the keys of the city. The mayor, when this photograph was taken in 1899, was L. J. Christen. (Nick Sanchez Collection, Yolanda Parker, Institute of Texan Cultures)

Chapter 17

George Washington's Birthday Celebration

Political enthusiasm for Theodore Roosevelt, the famous Rough Rider of San Juan Hill and president of the United States, is evident in the 1904 Washington's Birthday parade as Laredo was heavily Republican at the time. (Laredo Public Library)

Citizens gather in front of Market Hall for the annual George Washington's Birthday Parade in 1905. Less than two months later, a killer tornado hit the city destroying the cupola on Market Hall and leaving the business district of the city badly damaged. (Nick Sanchez Collection, Yolanda Parker, Institute of Texan Cultures)

Colorfully decorated animal-drawn carts and floats were an important part of the annual parade before the era of the motor car. On the far left, in this photograph taken in 1904, is Albert F. Muller, Sr., and on the far right is his sister, Louise Muller. Louise later married Edward D. Dwan, a colonel in United States Army who was stationed at Fort McIntosh. (Julia Ruhlman)

Maria del Refugia (Cuca) Trimble was one of the first young Laredo women to play the role of Princess Pocahontas in the annual celebration. In either 1901 or 1903 on the day of the parade, the young princess became frightened, and her horse had to be led along the entire parade route. (Ernesto Dovalina)

It has been traditional that local businesses enter colorful floats in the annual parade. This float, entered by the Muller Dairy, was in the 1900 parade. The Muller Dairy, run by Ida Muller, was one of the first in Laredo and was located off North San Bernardo in the vicinity of where Martin High School is located today. (Julia Ruhlman)

Decorated horse-drawn engines of the Laredo Fire Department make their way south along Santa Maria Avenue in the annual parade sometime prior to 1906. The photo can be dated because the steeple of St. Peter's Church was destroyed in the cyclone of 1905. (Laredo Public Library)

The Laredo National Bank, located in the Wilcox Building at the corner of Lincoln and Flores, is decorated with numerous American flags in preparation for the annual celebration. Later the Laredo National Bank constructed a larger, more modern building across the street where the Laurel Building is in this photograph which was taken by Jim Falvella in about 1913. (Laredo Public Library)

The annual parade passes in front of the Federal Building on Matamoros around 1910. Shown in the background on the left are the streetcars of the era. (Sam N. Johnson Collection, Nuevo Santander Museum)

This bicycle-drawn entry appears ready to take flight in the annual parade in the first decade of the twentieth century. (Sam N. Johnson Collection, Nuevo Santander Museum)

Several unidentified Laredo young ladies in an elaborately decorated wagon, complete with mounted escorts, prepare for the parade around 1910. In the background the recently completed Webb County Courthouse can be seen. (Bruna Sutton)

A patriotic parade during World War I progresses through the streets of Laredo. The young man is Rafael Valls, and the small girl with the red cross on her cap is Josephine Valls. The two women shown here are Lila Mendiola Ferrara who is holding Josephine's hand, and Antonia Ferrara who is dressed in black. (Carmen Nelson)

A small, beautifully-decorated parade entry halts in front of the old Webb County Courthouse as a photographer snapped this image sometime prior to 1906. (Laredo Public Library)

In 1917, Courtney Slaughter (Profitt) portrayed Pocahontas in the annual celebration. (Mary Cook, Neuvo Santander Museum)

This float, with Indian maidens rowing a canoe, passes down Houston Street. (Sam N. Johnson Collection, Nuevo Santander Museum)

Anne McKnight (Williams) and Lula Funk are ready for the parade in their horse-drawn carriage around 1910. (Mary Cook, Nuevo Santander Museum)

The float of Mrs. W. B. Jones, a local florist, presented a striking addition to the 1914 parade. (Sam N. Johnson Collection, Nuevo Santander Museum)

Children from the Puig and Sanchez Families, featuring the "Dario Sanchez Roundup with Puig Brother's Stock," was in the 1908 parade. From left to right, on horseback, are Baldomero Puig, Joseph Patrick Puig, Dan Sanchez, Maria Bruna Puig, Felipita Sanchez, Joe Sanchez, Luis F. Puig, and Robert Sanchez. John R. Puig is seated on the ground. (Joseph Puig, Laredo Public Library)

With large Mexican and American flags hanging from the Mexican side of the International Bridge, a Mexican band awaits the arrival of American dignitaries during the ceremonies in 1909. Note the cameraman in the center of the photograph and a second photographer on the automobile on the far right. (John Keck)

The annual parade proceeds south along Flores Avenue in front of Market Hall during the 1909 celebration in this vivid photograph. Note the band and the floats, as well as the clock on the west side of Flores near Reed's Drug Store. (John Keck)

The colorful decorations on Market Hall are seen in this Washington's Birthday Celebration around 1916. Although the automobile had now become an integral part of the yearly celebration, horse-drawn floats were still common. (Sam N. Johnson Collection, Nuevo Santander Museum)

The Ross Farm proudly prepares to display their Jersey calves at the 1915 George Washington's Birthday Parade. Note the clothing of the era, especially that of the unidentified man of the far left. At the 1915 parade, the Ross Farm also exhibited several, "Poland China Hogs." (Sam N. Johnson Collection, Nuevo Santander Museum)

Pamphlets and programs in both English and Spanish have traditionally been used to promote Laredo's annual February celebration. Carlota Warwick brightened the cover of the 1916 Spanish program. (Meli Coleman)

American and Mexican flags wave as this colorful mule-drawn entry passed down the parade route around 1908. (Sam N. Johnson Collection, Nuevo Santander Museum)

This float with a number of children on board passes in front of the old Webb County Jail on Houston Street around 1915. (Sam N. Johnson Collection, Nuevo Santander Museum)

Soldiers from Fort McIntosh drove the horse-drawn floats before automobiles and trucks became a part of the parade. In 1917, Belle Westbrook (Bobbit) protrayed Lady Liberty. (Mary Cook Collection, Nuevo Santander Museum)

Guests and local dignitaries head for the International Bridge on February 22, 1925, to greet their Mexican counterparts. The bridge ceremony, including the friendly "abrazo," has become an integral part of the annual celebration. (John Keck)

Since the commencement of the Mexican Revolution in 1910-1911, the United States military came to play an ever-increasing role in the social and economic history of Laredo. Here soldiers march in the 1917 parade. Two months later, the United States declared war on Germany, and the "Doughboys" were off to the trenches of France. (John Keck)

The "Girl's National Honor Guard" approaches the intersection of Matamoros and Santa Ursula during the annual parade sometime during World War I. Note the saloons, La Tosca and La Union, on the north side of Matamoros. The building had previously been the Ike Hirsh home. (Devine Collection, Jennie L. Reed)

With their flag waving, United States Custom employees march along Matamoros in the annual parade. From left to right in the lead are, Mrs. Pereira, Dr. W. W. MacGregor, and Mary Devine. (Devine Collection, Jennie L. Reed)

Mrs. Tom Leyendecker and Mrs. A. C. Hamilton are ready for the annual parade around 1920. For a number of years, Black drivers drove many of the parade entries. (Mary Cook Collection, Nuevo Santander Museum)

M. LALANDO Y S.FRANKLIN,
MATADORES

GRAN CORRIDA DE TOROS

The 1931 celebration featured a bullfight in
Nuevo Laredo with Spanish matador Marcial
Lalando and the well-known American
matador Sidney Franklin. In this panoramic
photo, American and Mexican bands are visible.
Unfortunately, Franklin, a "Brooklyn boy,"
was injured and collapsed in the contest, and
a horse was gored to death. The "Fox Sound
News" was present to film the entire celebration
including the gory bullfight. (Laredo Public
Library)

This photograph is thought to be one of the first
Noche Mexicanas. Through the years the Noche
Mexicana has become an integral part of the
George Washington's Birthday Celebration.
(T. R. Esquivel, Jr.)

In 1925 Matias DeLano, Sr., was in charge of making St. Augustine Plaza into a miniature Xochimilco. Small booths were set up around the plaza that sold a variety of food. In this photo the Knights of Columbus Orchestra poses with the floating gardens in the background. In the front row, left to right, are Leobardo Amparan, Pedro Garcia, Roberto Botello, Antonio Campos, F. Canseco, Tiburcio Gonzales, Director Rodriguez, Joaquin Mendez, V. Amparan, Jose Portugal, and Luis J. Cardenas. In the back row, left to right, are Mr. Herrera, Ramiro Sanchez, Narciso Montalvo, Hexiquio Amparan, Luis Perez Garcia, Jose Maria Martinez, Rafael Garcia, unidentified, Guadalupe Ornelas, and Mr. Aguilar. An unidentified man and Gonzales are on the ground in front. (Ramiro Sanchez)

The first Noche Mexicanas was in 1946. In the first row, left to right, are Magdaleno Aguilar, Mexican governor; the Herrera twins on each side of Governor Coke Stevenson of Texas; Bonifacio Salinas, Mexican governor; and Gloria Longoria Padilla. In the second row, left to right, are Lucha Reyes, entertainer; two unidentified women; Sylvia de Llano Barrera; Olga Rosenbaum Meyer; unidentified; Matilde Cardenas; Sophie Rosenbaum Snyder; Yolanda Magnon; Amanda Gutierrez Guerra; unidentified; and Oralia Dickinson, entertainer. Third row, left to right, are Dolores Compean; Modesto Compean; Arturo Montemayor; Jose Compean; Roberto Compean; Jose Compean, Jr.; Lorraine Da Camara; Elsa Gonzales Laurel; Josefina Benavides; and Jo Emma Da Camara. In the fourth row, left to right, are four unidentified dignitaries and Mayor Hugh Cluck of Laredo. (Laredo Public Library)

Gov. Allen Shivers and Parade Marshal J. C. "Pepe" Martin ride down San Bernardo Avenue during the annual parade in 1952. Citizens, including a number of nuns, gather on the porch and balcony of the A. M. Bruni mansion at the corner of San Bernardo and Washington. (Anita and J. C. Martin)

The route of the George Washington's Birthday parade has been changed a number of times since 1900. Here, the parade moves west along Matamoros Street. The 1928 parade used the following route: Start at corner of San Bernardo and Matamoros, north on San Bernardo to Houston, west on Houston to Santa Maria, south on Santa Maria to Lincoln, east on Lincoln to Juarez, north on Juarez to Matamoros, east on Matamoros to Salinas, south on Salinas to Grant, east on Grant to Flores, south on Flores to Zaragoza, east on Zaragoza to San Augustin, north on San Augustin to Iturbide, west on Iturbide to Flores, north on Flores to Hidalgo, east on Hidalgo to San Bernardo, north on San Bernardo to Matamoros, and east on Matamoros for disbandment. (T. R. Esquivel, Jr.)

Agapito Herrera died in a hail of bullets during the violence between Texas Rangers and citizens of Laredo during the smallpox epidemic of 1899. Herrera had previously been a city policeman. His sister, Refugia, was also wounded by the Rangers in the gun battle. (Humberto H. Herrera)

Yellow Flags of Death

In late 1898, the ugly head of smallpox spread out of northern Mexico like the black plague of the Middle Ages. By October of the same year, several cases a day were being reported in Laredo, and public officials were in a panic. Mayor L. J. Christen agreed to call a meeting in Market Hall at which time a number of leading citizens criticized the lack of controls in Monterrey and Nuevo Laredo. A committee was appointed to call upon the mayor of Nuevo Laredo to ask for a quarantine of the city. Additional requests were made to stay all trains from Monterrey and to deny entrance to travelers from the south.

By January 1899, despite the gallant efforts to contain the smallpox, the dreaded disease continued to run unabated in Laredo. On January 25, 1899, the Webb County Commissioners called a special meeting at which time Dr. W. T. Blunt, the state health officer, warned that stringent measures must be taken to control the disease. All clothing of those dead from the disease would have to be either burned or fumigated and it would be necessary to establish a "pest house" for those afflicted. Futhermore, several hundred children who were not in school would have to be vaccinated immediately. Commissioners unanimously agreed to join in the fight and appropriated a generous $500 to assist the city. By late February, however, the smallpox was still running wild. Every new day brought countless new cases and more deaths. City physician H. J. Hamilton, with a team of four physicians and five assistants, commenced to inspect every house beginning with Zacate Creek on the east and moving west into the downtown area. Although the medical teams encountered some resistance, as many as two hundred citizens were being vaccinated daily. But still people continued to die, and there was little indication that the epidemic was under control. Those most afflicted were young children under the age of six, almost all of whom were from the lower class. Most lived in small run-down wooden hovels and jacales. They were born in poverty and lived, played, and died in the dusty and dirty streets of the border city. Many of the young children were given hastily arranged funerals and buried in crude wooden caskets in unmarked graves.

By March, with the epidemic more than six months old, Mayor Christen was forced to take even more stringent measures than before. Anyone refusing to be vaccinated or refusing to allow a child to be vaccinated was to be immediately arrested. Those suspected of having the disease were to be taken to the "pest house" by force, if necessary. If the health officer found it necessary, their houses were to be burned, including all of the contents. Houses and yards were to be cleaned daily, and the trash collected by scavenger carts. Churches, schools, and places of public entertainment were to be closed indefinitely. Gatherings of large numbers of people, especially on the plazas, were to be prohibited. Beggars were to be removed from the streets, and peddlers were to be prohibited from plying their trade.

Chapter 18

On March 14, with thirty-three new cases reported in a single day, city and county officials were forced to ask Governor Joseph Sayers for help. He immediately wired Washington for five hundred tents to serve as makeshift infirmaries and detention camps and sent Dr. Blunt back to the border. Blunt arrived in Laredo three days later and was driven over the city by Dr. J. M. McKnight. Mayor Christen called for a meeting next morning at Market Hall where Blunt told a large gathering that the epidemic was the "worst he had ever seen anywhere." The situation was critical, he warned. Anyone thought to be sick must be immediately moved to the "pest house." Tents were to be erected and family members detained with the only exception being families who could afford a state appointed guard and whose house was not in close proximity to any other.

On March 17, with nineteen new cases reported in a single day, the old Davis, Caden and Company hide warehouse was procured as a hospital. Blunt felt the building was ideal because of its sturdy brick construction and the fact that it was fenced and could be easily guarded. A large vacant woolen mill along the east bank of Zacate Creek was rented as a detention camp, and large numbers of Laredoans were hired as cooks, guards, fumigators, and hack drivers.

With the heavy scent of disinfectant hanging low over the city, signs of trouble appeared on the horizon. Many of the lower-class citizens of the border city, those most afflicted and whose daily lives were most affected, distributed a circular in Spanish protesting what they called the concentration camp mentality of the state health officer and city and county officials. The author of the circular, Justo Cardenas, editor of a local Spanish weekly newspaper and spokesman for the city's poor, complained that only the lower-class neighborhoods of the city were being visited by the medical teams. The real reason for the heavy handed tactics of the authorities, Cardenas argued, was a desire on the part of local political leaders to achieve more power; all were accusations with which the lower class could easily identify. The circular helped to create a mood of wild hysteria in the city. Rumors were soon rampant on the streets that those being vaccinated were certain to die. Threats of violence became common. A number of individuals swore publicly that they would die before allowing a single member of their family to be taken from their home. When Dr. Blunt received word of the threats, he immediately wired Austin for help. Without hesitation, Governor Sayers decided to send in the Rangers.

On the nineteenth, a small squad of Rangers arrived by train and commenced to assist city officials in the removal of the victims to the "pest house." When those who were afflicted refused to acquiesce, City Marshal Joseph Barthelow and the Rangers commenced to break down doors and remove the victims by force. Within minutes, according to Ranger records, the streets became "crowded with excited Mexicans who manifested a disposition to riot." With the reputation of the Rangers for ruthlessness on the border, such was undeniably the case.

At the home of Juan Rodriguez on San Eduardo, a mob gathered when Rodriguez refused to allow the removal of his sister, diagnosed with the fearful disease. With City Marshal Barthelow, Assistant Marshal Idar, along with Aldermen Eugenio Christen and C. C. Pierce arriving on the scene, one man was arrested but was just as quickly set free by the frenzied mob. Encouraged by their success, the mob next began to shower the city officials with rocks. In the excitement, a shot rang out at which time the city officials drew their pistols and commenced firing. In the melee the crowd fled in every direction. Assistant Marshal Idar was seriously wounded by a rock, and Pablo Aguilar, a member of the mob, was shot in the leg.

By March 20, with the smallpox having spread to the Black garrison at Fort McIntosh, north along the line of the International and Great Northern and east to San Diego and Alice, the city continued in a state of panic. Furthermore, more Rangers arrived on the south-bound freight.

Sheriff L. R. Ortiz was greatly alarmed when word came that guns and a reported two thousand rounds of buckshot had been stored in a house along Zacate Creek in the poorer eastern section of the city. Fearing violence, Sheriff Ortiz set out with search warrants and a squad of Rangers, commanded by Captain J. H. Rogers, to seize the ammunition. At the first house, they met no resistance, but at the second, owned by Agapito Herrera, Ortiz was met by Herrera who protested most vehemently. As the two men argued, a teenager, who was standing at the entrance to the house, was heard to yell "ya" and run back inside. Fearing trouble, the Rangers drew their pistols just as several armed men charged out of the back of the house and across a narrow alley. Captain Rogers yelled for the men to stop and when they refused, the Rangers opened fire. In the excitement, Herrera, pistol in hand, was able to escape and make his way to a vacant house across the street.

A general gunbattle erupted. The first to fall was Captain Rogers, his shoulder bone shattered by a single shot from Herrera's pistol. Herrera, who had previously been a policeman, was able to get off three more shots before the Rangers gunned him down in the street. As he lay wounded in the breast, Private A. Y. Old ran up and fired two shots into Herrera's head, killing him instantly. Other casualties included Herrera's sister Refugia who was shot in the arm as well as Santiago Grimaldo, who was wounded in the stomach.

As the shooting subsided, the Rangers were able to place Rogers in a wagon and retreat to the Hamilton Hotel. In the process they were stoned by an angry mob of women. With reinforcements, they later returned to the scene of the shootout to find an angry crowd of one hundred citizens gathered around the fallen Herrera, twenty-five of whom were reported to be armed. Words were exchanged, and a second gunbattle erupted. Witnesses reported that the Rangers fired into the crowd wounding Margarito Herrera in the wrist and shoulder and Candido Garcia, who was hit four times, Antonio Pacheco, shot in the side and leg, as well as five other unidentified individuals who fled across the river, one of which was said to have died the following day. One Ranger had his pants leg shredded in the furious fusillade.

Later in the evening, as the Rangers regrouped around Market Hall, gunshots could be heard well past midnight and into the early morning emanating from the scene of the gunbattles. As the noise echoed throughout the dark and narrow streets, the Rangers realized they were being sent an ominous warning to stay away. With the breakdown of law and order and the Rangers unable to control the city, it was decided that the regular army from Fort McIntosh would have to be called out.

With the city taking on all appearances of a war zone, Capt. Charles G. Ayers and Second Lieutenant B. Kramer led Company E of the famous Black Tenth Cavalry into the city on the evening of March 20. The Buffalo Soldiers, all seasoned veterans of the Battle of San Juan Hill and the Spanish American War, were soon in control of the city. In some ways, however, the appearance of the military seemed to only make matters worse. People scurried about in the wildest excitement, and many of the city's more prominent businessmen were seen carrying shotguns.

Early on the morning of the twenty-first, Adj. Gen Thomas Scurry arrived in the city to take control of the situation, and additional Rangers were ordered in from El Paso. Cardenas, author of the original protest circular, along with twenty others, thought to be involved or implicated in the riot or the original gunbattle, were placed under arrest.

Considerable internal discord developed among the city and county officials when the powerful Independent Club allowed the body of Agapito Herrera to lay in state at party headquarters. A number of prominent Laredoans argued that the politicians were making a martyr out of Herrera.

For several days minor disturbances continued to erupt. One man in the eastern part of the city was "tapped" on the head with a Winchester in the hands of a Ranger when he refused to allow the authorities to enter his home. One man, crossing from Nuevo Laredo, was told he would have to be vaccinated or return to Mexico. He finally agreed to be vaccinated after he was struck over the head with a revolver. With all three hospitals full, those stricken with smallpox were now being taken to the detention camp.

With a large part of the household belongings and clothing of those in the hospitals destroyed, Mayor Christen and County Judge J. M. Rodriguez sent out a statewide alert for used clothing for the "pest ridden people of Laredo." Within days, a flood of clothing as well as food commenced to pour into the city from various parts of the state, all being distributed by the Sisters of Mercy from the Steffian Building on Market Plaza. Bishop Peter Verdaguer, who was in Los Angeles, California, convalescing, sent twenty-five dollars for the "suffering of my dear poor people of Laredo."

Throughout the latter part of March, the little children of Laredo, their crumpled bodies showing the full effects of the terrible disease, continued to die. Funeral processions, with tiny wooden coffins carried aloft, remained a daily ritual. By early April, however, the number of cases had subsided considerably, and by May 1, Dr. Blunt agreed to lift the quarantine. A. E. Vidaurri, elected mayor in the biggest political upset in Laredo history largely as a result of the turmoil of the smallpox riot, was gradually able to return the city to normal. Those who lived through the terrible days of March 1899 would never forget what the smallpox and the resulting violence had been like. Having experienced the worst of times, they could only look to the future for hope and consolation.

Chapter 19

The Killing Winds of April

For more than two hundred years the citizens of Laredo have cursed the stifling summer heat that stimies life on the Rio Grande Plain. Laredo, however, is located far enough inland that it does not receive the brunt of the killer hurricanes that ravage the gulf coast. Neither had the city felt the effect of tornadoes that frequently bring death and destruction to other areas of the state—that is—not until April 28, 1905.

Several days prior to April 28, citizens became alarmed when a terrific wind, rain, and hail storm broke over the city. Two inches of rain fell in less than an hour. Hail stones, as large as a hen's egg or a man's fist, pounded the city. Fruit trees were stripped bare, window panes were broken, and roofs were battered. The storm, however, proved to be little more than an ominous warning of what was to come.

On April 28, a Friday, at 7:00 P.M. many of the citizens of Laredo were going about their business as usual. Out of the southwest, across the rising waters of the Rio Grande, in the direction of Lampazos, a row of low, darkening clouds appeared to hover on the horizon. As the storm grew near and gathered strength, L. M. Bowden, a conductor on the International and Great Northern Railroad, walked out of the Hamilton Hotel for a closer look. "The gale had the appearance of an immense bank of clouds which sprang down upon the town," Bowden recalled. The conductor fearfully watched as a large black tornado fell on the city twisting "roofs off into the air." Some of the roofs "disappeared in the base of the tornado as if they . . . were tissue paper," he recalled. T. R. Gowan, a New York salesman who was also a guest at the Hamilton, watched in fright as houses were "wrecked until they looked like cigar boxes that had been struck with sledge hammers." "The memory of that storm . . . will linger long with those who saw it. I dream of the scene at night and cannot keep from dwelling upon it in waking moments," Gowan later recalled.

Another witness watched as "houses snapped and collapsed like card structures." Roofs, doors, shutters, and signs were sucked skyward as the tornado ravaged the city. All the telephone and telegraph poles in town snapped like match sticks and went crashing into the streets and buildings. Every house in town suffered some kind of damage as flying glass was everywhere. Ninety percent of all the shade and fruit trees in the city were ruined.

The dark and deadly twister was followed by a violent wind storm which was accompanied by hail. In all, the storm lasted for thirty-eight minutes. The rapidly approaching darkness only added to the terror as citizens rushed into the streets looking for friends and relatives.

Roaring across the Rio Grande at precisely 7:25 P.M., the tornado had first hit the Laredo Seminary on the southwestern outskirts of the city. Here more than two hundred students of Misses Nannie Emory Holding and Delia Holding were caught among "falling buildings and cracking timbers and brick." All of the major buildings at the school were severely damaged. One teacher, who was seriously injured, was bravely lowered with ropes by the school's students from a second-story window to a waiting ambulance. Although an elderly gardener at the school was instantly killed by the cyclone, school officials were thankful that there was not a larger loss of life. In all, damage at the seminary was estimated at fifty thousand dollars.

At nearby Fort McIntosh more than one hundred soldiers watched as the roofs of two of the large barracks were ripped off. One house was flattened, and the commissary was damaged. Debris from the fort was scattered over the parade ground. Damage was placed at sixty-thousand dollars.

Nearer the business district, the towering chimney at the waterworks fell across the boiler room causing tremendous damage. Downriver, two spans of the International Wagon Bridge, next to the Mexican side, were dislocated and sent hurtling into the river. The depot and roundhouses of the Mexican National Railway were flattened as were the Laredo Cotton Gin and the Ice House.

Both the Hamilton and Ross Hotels had their roofs ripped off. Both buildings suffered structural damage, and it was feared that the Hamilton would have to be condemned. Thousands of dollars in furnishings were ruined by the heavy rain that followed the twister.

The spire of St. Peter's Church went crashing into the street as did the ornate cupola of Market Hall. The west facade of St. Augustine Church was cracked and damaged. August C. Richter's clothing and department store suffered twenty-thousand dollars in damages while Eduardo Cruz's Las Dos Republicas, a large dry goods store, was also badly damaged. Grover C. Nye, who lived on Washington Street, watched in horror as his front porch disappeared into the heavens. Badly battered, it was later found in Nuevo Laredo. Hardest hit were the small, poorly-constructed neighborhood grocery stores, some thirty-eight of which were destroyed in the storm. In all, it was estimated that the city suffered more than one-half million dollars in damages.

Although the loss of life in Nuevo Laredo was less than in Laredo, the town was badly shaken. The Mexican Customhouse was severely damaged while the Sociedad Concordia, which was being used as an opera house, was destroyed.

Twenty-one people, sixteen from Laredo and five from Neuvo Laredo, died in the terrible storm. More than a hundred citizens were seriously injured. They included the old Confederate veteran, Bethel Coopwood, who had several ribs broken when a wall of his house caved in. Most of those who perished in the cyclone were from the poorer neighborhoods whose badly-built homes collapsed, trapping the occupants inside. Four members of the Guerrero Family, Tomas, Julia, Juan, and Panfila, all died when an adobe wall of their home fell on them.

During the tornado that hit Laredo on April 28, 1905, two spans of the International Bridge, next to the Mexican side of the river, collapsed into the Rio Grande. Construction to repair the bridge, shown here, commenced almost immediately. (Nuevo Santander Museum)

At sunrise on the morning after the tornado, citizens were seen to be walking through the ruins in a daze. All the physicians in the city continued to scurry about giving comfort and aid to the injured. Mayor Amador Sanchez sent an urgent appeal to Gov. Samuel Willis Tucker Lanham. "Laredo appeals to you, and through you, to the good people of Texas for immediate help," Sanchez wrote. "We need immediate assistance to relieve the suffering of the homeless," he continued. A number of leading citizens and political dignitaries pledged money to assist the homeless. Bishop Verdaguer sent thirty dollars from New York City. Congressman John Nance Garner pledged one-hundred dollars while James B. Wells, the powerful political boss of the Lower Rio Grande Valley, promised another two hundred. A. M. Bruni sent a hundred dollars, and George R. Page, John A. Valls, and Honore Ligarde promised twenty-five dollars each. A number of citizens agreed to take in the homeless, and the city's merchants offered to help rebuild the Laredo Seminary. "Noble Laredo, plucky Laredo," as the *Corpus Christi Caller* put it, was on its way to recovery.

Several days after the killer cyclone struck, Mayor Sanchez withdrew his call for help, stating that Laredo would take care of its own. An assessment of the damage revealed that four miles north of Laredo the twister had lifted into the heavens and had done no further damage.

In the days, weeks, and months that followed, Laredo Seminary would be repaired and rebuilt. The International Bridge would once again stretch across the Rio Grande. Businesses, hotels, and homes were reconstructed. The spire of St. Peters and the cupola of Market Hall, however, were gone forever. The City Council, quoting a figure of three-thousand dollars, felt the City Hall was better without a dome since it had never been "a thing of beauty anyway."

Laredo had survived Indian raids, revolutions, civil war, political riots, floods, and pestilence. It would also survive the terrible cyclone of April 28, 1905.

What remains of the depot and roundhouse of the Mexican National Railway can be seen in this photograph. Few homes and businesses escaped damage during the killer storm that swept across the Rio Grande in April 1905. (Sam N. Johnson Collection, Nuevo Santander Museum)

The lower portions of the partly destroyed International Bridge can be seen in this photograph. The storm took twenty-one lives, sixteen from Laredo and five from Nuevo Laredo. (Sam N. Johnson Collection, Nuevo Santander Museum)

The depot and round houses of the Mexican National Railways were completely destroyed by the tornado of 1905. The Laredo Cotton Gin and Ice House, as well as a number of other prominent businesses, including the Hamilton and Ross hotels, were severely damaged. The roofs were ripped off two of the large barracks at Fort McIntosh and Holding Institute suffered $50,000 in damages. (Sam N. Johnson Collection, Nuevo Santander Museum)

Damage at the depot of the Mexican National Railways following the tornado is quite visible in this photograph; moreover, so severely hit was the city that Mayor Amador Sanchez was forced to appeal to Gov. Samuel W. T. Lanham for help. Although Laredo was oppressively struck by the tornado, four miles outside of town, the twister lifted into the heavens and no further damage was recorded. (Sam N. Johnson Collection, Nuevo Santander Museum)

St Peter's
Church.
1905 Laredo, Texas.

The spire of St. Peter's Church was destroyed during the tornado of 1905. Only part of the tower supporting the steeple was rebuilt. St. Augustine Church suffered structural damage during the tornado but did not require extensive repairs. (St. Mary's University, Institute of Texan Cultures)

A number of citizens from the St. Peter's neighborhood came to see the damage to the church following the 1905 twister. Despite the damage to St. Peter's and a number of other historical landmarks, public officials were amazed that the damage and loss of life was not more severe. (Laredo Public Library)

The St. Augustine School for Boys was located on the parish grounds. In the doorway is Mr. Bryant, the teacher, and standing in front of him is Father Bracket. An old Ursuline scrapbook dates this photo back to 1873. (Ursuline Sisters)

Chapter 20

Education and Athletics

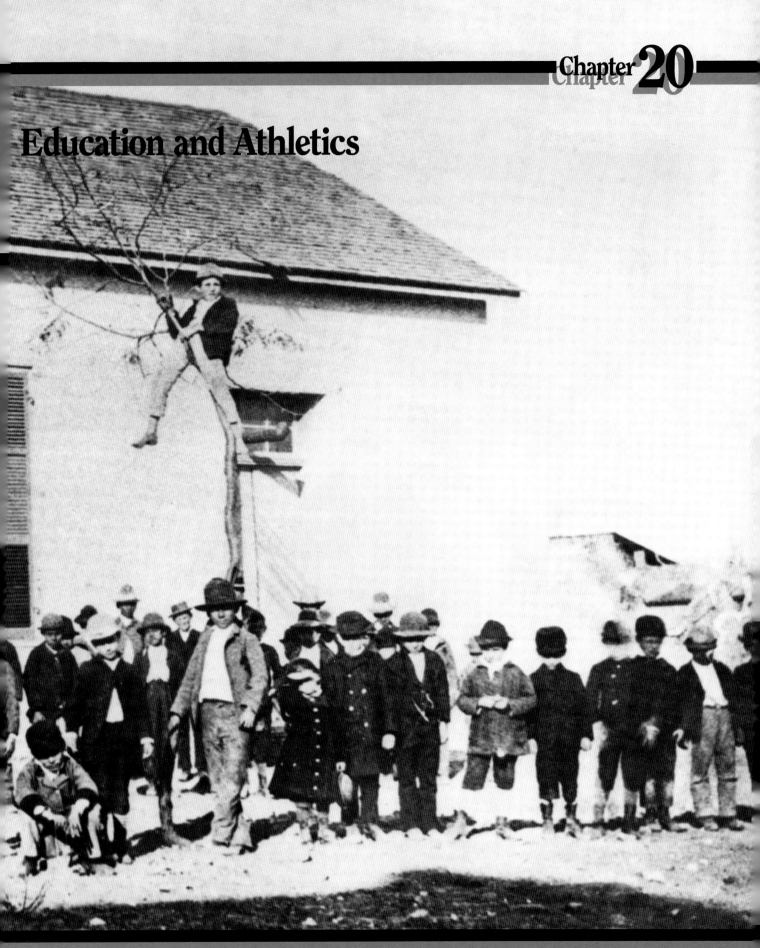

Holding Institute, shown here in 1882, was founded in 1880 on land donated by Elias Robertson. A. H. Sutherland and Joseph Norwood were responsible for establishing the school for Mexican children. (Sam N. Johnson Collection, Nuevo Santander Museum)

Nannie Emory Holding of Covington, Kentucky, arrived in Laredo in 1883 to take charge of the Laredo Seminary which had been founded in 1880 by the Methodist Episcopal, South. Miss Holding remained superintendent of what would become known as Holding Institute until her retirement in 1913. (A Decade of Mission Life)

A stagecoach arrives in front of the Laredo Seminary in 1882. During the administration of Nannie Emory Holding, the Laredo Seminary was enlarged to include seven buildings on a twenty-six acre campus. Bachelors degrees were conferred at the school before 1913. The tornado of 1905, followed by the floods of 1922 and 1932, badly damaged the school. Following the flood of 1954, the school was moved to a new location in North Laredo off Santa Maria Avenue. This photo is by Harry Stark. (Sam N. Johnson Collection, Nuevo Santander Museum)

Children in Miss Cumming's large private school gather in 1892 for their school photograph. Top row, left to right, are Mazil Winlock, Porter, Louise Galbraith, Robert Fly, Jodie Haynes, Friday (a man who worked for Miss Emma Cummings), Alma Brewster, Elsie Weeks, and Alma Pierce.

Second row from top, left to right, are Clara Murphy, Lizzie Mann Jackson, Lula Joseph, Mabel Sutherd Ryan, Lottie Pierce Gatewood, Edna P. Randolph, and Miss Cummings. Third row from top, left to right are Guss Buttron, Thadeus Winlock, Emilie Halsell, Ella Dimarest, Celita Vidaurri,

Elizabeth Murphy, Gallager, Dimarest, and Lilly Bollitor. Bottom row, left to right, are Mel Galbraith, Charles Pierce, Mat Ussery, Mark Porter, Geraldine Pierce Vidales, Alice May Watts, Prince Buttron, Fred Galbraith, and Hugh Polkinhorn. (R. C. Randolph Collection, Nuevo Santander Museum)

Miss Schultz School   May 9th 1893   59 pupils
First grade: 53 pupils present 6 absent.

This photograph of Julia Schultz's private school was taken on May 9, 1893. Ninety-three years later, only a few students can be identified. They include: bottom row, third from left, Jose Mendiola; sixth, Jose Garcia; seventh, Manuel Mendiola; eighth, Joe Benavides; ninth, Fred Vidaurri; tenth, James Kirkpatrick; and eleventh, Enrique Benavides. In the front row, far right, is Otto Withoff. Guadalupe Mendiola is seventh from the left in the third row. (Carmen Nelson)

Children in Miss Emma Cummings's private school gathered on the school steps sometime prior to 1900. The school was located on the east side of St. Peter's Plaza approximately where St. Peter's Elementary School is located today. (Anita Martin)

These children attended an unidentified private school that existed on West Victoria around 1910. Top row, fifth from left, is Jack Beretta. Middle row, third from left is Nick Sanchez. Bottom row, left to right, are first Ernst Buenz, second Eliza Bunn, fourth Evelyn Moore, and sixth Helen Richter. (Mary Cook Collection, Nuevo Santander Museum)

Boarders and day students at Ursuline Academy for girls pose in 1889. The priest (center) is Rev. J. Robert who taught religious classes. Third from left in the front row is Magdalena Martin, daughter of Raymond Martin and Tirza Garcia. (Ursuline Sisters)

St. Peter's School, on Victoria Street, was opened in 1899. The school consisted of three classrooms and a smaller room where the sisters took their noon meal as it was too far to walk to the convent. Shown in this 1912 photograph is front row, second from left, Maxine Taylor and third from left, in the same row, is Josephine Roberts. The boy in the middle row, center, with his arms crossed, is John Roberts. (Ursuline Sisters)

On April 11, 1910, the children of Margarita Gomez Colegio de Parvulos, at 1210 Hidalgo, pose with their musical instruments. (Luis Cardenas, Laredo Public Library)

This is J. T. Ward's private school around 1915. In the first row, fourth from left, is Mary Ward; fifth, Bobby Woodul; and sixth Daiches Brand. In the second row, first is Francisco Canseco, Jr. In the third row, first, is Elizabeth Kingman; second, Mary Besse MacDonald; third, Margaret Ward Peterson; fourth, Dorothy Borchers; eighth, Charlie Richter; and ninth, Abelarde Leob. In the fourth row, second is Ernestina Sanchez; fourth Jack Halsell; fifth, Emelie Halsell; and sixth Margarita Canseco. (Mary Cook Collection, Nuevo Santander Museum)

Students of the Fourth Ward School near Holy Redeemer Church, pose in 1917. First row, fifth from left, is Manuel Flores. Second row, second from left is Ernesto Dovalina. Third row, ninth from left, is Carmen Kazen. Standing in the upper right-hand corner is the teacher, Margarita Jarvis. (Ernesto Dovalina)

Members of the 1917 "wireless class" (telegraphy) of Laredo High School included: second from left, Ruth Simpson; fourth from left, standing, Mary Devine; and far right, Jennie Devine. (Devine Collection, Jennie L. Reed)

Behind the old Convent, students at Ursuline Academy participate in a badminton game around 1900. Mother St. Joseph and Sister M. Charles look on from the balcony while Sister M. Edwards remains seated. The tall girl on the right is the future Sister M. Gabriel. (Ursuline Sisters)

Taken around 1912, this photograph depicts Laredo High School students in one of the classes in the old public building called the Casa Consistorial which had previously served as city hall and jail before the completion of Market Hall and the Webb County jail in the 1880s. (Mary Cook Collection, Nuevo Santander Museum)

Teodora Viscaya taught this second grade class at Buenos Aires in 1927. (Meli Coleman)

Central School, the first large elementary school in Laredo, was built in 1906 on the site of the old Escuela Amarilla which had been built by Mayor Refugio Benavides in the 1870s. The building was demolished in the late 1970s and today a drive-in facility for the Laredo National Bank is on the site. (Laredo Public Library)

The old Laredo High School was located on the south side of St. Augustine Plaza. The building was constructed in 1917 on the site of the old Casa Consistorial. Today the building is part of La Posada Hotel. (1921 La Pitahaya)

Born in New Orleans, Louisiana, Louis J. Christen (1859-1929) began his career as a Guarache politician in the 1880s and early 1890s while he managed the Hamilton Hotel. In 1897, he was elected mayor on the Independent Club ticket. Christen is perhaps best remembered, however, for his long tenure as superintendent of the public schools (1902-1929). Today L. J. Christen School honors his memory. (Author's Collection)

Children from St. Peter's Elementary School are seen in front of their school on Victoria Street. The school, which had been established in 1899, had a reputation for excellence. Children in attendance usually came from the city's more prominent families. Holding the umbrella is Helen Bonugli. Next to Bonugli is Clare Derby. Seated in the second row on the extreme left is Reba Mims. In the front row, second from left, is Freddie Galo. Third from left, in the front row, is Claude Notzon. (Ursuline Sisters)

A group of young Laredo men gather for a formal photograph around 1900. In the front row, left to right, are Gibson and Charles Randolph. In the second row, left to right, are Rex Tarver, Charles Colman, George Fulton, Will Brennan, Royle Mims, and Maxy Pace. On the far left in the back row is Fitzgerald. The remainder are unidentified. (Mary Cook Collection, Nuevo Santander Museum)

The 1917 Junior Class of Laredo High School poses for its class portrait high above Flores Avenue on the balcony of Market Hall. Students included Ernest Buenz, Sue Brennan, Vida Bunn, Hillon Cline, Frank Eistetter, Marion Gray, Kenneth Hamilton, Rowena Loftus, Olivette Landrum, Cecilia Leyendecker, Emilie Merriweather, and Alice Thompson. A new high school on St. Augustine Plaza was under construction in 1917, and the second floor of Market Hall was being used temporarily. (1917 La Pitahaya)

The 1916 girls' basketball team at Laredo High School included: bottom row, left to right, Cecilia Leyendecker; Emilie Merriweather, and Genevieve Sharkey. In the second row, left to right, are Sue Brennan, Irene Moser, Lurlie Davis, Katherine Brennan, Courtney Slaughter, Mary Hall, and Olivette Landrum. At the top, in the back row, is Marcia D. Jarratt. (1916 La Pitahaya)

The 1922 Vocational Agriculture Club at Laredo High School included: Joe Condren, poultry; Lawrence Da Camara, dairy; George Derby, dairy; Frank Dickey, dairy; Herbert Foskett, dairy; Clarence Jefferies, poultry; Edward Leyendecker, poultry; Joe Leyendecker, poultry; Joe Puig, dairy; Joe Sanchez, poultry; David Slaughter, dairy; Lott Taylor, poultry; Edward Wright, dairy; and Clyde Wharton, dairy. (1922 La Pitahaya)

The 1921 Patrick Henry Club posed in front of Laredo high School for this formal photograph. (1921 La Pitahaya)

The Live Wire *was the Laredo High School newspaper for many years. A number of individuals who worked for the newspaper later went on to promising careers.* (1923 La Pitahaya)

Children at the Christ Church Episcopal sponsored this Halloween party and gathered on Flores Avenue near the intersection of Farragut Street in front of the old Webb County Jail in 1922. Standing, left to right, are Julieta Gonzales, Ignacio Guerra, Anita Otal Alvarado, Anita Rosenbaum, Horacio Guerra, Mercedes Centeno Verduzco, Bessie Gregg Rodarte, Judith Garza-Gongora, Elena Guerra Cardenas, Miss Garcia, Raul Guerra, Maria Luisa Canales, Elena Casasus, Anita Casasus, and Angelina Guerra San Martin. Seated, left to right, are unidentified, Sammy Gonzales, Jack Donaldson, unidentified, Beatriz Floyd Johnston, unidentified, and Sara Donaldson. (Bessie Gregg Rodarte)

Jose G. Garcia took this photograph of the 1926 Laredo High School Orchestra. Seated, left to right, are Henry Meyers, Ellenor Morrow, Lafayette Camp, Mario Salinas, and Richard Bryant. Top row, left to right, are Woodie Bunn, Rodolfo Quintana, Donald Ross, Mrs. Travis Bruce Bunn (director), William Ross, and Angelina Farias. (Meli Coleman)

The class of 1927 at Laredo High School included: Leopoldo Azios, Riley Barlow, Estela Barreda, Lilia Barrera, Beatriz Benavides, Lilia Benavides, Luis Benavides, James Walker Black, G. W. Bradberry, Bama Lee Bradley, Henry Bunn, Woodie Bunn, Garey Burr, Leopoldo Cardenas, Oscar Cass, Amado Cavazos, Feliciano Cerda, Bland Chamberlain, Ruby Coleman, Eusebio Contreras, Carolyn Cordero, Concepcion Cuellar, Jesus Cuellar, Josephine Daiches, Helen Davis, Bobbie Dees, Richard Derby, Kathleen Devine, Julius Deutsch, John Dickinson, Helen Dixon, Anne McKinney, Jennie Mae Edwards, Richard Edwards, Angelina Farias, Gonzalo Farias, Jr., Ernesto Flores, Agnes Garcia, Alicia Garcia, Candelario Garcia, Estela Garcia, Enriqueta Garcia, Maria Garcia, Flora Gonzales, Mary Lillian Graves, Jesus Guerra, Wendell Guinn, Arturo Gutierrez, Aurora Gutierrez, Alice Harper, Elizabeth Klein, Ofelia de LaChica, Katherine Landrum, Justo Lazo, Elena Leal, Sarah Leal, Willis Leyendecker, Joseph Leyendecker, George Loftus, Marjorie May, Dora Martinez, America Merriweather, Thomas Mudd, Maria Luisa Ostos, Abraham Palacios, John Puster, Ross Quinn, Amelia Ramon, Leonor Rico, William Ross, Elvira Saenz, Enriqueta Salas, Ezequiel Salinas, Gladys Sauvignet, Thomas Simms, John Sommerville, Eddie Stroud, Alvaro Trevino, Berta Uresti, Nicanor Valdez, Charlotte Vidaurri, Tasse Vidaurri, Maria Villareal, Dorothy Lee Webber, James Ward, Madeline Ward, Clayton White, George Wright, Harold Yeary, Evans Younkin, and Josefina Zapata. (1927 La Pitahaya)

Urban Elementary School, in the 1600 block of Victoria, was one of the more modern schools in the city when this postcard was made in the late 1920s. The school was named after Albert Urbahn who at one time owned the Callaghan Ranch. Urban, a popular political figure, also ran the Santa Rosa Farm, a model agricultural project located twelve miles downriver. Urbahn spent his last few years in poverty at the Bender Hotel and the school was vacated in 1985. (Laredo Public Library)

LAREDO'S HIGH SCHOOL, LAREDO, TEXAS—21

Martin High School, built during the Great Depression by the Works Progress Administration, was named after Tirza Garcia Martin and Raymond Martin and cost $353,000. It opened for the first time in September 1937. (Armengol Guerra III)

On August 28, 1940, Ursuline Academy dedicated its new $75,000 home at 1300 Galveston. A large crowd including the Ursuline Sisters from San Antonio, Sisters of Divine Providence, Sister Servants of the Sacred Heart, Sisters of the Incarnate Word from Corpus Christi, Sisters of the Incarnate Word from San Antonio, Salesian Sisters. Brothers of St. Joseph's Academy, Oblate Fathers, and numerous other clergy turned out for the ceremony. Alphonse Leyendecker was the architect while Peter P. Leyendecker and A. Medina Martinez were the contractors for the new building (Ursuline Sisters)

The 1904 Laredo professional baseball team included: standing, left to right, Elias Garcia, third base; C. Aguilar, outfield; Dave Craven, infield; James Collins, first base; Emilio Cadena, outfield; and Leo Fierros, pitcher and catcher. In the front row, left to right, are Cayetano Ancira, fielder; Polycarpio Marulanda, fielder; Jim Craven, infield and pitcher; and Francisco Pena, shortstop. Pena later became a colonel in the Mexican Army under Venustiano Carranza. (Francisco Pena)

Brothers Albert and Joe Martin pose in their baseball uniforms for this formal setting around 1912. Albert, after serving in World War I, became alderman and mayor from 1926 to 1940. Joe served as city tax assessor and as sheriff from 1932 to 1957. Commencing in the late 1920s until 1957, he was also president of the Laredo Independent School District. (Anita and J. C. Martin)

The 1913 Laredo High School Basketball team included these nine young men. Games were played in a small wooden frame building back of the old high school on St. Augustine Plaza. The gymnasium was later moved to a location near Christen Junior High School. Seated on the far left is Albert F. Muller, Sr. (Albert Muller)

The 1913 Ursuline girls' basketball team prepares for a workout on the court. In reality, the young ladies were unable to schedule a single game. Kneeling, left to right, are Margaret Simon, Mamie Cunningham, Leonor Lozano, and Guadalupe Alexander. Standing, left to right, are Alice Langford, Carmen (last name unknown), Amanda Feville, Josephine Roberts, and Francis Lozano. (Ursuline Sisters)

The 1922 Laredo High School baseball team included: E. Wright, catcher; F. Dickey, L. Da Camara, and O. McCauley, pitchers; R. Trout, first base; Joe Leyendecker, second base; D. Trevino, third base; G. Esparza, center field; P. Jeffreys, left field; L. Maher, center field; J. Condren and A. Zamora, right field; T. Garcia, D. Wright, and L. Taylor were substitutes. J. D. Tatley, Jr., was the coach. In the opening game of the season the high school players prevailed over the Boy Scouts by a score of 12 to 4. (Meli Coleman)

The 1909-1910 Laredo professional baseball team gather around their manager, George R. Page (1862-1920). Page, in civilian clothes, doubled as Webb County clerk (1890-1913) and manager of the Laredo "Bermudas" for a number of years. Page also served as county judge from 1913 to 1920. (Nuevo Santander Museum)

The 1928 Ursuline girls' basketball team, under the guidance of Sister Gerard, played Holding Institute, Laredo High School, and St. Augustine. (Ursuline Sisters)

The 1922 Laredo High School football team included: Perry Jefferies, Clarence Jefferies, Luther Almand, Joseph Puig, Frank Dickey, Clyde Wharton, Ben Rogers, Desiderio Trevino, Fred Rogers, Charlie Richter, and Delbert Wright. Highlights of the season included a 2-0 squeaker over Pearsall and a 65-0 drubbing of Lytle. (1922 La Pitahaya)

The 1925 Laredo High School tennis team included, from left to right, Lafayette Camp, Radcliffe Killam, and Evans Younkin. (1925 La Pitahaya)

In 1925 the Laredo High School freshmen basketball team, scheduled to graduate in 1928, posed for the camera of Jose G. Garcia. Players included: Webb Dickey, Gary Burr, Fernando Pena, Radcliffe Killam, Walter Stein, and Stuart Johnson. (Meli Coleman)

The 1926 Laredo High School baseball team included, front row, left to right, Robert Derby, Tom Hickey, R. Garcia, Henry Mejia, Woodie Bunn, Fernando Pena, and Tony Leyendecker. Standing, left to right, are Mateo Garcia, Ralph Connor, R. Garza, Oscar Hein, Robert B. Warwick, John Dickinson, Leon Fortassain, and Coach Shirley Da Camara. Photo by Jose G. Garcia. (1926 La Pitahaya)

The most valuable athlete at Martin High School in 1945 was Domingo Arechiga. Arechiga later served as president of Laredo Junior College from 1973 to 1985. (1945 La Pitahaya)

The 1948 Laredo Junior College Palomino football team included: front row, left to right, Ornelas, Sanchez, Meza, Laurel, Lozano, Sauvignet, Garza, Garcia, Villarreal, and Gloria. In the second row, left to right, are Lewis, Herrera, Munoz, Gonzales, Saenz, Jacaman, Sandoval, Aber, Villarreal, Starnes, Stewart, and Gissing. In the third row, left to right, are Coach Louvorn, Johnson, Arechiga, Campbell, Garcia, Sanchez, Hinojosa, Cruz, Lozano, Terry, Herrington, Quijas, Alebis, Swisher, and Coach Drennan. (1949 Laredo Junior College Spur, *Esther Stewart*)

Born on October 29, 1949, Dario Hinojosa, Jr., son of Dario and Eva Hinojosa, was one of the greatest athletes in Laredo schoolboy history. As a running back for Martin High School, Hinojosa had a promising college career ahead when he was tragically killed in an automobile accident on April 7, 1968. (1966 La Pitahaya)

One of the greatest accomplishments of a Laredo athletic team occurred when the 1956 Martin High School basketball team captured the state schoolboy championship. Although one of the shortest teams to ever win the title, the Tigers used a devastating fast-break to down Milby of Houston, 65-53, and North Dallas, 65-54. It has been thirty-two years since a Laredo team had made it to the state tournament. In the front row, left to right, are Jose Luis Novoa, manager; Guadalupe Guajardo; Enrique Mejia, Jr.; Agustin Molina; Isidro Garcia; Ramiro Hernandez; and Jimmy Rodriguez. In the back row, left to right, are Cruz Alejandro Soto, Leonard Anderson, Andres Santos, Willie Dickinson, Philip Trammel, Hector Chacon, and Walter Herbeck, manager. (1956 La Pitahaya)

Chapter 21

The Day the Great Commoner Came to Town

In 1896 he stood at the pinnacle of American politics. As a thirty-six year-old congressman from Nebraska, he had excited the country and electrified the Democratic Party at the Chicago Convention with his "Cross of Gold" speech. "You shall not press upon the brow of labor this crown of thorns," William Jennings Bryan had cried in one of the most famous perorations in American history. "You shall not crucify mankind upon a cross of gold!"

Not only had Bryan won the Democratic nomination that year, but even the upstart Populists had endorsed him. As a political messiah of the common man, Bryan stormed across the country advocating the free and unlimited coinage of silver, sometimes in three or four speeches a day. His followers called him the "Boy orator of the Platte." The Republicans mocked him, pointing out that the Platte River was six inches deep and a mile wide at the mouth. His political rallies resembled a revival meeting as Bryan, quoting passages from the Bible, drew huge crowds. The Eastern press called him a raving anarchist and compared him to the Jacobians of the French Revolution. Farmers, miners, and railroad workers everywhere flocked to his banner like rats to the Pied Piper of Hamlin. In response, factory owners told their immigrant laborers that "if Bryan was elected on Tuesday the whistle will not blow on Wednesday."

In that eventful year of 1896, Bryan went down to a crushing defeat at the hands of the "Robber Barons," the Republicans and William McKinley. Four years later he rose to challenge McKinley again but suffered an even worse defeat. By 1908 he was at the helm of his party again as he carried the Democratic banner into battle against William Howard Taft. Again, Bryan was soundly trounced. His political career appeared over. Many considered him a fallen and tarnished hero. Nevertheless, wherever he went, huge crowds gathered.

Despite the fact that the powerful and dominant Laredo Independent Club was solidly Republican during the Progressive Era, the name of William Jennings Bryan still evoked nostalgic pride and excitement. This was especially so when it was announced that Bryan would be traveling through Laredo on his way to Monterrey, Mexico, to do some hunting in the Sierra Madre.

Bryan first arrived in San Antonio on November 17 for some duck hunting. He then caught the train for Corpus Christi. On the twenty-second, after a brief rest by the sea, Bryan boarded the Texas-Mexican Railway for Laredo. Vast crowds gathered along his route to cheer Bryan. At Alice and San Diego he appeared on the rear platform of the train to address thousands of excited citizens. Hundreds of school children who had been given the day off to hear the "Great Commoner" gayfully waved small American flags and sang patriotic songs.

At 5:00 p.m. Bryan reached Laredo. He was met at a railroad crossing one mile outside of town by a committee of local dignitaries and politicians. They included Mayor Amador Sanchez; District Attorney John A. Valls; Webb County Democratic Executive Committee Chairman J. R. Moore; Republican Chairman James J. Haynes; ex-Democratic Chairman A. E. Vidaurri; Justo Penn, owner and editor of the *Laredo Daily Times*; and Priciliano Floyd, Clarence Jefferies, and W. M. Conway of the Associated Press. Bryan showed his political astuteness by reminding the greeting dignitaries that Webb and Zapata counties had been the only counties in the state to vote Republican in the 1908 general election.

As the train pulled slowly into the city and the shops of the Mexican National Railroad, Bryan was "greeted vociferously" by a large number of shop employees. Next the train proceeded to the Texas-Mexican Railway station where the Nuevo Laredo Municipal Band serenaded him as thousands cheered. As Bryan and his wife disembarked to make their way to the waiting cars of the Mexican National at the depot of the International and Great Northern, vast throngs of citizens, in their desire to get close to Bryan, rushed forward and had to be restrained by the city police. As he reached the waiting Pullman, several excited citizens were able to get close enough to shake his hand. At the station a large congregation of "little Mexican Boys" chanted "Viva Bryan, viva Bryan," and "No se vaya, no se vaya." Bryan was heard to remark: "Those are a lot of little bright-eyed urchins: I'll go and talk with them." He then descended from the train to shake hands with the children. This revived their vigor as they renewed their chants of "Viva Bryan, viva Bryan."

As the Mexican National train slowly pulled out of the station, the crowd continued to wave and cheer. After crossing the Rio Grande into Mexico, Bryan was greeted by another large crowd in Nuevo Laredo. As a Mexican band played "La Golondrina," one man came forward and was heard to tell Bryan in his broken English: "Mester Bryan, I am very pleased for know you for I theenk you great man." The expression was said to have come from the heart and was greatly appreciated by the "Great Commoner." With the ceremony concluded, the train pulled out of Nuevo Laredo toward Lampazos, the Sierra Madre, and Monterrey. Those citizens who came to see William Jennings Bryan on that brisk November afternoon in 1908, would remember for the rest of their lives the day the "Great Commoner" came to town.

William Jennings Bryan, the "Great Commoner" from Nebraska, had run three times unsuccessfully for president of the United States on the Democratic ticket. Although Laredo was heavily Republican during the Progressive Era, Bryan received a warm welcome when he visited the city following his defeat by William Howard Taft in 1908. (National Archives)

In February 1911, the Army Signal Corps brought one of its newest airplanes to Fort McIntosh for a series of test flights. The two individuals in this photograph are thought to be Aviator Philip O. Parmalee, right, and James H. Hare, left, photographer for Collier's magazine. The "Scout," a Wright brothers biplane, with Parmalee and First Lt. Benjamin D. Foulois aboard, made a flight on March 3, 1911, from Laredo to Fort Duncan at Eagle Pass. Although a number of records were set, the Scout crashed into the Rio Grande on the return trip. (San Antonio Express-News, Institute of Texan Cultures)

In February 1911, exciting news reached Laredo from San Antonio. The Army Signal Corps had decided to use Fort McIntosh as a base to test one of its newest "aeroplanes." Overnight, the town and the fort became a beehive of excitement and anticipation. It was even rumored that the Army would attempt a record-breaking cross country flight all the way from Laredo to Eagle Pass.

The "flying contraption" that caused all the excitement was a Wright Brothers biplane loaned to the Army by Robert Collier of New York. Thought to be clearly superior to the new monoplane, the biplane arrived in crates on the International and Great Northern from Fort Sam Houston. Anxious citizens of the border community stood by as the crates were unloaded and transported to nearby Fort McIntosh where the airplane was to be assembled. Also arriving from San Antonio for the great event were two pilots, First Lt. Benjamin D. Foulois and Aviator Philip O. Parmalee. When James H. Hare of Collier's magazine arrived to photograph the scene, Laredo had indeed become center stage to the world.

At Fort McIntosh, a tent hangar was quickly erected on the cavalry parade ground for the airplane which the Army was calling "Scout." Many citizens of Laredo crowded around the airplane, astounded at the thirty-five foot wing-span of the "monster bird."

On March 2, the Signal Corps mechanics announced that the Scout was ready for flight. In anticipation, a large crowd had gathered at the fort. Across the river in Nuevo Laredo, hundreds of others, hoping to catch a glimpse of the airplane, had gathered on housetops while a few bravely climbed trees and telephone and

Caught up in the excitement of the times, thousands of Laredoans rushed to Fort McIntosh to see the Wright Brother's "Scout" soar into the skies in preparation for an epic cross-country flight to Eagle Pass. Here a number of Laredo citizens inspect the plane. (Devine Collection, Jennie F. Reed)

Chapter 22

Wings Over Laredo

telegraph poles. A number of Laredoans, in their excitement, sped to the fort in autos and carriages.

With Aviator Parmalee at the controls, the airplane gently sped down the dusty runway and lifted off into the clear blue sky. For three minutes, the Scout circled around the parade ground each time gaining altitude. The crowd cheered as the airplane reached an altitude of several hundred feet. Observers were further astounded when the Scout made a "most graceful landing at the exact spot" from which it had taken off. Less than an hour later, the Scout again "rose quickly and easily" and headed north over an endless stretch of onion fields. This time both Parmalee and Lieutenant Foulois were aboard. In all, the Scout was able to travel over six miles before returning to the fort. On a third flight, photographer Ware was invited aboard. Six photos were hastily snapped from a height of over five hundred feet. Never before had photographs been taken from an airplane from such a height. Four more times the airplane landed, each time ascending into the skies again, all to the delight of the large crowd.

Most of the next day was spent in installing a wireless in the airplane as additional preparations were made for the flight to Eagle Pass. It was hoped that the Scout would be able to communicate with several wireless stations along the river such as Minera, Sullivan's Ranch, and Pagreache Crossing. An extra twenty-five gallon gasoline tank was installed for the long flight. Late in the afternoon, the Scout was able to make one brief flight with Parmalee waving to several hundred spectators.

Both the Army and the citizens of Laredo realized that the flight to Eagle Pass was a dangerous undertaking. The men would follow a course along the American side of the river roughly parallel to the wagon road leading to Eagle Pass, all the time scouting the Mexican side of the river. The wagon road to Eagle Pass was rough, and the countryside was full of deep arroyos. Any attempt at an emergency landing could easily mean disaster.

By Friday, March 3, everything was ready. With field glasses, a map, two days rations of food, an army revolver, forty rounds of ammunition, and a large quantity of chocolate bonbons, the two men climbed aboard the Scout. Observers remembered Parmalee as displaying a boyish enthusiasm while Foulois strutted around the parade ground with a big black cigar in his mouth.

At precisely 1:57 p.m., Parmalee gunned the Scout's powerful thirty-five horse power engine, and the airplane sped down the runway and rose gracefully into the sky. At an altitude of two hundred feet, the Scout circled once over the fort and then turned northwest for Eagle Pass. Skimming through the brisk March afternoon, the airplane was soon out of sight. Thirty-three minutes later, word arrived that the Scout was over Minera in a dense fog at one thousand feet.

Throughout the afternoon, anxious Laredoans awaited any news from the Scout. Well into evening, men could be seen on street corners and in the saloons talking of little else. At Fort McIntosh, a telegram arrived from Fort Duncan: "Arrived four seven without stop. Picket up air wireless stations en route. Didn't see a thing on Mexican side. Will probably start back Sunday. Foulois."

Laredo and the Scout had made history. The town erupted into wild jubilation. Foulois and Parmalee had set several world's records. The 116-mile flight by such a plane was the longest in aviation history. The two hours and seven minutes the Scout had remained aloft was also a record. It was, as the local press recorded, the "most remarkable aerial voyage ever made."

On March 5, the joy turned to fear, however, when Parmalee and Foulois failed to return as scheduled from Eagle Pass. A telegram arrived that the men had taken off as planned at 7:00 a.m., but they never arrived at Fort McIntosh. Laredo anxiously awaited any news of the fate of the two men.

One day later, it was announced that Parmalee and Foulois had been forced to make a hurried landing because of engine trouble. It was several weeks, however, before the true facts of exactly what had happened to the Scout were revealed. The Scout was some twelve miles downriver from Eagle Pass when Parmalee spotted a large flock of ducks taking flight from the waters of the Rio Grande. Hoping to point out the birds to Foulois, Parmalee had begun to gesture wildly with his hands. In the process, someone pulled a cord which released the compression from the camshaft of the Scout's engine. Before the two men could get the airplane under control, the Scout had taken a nose dive into the shallow water of the river and flipped over on its back. The men escaped injury, but the airplane was badly damaged.

The Scout was later pulled from the river, dismantled and carried in wagons to Fort McIntosh where, much to the sorrow of the town, it was shipped back to San Antonio.

Despite the crash of the Scout, the Army was impressed "with the possibilities of the airplane in signal, radio, and reconnaissance work." Shortly thereafter, Congress appropriated a generous $125,000 for military aeronautics. Laredo had, for one brief moment, played a critical role in the early history of aviation.

James Barney Compton, army veteran, drifter, and part-time railroad worker, was found guilty of the murder of G. J. Levytansky, a Laredo jewelry store owner. He was hanged at 11:10 a.m., March 15, 1912, in the old Webb County Jail. The hanging, which excited considerable public attention, was the last in Webb County. (San Antonio Express)

Lonnie A. Franks, a twenty-two-year-old unemployed veteran and gambler, was sentenced to life in prison for the murder of G. J. Levytansky. Franks escaped from the Texas State Prison on February 13, 1913, and although Texas Rangers remained on this trail for twenty-six years, he was never captured. (San Antonio Express)

The Day They Hanged

G. J. L evytansky, a thirty-nine-year-old Polish

immigrant, came to Laredo some time shortly before the turn of the century and opened a jewelry store in the Farrell Block on Flores Avenue, just two doors south of I. Alexander Men's store. His "New Jewelry Store" advertised solid gold jewelry and "all kinds of novelties." "Give me a trial," Levytansky asked the citizens of Laredo. "Levy," as he was commonly known in the city, was a small man less than five feet in height who weighed only 135 pounds. People remembered him as a balding bachelor, "quiet and unassuming;" someone who lived a "plain, unostentatious life."

James Barney Compton, age twenty-six, army veteran and drifter came to the border a decade after Levytansky. In Laredo he found a part-time job as a switchman for the International and Great Northern Railroad and fell in love with a local beauty, Delia Johnson, whom he hoped to marry, but was ashamed that he had little money to support a wife.

Over a game of poker one evening in a local saloon, Compton met Lonnie A. Franks, a twenty-two-year-old unemployed veteran attempting to scratch out a living gambling at pool and cards. Frank, described as standing five feet six inches in height and weighing 147 pounds, had chestnut hair, brown eyes, and a fair complexion. Franks and Compton soon became close friends. After being discharged from the Ninth Infantry, Franks had operated a pool hall in San Antonio for a time but had drifted down the I & GN to Laredo. He had been forced to fend for himself from the time he was a child of a large family in Midlothian, Texas. His mother died when he was only six, and he dropped out of school after finishing seventh grade.

It was in a pool hall one evening that the two men came to plot what came to be called "the most diabolical, dastardly and cold-blooded assassination ever committed in Laredo." Both men complained of not having enough money. Compton talked of getting married but was penniless. Franks suggested the two rob a well-known local lady reportedly worth thousands of dollars. When Compton objected, the discussion turned to Levytansky, also rumored worth thousands of dollars. Compton and Franks had heard that Levy had a safe full of precious jewels, and as Franks pointed out, Levy was "a single man and not having a wife and children . . . would not be missed by anybody."

By late December 1911, the two men completed their plans. Over the next few days they visited the New Jewelry Store several times to finalize in their minds the layout of the store including the location of Levy's safe. Three days before Christmas they were ready to strike. At seven in the evening Compton entered the store, telling Levy that a friend was anxious to have his watch regulated and inquired at what time Levy would be closing. Shortly thereafter, by prior arrangement, the two men met at a local saloon. Compton had a piece of steel pipe he found behind the hardware store of A. Duetz and Brother. He told Franks that "he

Chapter 23

J. B. Compton

would just tap the old fellow a little blow," and the two would "get away before he came to." He placed the pipe inside the waistband of his pants and would later recall how the cold steel felt against his flesh in the December night. Leaving the saloon, the two split up. Franks, dressed in a gray suit and a black hat, waited in a darkened entrance of Richter's Department Store across the street as Compton entered the jewelry store and engaged Levy in conversation. Within minutes Franks entered as planned and asked Levy to regulate his watch. As Levytansky bent over to examine the watch, Compton approached from behind and struck him a vicious blow over the head with the iron pipe wrapped in a brown paper bag. Levy fell to the floor, his skull crushed. To make sure of his deadly work, Compton struck Levy twice more with the pipe. Then with a long blade pearl-handle pocket knife, he stabbed the already dead victim several times in the heart. Franks quickly extinguished all the lights in the store as Compton dragged the body to a darkened corner beneath a window in the northwest part of the store. "My God, they will see you," Franks later recalled saying, as Compton's silhouette, reflected by a street lamp, passed across the store like a ghost in the night. The two men, acting almost as if they were morticians, placed the dead man's feet together and crossed his hands on his chest.

To their surprise, Levytansky had left his safe open. Inside they found twenty-nine packages of diamonds, $370 in Mexican currency and $54 in U.S. money. Within twenty minutes the safe had been looted, and the two had left through a back entrance where they were forced to jump over a brick wall. In his haste, Compton left the bloodied pipe on a wall between the jewelry store and the Western Union telegraph office. Through the city's darkened streets, the two men made their way to Compton's room where the diamonds were divided according to the value marked on the packages. Later the two walked along Houston Street toward the I & GN Railroad yards where Compton wanted to bury his share. As they scurried along through the night, Compton kept jabbing the bloodied pocket knife into a fence railing, breaking both blades. Disgusted, he threw the knife into a vacant lot.

Compton seemed obsessed with the idea that Texas Rangers would use bloodhounds to follow their trail. Reaching the darkened I & GN yards, Compton found a sand pile where he buried his nine small bags of diamonds which he had carefully wrapped in tissue paper. The two then took a solemn oath never to divulge their terrible crime. They then walked back to town and went to bed.

Early the next morning, Franks arose early and made his way to the post office where he mailed his share of the diamonds to a fictitious S. A. Austin in "McKienney," Texas; obviously misspelling McKinney in his almost illiterate scrawl. From the post office, Franks walked west to the I & GN depot and caught the northbound train to San Antonio. As the train carried Franks north, the citizens of Laredo went about their daily business, unaware of the terrible crime that had been committed the night before.

Promptly at 9:00 a.m., August Richter arrived at his clothing store as was his custom. He noticed that Levy had not yet opened his jewelry store. The store being closed was unusual as Levy was always punctual and one of the city's more responsible and hard-working businessmen. Richter felt that Levy had probably overslept. By 10:30, however, when the jewelry store was still not open, Richter became concerned. An hour later, he went to investigate. Finding the front door locked, he walked around to the back entrance, calling Levy's name several times. Not hearing a reply, he entered to find the jeweler cold in death. It was obvious at first glimpse that he had been murdered. Hurrying out the back entrance and racing around to the front of the store, Richter summoned Ike Alexander, who ran a nearby clothing store and Dr. O. H. Hodges, a dentist who had an office upstairs in the same building. Within minutes the city police arrived and with them a large crowd. One of those in the large congregation in front of Levytansky's store, who remained for over an hour until Levy's body was removed, was James Barney Compton.

Compton also followed Levy's body as it was taken to the Convery Funeral Home on the south side of Jarvis Plaza. Within days, two of his brothers, who were also jewelers, arrived from Yoakum and Victoria. From the Convery Funeral Parlor, Levy's remains were taken to the Masonic Hall where a large crowd gathered for an impressive funeral. With Annie Thaison at the organ, the Order of the Eastern Star Choir sang "Nearer My God to Thee." With his brothers accompanying his remains to San Antonio, G. J. Levytansky was buried in the Orthodox Jewish Cemetery two days later.

From the beginning Compton and Franks were suspected of the murder. They had left too many clues. On the day after the murder, Compton had initiated a conversation with a customs agent, W. G. Gilmore, about bloodhounds, asking a seemingly endless line of questions that would arouse anyone's suspicion. The next day he was arrested and taken to the Webb County Jail for questioning but was released when he steadfastly maintained his innocence. Taking no chances, City Marshal M. Brennan telegraphed Bexar County Sheriff John Tobin to be on the lookout for all suspicious characters arriving on the train from Laredo, especially one Lonnie A. Franks who was known to be a close friend of Compton.

Arriving in San Antonio, Franks decided to spend one or two days in the city before going on to McKinney. "I was going to McKinney and get my diamonds and just move on," he later admitted. He was having a good time at a saloon on Main Street when he happened to pick up a copy of the *San Antonio Express* which contained a front page article on the murder of Levytansky. Panic stricken, he took the diamonds and placed them in a knot

James Barney Compton was hanged in the old Webb County Jail on Houston Street, on March 15, 1912, for the murder of G. J. Levytansky. Compton was the last person hanged in Webb County. The jail shown in this photograph, actually the second Webb County jail, was built in 1902 and demolished when another facility was built on the site in 1936. (Nick Sanchez Collection, Yolanda Parker, Institute of Texan Cultures)

hole in a wall near a restaurant. The next day, Christmas Eve, he was picked up by Sheriff Tobin for questioning. For two days Tobin continued to tell Franks that the authorities in Laredo had already implicated him in the robbery and murder and if he would confess, Tobin would use his influence with District Attorney John A. Valls in Laredo, to save Frank's life. After two days of questioning, Franks finally broke, telling the sheriff the details of the robbery and murder. Tobin telegraphed the postmaster in McKinney who located the diamonds which were forwarded to San Antonio.

In Laredo, Compton had been arrested a second time, but once again maintained his innocence. When District Attorney Valls asked if he would like to make his peace with God, Compton, steely-eyed and confident, replied that he considered lawyers like Valls little better than outlaws. For a second time he was released. On New Year's Day 1912, he was arrested a third time but still refused to confess. This time, however, he was told of Frank's arrest in San Antonio and that Franks was blaming him for the murder. To convince Compton, Valls showed him a copy of the *Laredo Times* which detailed Frank's confession. Compton responded by asking Valls what his punishment would be if he also confessed. Valls replied that he would do everything possible to save his life and that it was conceivable he could get off with second degree murder which carried a punishment of from five to twenty-five years in the penitentiary. The next day Compton finally broke, asking the jailer to summon Valls and Marshal Brennan. Confessing every detail of the crime, Compton showed Valls and Brennan where he had buried the diamonds and led them to the vacant lot between Houston and Victoria streets where he had disposed of the bloodied knife.

On January 5, Franks was returned to Laredo from San Antonio under heavy guard. A large, angry crowd had gathered at the depot awaiting his arrival. To avoid any possible trouble, he was taken off the train at a crossing one mile north of town and placed in an open car. Guarded by Rangers, who galloped alongside on horseback, he was escorted to the county jail. Here, however, another large crowd, "anxious to get a glimpse" of the murderer, had gathered. As the car slowed in front of the jail, the crowd pushed forward and surrounded the automobile. The Rangers "made a charge to clear the crowd," and Franks was rushed inside. He was reported by the local press to be a "fair-looking chap" and neatly dressed. Upon entering the jail he asked only one question: "Where is Compton?"

Two days later, in a rare example of judicial expediency, Compton and Franks were indicted for first degree murder by a hastily called grand jury consisting of some of the more prominent and influential citizens in Webb County including L. R. Ortiz, P. P. Leyendecker, A. Bertani, Eugene Christen, and A. M. Bruni. With Compton and Franks unable to hire counsel, Judge John F. Mullally appointed local attorneys E. A. Atlee and Asher Smith to defend Compton, and T. C. Mann to represent Franks.

Only four days after the grand jury indictment, the trial convened in the Forty-ninth District Court. On the first day of the trial more than one hundred citizens of Laredo, including a number of prominent ladies, huddled for two hours in the January cold in front of the courthouse wanting to get seats. Some sat on the sidewalks. Others were wrapped in heavy blankets. All were anxious to witness what was perceived as the most important trial in decades.

Promptly at 9:00 a.m., Judge Mullally rapped the court into session. The anxious spectators had filled the courtroom to capacity. People stood in the aisles. Others, although unable to see or hear the proceedings, crowded in the hall outside. A number of individuals even climbed to the second story balcony on the outside of the building and watched in the cold through the windows. Compton and Franks were brought into the court handcuffed together and escorted by two Rangers and two Webb County sheriff deputies. Compton had pleaded with the jailer that he not be handcuffed, that he considered it humiliating and that his friends would see him. No one paid him any heed. As the two defendants entered the court, Compton's lips were seen to quiver. Neither man said a word.

With the state assembling an awesome array of forty-seven credible witnesses, the case revolved not around the guilt or innocence of the two men but whether their lives would be spared. Both pleaded guilty and when told by Judge Mullally that they had the right to change their plea, they refused. With practically every citizen in Laredo having either read or heard of the sensational murder, selecting a jury proved to be a difficult task. Of the first one hundred potential jurymen, only one man was qualified. The others had either formed an opinion in the case or were disqualified by either the defense or prosecution; some were neither registered voters of Webb County nor citizens of the United States. A second hundred potential jurors were called, and then another hundred and finally a hundred more. Fearing that it might be impossible to impanel a jury in the county, Judge Mullally asked that sheriff deputies "go into the remote parts of the county and secure the venirement in parts where the murder had not been so freely discussed." Finally on January 15, the jury was complete, consisting of a blacksmith, a farmer, several stockmen and ranchers, merchants, clerks, and bookkeepers.

After a number of witnesses testified not only to the guilt of the two men but to the brutality of the crime, T. C. Mann paraded several character witnesses, including Frank's brother from Midlothian, and army buddies from San Antonio, before the court in an attempt to save Frank's life. No such witnesses could be found for Compton, however.

As the trial proceeded, Compton and Franks seemed to loosen up and appeared on the best of terms. Handcuffed together, the two were seen to frequently whisper to one another and even smile. Their jovial mood, however, abruptly ended on January 17. Calling the two men "cold blooded premeditated murderers," District Attorney Valls, one of the toughest prosecutors in South Texas, asked that they both be hanged. T. C. Mann, calling Franks a poor orphan boy, pleaded for his life for over an hour. Asher Smith then rose to give an equally dramatic plea for Compton. After seventeen hours of deliberation, the jury returned to the courtroom. "We the jury, find the defendants James Barney Compton and Lonnie A. Franks guilty of murder in the first degree . . . and assess the punishment of the Defendant Compton at death, and assess the punishment of the Defendant Franks at confinement in the penitentiary for life." Compton's facial muscles were seen to tighten as he dropped his head and slouched in his chair. Franks, on the other hand, appeared relieved that his life had been spared.

In the days following the verdict, several citizens expressed concern that Compton would be hanged during the Washington's Birthday Celebration, and the entire affair would turn into a hedonistic circus. Judge Mullally, however, set March 1 as the date for the hanging. A number of local citizens, including several prominent clergymen, circulated a petition asking that Compton's sentence be commuted to life in prison. An equal number of Laredoans, especially local businessmen, asked that Compton be hanged as scheduled. Governor O. B. Colquitt did allow Compton a two week reprieve while his attorney filed for a new trial. When the new trial was denied, however, the hanging was set for March 15.

In the days preceding the execution, Sheriff Amador Sanchez was besieged with requests from Webb County citizens to watch the hanging. Since state law clearly stated that the execution must be held within the walls of the jail, the number of witnesses was limited by law to six, excluding the jailer, executioner, justices of the peace, physicians, and the necessary law enforcement officials. Those chosen to witness the gruesome proceedings were A. M. Bruni, Ygnacio Benavides, Charles Moser, W. M. Putman, A. V. Woodman, and M. C. Coleman.

On March 15, the day of his hanging, Compton arose early and had breakfast. The next two hours were spent in constant prayer with Father Leguyader, who, at 10:30 a.m., thirty minutes before the scheduled appointment with the hangman, baptized him a Catholic. Precisely at eleven o'clock, Compton was led from his cell to the hastily constructed scaffold. A crowd had gathered on the street outside. Approaching the crude platform, Compton asked for Sheriff Sanchez. Sanchez came forward, and a few words were exchanged. Next, Compton asked to speak with Marshal Brennan. "I want to forgive you for what you have done and I want you to forgive me too," Compton was heard to say. "I forgive you," the Marshal replied. Compton next asked for Valls who was not present. "I want to forgive him," Compton was heard to say, "for what he told the jury." As the noose was tightened around his neck, Compton in a last wish, asked everyone to read the Fourteenth Chapter of St. John. "Have faith in the Lord," he was heard to mutter. At precisely 11:10 the hangman, Sam McKenzie, a deputy sheriff, sprang the trap. Not a quiver could be seen as the body reached the end of the rope. No one muttered a sound. Three local physicians, W. W. McGregor, A. M. Horner, and M. T. Leal, came forth to pronounce Compton dead. At 11:25 the body was cut down and prepared for burial. Within hours James Barney Compton was buried in the Catholic Cemetery.

As Compton waited to die in Laredo, the northbound train took Franks to a life in prison, or so it seemed at the time. In San Antonio he told the local press that he had not been nervous during the entire trial. He did admit, however, that when he heard G. M. Campbell, jury foreman, pronounce Compton's sentence as death, he did become momentarily afraid but relaxed again when he realized he had been given life in prison. "My troubles have never worried me," Franks continued. Asked if he had his life to live again, he replied, "I would not lead a fast life. Life is whatever a fellow makes of it and I really haven't made much of mine." Asked about Compton, Franks would only say that "He was the best friend I ever had."

Lonnie A. Franks arrived in Huntsville five days before Compton was hanged in Laredo and was assigned to the Rusk unit of the state penitentiary. On September 2, 1912, less than six months later, he attempted to escape but was captured and given eighty-one hours of solitary confinement on bread and water. A later attempt on February 13, 1913, was successful.

Twenty-six years later in 1939, Weldon Bailey, a well-known Texas state patrolman, took up the hunt for Franks. Bailey became interested in the case when he learned that a brother of Franks, Robert, was confined to the Oklahoma State Penitentiary. Bailey asked for all of Robert Frank's correspondence and discovered that Robert had received a letter from a son named Burt who was awaiting execution in Texas for robbery and murder. One of the letters mentioned an individual named Steve who Bailey suspected was Lonnie Franks.

An examination of Burt's letters at Huntsville revealed that Burt, too, had received letters from the same Steve and that a blank page was always included. Bailey was now certain that Steve was Lonnie Franks. In a clever ruse, Patrolman Bailey began writing to Burt's mother, Mrs. Frank Watson, at Bonham, Texas, signing the letters Steve and always enclosing a blank piece of paper. Much to Bailey's delight, Mrs. Watson replied and after several letters, even referred to Steve by his last name which was Rockmore. Bailey also wrote to another brother, S. A. Franks, at Denton, Texas, and was able to learn that Steve had been in Chicago in 1936, but had moved to Sarasota, Florida, and later Wheeling, West Virginia, where he was known as Sy Austin, a name amazingly similar to that which Franks had used when he had mailed the stolen diamonds to McKinney, Texas, in 1911.

The trail of Steve Rockmore, alias Fred Rockman, alias Sy Austin, alias Lonnie Franks, led from Chicago to Sarasota to Wheeling, where Bailey discovered that Lonnie Franks was married. The trail continued to Ardmore, Oklahoma, and finally Columbus, Ohio, where he was described by authorities as a "well-known con man and gambler." Here the trail grew dim. Bailey checked with some twenty-three states but none had issued a drivers license to anyone with the name Franks. To complicate matters, neither the Federal Bureau of Identification nor the state of Texas possessed a set of Frank's finger prints. Surprisingly, no one bothered to check the 1912 newspapers in either Laredo or San Antonio, both of which had carried photographs of Compton and Franks. Lonnie A. Franks, drifter, gambler, convicted murderer, TSP convict #32675, had disappeared.

In San Antonio and Laredo, weeds grew on the graves of G. J. Levytansky and James Barney Compton. That terribly frightful night, three days before Christmas in 1911, had all but been forgotten. The last hanging in Webb County, Texas, had been relegated to the pages of history.

255

This view shows the approach to the 1889 International Bridge from the American side. Toll-booths can be seen on both sides of the entrance. (Laredo Public Library)

Chapter 24

Bridges and Floods

The first bridge to be built across the Rio Grande at Laredo was a temporary railroad structure erected in 1881 shortly after the arrival of the Texas-Mexican Railroad. This sketch shows Engine No. 4 of the Texas-Mexican crossing into Mexico on November 20, 1881. The event commenced a new era in the history of transportation and communication in South Texas and northern Mexico. (Laredo Public Library)

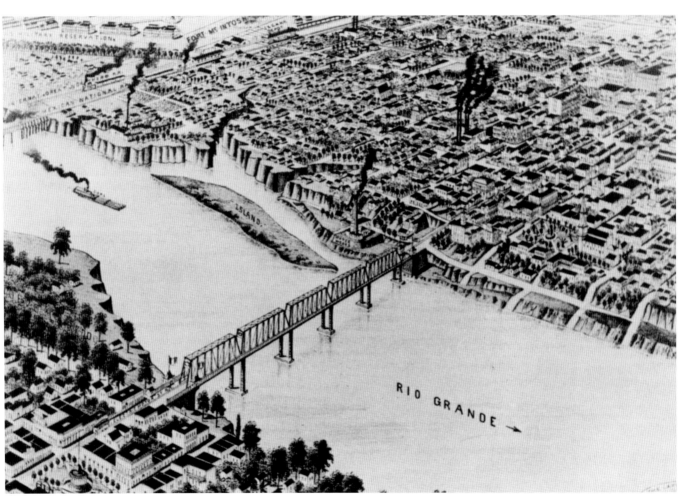

By 1890, the small village that Tomas Sanchez founded 139 years earlier was scarcely recognizable. This "Birdseye View" was made as an advertising souvenir by the Laredo Real Estate and Abstract Company. It was drawn from a point of view possibly two thousand feet above the eastern part of Nuevo Laredo. The artist was perhaps overly optimistic as trackage and terminal facilities (not shown in this photograph) for the San Antonio and Aransas Pass Railroad were included in the elaborate sketch. The "Electric Motor Street Railway" did materialize and is visible on the sketch. Laredo in 1890 still did not have a single paved street. (Sam Meyer)

258

This postcard view, made around 1900, shows women washing their clothes in the Rio Grande with the International Railroad Bridge in the background. Downriver, the International Foot and Wagon Bridge, which was completed in 1889, cost $150,000 and was owned by the Laredo Bridge Company of Laredo and New York. (Laredo Public Library)

Even after the completion of the International Foot and Wagon Bridge in 1889, large numbers of citizens continued to use the chalanes. The use of such boats on the Rio Grande date back to Tomas Sanchez and the founding of the town in 1755. (Sam N. Johnson Collection, Nuevo Santander)

This 1900 view of Laredo and the First International Bridge reveals the water tower and power plant of the Laredo Waterworks on the left while the three-story Ursuline Convent is in the center. (John Keck)

Three travelers, two on foot and one on a bicycle, enter Laredo after crossing the International Bridge from Mexico sometime around 1914. Notice the telephone lines connecting Laredo and Nuevo Laredo. (Nick Sanchez Collection, Yolanda Parker, Institute of Texan Cultures)

This 1916 view of Nuevo Laredo and the First International Bridge taken from the American side of the river, depicts the small houses on the flood plain near Water Street and the expanding skyline of Nuevo Laredo. (Laredo Public Library)

This daring view of the International Bridge and Ursuline Convent looking north was taken by an unknown photographer midway on the bridge sometime around 1912. (Sam N. Johnson Collection, Nuevo Santander Museum)

Wagons and automobiles continue to cross the First International Bridge on September 18, 1919, despite the fact that the Rio Grande was at flood stage. The flood, which reached a height of 34.2 feet, was the sixth largest at Laredo in recorded history. Flooding had resulted when 7.60 inches of rain fell on the city in a fifteen hour period. (Sam N. Johnson Collection, Nuevo Santander Museum)

At 2:00 p.m. on April 26, 1920, a small fire was detected about midway across the International Bridge. It was soon extinguished, and citizens continued to cross the river uninterrupted. By 4:00 p.m., however, the bridge was ablaze again, and huge clouds of black smoke bellowed into the sky. The Laredo Volunteer Fire Department, as well as volunteers from the American Legion and soldiers from Fort McIntosh, rushed to fight the blaze. Many observers were fearful that the flames would spread to the business districts of both cities. On the Nuevo Laredo side of the bridge, workers, shown here, hastily tore up the planks in the bridge floor to prevent the fire from spreading. (Sam N. Johnson Collection, Nuevo Santander Museum)

Three spans on the American side of the International Bridge were completely destroyed in the fire of 1920. The collapse of the bridge stranded several thousand citizens. Many residents of Nuevo Laredo were caught on the American side of the river while large numbers of residents of Laredo were trapped on the Mexican side. (Sam N. Johnson Collection, Nuevo Santander Museum)

The twisted girders of what was once the International Bridge shows the intensity of the fire that destroyed a large portion of the bridge on April 26, 1920. Volunteer fire fighters from Laredo were helpless against the blaze. It was never determined what caused the fire. Some thought it was a carelessly discarded cigarette or cigar that became caught in the planks of the thirty-two-year-old bridge. Others asserted that the fire had been intentionally set by Mexican revolutionaries. (Sam N. Johnson Collection, Nuevo Santander Museum)

Although M. M. Leyendecker, superintendent of the Texas-Mexican Railway Company, commenced to shuffle citizens across the railroad bridge by train following the 1920 fire, a number of citizens found it more expedient to use boats, reminiscent of the era prior to the completion of the bridge in 1889. (Sam N. Johnson Collection, Nuevo Santander Museum)

After the destruction of the International Bridge in the fire of 1920, J. K. Beretta, managing official of the Laredo Bridge Company, arrived in Laredo to announce plans for a new all concrete structure to replace the old steel and wood bridge. While construction on the new International Bridge progressed, a temporary wooden span, shown here, was constructed. (John Keck)

A surrey crosses the temporary wooden bridge into Nuevo Laredo in 1921 and, in contrast, the new International Bridge nears completion in the background. (T. R. Esquivel, Jr.)

Work on the second International Bridge had just been completed when this photograph was taken from the American side of the river looking southwest toward Nuevo Laredo. On the right is the new border station. (Sam N. Johnson Collection, Nuevo Santander Museum)

Workers put the final touches on the toll-booths on the American side of the river as the second International Bridge prepares to open in 1922. (John Keck)

Only a short time after the completion of the second International Bridge, the Rio Grande flooded in June 1922. Flood waters roared over the top of the bridge, and many citizens were fearful that the new structure would be swept away. The river reached its crest at 43.9 feet at 1:00 p.m. on June 20, making the flood the fourth highest at Laredo in recorded history. (Nuevo Santander Museum)

J. G. Garcia climbed to the top of a building on Zaragoza Street to snap this excellent photograph on June 20, 1922, as the Rio Grande reached flood stage. Large areas of the business district of Nuevo Laredo were already underwater, and many residents of the sister city feared further damage. (Sam N. Johnson Collection, Nuevo Santander Museum)

FLOOD AT LAREDO, TEX.
Sept. 3- 4, 1932
PHOTO BY
AIR CORPS, U.S. ARMY

The United States Army Air Corps took this aerial photograph of the 1932 flood. The old Zapata highway and the mouth of Zacate Creek are inundated by the rising waters. The Rio Grande reached a maximum height of 52.20 feet which was the third largest flood at Laredo in recorded history. (International Boundary and Water Commission)

In terms of human lives, the flood of 1932 was the worst in Laredo history. At least eighteen lives were lost when two spans, or 358 feet, of the International Railway Bridge fell into the Rio Grande. A number of railroad, immigration, and customs officials from Nuevo Laredo were swept into the raging current when the bridge collapsed. Those from Laredo who were lost included E. E. Starkey, a well-known Laredo railroad conductor, as well as Federico Saenz and Dionicio Espinoza. Three men, Vicente Gonzales Flores (from Laredo), and Jose Rodriguez Trigo, and Julian Lozano (from Nuevo Laredo) amazingly managed to swim to a pile of driftwood caught in the middle of the International Bridge. The three men, barely visible on the driftwood in this photograph, wave frantically as an airplane circles overhead. After sixteen frightening hours, they were rescued. (Sam N. Johnson Collection, Nuevo Santander Museum)

LAREDO, TEX. SEP. 3- 1932.

Creciente del Rio Bravo
10.30 H. 9-16-35.

10:30 A.M.

FROM BELOW BRIDGE
O LAREDO, SEPT. 5, 1932

The flood of 1935 reached a height of 35.10 feet and was the eighth largest in Laredo's recorded history. Because the Second International Bridge had been built several feet higher than the old 1889 Foot and Wagon bridge, the flood did little damage to it. (Albert Muller)

The debris from the 1932 flood—one of the worst in Laredo's history—is quite visible as more than two hundred families were left homeless in Laredo by the flood. In Nuevo Laredo, fifty blocks of the city had been underwater at one time. In the days and weeks that followed, the Red Cross and Salvation Army were able to muster large numbers of volunteers for the relief effort. Bodies of those who drowned in the flood continued to be recovered weeks after the flood, some as far as twenty and twenty-five miles downriver. The bodies of a number of those who drowned were never found. (International Boundary and Water Commission)

Millions of dollars in silver and gold bullion pass across the Second International Bridge into the United States. In the background, the outline of the Laredo Waterworks tower and powerplant can be seen. (Laredo Public Library)

A bus bound for Monterrey crosses the International Bridge during the 1930s. Although the Pan-American Highway was under construction, it would be years before the main highway stretching into the Mexican interior would be paved. (Webb County Heritage Foundation)

Holding Institute, located on a low plain south of Fort McIntosh in the bend of the river, caught the brunt of several of the Rio Grande floods. The flood of June 26, 1948, the fifth largest in Laredo's recorded history, swept over the campus, causing several thousand dollars worth of damage. It was the big 1954 flood, six years later, that virtually destroyed the school and convinced officials that they must seek a new location. The school was abandoned and relocated to a new, higher site in North Laredo off Santa Maria Avenue. (T. R. Esquivel, Jr.)

One of the worst floods in Laredo history was the one which occurred on June 29, 1954. Contrary to public belief, however, it was not the largest in recorded history. In 1865, a flood caused by a hurricane that swept up the Rio Grande watershed from Brownsville, was approximately one foot higher. In fact, the 1865 flood was said to have reached the steps of St. Augustine Church. Nevertheless, the 1954 flood was the largest in ninety-one years and the second largest according to archaeological evidence in at least three hundred years. (T. R. Esquivel, Jr.)

This aerial photograph taken from over Laredo, looking south into Nuevo Laredo, shows the 1954 flood at its crest. The flood reached a height of 61.35 feet, more than 10 feet higher than the disastrous 1932 flood. (International Boundary and Water Commission)

The Second International Bridge was inundated by the 1954 flood. At its height, the 1954 flood flowed at 715,900 feet per second. The extensive flooding in Nuevo Laredo is evident in this aerial photograph. Laredo, located on higher ground than its sister city, suffered, but not to the extent that Nuevo Laredo did. (International Boundary and Water Commission)

This aerial photograph taken over north-central Laredo shows the devastating damage to the city by the 1954 flood. Houses on both sides of Zacate Creek are underwater. The water reached such a height that water flowing into Manadas Creek in North Laredo had commenced to flow south into Zacate Creek, thus isolating a large part of West and North Laredo. The flood was 2.4 feet over the divide between the two watersheds. (International Boundary and Water Commission)

Laredoans by the hundreds gather near the International Bridge during the 1954 flood. This group of citizens watches from Zaragoza Street near Convent Avenue. (T. R. Esquivel, Jr.)

This easterly view of Matamoros Street shows extensive flooding along the banks of Zacate Creek. Hundreds of houses along both banks of the creek were severely damaged by the 1954 flood, and thousands had to be evacuated. (Ernesto Dovalina)

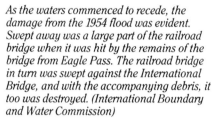

As the waters commenced to recede, the damage from the 1954 flood was evident. Swept away was a large part of the railroad bridge when it was hit by the remains of the bridge from Eagle Pass. The railroad bridge in turn was swept against the International Bridge, and with the accompanying debris, it too was destroyed. (International Boundary and Water Commission)

Within days following the 1954 flood, the Army Corps of Engineers had a pontoon bridge across the Rio Grande, and communications between Laredo and Nuevo Laredo were resumed. What remains of the International Bridge can be seen on the right. (Anita and J. C. Martin)

In this photo by Jose G. Garcia taken on June 22, 1913, two-thousand federal reinforcements under General Tellez arrive in Nuevo Laredo. The Mexican Army consisted of a large number of Indians from the interior. Many men brought their wives, as was the custom during the Mexican Revolution. (Falvella Collection, Laredo Public Library)

N.LAREDO- 22 de Junio de 1913.

By late 1913, the Mexican Revolution had spread from the jungles of Yucatan and mountains of Chiapas in the south, to the deserts of Sonora and Chihuahua in the north. Porfirio Diaz was in exile and Francisco Madero, who had previously fled Mexico through Laredo, had ridden triumphantly into Mexico City only to be murdered by the long arm of Victoriano Huerta. By 1913, the dictator Huerta was on the run. The armies of Venustiano Carranza, Alvaro Obregon, Emiliano Zapata, and Pancho Villa had

wiped out Huerta's forces in three-fourths of Mexico. The Federals were firmly entrenched in the capital and were still in the cities and villages of the gulf coast and they were also in Nuevo Laredo.

For some time, the Constitutionalists had hoped to seize Nuevo Laredo and by Christmas 1913, General Pablo Gonzales, with some three thousand Carranzistas, was moving upriver demanding the surrender of the city. With the approach of the Rebels, several thousand civilians, mostly women with little more

Chapter 25

The Battle of Nuevo Laredo

than a few personal belongings, commenced to flee to Laredo. Col. Gustavo Guardiola, the Federal commander, wired Lampazos and Monterrey for help and commenced to entrench his army. A ferocious battle appeared inevitable, and by December 31, the Rebels were on the outskirts of the city.

Laredo, too, was in a state of panic. At Fort McIntosh two companies of the Third Cavalry were dispatched to guard the railroad and the International Bridge. The Milmo Rifles, a local company of the National Guard under command of E. M. Matson, was mobilized. Eight engines of the Mexican National Railway sped across the Rio Grande to safety in Laredo.

The battle opened early on the morning of January 1, 1914. The Rebels sent several parties to probe the Federal defenses south, east, and west of Nuevo Laredo. Some of the heaviest fighting was on the western outskirts, just south of the Mexican National Depot. Here the Rebels had set up a machine gun that commenced to incessantly spray the Federal lines. Manning the machine gun was a Frenchman named Rene who drove off a series of furious cavalry charges, and on one occasion, killed eleven Federal soldiers in the process. During the day it was said he killed as many as twenty or thirty Federals and silenced a Federal artillery battery almost single-handedly.

Large numbers of Laredo citizens, some with field glasses, lined the river banks near the railroad bridge and south of Fort McIntosh to watch the fighting. So many citizens crowded around the International Bridge, that the Milmo Rifles had to be ordered out to restrain them. Others climbed on railroad cars at the Texas-Mexican Railway Yard to watch the fighting east of Nuevo Laredo. Some remained throughout the day.

What the citizens of Laredo saw on that New Year's Day of 1914 was a grisly site. West of Nuevo Laredo they watched as two hundred Federals set an ambush for seventeen Carranzistas, only to be set upon themselves by a band of Rebels who swarmed out of the chaparral. In their hasty retreat, the Federals were so anxious to reach the safety of their lines that they dove with their rifles head first into the trenches.

Later, Laredoans watched in disbelief as five captured Rebels were hanged from telegraph poles near the northwest outskirts of the town near the river.

In Laredo, bullets rained everywhere. Manuel Herrera, a merchant from Zapata, was standing in front of the Laredo National Bank when he was hit in the head by a stray bullet. Manuel Lugo, while walking near St. Augustine Plaza, was also struck in the head and died instantly. In the downtown area, a woman was wounded, and near the river a small girl was struck in the foot. Twelve year-old Bruna Sutton, who lived in the Ortiz home on Zaragoza Street, walked out into the courtyard with her brother to get a closer look at the fighting. A stray bullet splintered the gate only inches from where she stood. One elderly man in the western part of Laredo was sitting on his front porch in a rocking chair reading a newspaper when a bullet tore the paper from his grasp.

Mrs. Leonor V. Magnon and the ladies of the local Red Cross worked feverishly to help the wounded who were brought across the bridge in wagons. Makeshift hospitals, one in the Magnon Kindergarten school and another in the Villegas building, were hastily established. Yet the wounded continued to arrive and a third hospital had to be established. Local physicians and surgeons from Fort McIntosh were kept busy amputating arms and legs. The American Consul, fearing famine in Nuevo Laredo, wired Washington to lift the embargo on the exportation of provisions to Mexico.

As night crept across the battlefield, the campfires of both the Federals and the Rebels, less than one-hundred yards apart, could be seen burning into the crisp January night. Shortly after daybreak on the morning of the second day, Laredoans were awakened to the sharp crack of rifles and the booming of cannons. The Constitutional forces under General Gonzales, were in the process of renewing their attack on the Federal trenches. On the western outskirts of Nuevo Laredo, close to where the heaviest fighting had occurred the first day, the Rebels, under the cover of darkness, had dug trenches only a short distance from the Federal lines. Although the fighting slackened around noon, the bloodletting continued into the afternoon. After suffering several hundred casualties, Gonzales ordered a retreat. A number of captives were said to have been executed by both sides.

Although both armies deliberately underestimated their casualties, the Federals were reported to have lost on the second day alone, some 96 dead and over 100 wounded while the Rebels lost 175 dead and over 200 wounded.

Fires once again lit up the evening sky. This time, however, there was a strange odor to the flames. Fearing an epidemic, the Federals had put every wagon in Nuevo Laredo into use to gather the bodies of the dead. The fires were funeral pyres.

Doggedly, the Rebels limped downriver toward Guerrero to fight again. The Federals consolidated their forces and braced for another attack. Meanwhile, life back in Laredo returned to normalcy. The Mexican Revolution, however, had yet to run its course. Huerta would be forced out of Mexico. The gray-bearded Carranza, while attempting to make his way into exile, would be shot while he slept in a peasant's hut in the Sierra Madre. In the south, Zapata was treacherously murdered. Villa, too, would die in a hail of bullets at Hidalgo del Parral in the state of Chihuahua in 1923, before peace would return to Mexico.

General Tellez and his officers pose for the camera of J. G. Garcia on June 22, 1913. (Falvella Collection, Laredo Public Library)

Soldiers of the Third United States Cavalry, under Colonel A. P. Blocksom from Fort McIntosh, were sent to guard the railroad bridge during the Carranzista attack on Nuevo Laredo. Anticipating the attack, thousands of citizens from Nuevo Laredo fled to Laredo. (Sam N. Johnson Collection, Nuevo Santander Museum)

Laredo citizens crowd the top of a railroad building to watch the Rebel siege of Nuevo Laredo on New Year's Day 1914. In a bloody battle which included a number of executions and hangings, all of which were visible from the north bank of the river, the Rebels were driven off. (Falvella Collection, Laredo Public Library)

Thirty-seven-year-old James W. (Jim) Falvella, a crack reporter for the Laredo Times, holds a captured Mexican battle flag. The flag, with a diagonal white stripe and black lettering, bears the words, "Liberty, Equality, and Independence." (Falvella Collection, Laredo Public Library)

American reporters and Carranzistas gather for a group photograph at San Ignacio, Mexico, opposite San Ignacio, Texas, following the attack on Laredo on January 1-2, 1914. (Falvella Collection, Laredo Public Library)

Laredoans gather on top of a railroad boxcar to watch the Battle of Nuevo Laredo on January 1, 1914. Some citizens remained all day while bullets buzzed over Laredo like mosquitos. One man was killed and several were injured in Laredo from the fighting across the river. (Falvella Collection, Laredo Public Library)

Soldiers line up along the International Bridge during the Mexican Revolution. The photograph is dated February 2, 1914, one month after the Battle of Nuevo Laredo and four months before the Federal evacuation. (Falvella Collection, Laredo Public Library)

During the Mexican Revolution, a number of National Guard Units, including four regiments and three batteries of artillery from Missouri, as well as units from New Hampshire and Maine, were rushed to the Border. The entire band from the University of Maine, which had enlisted as a unit, came to Laredo. At one time, there were ten thousand National Guardsmen at Laredo. Fort McIntosh became so crowded that a number of the regiments were forced to set up make-shift camps north of town. (Nuevo Santander Museum)

Following the Battle of Nuevo Laredo and the lifting of a commodities embargo, large amounts of provisions were rushed through the streets of Laredo to help feed the citizens of Nuevo Laredo. During the fighting, one hundred wounded Carranzistas managed to escape to Laredo and received medical treatment from the Red Cross. Some remained in Laredo hospitals for over a month. (Falvella Collection, Laredo Public Library)

During the retreat of the Federal Army from Nuevo Laredo in April 1914, the business district went up in flames. An unidentified photographer climbed to the top of a building on Zaragoza Street to take this dramatic photograph. *(Mauricio Haynes)*

Following the burning of a large part of the downtown area of Nuevo Laredo during the Federal retreat in April 1914, citizens came to see the damage. Here, a lady with an umbrella seemed more concerned about the photographer than the burned-out ruins. *(Sam N. Johnson Collection, Nuevo Santander Museum)*

The customhouse, as well as a number of Nuevo Laredo civic buildings and businesses, fell victim to arson with the retreat of the Federals from Nuevo Laredo in April 1914. (T. R. Esquivel, Jr.)

A number of prominent women from Laredo await the arrival of the family of the famous Mexican revolutionary leader, Venustiano Carranza in 1916. After being taken through the city to the cheers of many townspeople, the family was entertained at a gala reception. (Laura Floyd)

In the first few years of the 1920s, the Ku Klux Klan spread its bigotry and hate across the country like a wildfire. Many times larger and more frightening than the old KKK of Reconstruction, the new Klan found some of its greatest support in Texas. In Houston, more than a thousand Klansmen swore to "maintain forever the God-given supremacy of the white race." The white-robed bigots carried their hatred from Houston and Beaumont into the piney woods of East Texas and to Dallas, Fort Worth, and beyond. By 1922, the Klan claimed more than two hundred thousand members in Texas. Texas was further embarrassed when

Earl B. Mayfield, a Klansman, was elected United States Senator. The Invisible Empire also swept the lower house of the Texas legislature, elected judges throughout the state, and carried every office in Dallas County, where the Klan celebrated in a wild street demonstration.

In Denton, the Klan took two Negroes from jail and flogged them. A Negro bellhop in Dallas was also flogged, and the letters KKK were burned on his forehead with acid. In Houston, where almost all of the police force were members of the Klan, a black dentist was kidnapped and brutally whipped. In Dallas, the

Chapter 26

Hooded Bigots at Laredo

national headquarters of the KKK, the Klan was credited with having flogged sixty-eight people during the bloody spring of 1922, most of them at a special Klan whipping meadow along the Trinity River. In Austin, theater goers walked out into the street to see two black men, tarred and feathered, running up Congress Avenue with a jeering mob at their heels.

But not all of the Klan's hatred was directed at blacks. A lawyer in Houston who frequently represented blacks in court was badly beaten. A divorced woman in Tenha was dragged from a hotel, whipped with a wet rope, and then tarred and feathered. Jewish businesses were boycotted, and Mexican-Americans watched uneasily.

Although most of Texas's nineteen congressmen refused to take a position on Klan violence, John Nance Garner, who represented South Texas, blasted the Klan in no uncertain terms. But in 1922, Garner even lost his home county of Uvalde.

Although the Klan marched in the streets of San Antonio, nothing was heard of the white-robed Kluxers in Laredo, that is not until March of 1922. Chief of Police Michael Brennan, Webb County Sheriff A. J. Condren, and Forty-ninth District Judge J. F. Mullally all received letters signed "KKK" announcing the intentions of the Klan to "parade in the city of Laredo on the 19th of March." A card arrived at the offices of *The Laredo Times* asking: "Do you know that the Ku Klux Klan is now organizing in Laredo?" Membership was to be by invitation only. *The Times* responded with a banner headline announcing that the Klan was now organizing in Laredo. With a small black population, it was obvious that the Klan's wrath in Laredo was aimed at the Mexican-American and Catholic communities.

Judge Mullally responded by calling a grand jury to investigate Klan activities in Laredo. In his charge to the jury, the judge stated: "I hoped and believed Laredo would be spared the indignity and disgrace of the establishment of such an organization as that in this country or this town, but it appears that there are a number of weak-minded men living here who believe that the Klan can establish an organization here and put it over on the good people of Laredo." Mullally warned that if the Klan marched in Laredo, they would be marching "unmasked straight to jail." Mayor L. Villegas and City Secretary A. R. Garcia wrote letters which were given front page coverage in the *Times*, warning the Klan not to come to town.

Judge Mullally received a telegram from the Anti Ku Klux Klan in Healdton, Oklahoma, congratulating him on his uncompromising stand. But as Sunday, March 19, neared, a mood of uncertainty and apprehension heightened.

When the day for the scheduled march arrived, local law enforcement officials were taking no chances. All city policemen and sheriff's deputies within fifty miles were called out and heavily armed. Three hundred World War I veterans, complete with

machine guns, rallied to the "defense of Old Glory" just as when they had been called out to fight the "Hun over there." To show that Laredo "was different from other areas of the country" citizens were urged to "prepare themselves, their homes, and their city against the devil Klansmen, and to have arms at their homes ready for use should any of the white-sheeted figures appear."

By early morning on the nineteenth, the veteran doughboys could be seen behind their machine guns on street corners while heavily armed deputies and policemen were visible everywhere. When word arrived that a line of cars was approaching from San Antonio, the Laredoans prepared to give the Klan a rude awakening, but nothing happened.

Either the Klan had been frightened off by such a show of force, or they never had plans of marching in Laredo in the first place. No one seemed to know.

In the days and weeks that followed, the Klan, nevertheless, remained the talk of the town. The grand jury reported that from fragmentary evidence there had been an attempt to organize a Klavern in Laredo, but no one could come up with any names. Special ordinances were rushed through city council prohibiting two or more individuals in "hoods, masks, cloaks, or any other device or regalia" from assembling or marching in Laredo. In a blazing editorial, Justo S. Penn of the *Times* took exception with Texas officers of the law for not bringing the "masked outlaws" to justice. To Penn, such negligence was clearly "an outrage upon the public." Penn continued for over a month to blast the Klan in the headlines of the *Times*: "Dallas Man Flogged by Masked Man," "Beaumont Man Whipped," "Old Man Mobbed," "Negro Catholic Church at Beaumont Threatened by KKK," "Klan Admits Floggings," and "Klansmen Deny Acts Now," were all examples.

Laredo could take great pride and consolation that it was one of the few cities in the Lone Star State where the Ku Klux Klan never marched during the 1920s. Had the KKK attempted to have done so, there was certain to have been violence. And the victims of that violence, unlike other places in Texas, would have been the white-robed bigots themselves.

In 1924, Miriam Amanda Ferguson campaigned for governor of Texas on a platform denouncing the Klan. "Ma" Ferguson, as she was called, wanted an antimask law, required publication of Klan membership, and the loss of tax exemption by churches used for Klan rallies. In the months following her election, Ma set out to cleanse the party and the state of the Invisible Empire. The Klan was on the ropes. Klan power crumbled. Thousands dropped out. Others claimed they had been forced to join the KKK or lose their jobs. A few apologized for having ever belonged to the Klan. The blazing cross atop the Klan headquarters in Houston was taken down, and the building was sold at public auction. Texas had become one of the most anti-Klan states in the South, and in Texas, there remained no more anti-Klan city than Laredo.

The Junior Choir at Christ Church Episcopal in 1921 included, from left to right, first row, Tom Greenstreet, Chris Kehl, Mendel Morgan, Edward Shahady, George Kehl, Anita Love, and Mary B. McDonald. Second row, left to right, were Evans Younkin, Mrs. C. L. Milton, Murray Cheston, Reverend C. W. Cook, Hunter Randolph, Emilie Halsell, Mary Cook, Anna May Mussett, Carolyn Brennan, and Marjorie Fish. Christ Church Episcopal was located at 1609 Farragut Street. (Mary Cook Collection, Nuevo Santander Museum)

The founders of Ursuline Academy included: seated Mother St. Joseph Aubert; standing left to right, Sister Mechitilde, Sister Angela, and Sister Teresa Pereida. Mother St. Joseph Aubert and Sister Teresa Pereida arrived in Laredo on May 30, 1868, having been brought from Galveston in a small horse-drawn cart by Mariano Gil. John Z. Leyendecker brought Sisters Angela and Mechitilde shortly thereafter. Asked by Bishop C. M. Dubuis of Texas to establish a school for girls in Laredo, the sisters found lodging in a small house east of St. Augustine Church and within months, had established a day and boarding school. (Ursuline Sisters)

Chapter 27

Religious Life

With the addition of a large number of nuns from France, the Ursuline Community had grown considerably by 1889. In the back row, left to right, are Sister Mary of the Cross, Sister St. Benedict, Madam Assumption, Madam Angela. In the second row, left to right, are Sister St. Agnes, Madam St. John, Mother St. Claude, Madam St. Pierre, Madam St. Joseph, and Madam St. Francis. In the front row, left to right are Sister St. Agatha, Madam St. Paul, Madam St. Luis, and Madam St. Mary. (Ursuline Sisters)

Shortly after the arrival of the Ursuline Nuns in 1868, a three story convent and school constructed of native stone, was built near the river. The Sisters and boarders lived on the second floor. The convent was demolished in 1939, and a Border Station was erected on the location. (Ursuline Sisters)

A new building was erected next to the Ursuline Convent on Zaragoza and Convent in 1896 by A. Eistetter. The third floor, or "Big Hall," of the building was used by the Knights of Columbus. It was later turned into an auditorium and later into a dormitory for the boarders. The second floor contained a parlor, offices, a guest room, and the priests' dining room. On the first floor were located two classrooms and the Sisters' dining room. In this photograph, a wagon is ready to take the Ursuline Nuns to Guadalupe and Holy Redeemer Grammar schools. (Ursuline Sisters)

St. Augustine Church is seen across a tree-less St. Augustine Plaza. Note the small bell tower on the right. The bells were taken from the old church, which stood only yards to the northwest of the present church, and which had been demolished about 1876. (Author's Collection)

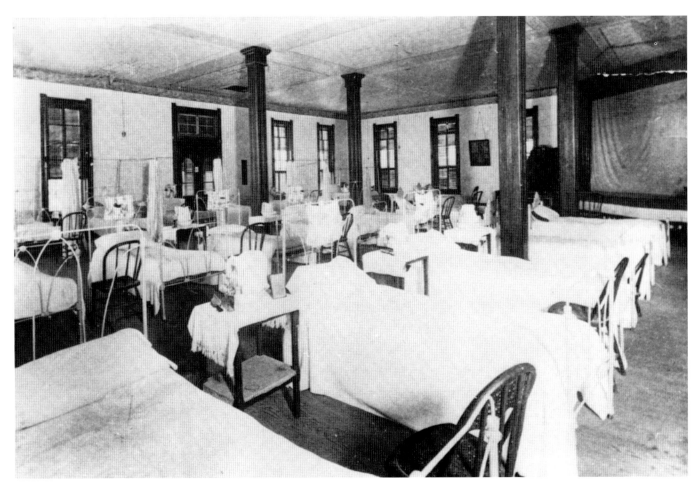

For many years, the "Big Hall" at the Ursuline Convent was used as a dormitory. The room, containing thirty beds, was airy and cool, for it had windows on three sides. On the stage, behind the curtain, slept one of the nuns who was in charge of the boarders at night. Because a fire escape on the west side went all the way to the yard below, a constant vigil was required. (Ursuline Sisters)

Bishop Peter Verdaguer, a native of Spain, arrived at St. Vincent Seminary, Cape Girardeau, Missouri, in 1860. He was ordained in San Francisco, California, two years later. He worked several years in the missions of San Bernardino, San Gabriel, Anaheim, and Santa Ana, California. In 1874, he became a parish priest in Los Angeles. While on a tour of Europe in 1890, he received a telegram from Pope Leo XIII making him Vicar Apostolic of Brownsville. On May 21, 1891, he arrived in Corpus Christi where he set up residence. He later moved his offices to Laredo. During the twenty years Bishop Verdaguer lived in Laredo, he did much to combat discrimination against Mexican-Americans which he found in the rural villages of the diocese. On October 26, 1911, he fell ill while on the road near Mercedes and died. He is buried in the large mausoleum at the Laredo Catholic Cemetery. (Ursuline Sisters)

In 1891, Reverend Benito Donato, on the left, and Reverend Miguel Puig, on the right, were serving in Laredo as assistant priests. (Ursuline Sisters)

The first Mercy Hospital is shown here shortly after its opening in 1894 at the J. P. Flynn residence on Rosario Street. The hospital was later moved to a location on the west side of Jarvis Plaza. In 1957, the Sisters of Mercy moved again, this time to the heights where the hospital would continue to grow and become Mercy Regional Medical Center. (Ursuline Sisters)

St. Augustine Church is shown here some-time prior to the addition of the clock in 1922. (St. Augustine Parish Archives)

Shown here is the first Guadalupe Church and School. Prior to 1913, Guadalupe School was a boarding and day school run by the Sisters of the Holy Ghost. In 1913, the Ursulines assumed control. (Ursuline Sisters)

In 1922, the steeple at St. Augustine Church was renovated. Also, the tower was made taller to accommodate the new large clock. (St. Augustine Parish Archives)

The new Guadalupe Church—a monument to the memory of Father David Rodriguez— neared completion by October 14, 1928. (Nick Sanchez Collection, Yolanda Parker, Institutue of Texan Cultures)

St. Augustine Church was the scene for this photograph of the Knights of Columbus, Council No. 2304, on June 18, 1922. One-hundred and sixty-four individuals are in the photograph, including two soldiers, and one man who defiantly holds his hat over his face to avoid the camera. (Dave Leyendecker)

The first Baptist Church in the 1600 block of Houston was built in 1901 in the Romanesque Revival style. The pointed portion of the tower was damaged in the 1905 cyclone and was later renovated. The church served Laredo's Baptist community for many years. The Rodolfo Aldape residence at 1612 Houston, can be seen in the background. Today, both buildings are used by the Laredo Independent School District. (Laredo Public Library)

Christ Church Episcopal, on the southwest corner of Farragut and Davis, was built in 1881 in the English Country Gothic Style. H. W. Elliott was pastor in 1883. He was followed by C. M. Hogo in 1885. (Anita and J. C. Martin)

Members of the St. Augustine Youth Band gather to celebrate the raising of the clock atop St. Augustine Church in 1922. Front row, seated on the ground, left to right, are Tiburcio Gonzales, Jr., unidentified, and unidentified. Second row, left to right, are unidentified, Ramiro Sanchez, Roy Alvarado, J. Negrete, C. Cordero, unidentified, Father Jose Rose, Director T. Gonzales, unidentified, unidentified, unidentified, Cecilio Herrera, and Diosdado. Third row, left to right, are Polo Botello, "Chorrey," Armando Leal, unidentified, Jose Salazar, unidentified, Eduardo Perez, unidentified, Cantu, unidentified, Martinez, and "El Tapon." Back row, left to right, are M. Garza, unidentified, Quijano, "La Cuba," unidentified, unidentified, unidentified, Munoz, Mauricio Didieu, and unidentified. (Ramiro Sanchez)

A number of clergy and laymen, most of whom are unidentified, gather for a formal portrait around 1930. Fifth from the left, in the back row, is Father J. C. Dubourgel of St. Peter's Church. After serving as pastor in Rockport, Texas, Father Dubourgel became pastor at St. Peters in 1922. In 1924, he was made Monsignor. He bought the old Cummings residence and turned it into a parish school. With over two hundred students in the building it proved to be inadequate, so Father Dubourgel rented two rooms in the Bender Hotel. For a number of years during the Depression, Father Dubourgel helped to operate St. Peter's High School for girls. It closed in 1940 when Ursuline Academy moved to the heights. (St. Augustine Parish Archives)

The St. Augustine Youth Bank, Oblate Fathers, missionaries, and sponsors pose by St. Augustine Church on March 21, 1926, as Samuel Serrano made this photograph. (St. Mary's University, Institute of Texan Cultures)

On February 27, 1929, a number of religious leaders gather for the dedication of the Sanctuary at Guadalupe Church. In the front row, fifth from left, is Father David Rodriguez, Pastor of Guadalupe Church. The man in civilian clothes in the front row is Juan Laine from Mexico City. Tenth from left in the front row is Father Dubourgel, Pastor at St. Peter's Church. (Ramiro Sanchez)

Chapter 28

Las Calles de Laredo

This rare photograph taken around 1890 is from the south side of St. Agustín Plaza, looking along Zaragoza Street toward the square-shaped Ursuline Convent on Convent Street. The two-story stone building on the left was the Casa Consistorial, which served as the city hall, jail, and school for more than eight decades. (From an album collected by Federico "Lico" Vidaurri. From the Collection of James C. Kirkpatrick. Courtesy of James E. Kirkpatrick. Digital restoration by Irene Vidaurri Zubeck.)

Iturbide Street looking north, circa 1900. South Carolina–born Dalziel H. Randolph's Botica del Rio Bravo *and* La Perla *(Almacen de Ropa) are seen on the west side (left) of the street. (From the Collection of James C. Kirkpatrick. Courtesy of James E. Kirkpatrick. Digital restoration by Irene Vidaurri Zubeck.)*

This view around 1900 looks north up Salinas Avenue at the intersection of Lincoln Street. A.M. Mann's grocery store advertising candy, ice, fish, and oysters is on the left. Fresh seafood arrived daily from Corpus Christi on the narrow-gauge Texas Mexican Railroad that reached Laredo in 1881. Also visible is the impressive two-story Milmo National Bank, the first bank in Laredo. Irene Vidaurri Zubeck notes a woman on the left sidewalk dressed in bulky clothing, indicating that it was probably winter. After 1911, the Vidaurri Printing Company occupied the Adolph M. Kahn building. (From the Collection of Federico E. Vidaurri. Digital restoration by Irene Vidaurri Zubeck.)

A stage with coachman and three well-dressed gentlemen pauses on Flores Avenue in front of the Laredo Times *Printing Office, around 1900. The passengers were likely on their way from the train station on the west side of Laredo to a downtown hotel. The small sign on the door on the right reads: "For Rent JR Moore." (From the Collection of James C. Kirkpatrick. Courtesy of James E. Kirkpatrick. Digital restoration by Irene Vidaurri Zubeck.)*

Two delivery wagons, each drawn by three mules with goods for the firm of L. Villegas, at the corner of Flores and Farragut, circa 1900. The photo was taken after the death of Joaquin Villegas since the sign has an "L" for Leopoldo, his son. (From the Collection of Federico E. Vidaurri. Digital restoration by Irene Vidaurri Zubeck.)

Around 1900, a political parade on Salinas Avenue turns west on Iturbide Street. Several in the parade prominently display American flags as children, some barefoot, scurry along. One man in uniform proudly carries a sword. The Spanish-born Nicolas Sierra's La Perla dry goods store advertises Sombreros and Zapatos as well as Ropa Hecha. This parade was similar to those of the Botas and Guaraches in 1886. (From the Collection of Federico Vidaurri. Digital restoration by Irene Vidaurri Zubeck.)

A sizeable crowd, some on foot and others with small two-wheeled carts, including a wagon of the Laredo Ice Factory, gathers in front of what is probably a Fourth of July celebration at a billiard and pool hall on Hidalgo Street. This image looks northeast. (From the Collection of Federico Vidaurri. Digital restoration by Irene Vidaurri Zubeck.)

This photograph was taken from the bell tower of San Agustín Church in 1924, showing houses and businesses lining the north side of Grant Street. Only one of the buildings remains today. Well into the twenty-first century, those in power in the border community had little inclination to protect the rich architectural history of the city. By the time the San Augustin de Laredo Historic District was proclaimed, it was too late to save many of the structures on the historic plaza. (La Pitahaya, 1924)

Numerous Laredo photographs in the late nineteenth and early twentieth centuries depicted the lives of the well-to-do, but few photographers bothered to record the lives of the very poor, who comprised the majority of Laredo's population at the time. In this strikingly rare image, a man is sitting with a child and three dogs. A water barrel indicating the lack of indoor plumbing, as well as a hand cart, illustrate the lifestyle of poor families. At the opposite end of the economic spectrum, a well-constructed brick two-story residence is seen in the background. (From the Collection of James C. Kirkpatrick. Courtesy of James E. Kirkpatrick. Digital restoration by Irene Vidaurri Zubeck.)

Lico Vidaurri poses with three other individuals at the Western Union Telegraph and Cable Office on Flores Street, circa 1910. The jewelry store of German immigrant Leon Daiches is next door at 414 Flores. (From the Collection of Federico E. Vidaurri. Digital restoration by Irene Vidaurri Zubeck.)

Bill Batey and the Boys of '56

On a warm overcast day in February 2007, an eighty-five-year-old former basketball coach, his head shining in the early afternoon sun, ambled slowly across the asphalt parking lot and up the steps into the "old" gym at Martin High School on San Bernardo Avenue. For many years, Coach William "Bill" Batey Sr. was a beloved figure at Martin High School, and the Laredo Independent School District had decided to dedicate the gym in his honor.

Hailed as "the man, the legend," Bill Batey coached basketball at Martin High School from 1953 to 1964. Against all odds, his 1956 team, said to have been the shortest team to ever compete in the 4A State Tournament, shocked the Texas basketball world by winning the state championship. For decades to come, there would be a sense of great pride and righteousness in the border city, and it was all due to the "Rabbit Runners of the Border."

The sturdy old L-shaped yellow-brick edifice at the corner of San Bernardo Avenue and Park Street was built with the help of Franklin D. Roosevelt's New Deal Depression-era dollars. It first opened its doors in 1937. The impressive two-storied high school was named for one of the city's more influential and powerful political *patrons,* the French-born Raymond Martin and his wife, Tirza Garcia.

As Batey slowly entered the gym, loud applause echoed forth. An instantaneous wide grin appeared on his face, along with a sparkle in his eyes. A number of former players rushed forward to hug the coach and pose for photographs. Others continued to applaud, and there were chants of "Once a Tiger, Always a Tiger."

Red, black, and white bunting provided a colorful background for the Laredo media. At one end of the gym, the old, badly tarnished 1956 championship trophy, rescued from a broom closet, was polished and prominently displayed on a neatly decorated table. The ceremony began with someone leading a prayer, and an impressive presentation of the colors by the high school ROTC. The Pledge of Allegiance came next, and then the singing of the school alma mater, with all of the students holding hands. This was followed by the cheerleaders in red and white skirts performing power lifts, jumping, and shouting.

After educators and politicians spoke with endless superlatives, the honoree's son, Bill Batey Jr., introduced members of the Batey family. Next, the assistant coach, John Valls, was presented. Like Batey, Valls was a veteran of World War II. Fighting with the highly decorated 9th Armored Division in Europe, Valls had been one of the first men across the Rhine after the Americans captured the Ludendorff Railroad Bridge at Remagen. Valls recalled how, in the final days of the war, he had personally accepted the surrender of a German general. But the war had taken a toll on him. First Lieutenant Louis Valls, John's brother, was shot down and killed during a bombing raid on the Orvieto Railroad Bridge in central Italy in January 1944. Returning home to Texas, Valls ran hurdles for the Baylor Bears. Part Catalan by birth, he had three brothers who were also athletes.

Valls even formed a semi-pro basketball team in Laredo called the Texaco Chiefs that was made up of coaches and officers from Laredo Air Force Base. Both Batey and Valls were central to the team that played mostly in San Antonio and Corpus Christi, but once drove to Durango, Mexico, for a game. With firepower in excess and a lightning-fast break offense, the Chiefs once won ten consecutive games by scoring more than 100 points in each game. That is, until they ran into an army team from Fort Sam Houston and were clobbered.

At Martin High School, Valls did a great job, Batey would remember, especially in helping to condition and motivate the championship team. Besides his coaching duties, Valls taught typing. "I could teach a monkey how to type," he would say.

Then the players themselves, several with silver hair and one or two with a limp, stepped forward to be introduced. Philip Trammell had been a superb scorer, roaming the key as forward with great skill and determination. He had a gifted hook shot that was indefensible, along with an impressive jump shot and a "sense of where to be at the right time." Moreover, he was a tremendous rebounder, the "Air Jordan" of Martin High School. A very reserved and likable kid, Trammell frequently led the team in scoring, but he had no ego and was certainly no "ball hog." Batey said that Trammell was one of the best players he ever coached. "In all the years I played basketball, he was the best pure shooter I ever saw," Andy Santos would say. After his sophomore year of sitting on the bench, Trammell's father, a wildlife manager on the sprawling Callahan Ranch, bought him a basketball, and from that day forth, Trammell was at the Boys Club practicing. Although he had small hands, he developed an indefensible hook shot with either hand.

At guard, Andres "Andy" Santos Jr. was the floor leader and the dedicated captain. He always worked hard and inspired others. Batey called Santos a "bell cow," someone who was always in charge and who consistently and fiercely competed, no matter how long or short the odds. Andy was, Odie Arambula would write in the school newspaper, a "terrific all-around player." He could do it all. Six feet tall and weighing a hefty 185 pounds, he was all spirit, "defense, offense, and ball hawk." Andy was only seventeen and would graduate with seven letters, including three in basketball, two in football, and two in baseball. Along with Trammell, Batey thought Santos was one of the best players he ever coached.

William "Willie" Dickinson came from a family of athletes. At six foot three, he was not only the tallest player on the team, but also one of the smartest. He was a "fighter," Batey remembered, and he knew how to "mix it up." Dickinson's inside game and his ability to pull down rebounds, even against players several inches taller, were the keys to the Tigers' success.

From El Trece neighborhood near the high school, Augustine Molina was indispensable as the seventh man. He was a good dribbler, ball handler, a great and reliable team player, and he played frequently.

Although only five foot six, Ramiro Hernandez rarely took a bad shot, frequently putting the ball up from the corner, long before the three-point rule was introduced. Hernandez was a great ball handler with blazing speed and guided the Cats' fast break. Although not a natural shooter, the five-foot-nine-inch Leonard Anderson was also a great ball handler, quick, and as Coach Valls remembered, a "wonderful kid." Batey remembered Anderson as someone who was tenacious and never got excited.

Baldomero Hector Chacón was the "utility man," springing off the bench to give the team energy and instant offense. Chacón could also be deadly from the free-throw line. When the Tigers went into their patented stall, his free throws were critical. Batey would remember Chacón as always being supported by his parents and family. Dependable and hardworking, Chacón was as skinny as a rail, and often sensitive, sometimes kidded by the other players. His pressure free throws in the final minutes of a game often made the difference between winning and losing.

Enrique "Kike" Mejia was small but smart, and a good ball handler. He was a great seventh man who played a lot. Mejia also ran track, especially on the Tiger mile relay team. Roberto "Pitin" Guajardo was an excellent ball handler, steady and composed, who knew the plays well. He was so versatile that he could play several positions. Guajardo "loved the game," Batey would remember, and he was so consistent that he "did not miss a practice all year."

Isidro "Chilo" Garcia handled the ball well and was also instrumental to the Tigers' success. Jimmy Rodriguez was the smallest player on the squad, but he was fast, spirited, could steal the ball, and was a team player. Both he and Cruz Alejandro Soto, who frequently got into the game in the fourth quarter, ran Batey's plays to perfection. Managers José Luis Novoa and Walter Herbeck both worked hard. They were always there when needed, and the coaches and the team respected them. Sadly, by the time the old gym was dedicated in 2007, two of the former players, Cruz Soto and Kike Mejia, had passed away. By June 2017, Ramiro Hernandez, the crafty, sharp-shooting, little guard was also gone.

Dickinson, Anderson, and Trammell were not Latino names, but the three young men were "puro Mexicano," one player remembered. They had Hispanic mothers, spoke Spanish, and roamed the dirt streets of the *barrios*. They were tough and did not back down from a fight. On the road, the three players, like other members of the team, were frequent victims of a biting and vicious racism that plagued Texas for more than a century. Sometimes taunted for being Latino, especially in the Lower Valley, they paid little heed to the jibes and played the game with intensity and dedication. At Martin High School and in Laredo, there were clear socioeconomic distinctions, but racial discrimination was something from afar.

Many of the Tigers, often referred to as the Bateymen, had played basketball almost from the time they could walk. They played in the Parish League for boys under thirteen and in the Boys Club League as teenagers.

As the dedication ceremony continued, the coach was finally asked to speak. Obviously overwhelmed by the large turnout, as well as the standing and prolonged ovation, Batey spoke passionately of his "unending" affection for his team, and how they had brought great pride to the city. His voice seemed to fade at times, and tears welled up as Batey recalled how the Tigers always "worked hard and had the right attitude."

At times, Batey spoke eloquently and forcefully, his enthusiasm for basketball obvious and unchallenged. At eighty-five, his energy seemed boundless. The Tigers used to practice seven days a week and twice on Sunday, Batey recalled. When asked what made the Boys of '56 so special, Batey responded that it was "team loyalty, and each player keeping himself in the best possible condition." The "height-shy" Tigers, as Batey called them, were consistent, and they never retreated. They played just as they were coached to play. With great joy, Batey remembered beating the Edinburg

Bobcats and the Harlingen Cardinals, the best teams in the valley at the time. But it was the surprising victories over the highly touted Houston Milby Buffaloes and the decidedly favored and high-octane North Dallas Bulldogs in the state tournament that everyone remembered, propelling the Cats into the hearts of every Laredoan. When Batey was asked exactly how the Tigers of '56 won the 4A state championship, the highest classification in the state at the time, the coach said that he thought it came down to "grit and determination and a love of the game."

It had been fifty-one years since the boys from the border, the courageous little band of brothers from the streets of Laredo, triumphantly raised the Texas 4A championship trophy before a capacity crowd of more than 8,000 at Gregory Gym on the Austin campus of the University of Texas. It was the first live schoolboy basketball telecast in Texas history with as many as 300,000 viewers in Austin, Temple, San Antonio, and Dallas tuned into the game. The 4A finals were also broadcast on twenty-six radio stations to more than a million listeners, all the way from the deserts and high plains of West Texas to the bayous and wetlands of East Texas; from El Paso to Texarkana; and from the Red River to the Rio Grande.

Salo Otero, longtime sports editor for the *Laredo Morning Times*, said that the bright and enthusiastic coach had vaulted to distinction and fame "on the legs and shoulders of a group of hard-playing, over-achieving youngsters from the downtown area of Laredo." They shocked the state and brought great delight and self-satisfaction to Laredo, the southernmost state-championship city since the tournament began in 1921.

At the helm of the Tigers, Batey dedicated his life to the game of basketball. "I am what you would call a road warrior," he would say. "The amount of miles I've ridden in a yellow hound number in the tens of thousands, but I knew that each mile would take me to the place that made the travel and time spent worthwhile—the gym of an opponent."

Few in Texas understood the intricacies of basketball as did Batey. If you asked him how the "pick-and-roll" had changed, Dan McCarney of the *Laredo Morning Times* wrote, "you'll get a five-minute overview on how the tandem post" had evolved over time. "He was always getting into chalk sessions," Victoria coach Mike Smith remembered. Batey spent hours "going over strategy, always looking for a new out-of-bounds play." Tuloso Midway's Bobby Craig recalled eating a sandwich in the hospitality room at a tournament and noticing

In his first year at Martin High School, Batey went 11–11, but in his second year, the Tigers went 15–8 and won their district. In 1956, they took it all by winning the state 4A state championship in Austin. Front row: Manager José Luis Novoa, Alfredo Wise, Agustin Molina, Leonard Anderson, Hector Chacon, Ramiro Hernandez, Oscar Ochoa, and Guadalupe Guajardo. Back row: Coach John Valls, José Ibarra, Pedro Rocha, Francisco Alvarado, Phillip Trammell, Willie Dickinson, Andy Santos, Francisco Santos, Manager Enrique Rosales, and Coach Bill Batey. (Courtesy of Andy Santos)

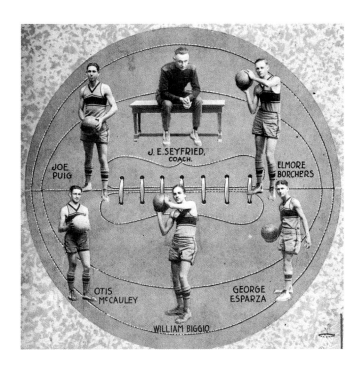

The 1924 Laredo High School basketball team went undefeated during the regular season. Victories included a 62–2 romp over Cotulla. The team practiced on a dirt court near the banks of the Rio Grande and had never played on a wooden court until they were decisively defeated, 10–36, by Dallas Oak Cliff Golden Bears in the last step before the state tournament. (La Pitahaya, 1924)

that Batey's "discarded paper plate was covered with plays he had diagrammed." There were even basketball drawings on the 1956 State Tournament program that Mary Frances saved for the family scrapbook. At halftime, Batey used a chalkboard, and he was known to talk and draw, and talk and draw. One coach said that Batey "had the best basketball mind" he had ever seen. "This guy was a genius when it came to the game of basketball," Valls would write. "It was his passion. He would not talk about anything but basketball."

Valls coached the B team and covered for Batey when he was off scouting. He "really cared for the kids," Valls would say. But he also drove his players hard. Batey "lived basketball. It was his life." "Be a fighter," Batey would tell everyone, even in the hallways. Valls once remembered riding in Batey's Studebaker when the head coach began excitedly talking basketball. They were twenty miles outside of town before Batey realized where they were.

The Tigers of '56 stood on the shoulders of other Laredo athletes. The 1924 Laredo High School basketball team had beaten a series of South Texas high schools, including Cotulla, 62–2, to face the Falfurrias Butter Boys, as they were known at the time, and then Dilley, and finally Raymondville, the Lower Valley champion, to compile a perfect 12–0 record. But the

Tigers had never played on an indoor court before, and they fell to Dallas Oak Cliff, the eventual state champions, 10–36. Attending the two-storied old high school on the south side of San Agustin Plaza, the team practiced after school on a dirt court near the riverbanks. "When we found out we had to play on a hard-wood gym, we cleared some of the chairs in the school auditorium and practiced for a day or so," Elmore H. Borchers remembered.

Another great squad was the 1927 Laredo High School football team, coached by the legendary Shirley DaCamara. Before the season started, the coach took his young recruits to the Nueces River at Cotulla, where they practiced in the stifling August heat for more than a week. Not counting an exhibition loss to the Kingsville Teachers, 6–13, they played undefeated and outscored their opponents 141–0. But at that time there were no playoffs, and the team had to be content with simply winning district. The last living member of the team, Radcliffe Killam, died in 2007, the day after Batey was honored at Martin High School.

The road to Gregory Gym and the state championship was not easy for the coach. He was born William Charles Batey on November 23, 1923, in Moulton, a small town in Lavaca County in east-central Texas, on a rise between the East and West forks of the Lavaca River where the Post Oak Belt meets the Gulf Coastal Plains. Many in Lavaca County were proud of the town and of Moulton's athletic teams.

Largely settled by Czech and German immigrants who grew mostly cotton, the town was said to have had a "heart as big as Texas." Batey came of age on the family farm on the edge of town among hundreds of hogs, cows, and chickens. One of Batey's first memories was bouncing a rubber ball against a wall in his childhood home, which was not far from the railroad, twenty miles north of Schulenburg. As a teenager, he would never forget the terrible days of the Great Depression. His mother often fed hungry, penniless, ragged, and demoralized hobos, all helpless victims of the worst economic disaster in American history, who came to the Batey house asking for food.

After starring in basketball at Moulton High School, Batey excitedly joined the freshman basketball team at the University of Texas in 1941. But in the summer of 1942, following the surprise attack on Pearl Harbor, he was swept up in war fervor and joined the U.S. Navy. Hitchhiking to a recruiting station in San Antonio, Batey and a friend caught a ride with a couple who (unbeknownst to them) had stolen the car in Louisiana. When police stopped the car outside Seguin, all of its occupants were arrested. Batey and his friend spent an uneasy night in the Guadalupe County Jail before telephone calls to Moulton verified their innocence the next morning.

In the Navy, Batey spent most of the time at the Kingsville Naval Air Station, where he played basketball for service teams. It was also at the naval air station where Batey came to know John Dick, a six-foot-four-inch forward and All-American from the University of Oregon. Dick had taken the

Webfeet, as the Ducks were known at the time, to the 1939 National Championship. He showed Batey how the Webfeet ran a lightning-fast break and breezed past Oklahoma and Texas to beat Ohio State 46–33 for the championship. Dick, who went on to become a rear admiral, strapped Batey in a plane while he was training as a pilot and took him through a series of aerial maneuvers. Dizzy and sick, but safely back at the naval air station, Batey swore that he would never fly in an airplane again. Discharged from the Navy in late 1945, he took advantage of the GI Bill and enrolled at Texas A&M University, where he was also offered an athletic scholarship.

With the Aggies, Batey won three letters. Guided by Slater Martin and Marty Karow, the 145-pound skinny forward led the Aggies in scoring for two years. His junior year, he had one of the highest free-throw percentages in the nation. During his senior year, Batey seriously sprained an ankle and limped through most of the season. Although the Aggies lost most of their games, Batey was able to see Chicago, Philadelphia, and the lights of Broadway. The one moment he recalled with great joy while at College Station was when he met his future wife, Mary Frances, at Catholic Youth Day.

Batey would pass his love of basketball and his athleticism on to his seven children, three boys and four girls, whom he called the "Live Wires." After graduating from Texas A&M, Batey was offered a contract to play professional basketball for the Anderson Indiana Packers of the National Basketball League, but the pay was so low that he was forced to turn down the offer.

Attending summer school at Texas A&M, Batey obtained an MA degree. He took a job at his alma mater, Moulton High School, where he taught history, a subject he admitted knowing little about, while coaching basketball, track, baseball, softball, tennis, and volleyball. The hometown coach made his skills known when he took the Bob Katz all the way to the state tournament in 1951, beating Blum 56–49 before losing to the legendary Livingston Big Sandy Wildcats in the semifinals, 53–24. Signing a two-year contract for $4,300 a year, Batey moved to Alice in 1952. He had managed to jump from B to 3A, and would then coach only basketball and football.

Batey learned quickly, mostly from other Texas coaches such as C. P. "Peck" Vass, who ran the "Duke shuffle" at Bryan High School and took his 1952 Vikings to the state tournament. He also admired and copied much of what he learned from Bill Corder at Moulton, his coaches at A&M, and the teams he had played against. He also liked what Henry Chovener did at Hallettsville. Batey was one of the first high school coaches in Texas to use the 1-3-1 defense. The defense was largely modeled on that of Milton Jowers, who won the state championship at San Marcos High School in 1940 and went on to take the Southwest Texas State University Bobcats to the 1960 NAIA National Championship. But over time, both Batey and Jowers came to rely more on a man-to-man defense. Batey also liked Jowers's offense that used both a high and low post with both guards and forwards setting screens.

After playing one year at the University of Texas at Austin, Bill Batey went on to play three years for the Texas A&M University Aggies, even leading the team in scoring his junior year. Batey had one of the highest free-throw percentages in the country. (Courtesy of the Batey Family)

Titled "a study in glum looks," Bill Batey sits on the bench with Coach Marty Karow at Texas A&M University during a decisive defeat by Baldwin-Wallace College. (Courtesy of the Batey Family)

*In 1956, Martin High School on San Bernardo and Park Street was Laredo's only public high school, which students from all over the city attended. In this aerial photograph, legendary Shirley Field can be seen behind the school, as well as Christen Junior High School in the upper left and Leyendecker Elementary School in the upper right. The entire four-block area was originally planned as a giant city park, similar to Central Park in New York City. (*La Pitahaya, *1956)*

At the time, almost everyone was influenced by the legendary Henry Payne "Hank" Iba, who won two national championships at Oklahoma State as well as three Olympic gold medals. Iba's career spiraled downward, however, following a controversial one-point loss to the Soviet Union in the 1972 Olympics.

Long before the advent of the shot clock, Batey would intentionally slow down a game, as did Iba, especially against a bigger opponent. In particular, Batey liked the way that Tony Burger at Austin High School could stall a game. He also loved the way Cotton Robinson, the icon at Buna, revolutionized Texas basketball with his fierce man-to-man, full-court pressure defense. But perhaps more importantly, Batey admired the way that Robinson played offense. The legendary small-town coach (who won seven state titles in fifteen years at Buna) built a set offense around discipline, spacing, precision,

and patience. "I always studied the game," Batey would say, even visiting locker rooms to see and learn as much as possible.

His players were always required to "dress up," at least with a nice coat, but Batey never required that they wear ties. Under no circumstance was tobacco or alcohol allowed. The first year Batey was at Alice, the Coyotes finished third in district. Then in 1953 they won the district crown, their season ending at the hands of San Antonio's Edison Bears in bi-district.

In 1953, the twenty-nine-year-old Batey, who was said to be a "basketball specialist," was highly recommended by the outgoing coach at Martin High School, M. R. Davis. Years later, Batey remembered driving from Alice to meet with J. W. Nixon in the Missouri-born superintendent's office on Houston Street, just off St. Peter's Plaza. Nixon thought Batey's record at Alice was impressive, but he was concerned that Batey might somehow be a rabble-rouser and become involved

Principal R. P. St. John presides over a predominantly female faculty at a meeting in the Martin High School Library. Many of the teachers had graduate degrees from prestigious universities, loved their disciplines, and were dedicated to their profession. (La Pitahaya, *1956)*

in local politics, thus bringing embarrassment to the Laredo Independent School District (LISD). Batey assured Nixon, who was an influential arm of the "Partido Viejo" (the local political machine that dominated Laredo and Webb County politics for six decades) that he was a basketball coach, not a politician. While coaching at Alice, Batey had been in the shadow of the ruthless "Duke of Duval" machine. "They shot people over there," Batey would say in reference to the rough-and-tumble world of San Diego and Duval County politics. In June 1953, the coach and the superintendent posed for the camera as Batey signed a two-year contract agreeing to coach the Tiger basketball team and also teach driver's education.

Before Batey arrived at the gym on San Bernardo, basketball had always been secondary at Martin High School. All of the previous basketball coaches had been primarily football coaches. On Fridays or Saturdays, thousands crowded into Shirley Field to watch football games, usually under the bright lights. When there were cuts in funding for public schools in Texas, no politician dared to touch football. Texas *was* football and football *was* Texas, and to play football in the Lone Star State was to be a man. It was a coming-of-age ritual that few young men who had the opportunity could pass up. Andy Santos would always remember one of the football coaches calling his brother Bobby "yellow" for his refusal to play football. Many of the young men who played football disliked the harsh discipline of the football coaches, saying in drills they were hit with switches from salt cedar trees, cursed at, and sometimes forced to run until they dropped from exhaustion. Having taken Freer to the state quarterfinals, J. W. Helms was hired to coach football at Martin High School and serve as athletic director, but he was envious of Batey's success, and the two never got along.

Batey liked what he saw at Martin High School. A wide green lawn fronted the building on the south and east sides. Here and there, hackberry trees provided shade from the relentless South Texas sun. There was even a rose garden and more than twenty palm trees. There were no fences around the school, and at lunch the students were free to leave. Some students sat on the lawn to eat, socialize, and sometimes flirt. Some students with money headed to the hamburger stands across Park Street, especially the Glass Kitchen, while others made their way to the school cafeteria. Some students who lived near the school went home for lunch.

There was no air conditioning, but the buildings were constructed for natural ventilation. The students were not uncomfortable, except in late August and early September, and late May, when afternoon temperatures soared over 100 degrees. To make learning bearable, every room was given a large, noisy fan.

R. P. St. John was principal, and Maj. August O. Hein, who would go on to become principal himself, was in charge of an award-winning ROTC program. Both men were proud graduates of Rice Institute, and the students liked them. They both had a sense of humor and frequently roamed the halls, always recognizing students by their first names. St. John was "never too busy to counsel with the newest freshman or the oldest teacher," the school yearbook, *La Pitahaya*, recorded. Each teacher was treated with great respect, by both the students and the administration, and they were told that they were the "captain of a ship."

A "Personal Grooming and Dress Code" was rigidly enforced at Martin High School. For boys, hair could not "rest on the shirt collar or overlap the collar." Mustaches and beards were strictly taboo, and boys were told to wear a "nice, clean shirt" and "underclothing" at all times. Girls were asked to wear only "a reasonable amount of makeup." Under no circumstances was the makeup to be excessive and "cause people of culture to question the good judgment of the particular girl and her parents." For girls, pants were forbidden, and dresses and skirts were to be no "higher than two inches below mid-thigh." If there were any doubt as to the proper length of the dress or lack of "essential underclothing," the principal would call on the "homemaking teacher to make judgment."

Students were grouped by motivation and ability. Such groupings were rarely discussed, although everyone was aware of the system. Students were motivated to make high grades, and many went on to pursue higher education and to become professionals.

St. John and Hein were stern disciplinarians, so there were rarely problems. For those who did transgress, the punishment could be harsh. Even in the heat of the afternoon, disciplinary cases were sometimes put to work near Shirley Field, pulling weeds. Once a teacher sent two students to run an errand, and when the boys cut through the gym where a girls' P. E. class was in progress, one of the coaches caught the boys and whipped them with a board. The unnamed coach "was a powerful man," one of the boys remembered, and "the whipping was quite a painful experience," but the student was more concerned that his "parents might find out." On rare occasions students were expelled, never to return. Once a young female was caught with marijuana, and everyone went into shock. Not only was the girl expelled, but also the school counselor, Guadalupe "Lupe" Cabrera, called the girl's family into her office and suggested that they move out of town; only then could the family regain a degree of respect.

Martin High School was the only public high school in Laredo, and kids from all walks of life went there. The Tiger athletic teams were the talk of the town, and they easily overshadowed the St. Joseph Antlers, St. Augustine Knights, and the Methodist-affiliated Holding Institute Golden Eagles. Kids from wealthy families in the heights rubbed shoulders with poor kids from the *barrios*. Saturday night dances in the gym were the highlight of social life. Batey and Valls and their players always stuck around after the dances to sweep and clean the gym so that the basketball team could practice on Sunday morning.

In an era when women were not welcomed into many professions, well-educated, dedicated females dominated the faculty at Martin High School, many with advanced degrees. Bess Lindheim, who taught English literature, was a favorite. Reading and rereading the works she assigned was a great pleasure for many students. Five decades later, former student Jim Whitworth could still take pleasure in reading Lord Byron's poetry. She "made us see that Byron could paint a picture with words in each line he wrote," Whitworth remembered. Everyone loved Josephine Baird, who taught several science classes, especially biology. With degrees from the University of Southern California and Texas A&I University, Baird always seemed happy and laughed frequently, often sharing personal stories with the students. Always dressed in a plain plaid dress, loose stockings, and orthopedic shoes, she got along well with the students and never sent anyone to St. John's office. Knowing his vocabulary needed improvement if he was to succeed in college, she asked Andy Santos for a special favor upon his graduation. Read a book. "What book," he asked, thinking she might recommend Leo Tolstoy's *War and Peace*. Read a page or two out of the dictionary every day. Ellen DeTournillion set high standards in chemistry, and students remembered making high scores in college as a result of her rigor. Bertha Treviño was a superb math teacher, and students seemed to appreciate her talents. At one time or another, every student ran into the sergeant-like Ruth Young, physical education teacher and sponsor of the Student Council and Pep Squad.

For popular male teachers, many students would never forget Jack Davis, who coached debate and drama. The teams Davis put together frequently won trophies in one-act plays and speech competitions at district. Everyone loved the always-patient Elmo Lopez, the band director, who was on his way to becoming "Laredo's Mr. Music." Fructosa G. Barreda was everyone's favorite. The Notre Dame graduate always dressed in nice slacks and a short-sleeve shirt; his class was "always fun and lively and he was a positive role model," one student

remembered. When students failed to complete an assignment, he had a saying that always brought laughter to the class: "A balloon for you." For decades, even in public, he was known affectionately as "Mr. Balloon," a name he reveled in. Two years before the Tigers won the state championship, Les Gillespie, a music teacher, was asked by the students to write a new school song. Students voted 1,041 to 93 to approve his lyrics: "All hail to Red and White; all hail to Martin High. We pledge our loyalty to thee, dear Martin High . . ."

The first year that Batey was at Martin, Laredo was struggling to recover from one of the worst floods in the long and difficult history of the community. In June 1954, Hurricane Alice came roaring out of the Bay of Campeche and swept over South Texas, dropping as much as thirty-five inches of rain in some places in less than twenty-four hours, leaving at least fifty-five people dead. A wall of water roared down the Rio Grande, sweeping everything in its path. The flooded river crested at Laredo on June 26 at an all-time record high of sixty-two feet, taking out the railroad and international bridges and sending water into the homes of thousands of citizens, especially on the Mexican side of the river.

In October, President Dwight D. Eisenhower came to Laredo to dedicate the recently completed Falcon Dam and Reservoir. The president landed at Laredo Air Force Base and then rode down San Bernardo in an open limousine as the Martin High School band gathered on the front lawn to play John Philip Sousa's "Stars and Stripes Forever." Not a single "heart was untouched as he made a deep bow to acknowledge the music and the applause," *La Pitahaya* proclaimed.

When Batey came to Laredo, the Tiger football team was little short of a disaster. During the previous year, 1953, the Tigers managed to win only one game, a 13–7 victory over Eagle Pass. During the entire season, the Tigers managed only five touchdowns. In fact, the lowly Tigers did not score for four consecutive games, losing to Corpus Christi Ray, 0–58; San Antonio Brackenridge, 0–26; Del Rio, 0–28; San Antonio Jefferson, 0–27; before closing out the season with a 6–46 embarrassing loss to McAllen. The following year, the football team did not win a single game, although the Tigers did manage a tie with South San Antonio and Corpus Christi Academy. Paul "Bear" Bryant, legendary coach at Texas A&M who had gone through a losing season himself, was brought to town to address the varsity players during their yearly banquet in the Maya Room of the Hamilton Hotel.

Many of those who tried out for the basketball team at Martin High School did not immediately adjust to Batey's discipline and hard work ethic. Some resented his regimentation and to practicing three to four hours Monday through Saturday and twice on Sunday. Others were slow to adjust to his 1-3-1 "wheel defense" and his hard-pressing full-court man-to-man. Batey was, a player would remember, someone "who did not put up with any bullshit." Behind his back, a few cursed and called him "El Diablo." But most of the Tigers had talent, and they caught on quickly. During his first season at Martin, Batey's team struggled in district, and the Tigers ended up 11–11.

The next year, Batey opened by beating up on St. Augustine before losing to the Laredo Air Force Jets that included several college graduates, 51–67. Batey always thought it was best to seek out the best competition to help his players prepare for district. The Tigers responded by reeling off three victories over Edinburg, Eagle Pass, and then Harlingen in overtime. For a second year, Batey took his Tigers to the Bryan Chamber of Commerce Tournament, where they lost to Dallas High and Houston Stephen F. Austin. Batey rarely complained about the officiating, but would later say that at Bryan "the Zebras did us in." But the Cats came home knowing that they could play with some of the best teams in the state. December proved to be difficult. The Tigers ran into a traveling team from Simsboro, Louisiana, one of the best high school teams in the nation. They could never get their offense going and were overwhelmed by a suffocating defense, 27–49. The Tigers star, Frank "Lefty" Santos, one of the best players Batey said he would ever coach, was held to 12 points. A few days later,

the Tigers rebounded with a 76–65 victory over the Harlingen Cardinals as "bean-pole" six-foot-three-inch Willie Dickinson and the hot-shooting Frank Santos combined for 45 points.

The Tigers opened district play in early January 1955 by beating Corpus Christi Miller. "The beautiful team work displayed by the Bengal Cagers was too much for the Miller Buccaneers, who, in spite of their advantage in height, had to bow to the Tigers," the *Laredo Journal* wrote. Jumping-jack Trammell had 23 points. Although the Tigers were upset by the hustling San Antonio Jefferson Mustangs on the road, they rallied two days later to edge San Antonio Brackenridge. At the end of January, they followed with a victory over a cold-shooting but scrappy Brownsville Eagles at the Tiger gym. At the end of the first half, the Cats were ahead 38–13. With two minutes left in the game, Batey pulled his starters, and the Tigers won by eight. A few days later, however, the Cats lost to San Antonio Tech.

Tragedy struck in the middle of the season when the Bateys' infant son, Michael Frank, suddenly became critically ill and died. The Batey family was plunged into mourning. The

In Batey's second year at Martin High School, the 1955 Tiger basketball team won the district title before falling to the Waco High School Lions in the bi-district. In front is Leonard Anderson. The second row includes (left to right) Phillip Trammel, Andy Santos, Willie Dickinson, Ramiro Hernandez, and Agustin Molina. Standing is Frank Santos, Hector Chacón, and Coach John Valls. Batey was absent. (La Pitahaya, 1955)

team, too, felt the sadness. Those days were difficult at Martin High School, but the season went on.

As the Bateys struggled to bury and mourn their son, Valls took the Tigers to Corpus Christi to meet the Ray Texans. In one of the most exciting games of the year, Andy Santos sank a field goal with three seconds left to throw the game into overtime, and the Cats went on to squeak out a victory, 58–56. The Tigers followed with wins over district rivals Miller, Jefferson, Brackenridge, San Antonio Tech, and then Ray again, and they were district champions. In the bi-district, the Cats ran into the much larger and more experienced Waco High School Lions in the best of three games. By the Brazos River in Waco, the Tigers were ambushed, 38–58, although Frank Santos had 22 points. Back on the border, in one of the most exciting games many of the Tiger fans had seen all year, the Cats nosed out the Lions, 60–58, as Phillip Trammell put in 18 points. Before a packed and excited audience the next evening, one game away from the state tournament, the Tigers were never able to gain any momentum and fell flat. The packed crowd sat in stunned silence as they lost, 65–50. The loss was devastating, and there were plenty of tears in the locker room.

"We lost to a fine team," Batey told the local press. "They were fast and well-coached. I am proud of my boys." The Tigers ended the season with a respectable 15–8 record. Waco went on to lose by two points to Dallas Tech in the finals of the state tournament.

Although Batey lost his star Frank Santos to graduation the following year, he went into the season with renewed determination and a sense of great optimism. He knew that his Tigers were capable of playing with the best teams in the state. With seven battle-tested juniors returning for their senior year, including Andy Santos, Phillip Trammell, and Willie Dickinson, Batey hoped that with hard work and discipline, the Cats could go far. But the nervous Batey always seemed to have doubts. "Our defense really looks sloppy," he told the local press at the beginning of the season. "If the boys have more desire than the other club and we play as a team and as a unit, we'll have a winning ball club. I think my boys have a pretty good chance to clinch the district crown again," Batey went on to say, although he admitted that the San Antonio Jefferson Mustangs were "a well-balanced quintet with plenty of height and speed." Corpus Christi Ray, Corpus Christi Miller, and San Antonio Fox Tech were also in the running. Batey was somewhat despondent when one of the most promising players he had ever coached, six-foot-four-inch junior Ed Hill, dropped out of school to support his family.

In the opening game at the Martin gym, Batey's Park Street boys took on the Laredo Air Force Jets. The Jets were older and more experienced, and they were not segregated, as were public high schools in Texas at the time. A few of the Jets who were training as pilots had even played basketball in college. But the Flyboys, as the Cats called them, were disorganized. They did not play well together or seem to run

During the games at Martin High School, Mary Frances Batey and the Batey children, (left to right) Carol, Bobby, Cathie, and Bill Jr., were always in the stands cheering for the Tigers and their hero coach. (La Pitahaya, 1955)

any plays. Although the Jets had four games under their belt, they got off to a clumsy start. Some spectators thought they were loafing, expecting an easy win. Stealing the ball several times from their taller opponents for easy layups, the Cats raced out to an impressive 28-point lead at halftime.

Anchored by their big six-foot-six-inch center, John McKinnie, the Jets fought back in the second half and cut the Tiger lead to ten. Pressing hard in the fourth quarter, the Jets drew to within three when Batey called a time out and went into his well-rehearsed stall. Trapping hard, the Jets stole the ball with only a few seconds left and raced in for a layup—but it was not enough. The Tigers shocked the much older and favored Flyboys, 52–51. Trammell was high for the Tigers with 22, while Santos chipped in with 13. As the crowd stood to cheer, Batey, who was never known to gloat, could only stand in amazement and offer words of congratulations. He went home that evening with Mary Frances and the children through the dirt streets of Laredo, knowing he had a team with tremendous potential that was capable of going far.

A few days later, with James Dean playing in *Rebel Without a Cause* on the screen at the Plaza Theatre across the street from City Hall, the Tigers got off to a quick start. They raced by the Harlingen Cardinals, only to turn cold. The much taller Cards featured six-foot-eight-inch center David Rozell, who was thought by some to be one of the best players in South Texas. The Tigers were amazed that the Redbirds were even taller than the LAFB Jets, with several other players well over six feet tall. The agile Cards pressed the Cats hard and had a 34–31 lead at halftime. As hundreds of spectators cheered, the Tigers came roaring back in the second half of the game.

Two Sinton players attempt to block a shot by Andy Santos as Hector Chacón waits for a possible rebound. (La Pitahaya, 1956)

They took a one-point lead at the end of the third quarter. In the fourth quarter, the Tigers built a ten-point lead and held on for an exciting 58–49 win.

There was also good news on another front. Sixteen-year-old Humberto Adame, Martin High School senior (and one of nine children) outran 129 other runners from all over the state. He captured the state high school cross-country championship, setting a new record of 9:45 over the two-mile course at Ziker Park in Austin. Track Coach Alfonso "Lefty" Valls and trainer Luis Novoa were ecstatic. In Adame, Martin High School had a state champion and a real hero.

A minor crisis developed when Trammell was caught reenacting a scene from *Blackboard Jungle* by pulling out a pocketknife in a drafting class, and as a result, St. John threatened to throw him out of school. Fearful their entire season would collapse in a cloud of dust, Andy was selected to approach Batey to warn that if Trammell was expelled or even suspended, the entire team would quit. "Fine," Batey said, calling their bluff, "go ahead and quit." In the end nothing ever happened, and the incident was largely forgotten.

The night after the Tigers beat Harlingen, they were brought back down to reality when a reorganized and newly energized LAFB team, thirsting for revenge and embarrassed by their earlier loss, clobbered the Cats at the Martin gym, 53–80. The Tigers never had a chance. In the fourth quarter, with the game out of hand, Batey ran in his reserves. "The Tiger defense went to pieces," the *Laredo Times* remarked. "They were walloped." The Cats "couldn't hit the basket," and they had trouble rebounding against the taller Jets. Batey took the defeat in stride, saying only that he hoped his Tigers learned something valuable from their trouncing.

When both the A and the B teams traveled together, the Tigers journeyed in the legendary "Blue Goose," an old, worn-out, beat-up 1940 bus that had seen its better days. The front door could only be opened with the support of bailing wire, and the engine often sputtered and coughed. When the A team traveled alone, the Tigers went in Batey's 1953 Studebaker, Valls's new four-door Oldsmobile, and Coach Helms's new Olds. The players preferred to travel with the more laid-back Valls, who allowed them to relax and listen to music on the car radio. The reserve players, including Guajardo, Garcia, and Soto, rode with Helms, and since the coach continuously puffed on cigars, the players always came home smelling like a cigar. On long road trips, the parents of the players packed tacos, and at the first stop, the Tigers would purchase cold cokes. Following games in the Lower Valley, the Cats always kept the coke bottles ready for defense.

Sometimes Valls would talk archeology and science, expounding on Charles Darwin's *The Origin of Species,* while asking, "Did we really come from monkeys?" Driving south of San Marcos at more than sixty miles an hour following one of the games, Valls had a blowout and was barely able to keep his Olds on the road. For a moment the situation looked perilous. When he finally steered the Olds to a stop, Dickinson calmly remarked, "God damn, Coach, you did a good job."

If you traveled with Batey, you talked basketball, coming and going, win or lose. Batey was always planning strategy for the next game. One player remembered returning from Corpus Christi in bad weather in the middle of the night with the windows of Batey's Studebaker fogging up, and the always-excited coach speeding down the narrow asphalt at sixty-five miles an hour, drawing plays for the next game on the window of the car with his finger.

Convinced that competing against the best teams possible would pay off in the long run, Batey again took his team 350 miles into the heart of East Texas to the Bryan Tournament, where the Tigers opened on a Friday afternoon with a 64–56 defeat of the Baytown Robert E. Lee Ganders. The next evening in the semifinals, however, the Tigers fought an uphill battle with the hometown Bryan Vikings. It was one of the most exciting games that fans had seen at Bryan in several years. The Tigers led 31–30 at halftime, and then with twenty seconds to go were up 65–64. But Bryan's six-foot-seven-inch center stole the ball and scored to give Bryan a one-point lead. With fourteen seconds left, the Vikings then stole the ball again and scored as the hometown crowd went wild. The Tigers lost a heartbreaker, 65–68, in a game that they should have won. Batey and his Tigers were bitterly disappointed.

The ride home was long, but the Cats returned a wiser and better team, the coach thought. A few days later, they defeated their valley rival, the Harlingen Cardinals, 55–46, at the Tiger gym. Dickinson had one of his better games, scoring 22 points, while Hernandez had 12. The Tigers outscored their opponents from the field, 28–12, although the Cards hit 22 of 29 free throws.

A few days later, the Tigers won back-to-back games against the very competitive Sinton Pirates, 54–37, on a Friday night, as the reserves played most of the second half, and a surprising squeaker on Saturday, 47–45. The Tigers were ahead by ten in the Saturday game, but the Pirates rallied to make the game close and missed a shot from center court at the buzzer that would have sent the game into overtime. The following week, at the Martin gym, the Cats ran over the Edinburg Bobcats for a second time, 67–55. Martin led all the way, and at one point had a 24-point lead before Batey began substituting.

The Cats then headed down U.S. Highway 83 and the Rio Grande to the Lower Valley for a much-anticipated game with the Harlingen Cardinals. Harlingen had the reputation of being one of the more racist towns in the Valley. The fouls were always hard, the fans were abusive, and there was always tension in the air. "They are going to kick the shit out of you," Batey warned the Tigers. Pressing throughout the game, the Cardinals led at halftime, 34–31, and although Santos was thrown out of the game after landing hard on one of the Cardinals while scrambling for a loose ball, the Cats went on to win in a thriller, 66–68.

Many on the Tiger team deeply resented the racism they saw in the Valley. At Weslaco and especially Harlingen, there

*Willie Dickinson (No. 35) scores two points as two Edinburg players try to stop him. Andy Ramos waits for a possible rebound. The Tigers went on to win the game 67–55. (*La Pitahaya, *1956)*

was always a shower of rocks as the Tigers departed in the Blue Goose. In Harlingen, there was nearly a brawl when several angry Harlingen fans began cursing and taunting Principal St. John after the game. Another time, a group of bullies showed up after a game at a restaurant where the Tigers were eating, threatening to "beat the shit out of the f------ Mexicans from Laredo," before the Harlingen coach intervened and chased the troublemakers away.

In 1956, there was a bigger problem when two hefty former Harlingen football players showed up at the same restaurant where the Martin cagers were eating. Trammell had received a threatening phone call at the restaurant from one of the ruffians only moments earlier, saying he and his buddies would be arriving to "kick the ass of some dirty Mexicans." Several of the Tigers sensed trouble when the waitress remarked to one of the individuals that she did not know he was out of jail. Fearing they would be attacked, several Tigers grabbed their table knives and forks. Realizing the seriousness of the situation, Valls jumped up from where he and Batey were eating and confronted one of the bullies. Placing his finger squarely in the chest of the hooligan, Valls warned him to back off. When the thug hesitated, Valls shoved him out of the restaurant. Batey and Valls feared there would be a brawl before the police showed up to escort the Blue Goose out of town.

The police presence, however, did not stop several angry Harlingen fans from throwing rocks and breaking several windows in the bus. As the Blue Goose clattered out of the city, cars followed with honking horns and individuals leaning out windows to shout racial epithets and make obscene gestures. Santos, who admitted years later he "was mean as hell," asked two of the Tigers to stand up and shield the coaches as he opened one of the back windows and hurled a coke bottle into the windshield of the lead car. It was a long, lonely ride upriver through the night, past orange and grapefruit trees, swaying palm trees in the night, through Rio Grande City, Roma, and the newly built Zapata. The Tigers hated the racism that seemed to permeate the Lower Valley.

The "now-hot, now-cold Tigers," as the local press called them, next headed north up U.S. 83 to the San Antonio Invitational Tournament. In an early morning game, they easily turned back the Victoria Stingarees, the 1955 State Tournament 3A champs, 65–47. In the quarterfinals, the Cats rolled over a much more competitive 4A San Antonio Fox Tech, 68–54, as Hernandez raced to a game-high 20 points. But then the Tigers ran into San Antonio Edison, one of the better teams in San Antonio. The always-difficult Bears featured the talented Rudy Davalos, future athletic director at three universities. From the opening tip, the game proved to be an absolute disaster for the Tigers. There were endless fouls and inconsistent officiating; the Cats were whistled 37 times while the Bears committed only 19 fouls. One by one the Tigers fouled out. By halftime, an emotional Batey, staring in disbelief, had lost everyone on his starting five except

Trammell. Although Trammell wound up with 31 points, the Tigers were demolished, 50–77. Years later, Batey still could not understand how so many fouls were called. The "zebras went absolutely wild," he would say. It was one of the few times he would ever blame the officials. It was an embarrassing defeat, and one of the worst the Tigers would suffer all year. "We were blown out. We lost our cool. The game should have been close. They are very good, but they are not as good as Martin High School," Batey would say in frustration and disbelief. "Everyone needs their oars in the water," the coach continued. "We learned from this. We were still experimenting at the time."

On January 5, 1956, the Tigers opened district play at home against Corpus Christi Ray, a seasoned team featuring a starting five that were all six feet tall or taller. From the opening tip, the Tigers dominated the offensive end of the court. The Cats outran and outplayed the Texans, and ended by clobbering Ray, 69–47. Trammell had 23 for the Tigers, while Santos added 15. In Brownsville two nights later, the Tigers looked sluggish and fell behind the Eagles at the end of the first quarter, 16–13. But with Batey pacing the floor and calling out plays, the Cats rallied for a two-point halftime lead and went on to win, 52–47. Batey said that he was satisfied with the results, although he "was not happy with the performance."

Before an overflow crowd at the Tiger gym three days later, the Cats clashed with another district rival, the San Antonio G. W. Brackenridge Eagles. Early in the game, the Tigers could not find the basket, but after some soul-searching and chalk-talk at halftime, the Cats were able to regroup and down the Eagles, 62–49, although the game was tied five times in the third and fourth quarters. The always-dependable Trammell hit eleven field goals and ended up with 24 points, while the crafty Santos had 14 points, and the sharp-shooting Hernandez dumped in 13.

The Tigers next headed north up U.S. Highway 83 again to the Alamo City to face San Antonio Fox Tech in a Saturday night showdown for the district lead. The Bateymen were at their best and rolled over the Buffaloes, 66–53, as Trammell and Santos combined for 47 points. Two days later, the Cats beat the red and blue San Antonio Thomas Jefferson Mustangs on the road in a defensive battle, 51–42. With alumni such as Tommy Nobis, Gabriel Rivera, and Kyle Rote, Jefferson had athletic pride unlike any other San Antonio high school. All of the games in Laredo were officiated by some of the best officials from San Antonio, and Batey rarely complained. He would always take pride in never having been ejected from a game.

Having dominated the first half of district, the Tigers were on a six-game winning streak. On January 21, in a warm-up for the second half of district, the Tigers took on the 2A district-leader Weslaco Panthers at the Tiger gym. Although Trammell sprained his ankle early in the game and was forced to watch from the bench, the Bengals raced to a 21–6 lead and never looked back, as Batey substituted with ease. Hernandez had 22 and Chacón contributed 13 as the Tigers prevailed, 59–48.

Now competing for the second half crown, the high-flying Cats took a tumble on January 27 and were upset at home by the Jefferson Mustangs in their first district loss, 54–66. The Mustangs stifled the Tigers with their height and their man-to-man defense. It did not help that the Cats were cold from outside, and shots that normally ripped the nets rolled off the rim. Once Jefferson got the lead, the Mustangs began stalling and it was all over. The mighty Tigers had fallen. Hundreds of disappointed fans walked out of the Martin gym in disbelief and silence, with their heads hung low.

In a fundraising effort on January 30, the Cats sat in the stands as the Martin High School coaches, including Batey as point guard, took on the traveling All-American Red Heads, the first professional women's basketball team in America. Dressed in colorful red-and-white-striped uniforms and wearing bright lipstick, the Red Heads raced up and down the court using men's rules. The women delighted the fans with their fancy dribbling, trick shots, expert ball handling and juggling, and they embarrassed the coaches, 44–40. The barnstorming women were not only taller; they were better. Some compared them to the Harlem Globetrotters.

The week after their depressing loss to Jefferson, the Cats rebounded in style and with championship flare when they unfeathered the Brownsville Eagles at the Martin gym, 65–54. At one time, the Tigers had a 38–8 lead on the poor-shooting birds from the Valley. Playing one of his best games to date, Dickinson had 19 points, while Trammell chipped in with 17. Santos's aggressive style won the ball several times, while Chacón came off the bench for 8 points. The Cats followed by clobbering Brackenridge in San Antonio. Ahead by only two points at halftime, the Bateymen put on a spurt in the final quarter that swept the Eagles away, 63–48, as Trammell hit for 21.

On February 7, students, parents, and Laredoans packed the Martin gym for the Tigers' final district home game against the hated Fox Tech Buffaloes. To wild cheers, Santos was unstoppable, hitting the nets for 22 points. The Tigers pulled away in the second half and downed the herd, 67–54. With Corpus Christi Miller Buccaneers leading the second half of district with a perfect record, it would come down to two final games in the bayside city against the W. B. Ray Texans and the Miller Buccaneers.

On Friday, February 10, using their lightning speed, rebounding, and superb ball handling skills, along with Santos's deadly right hand set shot, the Tigers jumped out to an 18-point lead over the Ray Texans. Playing in spurts and with a 12–1 run in the third period, the Cats took a 46–28 lead. It looked as if they would run the Texans out of the gym. But then Trammell fouled out in the third period and Hernandez in the fourth. The Texans pulled to within five points, with 1:30 left in the game, as the crowd got to their feet. At times tempers flared, and it appeared there might be fisticuffs at any moment.

When Dickinson was fouled with 53 seconds remaining, Coach Chip Guess of the Texans went wild and charged onto the court with a loud verbal tirade. He was tossed out of the

Before a packed crowd in the Martin gym on January 27, 1956, the Jefferson Mustangs won the opening tip as Willie Dickinson competes for the Tigers. Andy Santos and Phillip Trammel watch. The Mustangs upset the Cats, 54–66, although the Tigers had previously beaten Jefferson in San Antonio and would beat them again in a three-way playoff for the second half of district. (La Pitahaya, 1956)

Tiger seniors on the 1956 4A Texas state championship team pose before the opening game of the state tournament against Houston Milby. Left to right: Coach John Valls, Hector Chacón, Leonard Anderson, Ramiro Hernandez, Philip Trammell, Willie Dickinson, Andy Ramos, and Coach Bill Batey. (Courtesy of Andy Ramos)

game. Pressing hard against the Tiger stall, Ray pulled to within three as the crowd again jumped to their feet. Then the five-foot-nine-inch Chacón and the five-foot-seven-inch Molina, both coming off the bench, slipped in for layups, and the Cats held on for a crucial 63–56 win. Buccaneer fans were so agitated that the two officials had to be escorted to their dressing room. Ray tried to "run and shoot with the speedier Tigers . . . but couldn't match the Laredo speed," the *Corpus Christi Caller* reported. While carrying the rebound load, Dickinson had 17 points, Santos put in 15, and Trammell managed 11.

It would all come down to the Miller Buccaneers the next night. Located on Battling Buc Boulevard just south of what would become Martin Luther King Boulevard, the segregated Henry Pomeroy Miller High School was the oldest high school in the city and had long been the pride of Corpus Christi. On February 12, the largest audience to watch a high school game in the bayside city excitedly crowded into the Miller gym. From the opening tip, the game was close. In the first quarter and into the second, the lead went back and forth. Once the Cats held a five-point lead, but the Buccaneers surged back to go up by four.

"It was about as close as a game could be," Louis Anderson wrote in the *Corpus Christi Caller-Times*. In the second half, the game was tied six times and went down to the final emotional minutes. The Tigers "hit a huge percentage of their efforts and connected on what might easily be called phenomenal shots. The tougher the angle the easier the Tigers seemed to make the shots," Anderson continued. But Freddy Braselton, the long-armed and hustling Miller center and all-star, was able to match the Tigers goal-for-goal, and he kept the Bucs in the game. With two minutes remaining and the Cats up by four, Batey began stalling. With thirty seconds to go, Tommy DeSalme of the Bucs was called for a foul. When he angrily protested, he was hit with a technical. Tempers flared, both on and off the court. A few overzealous Buc fans charged the court and began cursing the San Antonio officials before

police escorted them out of the gym. When the final buzzer sounded, the Cats had prevailed, 63–59, and they had forced a three-way tie for the second half of district. Buccaneer fans were furious, and the two officials had to be escorted off the court by security.

To determine home court advantage and who would play first in the sudden-death playoffs, Batey met the Jefferson and Miller coaches at Alice, where he promptly lost two coin tosses. As a result, the Tigers were forced to face Jefferson on the road, while Miller rested in Corpus Christi. Since the Tigers had won the first half of district, a loss to Jefferson would still give the Cats a shot at the district crown, but Batey did not want to take any chances.

From the opening tip-off in the Alamo City three days later on February 14, the Tigers were all over the blue-and-gold Mustangs, a team they had lost to two weeks earlier by twelve points. At times it seemed as if the Cats were toying with the Mustangs, who were unable to slow the Tiger offense. At the end of the first quarter, the Cats were up 16–6. By halftime, they were leading 28–16. The Mustang defense was keyed to stopping Santos, but Dickinson broke loose for 21 points and Hernandez poured in 19. It was one of the most foul-free games of the year, as the Tiger starting five only committed five fouls during the entire game. Leading 46–28, Batey turned to his always-reliable bench. The Tigers won in a breeze, 69–43. As a result, the Mustangs were eliminated from the District 6-AAAA title race.

At the end of the game in San Antonio, Miller coach George Utterback and Batey met as Jefferson coach Harry Hamilton flipped a coin to determine who would have the home court advantage. Batey called the flip correctly this time, although the coin rolled across the gym floor before stopping. The Tigers had the consolation of knowing that the Buccaneers would have to beat them twice, but once again Batey did not want to risk a second game on the road. He was particularly worried about stopping Braselton, one of the best players the Tigers would face all year.

"The game tonight," Batey told the press before the game in Laredo two days later, will come down to the "team that wants the victory the most." On San Bernardo Avenue, more than an hour before the start of the game, there were long lines of students waiting to pay their forty cents, and adults their seventy-five cents. From the start of the game, the Cats were on fire, bombing from outside and making few mistakes. At halftime, they led 40–26. Anderson, who traveled to the border to cover the game for the *Corpus Christi Caller*, approached Miller's Coach Utterback at the half: "George, those guys can't keep hitting those fantastic shots from way out there, can they?" "Don't kid yourself," Utterback responded. "They can. I've been watching that for two years now. It's no accident." In the second half, the Cats held on for a 70–60 win, as Trammell hit for 20 points and Hernandez contributed 19. The Tigers were district champs for the second year in a row.

In the bi-district playoffs, the Tigers were forced to travel for ten hours, 575 miles north, all the way across the state, to take on the favored and much taller Wichita Falls High School Fighting Coyotes on the Red River. With facilities and resources of which the Tigers could only dream, Wichita Falls had long had one of the more successful athletic programs in the state. On February 22, 1,800 excited fans packed the Coyote field house on Coyote Boulevard. Wichita Falls started off like a house afire, rolling to an eight-point lead, 10–2. The Coyotes hit five of their first eight attempts from the field while the cold-shooting Tigers could only convert one of ten. After one quarter, the Coyotes led 18–14, and they held on for a 28–25 halftime lead. In the second half, Hernandez went wild from beyond the key. Willie Dickinson hit a critical fifteen-footer and added a free throw as the Cats surged to a 37–30 lead with 4:25 left in the third. Wichita Falls cut the lead to five, but that was the last time the Coyotes threatened. Trammell and the deadly shooting Hernandez pushed Laredo to a 45–36 advantage at the end of the period. With Hernandez and Santos continuing to hit crucial shots, the Cats jumped to a 52–38 lead with 5:30 remaining. At that point, Santos went into his ball-control act, and the game was over.

The "hot-shooting, ball-hawking" Tigers had roared from behind, Bud Worsham of the *Wichita Falls Record-News* wrote. "Laredo utilized some phenomenal long-distance shooting and a brilliant ball-control act by Andy Santos in the final five minutes," Worsham continued. For most of the game, the Coyotes refused to come out of their zone defense as the Bateymen dropped bombs from outside. Jim McKone of the *Corpus Christi Caller-Times* said the Coyotes' decision to stay in the zone "would go down in history as the worst mistake since armored cavalry let English long-bowmen shoot from outside." Called the "most accurate long-shooters in South Texas history," the Cats devoured the Coyotes with three men in double figures: Dickinson went for 21, Hernandez contributed 16, and Santos added 13. To a disappointed crowd of Coyotes, the Cats from the border had prevailed, 61–50. It would be a long but joyous ride back to the border.

Two days later, 2,200 Tiger fans, 200 over capacity, filled every corner of a sweltering Martin gym, including the stage and end zones, to watch the Tigers and the Coyotes continue their bi-district showdown. The two teams exchanged leads, Martin taking a ten-point lead, only to watch it disappear as the Coyotes battled back. Tiger hopes turned sour when Dickinson fouled out with two minutes to go in the third, replaced by Chacón. All of a sudden, the Tigers began having problems with the Coyotes' big center, six-foot-four-inch Bob Meyers. With no shot clock, Batey went into his patented stall. With two seconds left in the third quarter, Santos let fly with a set shot from thirty-five feet that swished through the net, giving the Cats a 44–38 lead. Early in the fourth quarter, Santos managed to miss four consecutive one-and-one free throws, and the Coyotes pulled to within two. The gym fell silent. But then Leonard Anderson hit two free throws, and Trammell tipped in a rebound. Chacón added five free throws, and the agile Cats went on to win, 56–52. The Coyotes had outscored the Tigers from the field, 17–15, but the Cats sank 26 of 35 free throws. Trammell, Santos, and Dickinson combined for 43 of the Tigers' 56 points.

Worsham of the *Record-News* said that Santos was the best ball-handler and dribbler he had ever seen. Under Batey's guidance, he had stalled the ball for almost two minutes while Wichita Falls pressed and double-teamed him, but "Andy dribbled right through them." Moreover, that "dead-eye kid Hernandez" was "one of the best set shooters ever seen as he consistently hit shots from twenty feet," Worsham complained. "It was a team victory," an excited Coach Batey told the local press.

Around 11:00 p.m. on February 27, three days later, less than a week before the state tournament, a fire broke out in the band room in the northeast corner of the Tiger gym, destroying most of the room and ruining thousands of dollars' worth of musical instruments. A sizable part of the maple floor of the gym was ruined by the large volume of water the firefighters poured into the building. Fire Chief George Renken estimated the damage at $200,000. At first it was feared that the entire building would go up in flames. Renken told the press that it was one of the "stubbornest fires he had seen in Laredo in several years." As soon as the firemen thought they had the blaze under control, it would flare up again. In fact, it took the fire department five hours to control the fire. The Tigers were now forced to practice at the Boys Club on Montezuma Street.

With the Tigers heading to the state tournament, everyone in Laredo seemed ecstatic. KVOZ radio sponsored a dinner in honor of the victorious Cats at Golding's Restaurant on Santa Maria. Days later, Batey and Valls headed north in their Studebaker and Oldsmobile, leading a fifty- to sixty-car caravan of excited fans. Someone taped a sign on Valls's car that read, "State Champions, Laredo." Valls always suspected that the sign had something to do with him getting a ticket as the Tigers passed through San Antonio. After all, it was usually a team from the Alamo City that went to the state tournament.

The seventy-eight-member Martin Pep Squad and students in chartered buses were escorted by P.E. teacher Ruth Young and her friend, the popular science teacher Josephine Baird. Hundreds of Laredoans took their cars and trucks. Some bought tickets on the Greyhound bus. Two crowded "migrant trucks" loaded with standing and sitting fans also headed north. A Laredo policeman, David Solis, drove another truck to Austin loaded with excited fans. "People did not know where to go in Austin," Walter Herbeck would remember, "they just took off."

A local rancher learned that a San Antonio television station would be televising the game and by putting up a tall antenna he could get the reception, so he erected a large tent and invited friends and relatives. The state tournament had become more than a basketball game. It had become a crusade of happy and excited fans decked out in red and white.

With little money but plenty of enthusiasm, some Martin High School students hitchhiked all the way to Austin. Unable to afford a place to stay, they slept in the fields near the capital city or crowded into dorm rooms of friends at the University of Texas. Without Batey or Valls knowing about it, a few slipped into the rooms of players.

Batey and his Tigers worked out at Travis High School in South Austin. They put the finishing polish on his 2-1-2

Elaine Wright, Dora Gonzalez, Bobby Jo Parker, and Nora Gonzalez perform a cheer at Gregory Gym on the campus of the University of Texas at Austin prior to the Tiger championship game against North Dallas. Laredo fans include Ruth Young, Josephine Baird, Elena Ramirez, Ofelia Ibarra, David Soliz, Pablo Garza, Joe Duncan, and Antonio Garibay. Three students from the "Laredo Club at Texas University" display a sign in support of the Tigers. (Photo by José Limón. La Pitahaya, 1956.)

defense, which he would rely on most of the time at the state tourney, but also his 1-3-1 "wheel," as well as his fierce man-to-man, which he would use to press following Tiger baskets before falling back into a zone. The team also went through their half-court trap one last time. On offense, they worked on their out-of-bounds and set plays. Batey, Valls, and all of the players could not believe the number of telegrams and telephone calls that arrived in Austin from Laredo banks and businesses, elementary schools, the fire department, and even public officials such as Mayor J. C. "Pepe" Martin, all wishing the Cats prayers and good luck. One telegram said simply, "The eyes of Texas are upon you." J. W. Nixon asked Batey to call him on the telephone, "collect."

After winning their 3A bi-district, the hated Harlingen Cardinals also arrived in Austin at the same hotel as the Tigers. There was so much animosity between the two teams, the managers of the hotel placed the two teams on separate floors with two floors in between. The Tigers took joy in watching as the Cardinals lost to the Beaumont French Buffaloes, 58–47, and then the Marshall Mavericks in the consolation game, 54–51.

Few in Texas gave the boys from the border a chance. They were the shortest team in the tournament. Father George Gloeckner of Blessed Sacrament Church, who had always been on the Tiger bench and prayed with the Cats in the dressing room before every game, gave each player a "Queen of Victory" medal. The Tigers wore the medallions with great pride. They were seen making the sign of the cross before taking the floor following a time out, after each goal, and before every free throw. "Each boy is of very strong faith," Batey told the press. "They take their faith into the game with them."

In the first round, the Tigers faced a much larger Houston Charles H. Milby Buffaloes team that had been in the tournament the previous year. The Buffaloes confidently arrived in Austin with twenty-five consecutive wins, the longest winning streak in the state. They were the pride of Houston's East Side. Batey personally liked the coach at Milby, Hal Lambert, who had played at Rice and went on to coach at Spring Branch. Using their blinding speed and remarkable outside shooting, the blue-and-gold Milby team had easily pushed aside Port Arthur in the bi-district, 65–53. But Milby's title hopes went up in smoke. After four minutes against the Tigers, the outcome of the game was never in doubt. Except for a very brief 4–1 lead, the favored Milby trailed for the remainder of the game. At the end of the first quarter, the Tigers were on top, 20–12, and by halftime they led 39–25. Always with a towel in his hand, sometimes wiping his bald head, Batey was often animated, shouting at the players.

The highly touted Milby guard, speedy Frank "Red" Portilla, had 21 points, including a tournament record of seventeen free throws for the Buffaloes as the Houstonians tried to rally, but it was not enough. The outside shooting prowess of the quick and crafty Tigers was too much. The Laredo Cats "played with their foes a cat toys with a rat, teasing and tantalizing them,

clowning and befuddling them, and soon throwing them into utter confusion," one sports writer would say.

In the other half of the state tournament, the North Dallas Bulldogs, who pushed aside Fort Worth Poly in bi-district, defeated the best team from West Texas, Odessa High out of the Permian Basin, 81–60. The 81 points was a state Class 4A record at the time. The Bulldogs, like Milby, now had a twenty-five-game winning streak. Although the Cats had raced by Milby, few gave them a chance of getting by the Bulldogs.

After the Milby victory, the Laredo Club at the University of Texas invited all the Laredo fans to the Hamburger Pit on the Dallas highway to celebrate. The manager had agreed to close at 11:00 p.m. so the Laredo fans could celebrate. Father Gloeckner even got special permission from the bishop of the Diocese of Austin for the fans to eat meat on a Friday.

With anticipation and great excitement on the afternoon of the big game, March 3, the Tigers arrived at Gregory Gym. Andy Santos was heard to say, "Coach, let's get it done." Surprisingly, however, the Cats were refused entrance to the arena. Somehow, their credentials had been lost or misplaced. Batey beseeched those at the gate, and the security guards who arrived, that these were indeed the Martin High School Tigers and they were in the championship game. It was not until someone found Abraham "Chick" Kazen, and the congressman arrived to flash his credentials and vouch for the Tigers, that they were allowed to enter.

The Tigers would be playing before a capacity audience of 8,200, the largest they had ever seen. Spectators included hundreds of Laredo citizens, teachers, administrators, and politicians, and students waving red-and-white pom-poms. Students from the Laredo Club at the University of Texas brought a large sign that featured a Tiger jumping on the back of a small helpless Bulldog, which was frequently seen on TV cameras throughout the game. The Tigers took an early lead on a shot by Trammell and never let up against the pressing North Dallas man-to-man defense. The Bulldogs did tie the game at 2–2 and again at 4–4, but after that it was all Laredo. Alternating between a zone press and a man-to-man defense, the Tigers rocketed ahead and were up 17–10 at the end of the first quarter. With Hernandez deadly from the corners, the lead increased to 25–12 as Tigers fans went crazy.

From the beginning, there was little doubt which team the overflow crowd, including the largest Laredo delegation to ever visit Austin, was cheering for. A few in the stands had never been south of San Antonio, but they had come to cheer for the underdog. "They let it be known throughout the game, and it seemed to inspire the Tigers," Dick Moore of the Fort Worth Star-Telegram wrote. But there were those in the stands who represented another time and another era of Texas history, who were trapped on the wrong side of history. William Valls, brother of the assistant coach, recalled hearing chants of "Pancho! Pancho! How many tacos did you eat today?" John Valls remembered a cry of "Pancho, did you buy shoes today or are you still barefoot?" Many in the stands saw the game as

The 1956 4A State Champions. Front row (left to right): José Luis "Fofol" Novoa (manager), Guadalupe "Pitin" Guajardo, Enrique "Kike" Mejia Jr., Agustín "Calaca" Molina, Isidro "Chilo" Garcia, Ramiro Hernandez, and Jimmy Rodríguez. Back row: Cruz Alejandro Soto, Leonard Anderson, Aandres "Andy" Santos, Willie Dickinson, Philip Trammel, Hector Chacón, and Walter Herbeck (manager). (Photo by José Limón. La Pitahaya, 1956.)

a contest between a bunch of "little Mexicans from the border and some big Anglos."

With flashbulbs popping, the Bulldogs cut the lead to 32–26, but at the end of the third quarter, the Cats with their full-court press and fall-back zone, were up by seven. Many thought the outcome of the game was never in doubt, although with 1:49 remaining in the third period, North Dallas pulled to within a point at 39–38. Just when it seemed that the Tigers were fading and about to lose momentum, they uncorked their passing attack, which seemed to stun the Bulldogs, and Laredo built a 48–40 lead.

With their "faking, dribbling, rebounding, and lightning-like basketball passes that traveled nearly the length of the 95-foot court several times," the Tigers were too much for the stunned Bulldogs. The cold-shooting Bulldogs could never catch up. Protecting a six-point lead, Batey called time out and went into a stall. At this point, with the shot clock a thing of the future, the floor man Andy Santos took over. His stall and "circus dribbling antics brought the enthusiastic crowd to its feet with roars of approval," Virginia Lee Kazen wrote in the *Daily Texan*. Santos "had the Bulldogs stumbling and falling in futile efforts to grab the ball." Time and again, "Santos would dribble deep into the player congestion under

the basket only to back out again while his defenders fell all over themselves trying to get the ball." The "bull-like Andy Santos," another reporter wrote, "dribbled in and out of the futilely-grabbing Bulldogs" like Marques Haynes of the Harlem Globetrotters. One Bulldog became so frustrated chasing Santos that he began cursing and openly weeping. Batey had simply "outfoxed" the highly favored North Dallas Bulldogs by abandoning his legendary run-and-shoot offense for the "shoot-and-stall" the Tigers knew well.

When the Bulldogs finally began to press in earnest with 3:15 left, Santos couldn't be caught as he dribbled all over the court. The Bulldogs "couldn't catch Santos and they couldn't catch up," it was said. The Tigers zone defense, the same defense they had used against Milby, "choked and crowded" the Bulldogs' highly touted center like "seaweed" and held North Dallas to 29 percent shooting. The Bateymen ran off nine consecutive points that vanquished the Dallasites in a smashing upset, 65–54. Given little chance of advancing beyond bi-district or the first round of the tournament, the Tigers were state champions. As the final buzzer sounded, hundreds of fans, some of them not even from Laredo, rushed the court, lifting Batey and several of his players to their shoulders. The coach's pent-up emotions burst forth as he wept openly.

"Unheralded, unsung and apparently unworried by the prominence given their foes in the finals, the Tigers ran through and around the bigger but slower Bulldogs," Harold V. Batliff of the Associated Press wrote. A "bunch of talented outside shooters that no type of defense could seem to stop" now reigned as the Class 4A state champions. Jim McKone of the *Corpus Christi Caller* said that Batey simply "outsmarted the other coaches by making them play Laredo's game." When the Tigers "wanted to run-and-shoot, they did," and when they "chose to play ball-control, they did that, too." The Cats had whipped the heavily favored Bulldogs, soundly and with great drama.

"Fiery little Laredo, short on height, but long on courage, cut down a tall North Dallas Quintet . . . in one of the most resounding upsets in tourney history," Verne Boatner of the University of Texas *Daily Texan* reported. The Tiger "formula was simple: run-run-run and uncork those unbelievable long shots, and they had it down to perfection." North Dallas and their touted big man, six-foot-seven-inch Allen Harris, did not know how to cope with the speedy Tigers "who caught them flat-footed with their fast breaks and defied the law of averages by relying almost wholly on outside shooting."

The Austin media marveled at the boys from Laredo and referred to them as the "Rabbit Runners of the Border." The key to the Tigers' triumph, the *Austin American Statesman* wrote, was that the Cats had "turned in an exhibition of dribbling and ball handling that would have made the Harlem Globetrotters envious." At one point in the game, Santos stood at center court and dribbled the ball for thirty seconds without moving an inch. He "was the most colorful man on one of the most colorful teams to ever appear in the annual meet," the *Houston Post* pronounced.

For many in the audience, Santos seemed to hold the ball for half the game, and as long as he held it, "Laredo was the only team with a chance to score." Santos "literally dribbled circles around North Dallas." Once he "made a referee grin with respect by the way he kept using up all 10 seconds to take the ball across half-court. Santos would hop across the line just as the referee counted 'eight, nine, t....'" The sight of Santos confidentially dribbling down court would long be remembered by the excited audience. Andy's on-the-button long passes, one sports writer recorded, "started the fast breaks and demoralized North Dallas. One of his throws traveled an incredible 80 feet." But it was a team victory. Trammell, who scored 28 points, was lauded by the *Dallas Morning News* for his "uncanny shooting" and his ability to sink goals "from any and all angles." When asked how he made so many difficult shots from such a distance, Trammell mumbled bashfully, "Just lucky. I don't know how to tell you all this," he concluded, "I'm so excited." In two games, he scored forty-seven points and set a state record. Some went so far as to say that Trammell was the best player to have ever played in the state tournament.

Frequently firing away from beyond the key, Ramiro "Deadeye" Hernandez added seventeen points. More than once, he ripped the net with a thirty-five-foot set shot. The two

Andy Santos, one of the best multisport athletes Martin High School would ever produce, starred in not only basketball but also baseball and football. In his senior year, Santos was selected as the Athlete of the Year. He was also chosen as the Most Valuable Player in the 1956 4A State Basketball Tournament. Basketball scholarship offers arrived from such NCAA schools as Kansas and the University of Texas at Austin. (Courtesy of Andy Santos)

Laredo "jackrabbits," Anderson and Hernandez, who ran the fast break to perfection, explained to reporters after the game how "Batey had taught them so well." When he was asked how he sometimes beat everyone down court, Anderson said that it was just determination. "I break for their basket whenever they shoot at ours, like coach taught us," Hernandez added. Dickinson, who had twelve rebounds in the game, said that Batey had taught him how to rebound against players such as those at North Dallas who were as much as five inches taller. Both Milby and the North Dallas team had skilled players over six foot five, and each team had a player over six foot eight, but Dickinson's skill at positioning himself under the basket and blocking out had made a big difference.

But it was the ball-handling and dribbling of Andy Santos that thrilled the audience. It was Santos's leadership and dribbling, Hernandez's expert outside shooting, Trammell's overall offense and defense, plus Anderson and Dickinson, along with Hector Chacón, that had made the difference. Their ascendancy to the heights of Texas basketball was a miracle on the Texas hardwood. "They are all great," Batey excitedly proclaimed.

Praise came from sportswriters across the state. One of the first questions for many in Austin and throughout Texas was, "Where did this team come from?" Laredo's phenomenal Tigers, "a dedicated team of destiny with unbelievable speed, spirit, and skill, blasted the proud North Dallas Bulldogs," the *Waco Tribune* reported. "There's a song that goes 'hold that Tiger,' but North Dallas couldn't catch 'em here Saturday,"

*The Martin High School Tigers were heralded as champions across the state of Texas. Many could not believe the Tigers beat two teams that were heavy favorites, Houston Milby and North Dallas. (*Laredo Times, *March 4, 1956)*

the Fort Worth *Star-Telegram* added. "Laredo, striking with awesome accuracy from the outside, squelched the longest current winning streak in Texas high school basketball," the *Houston Post* announced. "Showing bewildering speed and court savvy, the poised Tigers of Coach Bill Batey," were to be applauded by the entire state. Laredo's Tigers "rising to their dizziest athletic heights of all time turned their unique brand of basketball" into a state championship, the *Austin American-Statesmen* recorded. Batey was the biggest name in Laredo since someone wrote a plaintive little ballad called "The Streets of Laredo."

Laredo, which had long been something of a "soft touch" in most sports, now had its state champions. "They acted like champions, played like champions, and, in fact, were champions," Louis Anderson wrote in the *Corpus Christi Caller-Times*, an article Mary Frances Batey proudly clipped for the family scrapbook. The most lightly regarded team in the tournament, "Laredo's gallant Tigers . . . with speed, determination, and uncanny outside shooting" had come from nowhere to "glory" and had brought Laredo "a championship no one ever dreamed about," Harold V. Ratliff wrote in the *San Antonio Express*.

For weeks and months after the conclusion of the 36th State Tournament, Neal Ellison wrote, "they'll be talking about an unheralded Laredo team which came up from the border to humiliate the Class AAAA favorites with a style of basketball like none the tourney had seen in old timers' memory." The "flashy Laredo" Tigers wasn't the most talented team in the tournament, but "veteran sideliners couldn't remember a more colorful one." The "all-Latin outfit was a team with a mission," Ellis continued. The team "combined ball control with a fast break, uncanny dribbling with sensational rebounding and clowning with prayer."

The *Laredo Journal*, the Martin High School newspaper, compared the Boys of '56 who were "immortal" to those who gathered in Philadelphia in the summer of 1776 to sign the Declaration of Independence. Trammell was selected to the All-State team and would go on to play in the Texas Coaches' North-South All-Star game. Santos was named the Most Valuable Player in the tournament, and the coaches at Martin High School selected him as Athlete of the Year, not only because of his basketball prowess, but also for his leadership as captain on the baseball and football teams. Trammell and Santos were unanimous selections for the all-district team, while Dickinson and Hernandez were named to the second team.

Arriving at the outskirts of Laredo on the day after the state championship, the Tigers were greeted by hundreds of excited fans in cars, honking horns and cheering. Led by a police escort and flashing lights down San Bernardo Avenue to the high school, the team was greeted by another 700 fans. There was a big parade down San Bernardo, with sirens blaring and Batey riding in a big convertible. There were cheerleaders and the Martin High School band (performing with borrowed instruments). Rarely had the city seen such joy.

Back in Laredo, the champion Tigers pose for the camera of José Limón with their championship trophy. Left to right: Coach John Valls, Hector Chacón, Phillip Trammell, Ramiro Hernandez, Leonard Anderson, Willie Dickinson, and Andy Santos. (Photo by José Limón. Courtesy of Andy Santos.)

In front of the post office on Jarvis Plaza, excited students and fans watch as Coach Batey receives the keys to a new 1957 red and cream Ford station wagon from Al King, president of the Laredo Quarterback Club. After the state championship, Batey was selected as the Texas High School Basketball Coach of the Year. (Photo by José Limon. La Pitahaya, *1956.)*

Bill Batey addresses a crowd of hundreds on Jarvis Plaza as well as thousands on KVOZ radio. Arthur W. Lang, a member of the Quarterback Club and a former NFL player who would go on to teach social science at Martin High School, stands on the far left. Seated (left to right): Principal J. P. St. John, Coach John Valls, LISD Board Member Joe Brand, and Mayor J. C. "Pepe" Martin. (Photo by José Limón. Courtesy of Armando Lopez.)

The state champions were treated to a number of banquets in Laredo. A bronze plaque was presented to Batey, Valls, and the Tigers to be placed in the Tiger gym. Front row (left to right): Fr. George Glockner and Pitin Guajardo (holding the trophy), Hector Chacon, Jimmy Rodriguez, Cruz Soto, Ramiro Hernandez, Bill Batey, John Valls, Jose Luis Novoa, and J. P. St. John. Back row: Philip Trammell, Willie Dickinson, Andy Ramos, Leonard Anderson, Walter Herbeck, and Agustin Molina. (Courtesy of Andy Ramos)

At a huge gathering on Jarvis Plaza in front of the post office, Mayor J. C. "Pepe" Martin presiding, Batey was presented with the keys to a new 1957 red and cream Ford station wagon by the president of the Quarterback Club, Al King. Assistant Coach Valls was given a gold watch. The mayor read a proclamation announcing "Bill Batey Day" in Laredo.

"I think I have the most wonderful job and the most wonderful boys to work with. Gosh. I just want to say thanks to everyone," Batey muttered, wiping away tears. Batey was without a doubt, Felix Garcia wrote in the *Laredo Times*, "the best coach in the state of Texas." He was also one of the best public relations coaches in memory, the "friendliest, most talkative and cooperative coach in town."

Players were cheered at an elaborate banquet sponsored by the Chamber of Commerce and the Laredo League of United Latin American Citizens (LULAC) Council in the Maya Room of the Hamilton Hotel. Along with Father Gloeckner, they all posed for a photograph holding their trophy high. They were also presented with a large bronze plaque to be installed in the Martin gym. Colonel Walter Kerbel, commanding Laredo Air Force Base and also a former coach and basketball player, spoke on the occasion. National LULAC president, Oscar M. Laurel, and Leslie Winch, vice-president of the Chamber, acted as co-chairs. Mayor J. C. Martin and County Judge Carlos Palacios, along with 200 Laredoans, were in attendance. The highlight of the evening came when Superintendent J. W. Nixon was introduced, and the audience got to their feet when it was announced that Batey had agreed to a new two-year contract. Then Batey was introduced, and again the banquet attendees were on their feet. The coach took time to praise his players. Trammell was the "outstanding point-maker." He was so good that several times during the course of the year, teams had been forced to double- and triple-team him, Batey said. Ramiro Hernandez was the "long-shot artist." Leonard Anderson was "a fast learner who did not make mistakes and was always determined to win." Willie Dickinson was the "important tall man" who was "rough with his elbows." Hector Chacón, one of the best sixth-man players in Texas, was the "star substitute," with his "pinch-hit" performances. Agustin Molina was another fine substitute who played outstanding defense. Cruz Soto, Isidro Garcia, and Jimmy Rodriguez were the "backbone of the reserves." Even the managers, Luis Novoa and Walter Herbeck, were singled out for praise.

A few days later, the Tigers were guests of honor at the Optimist Club. "The seed for this team was planted three years ago," Batey would say. "That was when these boys began their determination to become state champions." Even Fr. George Gloeckner honored the boys with a *carne asada* at Blessed Sacrament Church. Scholarship offers poured in from leading Texas universities such as SMU, Baylor, TCU, and UT. In all, Santos and Trammell received more than twenty offers.

The Bateymen were also guests of honor at the weekly meeting of the Lions Club where Joe Puig, member of the 1924 Tiger basketball team that had gone to the state tournament, introduced Batey. Superintendent J. W. Nixon, Principal R. P. St. John, and Father Gloeckner stood to applaud. Everyone in Laredo seemed to vie with one another to honor the victorious Tigers.

A week after winning the state crown, Batey drove his new station wagon to Dallas for the Sports Achievement Dinner, where he was honored by the Texas Sports Writers Association as High School Coach of the Year. At the banquet he rubbed shoulders with Bobby Morrow, Olympic hero and sprinter from San Benito and Abilene Christian, and Paul "Bear" Bryant of Texas A&M, who were also being honored. In addition, Batey was invited to Kingsville to speak to forty high school basketball coaches from South Texas at a Texas A&I University clinic. He was even interviewed for the head coaching position at Texas A&M.

On May 25 at 8:30 in the evening, the second largest graduating class in Martin High School history, including two National Merit Scholarship finalists, walked across the stage at Shirley Field. There was a sense of optimism and promise in the warm Laredo night as 308 seniors received their diplomas, including most of the victorious Tiger basketball team. The entire atmosphere at Martin High School and throughout the city had been changed. For the Boys of '56, it was a season they would never forget.

In 1975, the "Rabbit Runners of the Border," as they were called, along with Batey and Valls, were inducted into the Latin American International Sports Hall of Fame. They would hold the distinction of being the only Laredo team to even win a state championship. It was amazing, Mike Farias wrote in the *Laredo Morning Times,* "how twelve Mexican American

The "Coach of the Year" and his players ride triumphantly through the fabled streets of Laredo in celebration of their 1956 state championship. (Courtesy of Andy Santos)

players were able to live an American dream and turn it into reality." It was a miracle on the Texas hardwood.

Three years after his crowning state championship, rebuilding and working hard, Batey would take another Tiger team to the state tournament in 1959. With a 27–5 record, almost identical to that of 1955–56, Batey ran into the Austin McCallum at Alamo Stadium Gym in San Antonio as 2,000 fans made their way to the Alamo City to cheer their Tigers. Led by Cat star Chalo Molina with thirty points, the undersized Tigers upset the Knights in a thriller, 63–58. Proudly carrying the Laredo banner the next week, the Cats headed north to the state tournament but were ambushed by Dallas Jefferson, 53–35. Demoralized and with little energy, they were then embarrassed by a much larger Houston Milby in the consolation game, 35–85.

A real dilemma came in 1964 when Batey was offered a coaching job across town at the newly established Nixon High School, the second public high school in Laredo. Batey was reluctant to leave Martin, but Nixon was a new school, with a new gym and new challenges. He could not turn down an opportunity to guide and shape another group of young athletes.

"He wanted the challenge of a new school," Mary Frances said. The Bateys and their seven children lived in the Nixon district, and "if Bill stays at Martin," Mary Frances theorized, sons Bill and Bobby, both budding basketball stars, would have to play at Nixon, and "there would be problems at home." At Nixon, one of Batey's greatest thrills would be coaching his sons for three years. Billy, a gifted guard with uncanny ball handling and outside shooting abilities, went on to play at Tyler Community College.

After thirteen years with the green and gold, including several seasons of beating the cross-town rival Martin Tigers, Batey was fed up with the politics at Nixon and decided to move to the gulf coast to coach the Corpus Christi Tuloso-Midway Cherokee. There he would enjoy coaching black athletes for the first time. In 1980 he was lured across town to Flour Bluff High School, not far from the sandy beaches of Nueces Bay and Padre Island. In his seven years at Flour Bluff, Batey twice led the Hornets to the 4A State Tournament. In 1983, they ran into the red-hot Waxachie High School Indians and the team was pounded, 76–57. Returning to the state tournament with

the Hornets the following year, Batey beat Jacksonville, 46–43, in the first round, only to fall to Port Arthur Lincoln, 61–52, in the championship. After a brief retirement, Batey was lured back to the border to coach at United High School, a growing school on the north side of Laredo. There he coached the burnt orange Longhorns for five years. However, pacing the sidelines, he was never able to gain the magic he once felt at Martin. In 1991, Batey agreed to step down and work as assistant coach with the Longhorn girls, but much of the charm was gone. "You know," he would say later, "I was pushed out."

Desperate to get back into the gym, Batey applied to coach the Lady Panthers at United South High School, a new school in South Laredo. He listed his qualifications as "experience, passion, intelligence, enthusiasm, and knowledge." At the age of seventy-three in 1991, after forty-nine years in education, forty-two of those years coaching basketball, Laredo's "Mr. Basketball" decided to retire for good. Six years later in an interview with Dan McCarney of the *Laredo Morning Times,* he was still excited while discussing his long and distinguished career. "It's great to hear the name coach before my name," Batey said. "A coach is somebody who has a great responsibility, who has an opportunity to mold and blend a diverse personality in his athletes. This is both exciting and rewarding."

Well into his eighties, Coach Batey could not be kept out of the gym. When he was not watching basketball on TV or dancing the night away at the Elks Lodge, he was frequently seen quietly sitting in the stands at United High School, sometimes alone, perhaps dreaming of another time and another place. Many of the young people who crowded the stands had no idea who he was. Once he was introduced at a Texas A&M International University game, sitting calmly at courtside, unable to climb the stands. "You know," he would say after the game, "I could teach that TAMIU coach how to run the trap much better from that one-three-one of his."

At the age of ninety, William "Bill" Charles Batey Sr. died quietly on Thursday, March 13, 2014, at Veterans Hospital in Temple, Texas. During his lifetime, the tall, proud man with the bald head won more than 700 games and took five teams to the state tournament, two of those from Martin High School. Decades after his triumph with the Boys of '56, Batey was asked to recall his days at Martin High School. "Lordy! Lordy! What a time!" he said simply.

Chapter 30

Aldo and the Fall of the Old Party

Under a warm Laredo sun on March 11, 2008, Gaby Canizales, once the bantamweight-boxing champion of the world, stood on the steps of Blessed Sacrament Church with tears in his eyes. Hometown hero Canizales had driven all the way from Houston to stand among hundreds of Laredoans, rich and poor, as they said goodbye to The Honorable Aldo J. Tatangelo Jr., mayor of Laredo, who had died at the age of ninety-four.

"He's my friend," Canizales said, choking back his emotions, unable to speak further. Aldo Tatangelo had once told Canizales how he, too, had boxed as a young man in Rhode Island. As mayor of Laredo from 1978 to 1990, Aldo had ushered in an era of reform and modernization that dragged Laredo into the twentieth century, although the twenty-first century was little more than two decades away.

Aldo "was very compassionate, and his heart was with the people of Laredo, especially those who were economically disadvantaged," one former councilman recalled. The mayor was honest, progressive, and his "heart was as big as his colorful personality," another mourner remembered.

"He set Laredo free and changed how people thought," Aldo's son, Aldo Jr., told Tricia Cortez of the *Laredo Morning Times*.

"There was something about Laredo that made Aldo feel that he belonged," Fernando Piñon would write in his *Patron Democracy*. "There was a lot of Italian in him, and perhaps it was his own ethnicity that drew him close to the people . . . There was his sense of family, of kinship, of community."

Aldo "really wanted to better Laredo," Mayor Betty Flores would say many years later, "he had good intentions and there was not a mean bone in his body."

Aldo was the second of five children born to Nicolo and Bettina Tatangelo in the rough Italian borough of Federal Hill, Providence, Rhode Island, on *diez y seis de septiembre*, 1913. Hoping for a better life for their children, the Tatangelos had immigrated to America three years earlier from the province of Frosinone, southeast of Rome. Aldo came of age on the rough cobblestone streets and in the tough outdoor food markets in what was called "Little Italy," rubbing shoulders with poor Irish laborers, recently arrived immigrants from southern Italy, and puritanical Yankees. Decades later, Aldo recalled the difficult days of the Great Depression and having once been shot at by a gang of Irish bootleggers. He dropped out of high school at sixteen to assist his father in the jewelry business. Then in 1943, at the height of World War II, he enlisted in the Navy. After the war, Aldo continued to work for his father while completing his high school education at night. After graduation, he enrolled at Bryant and Stratton College in Buffalo, New York, where he earned a degree in plastics engineering. With only $380 in his pocket, Aldo built a successful company of his own, Atlantic Optical Products. In time, the company would open factories in Mexico City; Havana, Cuba; and a maquiladora in Nuevo Laredo that employed 168 workers and produced 5,000 sunglasses per day. Aldo and his wife, the former Natalie Alice De Long, lived in Mexico City for five years, where they raised three children. It was here that Aldo learned his broken Spanish.

"I had always felt like a foreigner in Mexico," Aldo would say. "I liked the city, but I didn't think it was a place for my children to grow up." After selling his business in 1965, Aldo came north to Laredo, where he opened a wholesale business called Frontier Novelty on Lincoln Street.

Not long after arriving in Laredo, Aldo met Joseph Claude "Pepe" Martin Jr., the powerful and influential mayor of the city. Martin was head of the Independent Club, or *Partido Viejo* (Old Party) as it was known locally, that had dominated Laredo and Webb County politics for seven decades. Born on August 1, 1913, Pepe, as everyone knew him, was only a few months older than Aldo. In 1954, Hugh S. Cluck stepped down as mayor after twelve years. Pepe Martin was selected as the Independent Club candidate for mayor and was easily elected. Only months later, Pepe ably managed one of the greatest crises in the long history of the city when a devastating flood swept down the Rio Grande, destroying homes and sweeping away the pedestrian, car, and truck bridge, as well as the railroad bridge—the city's commercial lifeline to its sister city of Nuevo Laredo.

Martin proudly traced his ancestry back to Tómas Sánchez Barrera y de la Garza, founder of the rough frontier settlement of San Agustín de Laredo in 1755. In fact, Pepe was the eleventh member of his family to serve as either mayor or *alcalde*. Martin was also a millionaire several times over, having inherited a vast ranching empire that spread across 70,000 acres of South Texas brush land that provided abundant oil and gas revenues.

CBS News described Pepe Martin as rich, powerful, feudal, and politically unbeatable. He and the well-oiled political machine, the powerful Independent Club, controlled as many as 8,000 to 10,000 votes. Prominent politicians both in Austin and in Washington, D.C., including Lyndon B. Johnson and John F. Kennedy, sought Pepe's influence and the blessing of the Independent Club. His influence greatly eclipsed that of the more infamous Parr Machine in neighboring Duval County. In fact, it was the Independent Club's endorsement of Lyndon Johnson that made possible his "landslide" victory over Coke Stevenson for the U.S. Senate in 1948. Martin dispersed patronage on a grand scale, making decisions about which candidate would run for what office. The Old Party not only controlled the city and the county, but the Democratic Party as well. Even in the local district courts, grand jury commissioners were always loyal members of the Independent Club.

Before they were hired, prospective teachers who applied at the Laredo Independent School District first had to obtain Pepe's blessing. In advance of any election, teachers at Martin High School and the elementary schools in the city would gather and be told how they were expected to vote. The same was the case with city and county employees. In fact, every city and county employee was also responsible for ten relatives or individuals whom they would personally usher to the polls on Election Day to vote the Independent Club ticket.

The Traffic Captain of the Laredo Police Department, J. C. Davila, admitted to Fernando Piñon that he had achieved his position because of his association with the Old Party. "I do not deny this," Davila said. "The party has been good to me and I intend to continue working for the party . . . You have to learn how to play the game. You take care of the party and the party will take care of you."

Carmina Danini wrote in *Texas Monthly* that anyone who walked into Martin's City Hall office on Market Plaza was "likely to find an elderly woman capped in black *mantillas* pleading for help in paying the rent and the light bill." Older Laredoans recalled how Albert Martin, Pepe's uncle who was mayor during the depths of the Great Depression, would stand in Jarvis Plaza on Saturday mornings with rolls of coins and hand out dimes to long lines of children from the poorer neighborhoods so they could buy a bag of popcorn and attend an afternoon matinée.

"I know of my own knowledge that Pepe Martin has devoted from 10 to 14 hours a day to the affairs of his office. He is an untiring worker. He is gracious and courteous and never turns anyone away who has business with his office," State Senator Abraham Kazen Jr. told the local press during the 1956 mayoral campaign.

Simply put, Pepe "was a really good guy," one Laredoan recalled. "We were very poor and had no heating in our small house in the Guadalupe neighborhood. One winter when it was very cold, my father went to see Pepe, and the next day two trucks arrived loaded with mesquite wood. All Pepe asked was that we share the wood with our neighbors."

To many of Laredo's poor, Pepe was a saint straight from heaven, always there for those in need. When there was an illness, a family member would go to see Pepe, and the mayor would give them a voucher for their medical expenses.

If a family was out of food, Pepe would provide vouchers for a neighborhood grocery store. As the patrón, Pepe was everything to everybody. Judge Solomon J. Casseb Jr. recalled an elderly lady once calling the mayor on the telephone late one Saturday night, complaining that her toilet would not flush. Billy Cowart, the founding president of Texas A&I University at Laredo, said that the creation of a university at Laredo would not have been possible had it not been for Martin's far-reaching political influence. One scholar of border politics and economics, Elaine Peña, said that of all the politicians she has studied, Pepe Martin had to be the smartest. At an early age, even while he was attending high school at St. Edward's in Austin, Pepe was introduced to politics by his father, J. C. Martin Sr., who served as Webb County sheriff for many years. In 1936, in the pits of despair of the Great Depression, Martin became deputy tax-assessor collector, and in 1940, on the eve of World War II, he was named district clerk. Fluent in Spanish and active in the Community Chest, Boys Club, and Chamber of Commerce, J. C. Martin Jr. was elected mayor in 1954, inheriting the leadership of the Old Party.

In 1932, the Old Party's control over Laredo and Webb County was bitterly contested by the Progressive Peoples' Party known as *Partido de la Garra*, but the opposition failed to capture a single office. In 1939, William Prescott Allen, publisher of the *Laredo Daily Times,* launched a campaign against the Old Party, but he, too, got nowhere. It was not until after World War II that cracks began to appear in the armor of the Independent Club. In Old Party circles, there was little new blood and few new ideas. It was as if the century was passing the party and the city by. In 1956, the Reform Party launched a frontal attack on the Old Party, even establishing its own newspaper, the Laredo *Free Press,* to counter the Old Party's *Independent.* The Reform Party was supported by a few wealthy landowners and several World War II veterans. With A. W. "Lonnie" Gates as candidate for mayor, the reformers fell short by a two-to-one vote. Two years later, the Reform Party ran Guillermo "Memo" Benavides, a well-to-do rancher, against Martin. Once again, they were decisively defeated. Three years after that, however, reformers Norma Zúñiga Benavides, well-mannered and energetic wife of Guillermo Benavides, and George Byfield were elected to help guide the Laredo Independent School District. Benavides was the first woman elected to a citywide office. The reformers were unable to sustain their energy, however, and any kind of meaningful reform quickly abated as the Old Party again reigned supreme.

A decade later, in 1972, the Independent Club watched as a charismatic Alfonso "Poncho" De la Garza, best known in Laredo for his TV commercials of "un dolar nada más" while advertising furniture, was elected county commissioner. He defeated a dull Mario Novoa of the Independent Club. Two years later, Cruz Cabello, a forwarding agent, was inspired to challenge the Old Party candidate, Alberto J. de la Chica, for county commissioner of Precinct 4 in west Laredo. Cabello and a number of the old reformers sensed that the Old Party was not as invincible as previously perceived. Cabello bought thirty minutes of KGNS-TV prime time air and carefully arranged for himself and five of his supporters, including Aldo, to speak for five minutes apiece. Aldo went first and took up twenty-six of the allocated thirty minutes. In the Democratic primary, Cabello defeated de la Chica, and the Reformers smelled blood.

It was an exciting time in Laredo and South Texas political circles. *Brown vs. Board of Education of Topeka* was the law of the land, and *La Raza Unida* had started a political revolution in Crystal City and Manuel "Chaca" Ramirez was trying to start one in Laredo. In the governor's race, traditionally dominated by conservative Democrats, progressive Frances "Sissy" Farenthold, a former state representative from Corpus Christi, made it into the primary runoff against wealthy Uvalde banker and rancher Dolph Briscoe, the largest landowner in Webb County. Although many young people in Laredo rallied to Farenthold's support, the Independent Club endorsed Briscoe, and he easily prevailed in Laredo and statewide.

Not long after arriving in Laredo, Aldo became more and more interested in reforming what he perceived as the corruption-riddled municipal government. At first he had tried to avoid politics, as being involved in partisan politics, especially in opposition to the Old Party, was not good for business. But Aldo met and befriended Lawrence Berry, a lanky outsider who was convinced there was massive corruption in the Laredo Street Department run by an Old Party stalwart, Pepe Martin's right-hand man, José R. "Pepe" Rodríguez. A drifter by nature, Lawrence Berry had hitchhiked from Canada to Florida and somehow made his way to the Texas-Mexico border. He married a local woman, worked at Laredo Junior College as a maintenance supervisor, ran a print shop for a while, and repaired lawnmowers. Frequently when he was unemployed, a reporter would remember, Judson Twiss, a reform-minded businessman with an intense disliking for the Old Party, would give Berry "living expenses" to keep him around and "digging up the skeletons." Berry became notorious for getting under the skin of councilmen who, in their anger, sometimes invited him to step outside to settle matters with fisticuffs. Obnoxious, uneducated, ego-driven but tenacious, and clearly enjoying his role as provocateur, Berry consistently told voters that there was more to Laredo politics than barbecue and beer.

"Do you like living in all this filth and garbage?" he would shout out. Berry told anyone who would listen that since Laredo was so corrupt, it would be more appropriate for the Society of Martha Washington to celebrate a bandit than to dress their debutantes in dresses costing thousands of dollars for a Colonial Ball, flaunting their wealth in a parade down San Bernardo Avenue before a populace that was dirt poor. At City Council meetings, Berry consistently asked Mayor Martin to resign, while demanding a more democratic form of government.

"Laredo will never be the same again because I am here," Berry proudly told CBS News. Hoping to bring more transparency to the city and county, Berry, Aldo, Joe

Poverty plagued Laredo well into the twenty-first century. Manuel "Chaca" Ramirez snapped this striking photograph in 1973 in his El Cuatro neighborhood. (Photo by Manuel Ramirez. Courtesy Benson Latin American Collection, University of Texas at Austin.)

In 1974, Cruz Cabello (seated right in center) was elected county commissioner in Precinct One by defeating the Old Party candidate, Alberto de la Chica. Several nephews and party activists, along with children from the El Cuatro *neighborhood, look on. (Photo by Manuel Ramirez. Courtesy Benson Latin American Collection, University of Texas at Austin.)*

Guerra, Cruz Cabello, Margarito Flores, Judson Twiss, and a few others formed an organization called TOPS (Taxpayers Organized for Public Service) that was modeled after COPS, a similar organization in San Antonio. Almost every morning, the reformers would meet at a restaurant, El Aguila, for coffee and to strategize.

While Berry was abrasive and confrontational, Aldo could be mild-mannered and cooperative. Yet Aldo, too, was stubborn and resolute at times, and he began to take politics seriously. He managed to nudge his way into neighborhood meetings, where he dominated the agenda and droned on in his sometimes-incomprehensible Spanish for hours. As a businessman, Aldo was selected to chair a beautification committee at the Chamber of Commerce, where he and Pepe proudly posed together for the local newspaper. Aldo was active in the Boy Scouts, Little League baseball, and was also a regular and devout worshiper at Mother Cabrini Church, where he was lured into the anti-abortion crusade. Named president of the Laredo chapter of the American Cancer Society, chairman of the local American Red Cross, as well as president of the Webb County Association for Retarded Children, Aldo was becoming well known. LULAC (League of United Latin American Citizens) gave Aldo an award, and the Optimist Club named him "Man of the Year."

In 1978 Laredo had a population of 80,000, one half of whom lived below the poverty level. One in three received food stamps. Unemployment was known to reach 26 percent. Many of the poor lived in less-than-ideal conditions, on unpaved streets, and corruption in the city and county abounded. Millions of gallons of raw sewage every day emptied into the once-pristine Rio Grande from both sides of the river, and no one seemed to care. Local physicians urged fishermen not to consume fish from the river or even Falcon Reservoir. Many realized there was corruption in the city and county, but they were either dependent on the Old Party for their livelihoods or felt helpless.

One idea dominated Aldo's thoughts: At every opportunity, he urged Pepe Martin and the City Council to pave the streets. Aldo correctly calculated there were 3,400 city blocks that were unpaved. When there were months without rain, vehicles would stir up so much dust that a dark gray cloud hung over the city for days. In the neighborhoods, people hurried outdoors in the early morning to water the street in front of their houses in an attempt to tamp down the dust. Physicians told Aldo that the rate of emphysema in Laredo was several times the state and national averages because there was so much dust in the air. Aldo even offered to donate $6,500 of his own money to purchase paving equipment for the city. In March 1974, he carefully drafted a letter to Mayor Martin and the City Council calling for a comprehensive paving plan and the creation of a Public Works Department to replace Rodríguez's corrupt Laredo Street Department. Aldo argued that a $5 million bond would pave 776 blocks, complete with curbs and drainage, but Pepe and the City Council countered that property taxes were already too high and turned a deaf ear to his request.

Continuing his argument, Aldo offered data from the street commissioner in Cranston, Rhode Island, showing how streets that could carry thirty-ton trucks could be constructed with a foot of gravel and three inches of asphalt, 30 feet wide by 210 feet long, complete with curbs, for $2.70 per square yard or $2,400 per block. For the next several years, paving the streets became Aldo's relentless mantra.

A growing number of angry citizens joined Aldo and Lawrence Berry as they appeared at every Laredo City Council meeting to hound Martin and his aldermen. Berry was always the abrasive, sometimes-insulting newcomer, demanding that Pepe resign, while Aldo acted as the diplomatic "good cop." Although Martin argued that paving the streets was not a priority, he did agree to an experimental program that would pave six streets in the Guadalupe neighborhood. At last, Aldo felt that he had his foot in the door. But Martin appeared on KGNS News to say that street paving was not a priority, and that it would not be on the City Council agenda in the foreseeable future. Moreover, Pepe said that he did not think it was a good idea for the city to get into "the street paving business."

But Aldo and Berry and their followers refused to give up. Aldo appeared at the City Council meeting three months later with a longer and more detailed outline of how he thought the Laredo Street Department should be reorganized to function in an "efficient and well-organized manner," including the hiring of a competent director, assistant director, and professional engineer, all with no conflict of interest. Adding that he was motivated as a good citizen to "contribute something constructive to the community," Aldo was always present at the City Council chambers at City Hall, asking question after question: How exactly was money from the Community Action Agency to be used? Why wasn't a comprehensive plan for paving the streets being considered, as he had recommended? Would storm drainage be included?

Street paving was a "topic of great concern to the residents of Laredo," he argued. "I would go to the City Council meetings and nobody would pay attention to me. I said, 'Maybe I should be inside, instead of outside looking in,'" Aldo finally concluded.

By the spring of 1975, Aldo was becoming better organized and more assertive. A group of reformers including Margarito Flores, Alfonso "Poncho" de la Garza, Angel R. Laurel, Cruz Cabello, Joe M. Guerra, and Judson Twiss wrote a letter to Martin, recommending Aldo as a member of the South Texas Development Council. Aldo was "a civic-minded businessman" and an "independent thinker," the six wrote. But again, the City Council paid little heed to anything that did not originate with Pepe Martin.

Finally in 1978, Aldo announced that he would be a candidate for mayor. He drew up a fifteen-point program that called for the complete reorganization of the Street Department, establishment of a department of Parks and Recreation, creation of a pension system for city employees, plans for amending the antiquated city charter, regular City Council meetings, more low income housing, public works for migrant workers during the months they were unemployed, dependable water and sewage, and an all-out effort to preserve the city's treasured historic sites.

"The city must commit itself to the preservation of sites and homes and work closely with the Historical Society making available money and public works department equipment and assistance," Aldo wrote. Somewhat of a utopian dreamer, Aldo concluded that property owners who were unable to pay their taxes should be "given jobs instead of delinquency notices." For youth and the unemployed, Aldo wanted more technical-vocational programs at Laredo Junior College and in the Laredo Independent School District. But most important of all, Aldo would implement a comprehensive long-range paving program that would pave the dusty streets of the border city.

As Aldo was marshaling his small band of supporters for a campaign in which he was certain to be the underdog

Gloria Murray prepares to speak at one of the many rallies Aldo Tatangelo held in Laredo during his race for mayor in 1978. Murray previously worked with Aldo and Mayor J. C. "Pepe" Martin in an effort to clean and beautify Laredo. (Tatangelo Collection, Special Collections and Archives, TAMIU)

Aldo Tatangelo addresses a gathering just east of IH-35 in his mayoral campaign in 1978. (Special Collections and Archives, TAMIU)

Aldo Tatangelo poses outside his campaign headquarters with family and friends during his campaign for mayor, 1978. (Special Collections and Archives, TAMIU)

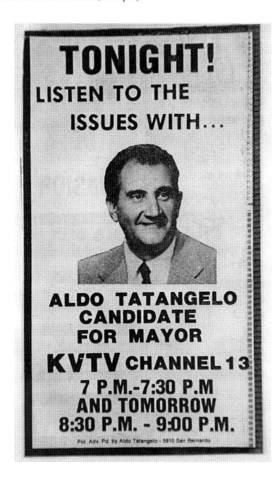

With much of his own money and hundreds of excited reformists by his side during his race for mayor in 1978, Aldo mounted an effective campaign that included buying considerable media time. (Laredo Times, March 30, 1978)

against Pepe Martin, Lawrence Berry and TOPS scored a major victory in their investigation of Pepe Rodríguez's Street Department. A close scrutiny of the records indicated the department was spending a third of its annual budget to repair and maintain eighty-seven vehicles. Moreover, an audit revealed that during a four-month period, the Street Department had purchased 115 radiators, at a cost of $340 each. In the previous fifteen months, 906 batteries had also been purchased for eighty-seven vehicles, many of them inoperable. More than $10,000 was spent for engine repairs.

Aldo and TOPS estimated the Street Department, riddled with kickbacks and bribery, was squandering $1.2 million per year, and that was only the tip of the iceberg. In a meticulous examination of the records, Berry continued to uncover massive corruption. The Street Department was spending $250,000 a year for oil and gas for its vehicles, while McAllen, a city of comparable size, was spending only $80,000. Most revealing of all was the discovery that the Street Department had several dozen "phantom workers." Some of them were Pepe Rodríguez's family members, receiving paychecks while working elsewhere or not working at all. Some received a full-time check for playing on the B-29 softball team that represented the bar Pepe Rodríguez owned near the railroad tracks off Market Street. Bill Bouldin, a crack reporter at the *Laredo Times* who had the instincts of a sharp-witted detective, discovered that many of the checks at the Street Department were going to longtime employees who, instead of getting a raise, simply got an additional paycheck made out to a relative. According to Bouldin, when Rodríguez's right-hand man who ran the day-to-day activities of the Street Department, Luis Guardiola, was unable to obtain a raise from the City Council, he simply put his wife on the payroll at $5,000 a year. The number of workers receiving checks at the Street Department, investigators discovered, doubled in the spring during the Democratic primary. On the next payday following the revelation of the corruption, with TOPS closely watching, fifty to seventy-five people did not show up to pick up their checks.

When KVOZ and the *Laredo News* first broke the story of the staggering expenditures at the Street Department, the City Council did nothing. But after weeks of prodding, angry questions, and accusations by Aldo, Berry, and others, the City Council agreed to an independent audit.

Luis Guardiola later told Bill Bouldin an incredible story of how he would act as a courier, taking envelopes of cash from Pepe Rodríguez to Martin every other week. According to what Guardiola told Bouldin, he would "deliver the envelopes to Martin via the little alcove that opened on the back door to the mayor's office in City Hall." Guardiola said, "Martin was always there at 5 p.m., waiting for the envelope." In fact, "that was the only time you could count on Martin being in his office." Guardiola said he "didn't know how much was in the envelopes, but he understood the amount varied depending on the mayor's needs."

Laredo's Municipal Court collected $157,000 in fines, while McAllen collected twice that amount. Laredo spent $413,000 on parks and recreation, while McAllen spent $293,000, with thirty-one organized programs to show for it. Laredo's civic center revealed an operating loss of $61,000; McAllen's civic center had a profit of $25,000. An additional loss of $47,000 was experienced by the Laredo Civic Center swimming pool. The Laredo Transportation Company, known by citizens for the excessive diesel exhaust fumes and old, run-down buses, was purchased from Martin for $160,000. Only six of twenty-six buses were in operation, and the city had spent $245,000 for maintenance. A local merchant spotted six county vehicles and employees at work on one of Martin's ranches.

Facing federal prosecution and reeling from more than one investigation of his corrupt Street Department, Pepe Martin announced that he would not seek reelection. With the collapse of the Old Party, forty-two candidates filed for city offices. In what was called a "Saturday night melee" on election night, 1978, hundreds crowded into the Abraham Kazen Student Center at Laredo Junior College to excitedly watch the election returns written on chalkboards.

With Pepe Martin presiding over the returns, someone asked him in a friendly way, "Well, Pepe, where do you go from here?"

"Probably to jail," he responded, half laughing.

"I don't know if Laredo is ready for democracy, but they sure got it," Martin told the press. "I just stayed too long," he continued.

With the local district attorney, Charlie Borchers, failing to take any action to help end the corruption, TOPS pressed Texas Attorney General John Hill for action, but Hill, a loyal Democrat, wasn't thrilled about prosecuting the leaders of the "last really productive political machine in the state," Bill Bouldin would write. Despite several pleas by members of TOPS, Hill maintained he could not enter the case unless asked to do so by Borchers. In May 1978, U.S. Attorney for the Southern District of Texas Tony Canales stepped in and empaneled a federal grand jury. A confidential source inside the grand jury revealed the details of their laborious workings to Bouldin. Among those testifying were twelve vaqueros Canales brought in from Martin's large Colorado Ranch. All of the vaqueros told how the City of Laredo had paid them every two weeks for twenty years. All had great respect for the mayor and spoke of him with reverence and awe. Each of the men could remember with great detail every time the mayor spoke to them and his exact words. According to Bouldin, the vaqueros related an amazing story of how, every spring and fall, they and their horses would be packed into gooseneck trailers and driven about a half-day's drive north, where they rounded up cattle on the prettiest ranch they had ever seen. There were rolling hills, lush grass, and a meandering stream. The vaqueros were never able to identify the stream, but Canales was sure they were talking about Lyndon Baines Johnson's ranch on the Pedernales River in the Hill Country.

At the time of the Street Department scandals, a photographer for the Laredo News *snapped this image of City of Laredo Street Department workers in a battered truck. Aldo clipped the image from the newspaper for a large album he and his wife were keeping at the time. (Aldo Tatangelo Papers, Special Collections and Archives, TAMIU)*

Despite most of the city financial records being stored in a private home or lost, the grand jury considered more than three hundred counts of mail fraud, but Martin's attorney, Roy Barrera Sr., successfully argued the number down to three and eventually one. Martin was finally indicted and plead guilty to a single count of mail fraud stemming from his sending a city check through the mail to pay for $250 worth of paint used to spruce up one of his ranches. At the *Laredo Times*, editors Jim Johnson and Bill Bouldin calculated that over the course of his administration, Martin stole as much as $12 million.

After considerable legal haggling, Martin entered a guilty plea before U.S. District Judge Reynaldo G. Garza—an old family friend—in Brownsville, and was sentenced to four years in prison. The sentence was later reduced to ninety days in the Webb County Jail and four years' probation. Garza also specified that Pepe not be quartered with the main jail population and that he be given a private room on the first floor near the dispensary. Webb County Sheriff Mario Santos was instructed that the sixty-five-year-old former mayor would require "extra-fine bedding with a board underneath." Pepe's physician also asked that he be given a salt-free diet. Some asserted the lenient sentence was laughable, further evidence of how the judicial system in South Texas was badly broken.

For thirty consecutive weekends, Martin served his sentence in a twenty-by-seven-foot cell at the Webb County Jail that his father had built. He reported there every Friday evening and returned home to his colonnaded colonial two-story mansion on Clark Boulevard every Sunday morning promptly at 8:00 a.m., as Judge Garza had directed. During his sentencing, Judge Garza "suggested" that Martin repay the city $200,000, a figure the FBI estimated Martin had taken in goods and services over the previous four years. Pepe would eventually pay a fine of $1,000 and compensate the city $201,118 in restitution.

Aldo proudly poses for the camera after becoming mayor following the election of 1978. (Aldo Tatangelo Papers, Special Collections and Archives, TAMIU)

Thus, $250 worth of paint brought down a dynasty that had dominated Laredo and Webb County for eighty-four years. There was little doubt that Pepe was the last of his breed. Carmina Danini, who covered Laredo politics as a reporter for the *Laredo News* at the time of Martin's fall, wrote in *Texas Monthly* that if Richard King was the first South Texas patrón, Pepe Martin was the last. Following investigations by a Webb County grand jury, the Texas Rangers, and the Texas attorney general's office, twenty-four of Martin's henchmen were indicted on charges that included theft and bribery.

But the Old Party died hard, and there were many who defended Pepe to the end. "Pepe Martin was no political boss and there was no political machine," Martin's brother-in-law, Honore Ligarde, vehemently argued. Although Pepe had helped Ligarde become state representative, Ligarde argued that it was "ridiculous to say he was 'el patrón.' There was no machine for him to boss." Pepe was tired, Ligarde went on to say. "He wanted out of politics, but his ego wouldn't let him. He thought he was irreplaceable."

During the time Aldo was mayor, Pepe never refused to help when he was called on, Aldo would say. For more than twenty years, Aldo always called Pepe on his birthday, on August 1, to wish him well. "I respected him," and "he had respect for me," Aldo remembers. "You were the cause of my fall," Pepe once tersely told Aldo, however. "No, you are the cause of your fall," Aldo remembered saying. With a kind heart yet nerves of steel, Pepe's wife, Anita, never spoke to Aldo after 1978.

Joseph Claude "Pepe" Martin, the last of the old-time South Texas patrones, died at the age of eighty-five in a San Antonio hospital on November 11, 1998. After High Mass at St. Augustine Cathedral and as hundreds watched, he was laid to rest in the Calvary Catholic Cemetery, not far from the remains of several prominent ancestors who had reigned over the city and county with an iron fist for almost a century.

In a six-candidate, nonpartisan scramble for mayor in 1978, Aldo claimed that he visited 10,100 homes, shook thousands of hands, attended countless *pachangas*, and lost twenty-five pounds. On election night, the sixty-five-year-old son of a struggling Italian immigrant who was a political oddity, an anachronism, a man born in distant Rhode Island, who spoke broken Spanish and bad English, was easily elected mayor of Laredo, besting his five opponents without a runoff. Riding the flood crest of popular indignation, Aldo received 9,748 votes, while his nearest competitor, Oscar Laurel, backed by remnants of the Old Party, received 4,833 votes. For the first time in anyone's memory, David McLemore of the *San Antonio Express News* recorded, "the people went to the ballot box and voted in the mayor of their choice, not someone selected for them." Pepe Martin's twenty-four-year reign had ended in a calamity.

Aldo's election was "a new beginning . . . with new ideas, new things to do. The rest, as you know, is history," one observer wrote. Aldo clearly represented the "chief catalyst to the destruction of one of the last genuine political machines in the area." Pepe admitted that he had been in office too long, that the "city grew from under us." Aldo, Berry, and their followers had not only brought down a mayor; they had brought down a system.

As expected, Aldo's first priority as mayor was paving the streets. He immediately drew up specifications for the paving of 400 blocks. One of the first things Aldo did was to call the mayor of Cranston, Rhode Island, for advice. Just south of Providence on the Pawtuxet River, Cranston was comparable in size to Laredo. It had all its streets paved, and a $1 million budget. Laredo had a $3 million budget, and 150 miles or at least 75 percent of its streets remained unpaved. Cranston also had to earmark funds for snow removal. Aldo borrowed Carmino Pupolo from Rhode Island to revamp the Street Department. Sixty-one years old and grandfather of six, Pupolo worked as director of Johnston's Public Works for more than a decade. He and Aldo had grown up together on Federal Hill in Providence, and they trusted one another. From the beginning, Pupolo realized that to pave 150 miles of dirt streets would be a formidable task, while he also struggled to streamline the garbage collection in the city. Not only was there no paving equipment, but also many of the trucks and vehicles were inoperable.

"Everything was in shambles," he recalled. With the "phantom workers" from the Old Party no longer on the books, Pupolo was able to reduce the number of employees in the new Department of Public Works from 297 to 204. Yet, he was also able to restore morale in the department. With new equipment, a street a day was either paved or resurfaced. But the cost of Aldo's paving program quickly outpaced the city budget. Not wanting to call for a bond election, the mayor gained national attention by resorting to simply selling streets that were infrequently used or ones that were a dead end. A 50 percent drop in the Mexican peso, which caused hundreds of downtown businesses to fail, as well as a decline in bridge revenues did not help city coffers either.

During his first year in office, Aldo and the City Council scheduled meetings three or four days a week in the city's fourteen *barrios*. Sometimes the meetings would go on for hours as residents complained of everything conceivable. Grassroots democracy had come to Laredo.

From the beginning, Aldo realized (as he had recommended to Pepe Martin) that the city badly needed an Engineering Department. Aldo recruited a talented Laredoan, Carlos Mejia, who left his job in California to head the department. Other departments went through dramatic changes. The Police Department went from 89 officers to 143 in four years. At the same time, Aldo worked at beautification of the city, a long-held passion of his. Hundreds of junk cars were removed from public property, as were thousands of abandoned tires.

Aldo also worked to modernize the Azteca neighborhood, just east of downtown. In blistering heat, he walked Zacate Creek from the Market Street Bridge to the Rio Grande and was shocked at what he saw. The rocky, picturesque creek ran through the heart of the city from north to south, and it had been used as a garbage dump for more than one hundred years. Not only was household trash dumped into the creek, but also rotting abandoned tires and raw, putrid sewage that flowed into the Rio Grande. Numerous rodents were spotted, and Aldo heard that there was an alligator in the creek. With the assistance of Congressman Abraham "Chick" Kazen, the city was able to obtain a $3 million grant in conjunction with the Army Corps of Engineers to clean the creek and remove tons of garbage.

Every day Nuevo Laredo unleashed twenty-seven million gallons of raw sewage into the Rio Grande, some of it entering the river near the international bridge. It took him four years, but Aldo was finally able to broker a deal with the governor of Texas, Bill Clements, to help fund a multimillion-dollar treatment plant for the sister city.

Streets in northern Laredo were widened. An onion field just east of the interstate became one of the largest malls in South Texas, and nearby pastureland was turned into a lively middle-class neighborhood called Hillside. Aldo would laugh when recalling how a pastor on Calton Road refused to give up property in front of his church so the road could be widened to four lanes. Aldo asked the pastor if God really cared if parishioners entered the church through the front door or the back door.

When two Laredo firefighters, Gregorio Lerma and Armando Peña Jr., died heroically in a raging wildfire on the campus of Laredo Junior College, Aldo wrote personal checks to each of their families for $250. Large earthen pits in the Ladrillera neighborhood in west Laredo that had been used to extract earth for bricks in the late nineteenth and twentieth centuries were filled and turned into playgrounds. Aldo loved boxing, and he became close friends with Gaby and Orlando Canizales, bantamweight world champions. Aldo had an old fire station on Guadalupe Street converted into a boxing gym and named for the Canizales brothers. The mayor also loved baseball, and he and the mayor of Nuevo Laredo could frequently be seen together watching the sister cities' beloved *Tecolotes*. The mayor also led a delegation to Taiwan, where Tainan Shen, along with Nuevo Laredo and Laredo, Spain, was proclaimed as a sister city.

Aldo "threw the doors wide open to a formerly closed, cliquish and stuffy city government many said provided minimal municipal services to its people," Tricia Cortez would write in the *Laredo Morning Times*.

Aldo once bragged to a civic group about a recent trip he had made to Washington, D.C., and his visit to the White House. Before meeting with President Ronald Reagan in the Oval Office, Reagan's assistants told the mayor that the president's schedule was crowded, but they had arranged for ten minutes but no more.

"I just took thirty minutes, and I told him all about our problems here on the border," Aldo bragged to the civic leaders, "and when I was finished, I went up to the president and I gave him my card and I said, 'Mr. President, don't you forget us down there on the border.'"

"Aldo, I will never forget you," Reagan announced.

When a high-ranking official from Washington came to Laredo, Aldo introduced him at a formal luncheon at La Posada, with no malice or intended racism whatsoever, as "the Chinaman from Washington."

Aldo "had notorious one-liners and of course was famous for always saying 'Youse guys,'" Odie Arambula remembered. Laredoans from all political stripes cheered Aldo when he threw his weight behind building a third bridge, which Aldo, in his Italian accent, referred to as a "turd" bridge. He once called one of the history professors at the university to say that he wanted to do "something for 'de Yute.'" Puzzled that Aldo would be bringing Ute Indians for the traditional George Washington Birthday celebration from Utah or Colorado, the professor inquired further, only to learn that Aldo was deeply concerned about the future of "the youth" of Laredo. They needed more recreational facilities that would keep them off the streets, he said.

Aldo often joked about being trilingual, but Elmer Buckley, the mayor's trusted lieutenant, confessed that Tatangelo "couldn't speak good Italian, or good Spanish or good English, but he had heart, and everybody understood what he was saying and trying to do."

Webb County had always been among the bluest of the blue counties. Aldo voted in Democratic primaries and called himself a Democrat. In reality, he was a closet Republican, as

Aldo and the City Council following the municipal elections of 1982. One member of the council, Saul Ramirez, would succeed Aldo as mayor in 1990. Two members of the council would go on to serve on the Board of Education of the Laredo Independent School District. Andy Ramos Jr. would become county judge. One member would become a county commissioner and then go to jail. (Aldo Tatangelo Papers, Special Collections and Archives, TAMIU)

were many of his closest advisors. He donated money to the campaigns of John Tower and Bill Clements, as well as George Herbert Walker Bush and George W. Bush. When Ronald Reagan died in 2004, Aldo wept like a baby and gave $750 to the Republican National Committee. Although he pursued what was perceived by many as a progressive agenda, Aldo remained deeply conservative in many ways. But the populace, especially in the city's several *barrios*, loved him.

In 1982, there was little doubt that Aldo would be easily reelected. He came up with a seventeen-point plan that would center on what he called "growth and development." At the center of his proposed program was, of course, paving and then more paving. Plans also called for more sidewalks, especially in the vicinity of schools and churches. At the same time, he continued to push for the beautification of Zacate Creek. In addition, he wanted more low-income housing and a plan to annex a middle-class northern subdivision called Del Mar Hills. Aldo was also pushing for a third bridge. Moreover, there were plans to increase the number of policemen and firemen in Laredo.

Seeking reelection in 1982, Aldo faced two formidable opponents: Mercurio Martínez and Alfonso "Poncho" De la Garza. Martínez had deep roots in the South Texas ranching and banking community, and he had been a popular business instructor at Laredo Junior College for a number of years. De la Garza was a sitting county commissioner, and he was popular in many of the *barrios*, especially in the southern part of the city, the same area of the city where Aldo had won overwhelmingly four years earlier. On Election Day, Martínez received the most votes but not the necessary 50 percent to avoid a runoff. Aldo was second, and De la Garza finished third. In the runoff, everyone expected Martínez to easily prevail, but at the last moment, De la Garza threw his support behind Aldo. On April 3, the incumbent prevailed by a vote of 7,322 to 6,279. Aldo thought his victory was due, in part, to the fact that Martínez was identified with the Independent Club and never repudiated their support.

"I think, all in all," Aldo told the local press, "the voters of Laredo have shown political maturity. Under the old party's administration, voters looked for help for their day-to-day needs. Now, I think they voted for the future."

Four years later, Aldo was reelected again. On the night of the city elections, several hundred supporters crowded into the Huisache Room at the Holiday Inn to watch the returns on television. It was evident early in the evening that Aldo would have a third term, trouncing his nearest opponent, Victor Solis, by a vote of 9,018 to 1,997.

"The people in Laredo have voted for what they want and what they want is good government," Aldo proudly said, amid chants of "5-to-1, 5-to-1."

At about 9:00 p.m., Solis "appeared briefly at the Civic Center election control center," Tom Pfeil of the *Laredo News* wrote, "glanced at the voter board totals, greeted supporters and left."

But in time, much of the excitement over the fall of the Old Party and Aldo's election abated, and a sense of smugness set in. Aldo grew bitter with the pace of events and with the apathy and complacency that seemed to settle over the city.

"Nobody comes to the office anymore," the mayor complained. "I simply do not understand the game," Aldo told Fernando Piñon of the *Laredo Times*. "There have been times when councilmen tell me something right to my face then do the opposite in public."

Aldo threw one councilman out of his office, telling him never to come back. At council meetings, he consistently told one alderman, Henry Treviño: "I am the mayor; you are just a councilman."

There were many times he thought about resigning. "This is a very lonely job," Aldo went on to say. "If things don't work out, I am going to go directly to the people. I will go to every *barrio*, talk before every group, and appeal to everyone."

One anonymous alderman complained to the *Laredo Times*: "Aldo only broadcasts. He doesn't receive. Tatangelo has become overly enamored with the power, political and economic, of elected officialdom."

Very "few people really understood him or his motives," Elmer Buckley, Aldo's aide and close friend, said. "They were always looking for a secondary motive or for something other than what he wasn't saying. But Aldo did not have ulterior motives, none whatsoever." As mayor, he demanded results, Buckley remembered, he "did not tolerate laziness."

At City Council meetings, Aldo completely dominated the conversation, and he frequently paid little heed to the opinions of the council. Frequently, the chaotic meetings would last well past midnight.

Frustrated when others failed to agree with what he wanted, Aldo would refer to anyone who opposed him as "crooks, tibes, and tings [crooks, thieves, and things]." Other times, they were "mental retards."

"He calls us names," one councilman complained.

Moreover, the mayor seemed to talk endlessly, without recognizing members of the council. With no knowledge of parliamentary procedure, council meetings were more of a prolonged Tatangelo lecture or tirade. When complaints continued, Aldo agreed that a local history professor, Rex Ball, could be appointed as the official parliamentarian. Ball first learned of his appointment by reading the *Laredo Times*. He met personally with the mayor and members of the council to brief them on *Robert's Rules of Order*.

"I can't do dat," was Aldo's initial response.

Ball said the first meeting he attended was the "worst meeting I ever had anything to do with."

In one instance, a councilman blurted out "point of order" with the mayor responding: "I can do anything I want." Years later, Ball would remember Aldo as "a really nice man who was good for the city and the people, although there were times I thought he would drive me crazy."

When Aldo took office, he inherited a city charter that gave the mayor most of the power. A large committee of citizens, headed by Arturo Nava of Laredo Junior College, was authorized to draft a new city charter. The new charter was approved in a referendum and would take effect with the municipal elections in the spring of 1982. The office of the mayor was made largely ceremonial, and an eight-member City Council was to be elected by districts. A professional manager was authorized to handle the day-to-day activities of the city. Moreover, by the new charter, mayoral terms were limited, and Aldo could not seek reelection in 1990.

Unable to stay away from the cauldron of local politics, however, Aldo threw his hat into the ring as a write-in candidate against Mercurio Martínez for Webb County Judge. Martínez had served on the City Council when Aldo was first elected and had run unsuccessfully against him for mayor in 1982. Although Aldo made a strong showing for a write-in candidate, Martínez prevailed, with nearly 75 percent of the vote. It was the end of Aldo's political career.

Aldo had open-heart surgery in 1998 that slowed his civic and political activities. "I still have many ideas, but physically the doctors don't want me to get too involved," Aldo said.

"I miss . . . being able to sit down and trying to figure out problems," he told a local newspaper. He did come out in opposition to the construction of a large events center on Bob Bullock Expressway in northeast Laredo, arguing that it should be built at a downtown location to revitalize the central city. Two years later, he created a scholarship at Texas A&M International University and gave his papers to the university, including an oversized album wherein he and his wife had carefully saved all the articles relating to his career as mayor.

Aldo remained restless and missed the limelight of being mayor. In 1990 he suffered a massive heart attack, but survived. The following year, he established a $25,000 scholarship endowment at TAMIU. Worrying about his legacy, Aldo commissioned a biography by a well-known local editor, Fernando Piñon, entitled *Patrón Democracy*.

Aldo died on March 7, 2008, and was laid to rest in the Calvary Catholic Cemetery not far from where Pepe Martin had been buried a decade earlier. Two weeks later, the City Council voted to name the new City Hall in his honor, but the name change was never formalized, and most people continued to refer to the building as simply, "City Hall." He was honored with the "Aldo Tatangelo Parkway," a quiet, shaded area just off busy San Agustin Plaza in the heart of the old city.

Aldo would always be remembered, one councilman remarked, "for his unselfish contributions to the community for over thirty years, for his unwavering commitment to helping the poor and disadvantaged."

Andy Ramos, who was on the City Council when Aldo was mayor and who later became Webb County Judge, remembered Tatangelo as someone who "wanted everything done today." He was "always asking the City Council for support in getting projects done as fast as we could with the money we had available. He was very compassionate, and his heart was with the people of Laredo, especially those who were economically disadvantaged."

It did not matter "where you came from," Aldo's daughter Linda McKinney, would say. "If you were from the *barrio* or if you were a multimillionaire, he would treat you the same. He accepted everyone."

Perhaps Aldo's greatest joy was knowing that several children in Laredo were named after him. "There are a lot of little Aldos running around now," he said, beaming like a new grandfather.

Aldo Tatangelo had become, as Eppy Palacios Jr. wrote, an integral "part of Laredo's history."

Making their way home from Aldo's funeral on that warm spring day in 2008, the people of Laredo drove on paved streets.

Mourners carry the casket of Sgt. John B. Alexander from St. Agustín Church for burial in the Catholic Cemetery. Only weighing 105 pounds and standing five foot six, Alexander was a Laredo favorite. He was wounded in action on June 11, only five days after his regiment landed on Utah Beach on Normandy. After receiving the Purple Heart, he rejoined his regiment, only to be killed on July 23, 1944. A graduate of Laredo High School, Alexander received a law degree from Cumberland Law School in Lebanon, Tennessee, and was said to be a favorite in the Laredo Bar Association. Inducted into the army at Fort Sam Houston in San Antonio on March 2, 1942, Alexander was sent to Camp Barkeley for training before going on maneuvers with his division in Louisiana and the Mohave Desert in California. "John was a great American," Porfirio Flores, president of the local LULAC chapter where Alexander was an active member, said in a somber memorial service. "He was a loving son and a loyal friend." On the same day that the Alexander family received the news of the death of their son and brother, the Laredo Times reported that Sgt. Richard Leyendecker was missing in action after a bombing raid over central Europe. (Courtesy of Ricardo Alexander)

Chapter 31

Warriors, Artists, Reformers, and Sports Figures

After an overnight stay in Victoria, a visit to a CCC camp at Goliad, and a stop for coffee and doughnuts in Alice, First Lady Eleanor Roosevelt arrived to great excitement at the Plaza Hotel December 5, 1940. People lined the streets while the Martin High School band played "patriotic airs." City and county dignitaries, along with officers from Fort McIntosh and U.S. consular officials, waited in the lobby where young girls dressed in Chino Poblano costumes distributed gardenias. A marimba orchestra played in the background. In Laredo, a large friendly crowd and reporters scurrying for an interview, greeted the First Lady. Escorted by Mayor Hugh S. Cluck and members of the Pan American Round Table, along with city and county officials, the First Lady accepted an invitation to tour Nuevo Laredo, where the Mexican Consul, Efrain G. Dominguez, greeted her. The First Lady visited the new municipal building and a recently constructed swimming pool where youth from both sides of the border gathered during the long hot summers. Hundreds of people in the sister city lined the street to cheer the charming First Lady as she stopped frequently to greet and shake hands with small children. Shopping on Guerrero Street, Eleanor purchased some "delightful French perfume," a few pieces of Mexican silver jewelry, and an "Indian weaving." The First Lady came to the border to address the Pan American Round Table in a lecture entitled "Strengthening the Bonds of Friendship Between the Americas by Cultural Ties." Fighting Nazism and Fascism was becoming more and more important, she warned. Before a crowded high school auditorium, the First Lady proved to be a "charming, brilliant speaker," Mabel Cogley Wall wrote in the Laredo Times. "She is in every sense of the word, an outstanding Lady and a living example of Democracy." Leaving for San Antonio by car the next morning to catch a flight back to Washington, the First Lady was more convinced than ever that, "If we are to defend ourselves in this hemisphere and preserve our democracy, we must have unity in the Americas" that would come "only through the understanding of our various cultures." With the Japanese attack on Pearl Harbor exactly one year later, the United States was at war. (La Pitahaya, 1940)

Magdalena Carmen Frida Kahlo y Calderón poses for the camera of her friend, Lucienne Block, in Laredo during her visit to the United States in October 1932. Highly critical of the segregated facilities she found north of the Rio Grande, Kahlo later posed under a sign in Laredo that read "For Negroes," and referred to the United States as "Gringolandia." "It is like being in another world to see such outrageous medievalism!" Kahlo wrote when seeing the "White" and "Colored" signs north of the border. Considered one of Mexico's greatest artists, Kahlo was twenty-five at the time this photo was taken and was married to Diego Rivera, an equally famous Mexican artist. During their stormy marriage, the couple was often referred to as the Elephant and the Dove. Kahlo's surrealist art often depicted her personal tragedies, both physical and psychological. A dedicated communist and feminist, Kahlo was also bisexual and was known to have had an affair with Leon Trotsky. She died in Mexico City on July 13, 1954. A pre-Columbian urn holding her ashes is on display in her former home, La Casa Azul, in Coyoacán. (Courtesy of Benham Gallery)

McCarthyism, the Second Red Scare, was alive in Laredo during the Cold War, especially the 1950s and 1960s. In this photograph, Martin High School students proudly display their "Americanism." Teachers in the Laredo Independent School District, as well as county and city employees, were required to sign a loyalty oath affirming they did not belong to any of 168 organizations that were deemed to be subversive. A Martin High School football coach, known to players as the "Senator," consistently referred to Tiger opponents as communists. When the Mexican American Youth Organization (MAYO) staged a demonstration in front of Martin High School, students on the second floor came to the windows to shout obscenities and call the demonstrators communists. (La Pitahaya, 1956)

On November 9, 1917 (two days before the end of the war), near Pouilly, France, Pvt. David Barkley-Cantu volunteered to swim the frigid waters of the Meuse River under heavy enemy fire to gain a position behind enemy lines, in hopes of obtaining as much information as possible. "Having obtained his information, he again entered the water for his return, but before his goal was reached, he was seized with cramps and drowned," his Medal of Honor citation reads. For his heroism, the private also posthumously received the French Croix de Guerre and the Italian Croce Merito de Guerra. (Author collection)

In the fall of 1964, Mayor J. C. "Pepe" Martin and Anita Martin greet Lady Bird Johnson at a reception and rally at La Posada on San Agustín Plaza. Lady Bird was visiting Laredo during Lyndon Johnson's contest for president against Republican Barry Goldwater. On the left is Mary Alice Corrigan. Virginia Goodwin is on the far right. (Courtesy Laredo Chamber of Commerce)

Thomas Clulley, Laredo's famous "Whistling Cop," spent more than thirty years with the Laredo Police Department. It was said that Clulley (or Cluley) had a "nationwide following of friends who stopped to enjoy his imitation of bird songs while directing traffic on the streets of Laredo." Laredo's population of 59,350 indicates the photograph was taken in 1959 or 1960. (Author collection)

339

DRAFTEES-FOR THE- N

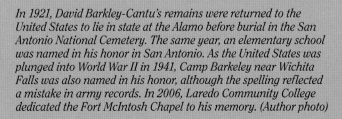

In 1921, David Barkley-Cantu's remains were returned to the United States to lie in state at the Alamo before burial in the San Antonio National Cemetery. The same year, an elementary school was named in his honor in San Antonio. As the United States was plunged into World War II in 1941, Camp Barkeley near Wichita Falls was also named in his honor, although the spelling reflected a mistake in army records. In 2006, Laredo Community College dedicated the Fort McIntosh Chapel to his memory. (Author photo)

By 2017, less than 5 percent of America's "Greatest Generation," veterans who survived both the privations of the Great Depression and the bloodletting of World War II, were still living. Even veterans of the Korean War and Vietnam War were passing fast. In World War II, 165 young men from Laredo lost their lives. Twenty-four died in World War I, twenty-two in the Korean War, and twenty-six in Vietnam. The ever-growing Veterans' Section of the City Cemetery is shown here. (Author photo)

MAY-25-1944

John B. Alexander, a sergeant in Company E of the 358th Regiment of the 90th Infantry Division, the "Bad Hombres" as they were known, was killed in action on July 23, 1944. His company was attempting to hold a small marshy island, the Island of the White Witches, in the Seves River near the small French village of Saint-Germain-sur-Sèves in Normandy, not far from the coast. Without air support and in bad weather, the Americans attacked against overwhelming odds and gained a foothold on the island on July 22, only to face a fierce counterattack by the elitist German 6th Parachutist Regiment. Driven back, the Americans lost 100 soldiers, with 400 wounded and 250 taken prisoner. The ferocious battle was the last successful action fought by the Germans in Normandy. A few days later, the Americans took the island and the village, and the race for Berlin began. Sergeant Alexander's regiment landed at Utah Beach on June 6 and fought their way ashore and through hedgerows, despite heavy casualties. (Courtesy of Ricardo Alexander)

Forty-nine Laredo draftees proudly pose for the camera of T. R. Esquivel as they prepare to board a bus for San Antonio on May 25, 1944. With the war raging in the Pacific, as well as in Europe, many of the young men in this image found themselves with the Marines on Peleliu, Iwo Jima, and Okinawa, as well as with the Army in the Hurtgen Forest, the Battle of the Bulge, and the race for Berlin. Several young men in this image did not return. (Courtesy of Jose E. Arredondo)

Born and raised in the El Cuatro neighborhood of Laredo, Manuel "Chaca" Ramirez studied photojournalism at the University of Texas at Austin and began his career in Laredo during the 1960s. Before his death, Ramirez donated 875 of his photographs and thousands of his slides to the Nettie Lee Benson Latin American Collection at the University of Texas. These unique images depict the Poor People's 1968 March on Washington, D.C., the striking contrast between poverty and luxury in Laredo in the 1970s, the Texas Farmworkers' March from the Lower Valley to Austin in 1977 to reform labor laws in Texas, several protests against police brutality, as well as examples of neighborhood activism. Ramirez also recorded the work of Mexican American artists Amado Maurillo Peña Jr. and Consuelo "Chelo" Gonzalez Amezcua. A recognized leader in the Chicano movement, Ramirez started an underground newspaper at Laredo Junior College called the Ground Up, and helped lead protests in Laredo that included a picketing of the Colonial Ball, demonstrations at Martin High School, and local restaurants that paid workers far below minimum wage. Ramirez entered a float in the annual George Washington Birthday Parade under the title "Children for Education" that turned out to be a protest against Mayor J. C. "Pete" Martin and Gov. John Connelly. In the latter years of his life, Ramirez turned his attention to the environmental movement in Austin and Laredo. (Courtesy of Richard Geissler)

Almost a century after his death, the city of Laredo finally honored its most decorated war hero, Pvt. David Bennes Barkley-Cantu, who had posthumously received the Medal of Honor. Born in Laredo on March 13, 1899, to Josef Barkley, a soldier at Fort McIntosh, and Antonia Cantu, Barkley was taken to San Antonio at an early age, only to be abandoned by his father and forced to drop out of school at the age of thirteen. Four years later, he enlisted in the U.S. Army and was assigned to the 89th Infantry Division, the "Rolling W," on the Western Front in France. Fearful of being removed from the army or relegated to a menial task because of his ethnicity, Barkley-Cantu cautioned his mother in her letters not to use her maiden name. Behind Barkley-Cantu's bronze statue is a granite wall bearing the names of all Latino recipients of the Medal of Honor. (Author photo)

A native of Laredo, Helen Richter Watson (1926–2003), daughter of Helen Richter and Horace Watson, was one of the community's most gifted artists. Educated at California's Scripps College, she won a fellowship from the Swedish government and later became chair of the Ceramics Department at the famed Otis Art Institute. A dedicated educator, Watson taught at the Los Angeles Art Museum, the Art Institute of Chicago, and Claremont McKenna College, while she exhibited and lectured nationally. Today her works dot the country in churches and private collections. (Special Collections and Archives, TAMIU)

Lady Bird Johnson addresses a political rally at La Posada in the fall of 1964, as city officials, dignitaries, and Golden Spurs from Nixon High School watch and cheer. Signs reading "Bienvenidos Lady Bird" and "Johnson, Humphrey, USA" are seen in the crowd. On Tuesday, November 3, 1964, Lyndon Johnson swept over his Republican opponent, Senator Barry Goldwater of Arizona. Johnson carried Texas with 63 percent of the vote and Webb County with more than 90 percent, and he won a nationwide mandate with 61 percent, the highest percentage of the popular vote since James Monroe's reelection in 1820. Johnson also won an Electoral College landslide, 486–52. (Courtesy Laredo Chamber of Commerce)

Graduate of Texas A&I University and a proud descendant of Tomás Sanchez, the founder of Laredo, Armando Garcia Hinojosa is one of Laredo's celebrated artists. He is best noted for his Tejano monument on the Austin state capitol grounds. The impressive bronze monument includes a Spanish explorer, a well-heeled hacendado *riding a stubby-legged mustang, a mother and father with their newborn infant, a boy with a strong-willed goat, a girl filling a water jug, and two longhorn cattle. Other Hinojosa works include a life-sized replica of Adm. Chester Nimitz at the entrance to Sea World in San Antonio, the nine-foot-high Double Eagle with a fourteen-foot wingspan at San Antonio's Six Flags Fiesta Texas. Other Hinojosa sculptures include that of Juan Seguin in Seguin, Texas, and Knute Rockne and Ara Parseghian at Notre Dame University in South Bend, Indiana, plus the impressive life-size "Among Friends There Are No Borders," statues depicting a South Texas* vaquero *and a Texas cowboy sharing a campfire, on display at the Laredo International Airport. His works today can be found in the collections of former President Richard M. Nixon and the late Governors Allan Shivers, Dolph Briscoe, and Bill Clements. (Courtesy of Armando Hinojosa)*

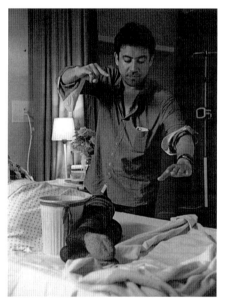

At St. Augustine High School, it was said that Alfonso Gomez-Rejon would borrow a friend's camera and "make shorts in lieu of presenting a report in front of the class." Born and raised in Laredo, the well-known film and television director received a BFA from New York University and an MFA from the American Film Institute. He began his professional career as personal assistant to Martin Scorsese, Robert De Niro, and Alejandro Gonzalez Iñárritu, spending his time on the sets of major motion pictures. His television credits include several episodes of* Glee *and* American Horror Story. *He was nominated for an Emmy for Outstanding Directing for a Miniseries for* American Horror Story: Coven. *In 2014 he directed* The Town That Dreaded Sundown. *Gomez-Rejon is best known for his feature film* Me and Earl and the Dying Girl, *which was selected for and won the U.S. Dramatic Competition at the 2015 Sundance Film Festival. Dedicated to his father, Dr. Julio C. Gomez-Rejon, the film also won the U.S. Drama Audience Prize. (Photo by Chung-Hoon Chung. Courtesy of Alfonso Gomez-Rejon.)*

Proud Martin High School graduate and "Tiger Legend" Amado Maurillo Peña graduated from Laredo Junior College before going on to Texas A&I University in Kingsville, where he obtained a bachelor's degree in art in 1965 and a master's in art education four years later. Peña's bold and colorful early work reflects the Mexican ancestry of his father and the Yaqui roots of his mother. After teaching for several years, including heading the art department at Crystal City High School, Peña's art took a more serious turn when he traveled to the southern part of Mexico and portrayed the day-to-day activities of the people in simple, primitive style. The lively mix of Native American and European cultures evolved even more when he moved to Santa Fe in the early 1980s. He was inspired by such places as Canyon de Chelly, Monument Valley, Enchanted Mesa, Acoma, and Black Mesa. His bold, colorful paintings grace the walls of art galleries, museums, universities, businesses, and private homes around the world. (Photo by Danny Zaragoza. Courtesy of the* Laredo Morning Times.)*

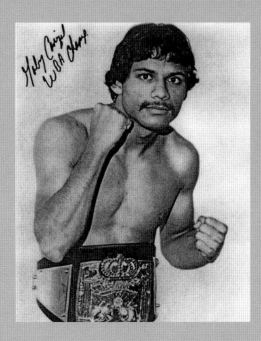

José "Gaby" Canizales turned pro in 1979 and four years later challenged Jeff Chandler for the World Boxing Association (WBA) bantamweight title, but lost in a decision. Three years later, he fought Richie Sandoval for the WBA title, a fight Canizales dominated by knocking Sandoval down in the first, third, and three times in the seventh round, then winning via a knockout. Canizales is shown here on March 10, 1986, in the WBA Bantamweight Championship bout he won with Richie Sandoval. (Photo by Cuate Santos. Courtesy of the Canizales Family.)

Gaby Canizales lost the title in his first defense against Bernardo Pinango via decision and in 1990 challenged Raul Perez for the World Boxing Organization (WBO) bantamweight title, but lost a decision. Canizales later challenged Miguel Lora for the vacant WBO title and won by a second-round knockout. He lost the belt in his first defense to Duke McKenzie via decision and retired after the loss. During his boxing career, Canizales compiled a record of 48–8–1. Of his forty-eight victories, thirty-six were by KO. (Courtesy of the Canizales Family)

Five years younger than his brother Gaby, the five-foot-four-inch Orlando Canizales began training when he was only ten, at the Boys and Girls Club on Moctezuma Street. He turned professional in 1984 and was undefeated in twelve consecutive fights. In 1986, Canizales took on Olympic gold medalist Paul Gonzales, but lost in a twelve-round decision. Canizales rebounded on July 9, 1988, when he won the IBF bantamweight title by knocking out defending titlist Kelvin Seabrooks. He defended his title a division-record sixteen consecutive times, including a victory over his old foe Paul Gonzalez. In January 1995, Canizales attempted to win the WBO junior featherweight title but lost a twelve-round split decision to Wilfredo Vazquez. Canizales continued fighting until 1999, when he lost a ten-round split decision to future champion Frank Toledo. He retired after the fight. Canizales is shown here at Atlantic City on July 9, 1988, in his victory over Seabrooks for the IBF Bantamweight Championship. (Photo by Peter Goldfield. Courtesy of the Canizales Family.)

Graduate of Nixon High School and slick fielding shortstop with excellent speed but little power, six-foot-two-inch Freddie Benavides started for three years for the Texas Christian University Horned Frogs before being drafted by the Cincinnati Reds in the second round of the 1987 free agent draft. In his first year in professional baseball, Benavides played for Cedar Rapids in the Class A Midwest League. In 1990 at Chattanooga in the Double-A Southern League, he was voted the best defensive shortstop. The following year, Benavides moved up to Triple-A Nashville before being called up by Cincinnati to make his major league debut on May 14, 1991. After three years, Benavides was traded to the Montreal Expos, and was then with the Colorado Rockies for their inaugural season. Benavides compiled a major league batting average of .253. He spent fifteen years in the Reds minor league system, including managing Billings in the Pioneer league in 2007. In 2017 he was the Reds' first-base coach. (Courtesy of Violeta Benavides)

The Canizales brothers, both graduates of Martin High School, were champions in the same class weight at the same time. Today, the Orlando & Gaby Canizales Boxing Gym on Guadalupe Street honors their memory. (Courtesy of the Canizales Family)

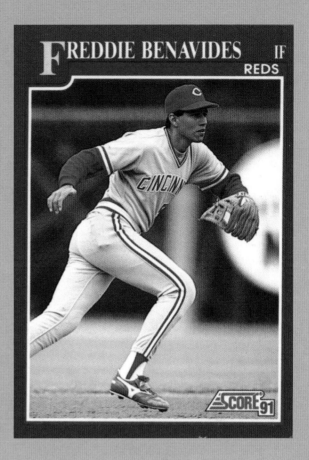

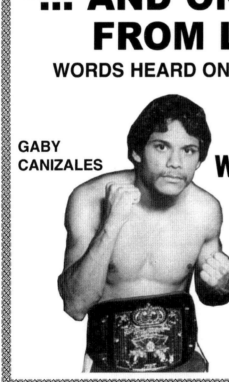

"... AND ON THIS CORNER FROM LAREDO, TEXAS ..."

WORDS HEARD ON BOXING RINGS AROUND THE WORLD

GABY CANIZALES

ORLANDO CANIZALES

WORLD BOXING CHAMPS

NATIVE SONS OF

LAREDO

LOS HIJOS

DEL PUEBLO

Saul N. Ramirez Jr. and President Bill Clinton shake hands in the White House in 1993. When Aldo Tatangelo was term limited by a new city charter, Ramirez defeated Maria "Bebe" Zuniga in a runoff, becoming the youngest mayor in the history of Laredo at the age of thirty-one, in 1990. Although born in Los Angeles, California, Ramirez was raised in Laredo and educated at St. Augustine High School before going on to Southwest Texas State University. Reelected in 1994, Ramirez helped to secure the permit for the construction of the World Trade Bridge. He worked to build four recreation centers, three fire stations, and a new public library on McPherson Road. With several months remaining in his second administration, Ramirez stepped down to take a position in the Clinton administration, in the Department of Housing and Urban Development. From 1997 to 1998, he served as the HUD assistant secretary of community planning and development, and then as deputy secretary of HUD. (Courtesy of Saul Ramirez)

The always smiling and friendly Mayor Betty Flores proudly poses with the distinguished federal judge, George Philip Kazen. In the late 1970s, the bright and articulate Kazen was thought by many to be the heir to the crown of the Independent Club, but he displayed little interest in politics. Kazen was a distinguished graduate of the University of Texas School of Law. He worked for a year as a briefing attorney for the Texas Supreme Court before becoming a captain in the U.S. Air Force in the Judge Advocate General Corps for three years. In 1965, he entered private practice in Laredo and served on the Laredo Community College Board of Trustees but, in March 1979, was nominated by President Jimmy Carter to a new seat on the United States District Court for the Southern District of Texas. He served as chief judge from 1996 to 2003 and was a member of the U.S. Foreign Intelligence Surveillance Court from 2003 to 2010. He assumed senior status in March 2009. That same year, the Federal Courthouse at 1300 Victoria was named in his honor. Kazen's father, E. James Kazen, was a long-term Democratic district attorney and district judge for the 49th Judicial District of Texas and an influential member of the Independent Club. Kazen's uncle, Abraham "Chick" Kazen, represented Laredo and other South Texas communities in the U.S. House of Representatives from 1967 to 1985. (Courtesy of Betty Flores)

In 1998, Elizabeth "Betty" Flores, a successful banker for more than twenty-five years, was elected the first woman mayor of Laredo. Flores long remembered the gender discrimination she faced in her youth and early career. Four years after being elected mayor, she was easily reelected to a second four-year term. Perhaps her most noted accomplishment was being the driving force behind the completion of Laredo's fourth international bridge, the World Trade Bridge, which became necessary after truck traffic clogged much of IH-35 following the implementation of NAFTA. It was also during her administration that the community voted to build a large multipurpose entertainment center off Bob Bullock Loop, known as the Laredo Entertainment Center. For a time, the LEC was home to a successful ice hockey team, the Laredo Bucks. A Democrat, Flores took great pride in her personal relationship with both Bill Clinton and George W. Bush. (Courtesy of Betty Flores)

Mayor Betty Flores, members of the City Council, Luis de León, along with family and friends, honor Gold Star Mother Francisca J. Martinez. "Panchita," as she was affectionately known, was born in Linares, Nuevo León, on September 3, 1911. She immigrated to the United States when she was only fourteen, settled in Laredo, became a U.S. citizen, and in 1939, married Enrique Martinez. Martinez was the mother of eight children. Five of her sons served in the U.S. Army. Her oldest son, Estanislado Martinez, was wounded in the Korean War. Her second eldest son, Sgt. Guadalupe Martinez, a Green Beret, was killed in action during the Vietnam War. Francisca Martinez died on September 15, 2016, at the age of 105. Congressman Henry Cuellar introduced a resolution shortly after her death honoring her in the U.S. House of Representatives. Members of the City Council (left to right) include Juan Ramirez, Jose Valdez Jr., Joe A. Guerra, Eliseo Valdez Jr., Mayor Flores, Johnny Amaya, John C. Galo, and Luis Bruni. (Courtesy of Betty Flores)

Alice native and graduate of the University of Maryland, Raul Gonzalez Salinas was a former agent for the Federal Bureau of Investigation who was elected to the first of two terms as mayor of Laredo on June 17, 2006. He defeated eight-year City Council member John Galo. In an election with a low turnout, Salinas received 52.7 percent of the vote. His first term was extended to four and one-half years so that city elections would coincide with the November general election of non-even presidential years. Seeking a second term and claiming he was "Still, the Right Man," Salinas was forced into a runoff. He defeated his opponent, outgoing eight-year City Council member Gene Belmares, by a two-to-one margin. (Photo by Billy Hathorn. Courtesy of Billy Hathorn.)

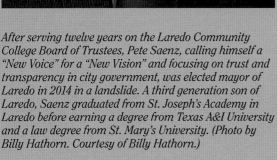

After serving twelve years on the Laredo Community College Board of Trustees, Pete Saenz, calling himself a "New Voice" for a "New Vision" and focusing on trust and transparency in city government, was elected mayor of Laredo in 2014 in a landslide. A third generation son of Laredo, Saenz graduated from St. Joseph's Academy in Laredo before earning a degree from Texas A&I University and a law degree from St. Mary's University. (Photo by Billy Hathorn. Courtesy of Billy Hathorn.)

Antonio Sanchez Sr., Brian O'Brien, and Antonio Sanchez Jr. symbolize the economic future of South Texas. In 1971 the three men formed the Sanchez-O'Brien Oil and Gas Company. By developing the largest pool of natural gas (mostly in Webb, Zapata, and Starr counties) to be discovered in the continental United States in thirty years, the company grew to become one of the largest in the country. Antonio Sanchez Sr. survived the Great Depression by selling newspapers and milk on the streets of Laredo and by following trains to gather spilled coal to heat the Sanchez family home. Tony Sanchez Jr. ran unsuccessfully for governor of Texas as a Democrat in 2002. (Courtesy of Tony Sanchez Jr.)

One of the most influential political figures in Laredo and South Texas over three decades has been Senator Judith Zaffirini, the first Mexican American woman elected to the Texas Senate. In the Democratic runoff primary in 1986 to succeed John Traeger, Zaffirini decisively defeated State Representative William N. "Billy" Hall, then turned back Republican businessman Bennie Bock in the general election. In the next six elections, Zaffirini was consistently reelected with more than 60 percent of the vote. In 2008 she carried all seventeen counties in the 21st Senatorial District, beating Democrat-turned-Republican Louis H. Bruni, a former Webb County Judge. During her early political career, Zaffirini worked closely with Lt. Gov. Bob Bullock, for whom the Laredo Loop 20 was named. A tireless advocate for young people, she is remembered for her ability to work across party lines with Lt. Gov. David Dewhurst. With the exception of July 2003, when she joined her fellow Democrats who fled to New Mexico to prevent a quorum and to defeat Republican plans to redraw the Texas congressional map along partisan lines, Zaffirini has had a 100 percent voting record, casting more than 52,000 consecutive votes. Senator Zaffirini Elementary School in UISD, the Senator Judith Zaffirini Library at the Laredo Community College South Campus, and the Student Success Center at Texas A&M International University all honor her. Senator Zaffirini holds BS, MA, and PhD degrees from the University of Texas at Austin. She is shown here in the senate chambers with her son, Carlos M. Zaffirini Jr., when she was first sworn in as senator. Young Carlos went on to follow his father into the law profession and in 2016 established the Senator Judith Zaffirini Endowed Scholarship Fund to support students attending Baylor College of Medicine and the University of Texas at Austin. (Courtesy of Senator Judith Zaffirini)

Chapter 32

Education and the Growth of a Border City

Entering the "Border Town" of Laredo on the Zapata Highway (U.S. 59) near the Three Points Neighborhood, drivers are cautioned to slow their speed. This image was taken just before World War II. (Author Collection)

The New Deal of Franklin D. Roosevelt helped to relieve the massive unemployment in Laredo during the Great Depression. Hundreds of young men between the ages of eighteen and twenty-three left town as part of the Civilian Conservation Corps, one of the more popular public relief programs. The CCC was so successful that it was later expanded to include young men between the ages of seventeen and thirty-five. Another vital New Deal program in Laredo was the Works Progress Administration, which helped to construct Martin High School, street curbs and sidewalks, bridges on the Mines Road, the Boys Club on Moctezuma Street, an impressive stone wall around Fort McIntosh, as well as a reconstruction of the old Star Fort at the post. The Work Projects Administration was a successor to the Works Progress Administration. With World War II raging, the agency was abolished in December 1942, only months after the completion of a stone building at Fort McIntosh that has this marker from a bygone era. (Author photo)

FLAG & SALUTE GUN, FT. McINTOSH, LAREDO, TEXAS (RESTRICTED)

One of the most impressive buildings on the Laredo Community College campus is the Visual and Performing Arts Center, which opened in 2012. The building was one of the crowning achievements in the college's multiphase, multimillion-dollar facilities master plan to modernize existing buildings and infrastructure. (Author photo)

In 1947, newly created Laredo Junior College began using space at historic Fort McIntosh. This view (circa 1940) looks northwest across the parade ground. Although several historic buildings, including two of the storied barracks buildings, were demolished in 1967–1969 to make way for new classrooms, other buildings, including those on the north side of the parade ground, are still in use today by Laredo Community College. (Author Collection)

With fireworks and pageantry, Laredo Community College celebrated the opening of a new campus in South Laredo on April 16, 2014. The second campus was constructed primarily to provide accessible education to Laredo's growing neighborhoods on the south side of the city. (Courtesy Laredo Community College)

At 1700 East Saunders, the for-profit Laredo Medical Center, a 326-bed facility, is the largest medical building in Laredo. The Sisters of Mercy built the impressive structure in 1999. The Sisters had previously opened a seven-story hospital in the Heights in 1954, a structure that was later abandoned. In 1894, the motherhouse of the Sisters of Mercy of South Texas was moved from Refugio to Laredo, under the leadership of Mother Mary Clare O'Connell. Along with another Sister and a postulant, she established Laredo's first hospital, a twelve-bed facility at 1320 Rosario Street. The Sisters later moved to a much larger facility on the west side of Jarvis Plaza. Another for-profit large medical facility, Doctors Hospital of Laredo, was opened in north Laredo in 1974. (Author photo)

Texas A&M International University began with a stranger, Billy F. Cowart, in a carrel at the Yeary Library at Laredo Junior College in August 1969. Arguing that Tejanos had consistently been discriminated against in higher education, 8,000 Laredoans petitioned the Texas Coordinating Board for Higher Education to create an upper-level senior institution as a branch of Texas A&I University. In 1976, the name of the school was changed from Texas A&I at Laredo to Laredo State University. Shown here in 1972 is the chancellor and president of Texas A&I in Kingsville, James C. Jernigan, the president of Texas A&I at Laredo, Billy F. Cowart, and the president of Texas A&I at Corpus Christi, Whitney Halladay. (Tusk, May–June 1972)

In 1995, President Leo Sayavedra, the administration, and staff of Texas A&M International University proudly pose on the site of the future TAMIU campus in northeast Laredo. At the same time, on the twenty-fifth anniversary of the university, the school changed its name from Laredo State University and expanded to include freshmen and sophomores for the first time. At the time, the campus was the newest in the country. (Special Collections and Archives, TAMIU)

Billy Cowart, president of Texas A&I at Laredo, and his secretary, Linda Beverly, work in Cowart's office in Laird Hall on the campus of Laredo Junior College about 1970. After fifteen years at the helm of Laredo State University, Cowart left in 1984 to become provost of Oregon State College in Monmouth, Oregon. Manuel Pacheco succeeded Cowart as president. Retiring from the office of provost, Cowart served as interim president of Oregon State College for a year. (Courtesy Billy Cowart)

This aerial view of TAMIU was taken after the completion of a large part of the campus. Other buildings, including the Fine and Performing Arts Center, the Zaffarini Student Success Center, a recreational center, as well as the Laredo Independent School District Early High School, would be built on the southern part of the campus. (Office of Public Relations, TAMIU)

IH-35 and access roads at the intersection of Calton Road can be seen in this 1990 aerial photograph of north Laredo showing the growth of the city. By 2017, Webb County had a population nearing 300,000. (Courtesy Laredo Chamber of Commerce)

The second international bridge and the border station on the American side of the river, as well as downtown Laredo and the big bend of the river in west Laredo, can be seen in this aerial photograph circa 1990. (Courtesy Laredo Chamber of Commerce)

By 2017, Texas A&M International University had an enrollment of more than 7,600, including students from more than thirty countries. Situated on 300 acres of land in northeast Laredo donated by the Killam family, the university offers more than eighty degrees for undergraduate, graduate, and doctoral students. Shown here is the largest building on campus, the Killam Library. With an abundance of wildlife, some believe the campus to be one of the most beautiful in Texas. (Author photo)

BIBLIOGRAPHY

BOOKS

Acuna, Rodolfo. *Occupied America: A History of Chicanos.* (New York, 1981).

Adjutant General's Report, 1873. (Austin, 1874).

Allhands, James Lewelleyn. *Gringo Builders.* (Iowa City, 1931).

Almaraz, Felix D. *Tragic Cavalier.* (Austin, 1971).

Anders, Evan. *Boss Rule in South Texas: The Progressive Era.* (Austin, 1982).

Ashford, Gerald. *Spanish Texas.* (Austin, 1971).

Ashley, George H. *The Santo Tomas Cannel Coal, Webb County, Texas.* (Austin, 1918).

Atkinson, Mary Jourdan. *The Texas Indians.* (San Antonio, 1953).

A Twentieth Century History of Southwest Texas. (Chicago, 1907).

Audubon, John Woodhouse. *Audubon's Western Journal, 1849-1850.* (Cleveland, 1906).

Bancroft, Hubert Howe. *History of Mexico.* (San Francisco, 1886-1887, 2 vols).

_____. *History of Texas and the North Mexican States.* (San Francisco, n.d., 2 vols).

Bannon, John Francis. *The Spanish Borderlands Frontier, 1531-1821.* (New York, 1970).

Barker, Eugene C. *Mexico and Texas, 1821-1835.* (New York, 1965).

_____. *The Life of Stephen F. Austin.* (Austin, 1969).

Bartlett, John Russell. *Personal Narrative of Exploration and Incidents in Texas, New Mexico, California, Sonora, and Chihuahua in 1850-1853.* (Chicago, 1965).

Barton, Henry W. *Texas Volunteers in the Mexican War.* (Waco, 1970).

Bell, Thomas W. *A Narrative of the Capture and Subsequent Sufferings of the Mier Prisoners in Mexico, Captured in the Cause of Texas, Dec. 26th 1842 and Liberated Sept. 16th 1844.* Edited by James M. Day. (Waco, 1964).

Benedicto, Luis *Historia de Nuevo Laredo.* (Nuevo Laredo, 1956).

Bolton, Herbert Eugene. *Athanase de Mezieres and the Louisiana-Texas Frontier, 1768-1780.* (Cleveland, 1914).

_____. *Bolton and the Spanish Borderlands.* Edited with an introduction by John Francis Bannon. (Norman, 1964).

_____. *The Spanish Borderlands: A Chronicle of Old Florida and the Southwest.* (New Haven, 1921).

_____. *Spanish Exploration in the Southwest, 1542-1706.* (New York, 1959).

_____. *Texas in the Middle Eighteenth Century.* (Austin, 1970).

Bradley, Haldeen. *Mexico and the Old Southwest.* (Port Washington, 1971).

Brown, John Henry. *History of Texas, from 1685-1892.* (Saint Louis, 1892-1893, 2 vols).

_____. *Indian Wars and Pioneers of Texas.* (Austin, 1891-1892).

Byfield, Patsy Jeanne. *Falcon Dam and the Lost Towns of Zapata.* (Austin, 1971).

Callott, Wilfrid Hardy. *Santa Anna.* (Camden, 1864).

Casey, Robert J. *The Texas Border.* (New York, 1950).

Castaneda, Carlos E. *The Mexican Side of the Texas Revolution.* (Dallas, 1928).

_____. *Our Catholic Heritage in Texas.* (Austin, 1936-1950. 7 vols).

Cazneau, William L. (Mrs.). *Eagle Pass, or Life on the Border.* Edited with an introduction by Robert Crawford Cotner. (Austin, 1966).

Celebracion Del CXXCIV Aniversario Del Natalicio De Washington. (Laredo, 1916).

Chamberlain, Samuel E. *My Confession.* (New York, 1956).

Clendenen, Clarence C. *Blood on the Border: The United States Army and the Mexican Irregulars.* (Toronto, 1969).

Cline, Howard F. *The United States and Mexico.* (New York, 1969).

Da Camara, Kathleen. *Laredo on the Rio Grande.* (San Antonio, 1949).

Daddysman, James W. *The Matamoros Trade: Commerce, Diplomacy, and Intrigue.* (Newark, 1984).

Daniell, L. E. *Successful Men of Texas.* (Austin, 1890).

Davis, Ellis A. and Grobe, Edwin H. (ed.). *The New Encyclopedia of Texas.* (Dallas, n.d.).

Day, James J. *Black Beans and Goose Quills.* (Waco, 1970).

De la Garza, Lorenzo. *La Antiqua Revilla.* (Cuidad Victoria, 1944).

De Leon, Arnoldo. *They Called Them Greasers: Anglo Attitudes Toward Mexicans in Texas, 1821-1900.* (Austin, 1983).

_____. *The Tejano Community, 1836-1900.* (Albuquerque, 1982).

Dewees, W. B. *Letters From an Early Settler of Texas.* (Louisville, 1852).

Dufour, Charles L. *The Mexican War.* (New York, 1968).

Durham, George. *Taming the Nueces Strip.* (Austin, 1962).

Emory, William H. *Report on the United States and Mexican Boundary Survey, Made Under the Direction of the Secretary of the Interior.* (Washington, 1857).

Farber, James. *Those Texans.* (Waco, 1965).

Flavella, James William. *A Souvenir Album of Laredo 'The Gateway to Mexico:' Historical, Pictorial, and Descriptive Stories of Laredo, Webb County, the Military and Other Forces on the Rio Grande Frontier and a Pictorial and Descriptive Story of Our Sister City, Nuevo Laredo, Mexico.* (Laredo, 1917).

Frazer, Robert W. *Forts of the West.* (Norman, 1965).

Freeman, Douglas Southall. *R. E. Lee: A Biography.* (New York, 1934. 2 vols).

Friend, Llerena B. *Sam Houston: The Great Designer.* (Austin, 1969).

Fugate, Francis. *The Spanish Heritage of the Southwest. (El Paso, 1952).*

Fundacion de la Colonia del Nuevo Santander: Estado General de las Fundaciones Hechas por D. Jose de Escandon en la Colonia del Nuevo Santander, Costa del Seno Mexicano. (Mexico City, 1930).

Galarza, Ernesto; Gallegos, Herman; and Samora, Julian *Mexican-Americans in the Southwest.* (Santa Barbara, 1969).

Gallaway, B. P., ed. *The Dark Corner of the Confederacy.* (Dubuque, 1972).

Garcia, Felix. *The Children of John Z. Leyendecker.* (Laredo, 1984).

Garcia, Rogelia O. *The Bells of St. Augustine.* (Laredo, 1962).

_____. *Dolores, Revilla, and Laredo: Three Sister Settlements.* (Waco, 1970).

_____. *Song of La Grande Agua.* (Laredo, 1973).

Garrett, Kathryn. *Green Flag Over Texas: A Story of the Last Years of Spain in Texas.* (New York, 1939).

Goetzmann, William H. *Army Exploration in the American West, 1803-1863.* (New Haven, 1965).

Goldfinch, Charles W. *Juan N. Cortina, 1824-1892: A Reappraisal.* (Chicago, 1949).

Grebler, Leo; Moore, John W.; and Guzman, Ralph C. *The Mexican-American People, The Nation's Second Largest Minority.* (New York, 1970).

Green, Thomas J. *Journal of the Texan Expedition Against Mier.* (Austin, 1936).

Grimm, Agnes G. *Llanos Mestenas.* (Waco, 1968).

Heitman, Francis B. *Historical Register and Dictionary of the United States Army.* (Urbana, 1965, 2 vols).

Henderson, Hary McCorry. *Texas in the Confederacy.* (San Antonio, 1955).

Hill, Lawrence Francis. *Jose de Escandon and the Founding of Nuevo Santander.* (Columbus, 1926).

Hinojosa, Giberto Miguel. *A Borderlands Town in Transition: Laredo, 1755-1870.* (College Station, 1983).

Historical Sketch of Laredo, Texas. (Laredo, 1925).

History of Twentieth Century Southwest Texas. (1907).

Hobsbawn, E. J. *Primitive Rebels: Studies in Archaic Forms of Social Movement in the 19th and 20th Centuries.* (New York, 1965).

Holding, Nannie Emory. *A Decade of Mission Life in Mexican Mission Homes.* (Nashville, 1895).

Hollon, W. Eugene. *Beyond the Cross Timbers: The Travels of Randolph B. Marcy, 1812-1887.* (Norman, 1955).

Horgan, Paul. *Great River: The Rio Grande in North American History.* (New York, 1954).

Hughes, William J. *Rebellious Ranger: Rip Ford and the Old Southwest.* (Norman, 1965).

Hutson, Cleburne. *Deaf Smith: Incredible Texas Spy.* (Waco, 1973).

Jackson, Jack. *Los Mestenos: Spanish Ranching in Texas, 1721-1821.* (College Station, 1986).

James, Marquis. *The Raven: A Biography of Sam Houston.* (Indianapolis, 1929).

Jarrett, Rie. *Gutierrez de Lara, Mexican Texan: The Story of a Creole Hero.* (Austin, 1949).

Jenkins, John H. (ed.). *Papers of the Texas Revolution*. (Austin, 1973. 10 vols.).

John Armengol Onion Farm. (Laredo, n.d.).

John, Elizabeth A. H. *Storms Brewed in Other Men's Worlds: The Confrontation of Indians, Spanish, and French in the Southwest, 1540-1795*. (College Station, 1975).

Johnson, Francis W. *A History of Texas and Texans*. Edited by Eugene C. Barker. Five Volumes. (New York, 1914).

Jones, Oakah L. Jr. *Santa Anna*. (New York, 1968).

Jones Jr., Oakah L. *Los Paisanos: Spanish Settlers on the Northern Frontier of New Spain*. (Norman, 1979)

Kinnaird, Lawrence. (trans.). *Frontiers of New Spain*. (Berkeley, 1957).

La Defensa de Nuevo Laredo. (Laredo, 1914).

Lafora, Nicholas de. *Relacion del Viaje que hizo a los Presidios Internos situados en la Frontera de la America Septentrional Perteneciente al Rey de Espana*. (Mexico City, 1939).

Lamar, Maribeau Buonaparte. *The Papers of Maribeau Buonaparte Lamar*. Edited by Charles Adams Gulick, Jr., and Winnie Allen. (Austin, 1924, 6 vols.).

Lamego, M. A. Sanchez. *The Second Mexican-Texas War, 1841-1843*. (Hillsboro, 1972)

Lane, Lydia Spencer. *I Married a Soldier or Old Days in the Old Army*. (Albuquerque, 1964).

Laredo Police Department. (Laredo, n.d.).

Lea, Tom. *The King Ranch*. (Boston, 1957).

Lindheim, Milton. *The Republic of the Rio Grande*. (Waco, 1964).

Lott, Virgil N., and Fenwick, Virginia M. *People and Plots on the Rio Grande*. (San Antonio, 1957).

Lott, Virgil N., and Martinez, Mercurio. *Kingdom of Zapata*. (San Antonio, 1953).

Madsen, William. *The Mexican-Americans of South Texas*. (New York, 1963).

Marcy, Randolph B. *Thirty Years of Army Life on the Border*. (New York, 1963).

Martinez, H. L., and Villarreal, A. O. *Laredo's Own: An Album of Laredo's Own Native Citizens Who Served So Faithfully in World War II*. (Laredo, 1947).

Matthussen, Peter. *Sal Si Puedes*. (New York, 1968).

McCaleb, Walter F. *Spanish Missions of Texas*. (San Antonio, 1954).

McIntyre, Benjamin F. *Federals on the Frontier: The Diary of Benjamin F. McIntyre, 1862-1864*. Edited by Nannie M. Tilley. (Austin, 1963).

McWilliams, Carey. *North from Mexico: The Spanish Speaking People of the United States*. (Philadelphia, 1949).

_____. *Al Norte de Mexico: El Conflicto Entre Anglos e Hispanos*. (Mexico, D. F., 1968).

Mexican-International Railway Views, Series No. 1. (Laredo, 1888).

Mexican-Texans. (San Antonio, 1971).

Moorehead, Max L. *The Presidio: Bastion of the Spanish Borderlands*. (Norman, 1975).

Morfi, Juan Agustin. *History of Texas, 1673-1779*. Translated by Carlos E. Castaneda. (Albuquerque, 1935).

Morin, Raul. *Among the Valiant: Mexican-Americans in World War II and Korea*. (Los Angeles, 1963).

Morrow, William W. *Spanish and Mexican Private Land Grants*. (San Francisco, 1923).

Moquin, Wayne, (ed.). *A Documentary History of the Mexican-Americans*. (New York, 1971).

Myres, Sandra L. *The Ranch in Spanish Texas*. (El Paso, 1969).

Nance, Joseph Milton. *After San Jacinto: The Texas-Mexican Frontier, 1836-1841*. (Austin, 1964).

_____. *Attack and Counterattack: The Texas-Mexican Frontier, 1842*. (Austin, 1964).

Nava, Julian. *Mexican-Americans: A Brief Look at Their History*. (New York, 1969).

Newcomb, W. W., Jr. *The Indians of Texas: From Prehistoric to Modern Times*. (Austin, 1961).

Oates, Stephen B. (ed.). *Rip Ford's Texas*. (Austin, 1963).

Official Program of the Seventeenth Annual Celebration of the Birthday Anniversary of Washington. (Laredo, 1916).

Owsley, Frank Lawrence. *King Cotton Diplomacy: Foreign Relations of the Confederate States of America*. (Chicago, 1959).

Paredes, Americo. *With His Pistol in His Hand*. (Austin, 1966).

Perrigo, Lynn I. *The American Southwest*. (New York, 1971).

_____. *Our Spanish Southwest*. (Dallas, 1960).

Perry, Carmen. (ed. and trans.). *San Jose de Palafox*. (San Antonio, 1971).

Phares, Ross. *Cavalier in the Wilderness: The Story of the Explorer and Trader, Louis Juchereau de St. Denis*. (Baton Rouge, 1952).

Pierce, Frank Cushman. *A Brief History of the Lower Rio Grande Valley*. (Menasha, 1917).

Pinon, Fernando. *Patron Democracy*. (Mexico City, 1985).

Price, Glenn W. *Origins of the War with Mexico*. (Austin, 1967).

Prieto, Alejandro. *Historia Geografica y Estadistica del Estado de Tamaulipas*. (Mexico City, 1873).

Prucha, Francis Paul. *The Sword of the Republic: The United States Army on the Frontier, 1783-1846*. (Toronto, 1969).

Rayburn, Virginia Kemp and Rayburn, John C. (eds.). *Century of Conflict*. (Waco, 1966).

Record of the Southwest. (Chicago, 1894).

Report of the Committee who Visited Washington on the Affairs of Western Texas. (New York, 1862).

Richer, Juan E. *Resena Historica de Nuevo Laredo*. (Nuevo Laredo, 1900).

Rippy, J. Fred. *The United States and Mexico*. (New York, 1926).

Rivera, Feliciano and Meir, Matt S. *A Bibliography for Chicano History*. (San Francisco, 1972).

_____. *The Chicanos: A History of Mexican-Americans*. (New York, 1972).

Rives, George Lockhart. *The United States and Mexico, 1821-1848*. (New York, 1969).

Rodriguez, J. M. *Rodriguez Memoirs of Early Texas*. (San Antonio, 1913).

Roel, Santiago. *Nuevo Leon*. (Monterrey, 1944).

Rosenbaum, Roberto J. *Mexican Resistance in the Southwest*. (Austin, 1981).

Ruiz, Ramon E. and Tebbell, J. *South by Southwest: The Mexican-American and His Heritage*. (Garden City, 1969).

Salinas Dominguez, Manuel Ignacio. *Origenes de Nuevo Laredo*. (Ciudad Victoria, 1981).

Samora, Julian. *La Raza: The Forgotten Americans*. (South Bend, 1966).

Sanchez, Ramiro. *Frontier Odyssey: Early Life in a Texas Spanish Town*. (Austin, 1981).

Santos, Richard G. *Santa Anna's Campaign Against Texans, 1835-1836*. (Waco, 1968).

Schmitt, Karl M. *Mexico and the United States, 1821-1973*. (New York, 1974).

Scott, Florence Johnson. *Old Rough and Ready on the Rio Grande*. (Waco, 1969).

_____. *Historical Heritage of the Lower Rio Grande*. (Waco, 1970).

_____. *Royal Land Grants North of the Rio Grande, 1777-1821*. (Waco, 1969).

Sequin, Juan N. *Personal Memoirs, 1834-1842*. (San Antonio, 1858).

Servin, Manuel P. *The Mexican-Americans: An Awakening Minority*. (New York, 1970).

Smith, Justin H. *The War with Mexico*. (New York, 1919, 2 vols.).

Sonnichsen, C. L. *Ten Texas Feuds*. (Albuquerque, 1971).

Stambaugh, Lillian J. and Stambaugh, J. Lee. *The Lower Rio Grande Valley of Texas*. (San Antonio, 1954).

Stapp, William P. *Prisoners of Perote*. (Austin, 1936).

Steiner, Stan. *La Raza*. (New York, 1970).

Su Vida y Su Espiritu: Webb County Family Histories. Volume I, (Laredo, 1982).

The Syrian and Lebanese Texans. (San Antonio, 1974).

Tarver, E. R. *Laredo: The Gateway Between the United States and Mexico*. (Laredo, 1889).

Taylor, Paul Schuster. *An American-Mexican Frontier; Nueces County, Texas*. (New York, 1934).

Thomas, Alfred Barnaby. (ed.). *Teodoro De Croix and the Northern Frontier of New Spain, 1776-1783*. (Norman, 1941).

Thomas, George H. *Memoirs of Major-General George H. Thomas*. Edited by Richard W. Johnson. (Philadelphia, 1881).

Thompson, Jerry. *Mexican-Texans in the Union Army*. (El Paso, 1986).

_____. *Sabers on the Rio Grande*. (Austin, 1974).

_____. *Vaqueros in Blue and Gray*. (Austin, 1977).

Tilden, Bryant P., Jr. *Notes on the Upper Rio Grande: Explored the Months of October and November, 1846, on board the U.S. Steamer Major Brown, Commanded by Captain Mark Sterling of Pittsburgh, By Order of Major General Patterson, U.S.A. Commanding the Second Division, Army of Occupation, Mexic.* (Philadelphia, 1847).

Tyler, Ronnie C. *Santiago Vidaurri and the Southern Confederacy.* (Austin, 1973).

U.S. War Department *The War of the Rebellion: A Compilation of the Union and Confederate Armies.* (Washington, 1889, 127 vols.).

Viele, Egbert L. *Handbook for Active Service: Containing Practical Instructions in Campaign Duties.* (New York, 1861).

Wallace Ernest. *Texas in Turmoil.* (Austin, 1965).

Webb, Walter Prescott. *The Texas Rangers.* (Austin, 1969).

Webb, Walter P., and Carroll, H. Bailey. (eds.). *Handbook of Texas.* (Austin, 1952, 2 vols.).

Weber, David J. (ed.) *Foreigners in Their Native Land.* (Albuquerque, 1973).

_____. *New Spain's Frontier: Essays on Spain in the American West.* (Albuquerque, 1979).

Weddle, Robert S. *Wilderness Manhunt: The Spanish Search for La Salle.* (Austin, 1963).

_____. *San Juan Bautista: Gateway to Spanish Texas.* (Austin, 1968).

Wellman, Paul I. *The Callaghan, Yesterday and Today.* (Encinal, n.d.).

Wessels, William L. *Born to be a Soldier.* (Fort Worth, 1971).

Wharton, Clarence R. *El Presidente: A Sketch of the Life of General Santa Anna.* (Houston, 1924).

Wilkinson, J. B. *Laredo and the Rio Grande Frontier.* (Austin, 1975).

Williams, Amelia W. and Barker, Eugene C. (eds.). *The Writings of Sam Houston.* (Austin, 1970).

Williams, R. H. *With the Border Ruffians: Memories of the Far West, 1852-1868.* Edited by E. W. Williams. (London, 1908).

_____. and Sansom, John W. *The Massacre on the Nueces River.* (Grand Prarie, n. d.).

Woodman, Lyman L. *Cortina, Rogue of the Rio Grande.* (San Antonio, 1950).

Wright, Marcus Joseph. *Texas in the War, 1861-1865.* Edited by Harold B. Simpson (Hillsboro, 1965).

Zapata County Folklore. (Zapata, 1982).

ARTICLES

Bolton, Herbert Eugene. (trans.). "Tienda de Cuervo's Ynspeccion of Laredo, 1757," *Quarterly of the Texas State Historical Association*, VI (1902-1903), 187-203.

Broussard, Ray F. "Vidaurri, Juarez and Comonfort's Return from Exile," *Hispanic American Historical Review*, XLIX (May, 1969), 268-280.

Carnes, Cecil, and Wheat, James. "Laredo," *Texas Parade.* (May, 1949).

Castaneda, Carlos E. (trans.). "A Trip to Texas in 1828 by Jose Maria Sanchez," *Southwestern Historical Quarterly*, XXIX (April, 1926), 249-257.

Cheney, Louise. "Blood and Thunder at Old Fort McIntosh," *Real West*, (March, 1973).

Christian, A. K. "Maribeau Buonaparte Lamar," *Southwestern Historical Quarterly*, XXIII (1919-1920), 153-170, 231-270; XXIV (1920-1921), 39-139, 194-234.

Clendenen, Clarence C. "Mexican Unionists: A Forgotten Incident of the War Between the States," *New Mexico Historical Review*, XXXIX (1964), 32-39.

Cox, I. J. "The Southwest Boundary of Texas," *Quarterly of the Texas State Historical Association*, VI (1902-1903), 81-102.

Cohen, Barry M. "The Texas-Mexico Border, 1858-1867," *Texana*, VI (Summer, 1968), 153-165.

Crimmins, M. L. (ed.). "W. G. Freeman's Report of the Eighth Military Department," *Southwestern Historical Quarterly*, LI (1947-1948), 54-58, 167-174, 252-258, 350, 257; LII (1948-1949), 100-108, 227-233, 249-353, 444-447; LIII (1949-1950), 71-77, 202-208, 308-319, 443-473; LIV (1950-1951), 204-218.

_____. (ed.). "Colonel J. K. F. Mansfield's Report of the Inspection of the Depatment of Texas in 1856," *Southwestern Historical Quarterly*, XLII (October, 1938), 122-148; (January, 1939), 215-257; (April, 1939), 351-387.

_____. (ed.). "Robert E. Lee in Texas: Letters and Diary," *West Texas Historical Association Year Book*, VIII (June, 1932), 7-18.

Davenport, Herbert. "General Jose Maria Jesus Carbajal," *Southwestern Historical Quarterly*, LV (April, 1952), 475-483.

_____. "Notes on Early Steamboating on the Rio Grande," *Southwestern Historical Quarterly*, XLIX (October, 1945), 286-289.

Day, James M. (ed.). "Diary of James A. Glasscock, Mier Man," *Texana*, I (Spring and Summer, 1963), 85-119, 225-238.

_____. (ed.). "Israel Canfield on the Mier Expedition," *Texas Military History*, III (Fall, 1963), 165-199.

Delaney, Robert W. "Matamoros, Port of Texas During the Civil War," *Southwestern Historical Quarterly*, LVIII (April, 1955), 473-487.

Elliott, Claude. "Union Sentiment in Texas, 1861-1865," *Southwestern Historical Quarterly*, L (1946), 449-477.

Green, Stanley. "Laredo 1755-1920: An Overview," *Nuevo Santander Occasional Papers*, 1981.

Harby, Lee C. "Mexican-Texas Types and Contrasts," *Harpers Magazine*, (July, 1890), 229-246.

Hatcher, Mattie Austin. "Joaquin de Arredondo's Report of the Battle of Medina," *Southwestern Historical Quarterly*, XI (1907), 220-236.

Hendricks, Sterling Brown. "The Somervell Expedition to the Rio Grande, 1842," *Southwestern Historical Quarterly*, XXIII (October, 1919), 112-140.

Jones, Rufus. "Laredo, a Texas Gateway," *Texas Magazine*, (April, 1910).

Juarez, Jose Roberto. "La Iglesia Catolica y el Chicano in Sud Texas 1836-1911," *Aztlan*, Vol 4, No. 2, 1974, 217-255.

Limon, Jose E. "El Primer Congreso Mexicanista de 1911: A Precursor to Contemporary Chicanismo," *Aztlan* V (Spring and Fall, 1974), 85-118.

Kress, Margaret Kenny. (trans.). "Diary of a Visit of Inspection of the Texas Missions Made by Fray Gaspar Jose de Solis in the Year 1767-1768," *Southwestern Historical Quarterly*, XXXV (July, 1931).

"Laredo: Gateway to Latin America," *Texas Weekly*, (January, 1937).

Larios, Avila, "Brownsville-Matamoros: Confederate Lifeline," *Mid-America*, XL (April, 1958), 67-69.

Nordyke, Lewis. "Laredo: The Belle of the Border," *Texas Parade*, (April, 1958).

_____. "Laredo: Trade Gate to Mexico," *Texas Parade*, (April, 1959).

Oates, Stephen B. "Los Diablos Tejanos!" *American West*, (Summer, 1965), 41-50.

Rippy, J. Fred. "Border Troubles Along the Rio Grande, 1848-1860," *Southwestern Historical Quarterly*, XXIII (October, 1919).

Sanchez, Jose Maria. "A Trip to Texas in 1828," *Southwestern Historical Quarterly*, XXIX (April, 1926), 249-88.

Shearer, Ernest C. "The Callahan Expedition," *Southwestern Historical Quarterly*, LIV (April, 1951), 430-451.

_____. "The Carvajal Disturbances," *Southwestern Historical Quarterly*, LV (October, 1951), 430-451.

Smith, Mitchell. "The 'Neutral' Matamoros Trade, 1861-1865," *Southwest Review*, XXXVII (Autumn, 1952), 319-324.

Smyrl, Frank H. "Texans in the Union Army, 1861-1865," *Southwestern Historical Quarterly*, LXV (1961), 234-250.

_____. "Unionism in Texas, 1856-1861," *Southwestern Historical Quarterly*, LIV (April, 1951), 430-451.

Sosa, Octaviano. "Creacion y denominacion de la Villa de Nuevo Laredo," in *Centenario de Nuevo Laredo.* (San Antonio, 1948).

Swisher, Bella French. "The Two Laredos," *American Sketch Book.* VII, (1882).

Thompson, Jerry. "A Stand Along the Border: Santos Benavides and the Battle for Laredo," *Civil War Times Illustrated*, XIX (August, 1980).

_____. "Mutiny and Desertion on the Rio Grande: The Strange Saga of Captain Adrian J. Vidal," *Military History of Texas and the Southwest*, XI, No. 3 (1975).

_____. "The Republic of the Rio Grande," *Nuevo Santander Museum*, (1985).

Tyler, Ronnie C. "Cotton on the Border, 1860-1865," *Southwestern Historical Quarterly*, LXXIII (April, 1970), 456-477.

_____. "Santiago Vidaurri and the Confederacy," *The Americas*, XXVI (July, 1969), 66-76.

_____. "The Callahan Expedition of 1855: Indians or Negroes?," *Southwestern Historical Quarterly*, LXX (April, 1967), 574-585.

Viele, Egbert L. "Our Southern Frontier, The East and West Boundary Line Between the United States and Mexico," *Frank Leslie's Popular Monthly,* (June, 1878), pp. 725-734.

Vigness, David M., trans. and ed. "Nuevo Santander in 1795: A Provincial Inspection by Felix Calleja," *Southwestern Historical Quarterly,* LXXV (April, 1972), 461-506.

_____. "Relations of the Republic of Texas and the Republic of the Rio Grande," *Southwestern Historical Quarterly,* LVII (1953-1954), 312-321.

_____. "Don Hugo O'Conor and New Spain's Northeastern Frontier, 1767-1776," *Journal of the West,* VI (January, 1967), 18-30.

_____. ed. "Nuevo Santander in 1795: A Provincial Inspection by Felix Calleja," *Southwestern Historical Quarterly,* LXXV (April, 1972), 461-506.

_____. "Indian Raids on the Lower Rio Grande, 1836-1837," *Southwestern Historical Quarterly,* LIX (July, 1955), 14-23.

Weber, David J. "Mexico's Far Northern Frontier: Historiography Askew," *Western Historical Quarterly,* VII (July, 1976), 279-93.

Weinert, Richard P. "Confederate Border Troubles With Mexico," *Civil War Times Illustrated,* III (October, 1964), 36-43.

West, Elizabeth H. (ed.). "Diary of Jose Bernardo Gutierrez de Lara, 1811-1842," *American Historical Review,* XXXIV (1928), 55-77, 281-294.

Wilcox, Seb S. "Laredo During the Texas Republic," *Southwestern Historical Quarterly,* XLII, (October, 1938), 83-107.

_____. "Laredo and Fort McIntosh Furnish Much Colorful History," *Epic Century,* (September, 1938).

_____. "Laredo City Election and Riot of 1886," *Southwestern Historical Quarterly,* XLV (July, 1941), 1-23.

_____. "The Spanish Archives of Laredo," *Southwestern Historical Quarterly,* XLIX (January, 1946), 341-360.

_____. "The Story of the Washington's Birthday Celebration of Laredo," *Washington Birthday Celebration Program,* (Laredo, 1947).

Winfrey, Dorman H. "John Coffee Hays," *Rangers of Texas,* (Waco, 1969).

_____. "Maribeau B. Lamar," *Heroes of Texas,* (Waco, 1964).

Worcester, Donald E. "The Significance of the Spanish Borderlands to the United States," *Western Historical Quarterly,* VII (January, 1976), 5-18.

Yeaman, Jack. "Laredo—International Town," *Texas Parade,* (February, 1951).

_____. "Seven Flag City: Laredo's First 200 Years," *Texas Parade,* (May, 1955).

ARCHIVAL COLLECTIONS

Acta de la General Visita al Pueblo de San Agustin de Laredo, 1767. Laredo Public Library, Laredo, Texas.

Baptismal, Burial, and Marriage Records. St. Augustine Parish Archives, Laredo, Texas.

Papers of Governor Peter H. Bell, Texas State Archives, Austin, Texas.

Muster Roll of Santos Benavides' Company. Texas State Archives, Austin, Texas.

District Court Civil and Criminal Records, 1848-1920. Pan American University Library, Edinburg, Texas.

Election Returns. Webb County Clerk's Office, Laredo, Texas.

Election Returns for Webb and Zapata Counties, Secretary of State's Office, Texas State Archives, Austin, Texas.

John S. Ford Military Correspondence. Daughters of the Confederacy Museum, Austin, Texas.

John S. Ford Papers, 1836-1892. University of Texas Archives, Austin, Texas.

Lonnie Franks, Prison Records. Texas Department of Corrections, Huntsville, Texas.

John L. Haynes Papers. Barker Texas History Center, University of Texas, Austin, Texas.

Samuel M. Jarvis Papers. Nuevo Santander Museum, Laredo, Texas.

Scrapbook of the Career of Albert Martin. Private Possession. Texas.

George R. Page Papers, County Clerk's Office, Laredo, Texas.

Laredo Archives. St. Mary's University Library, San Antonio, Texas.

John Z. Leyendecker Papers. Barker Texas History Center, University of Texas, Austin, Texas.

General George Brinton McClellan Papers, 1826-1885. Manuscript Division, Library of Congress, Washington, D. C.

War Department Records. The National Archives. Washington, D. C.
    Adjutant General's Office.
        Letters Received.
        Medical History of Fort McIntosh.
        Post Returns of Fort McIntosh.
        Register Book of Letters Received.
        Reservation File of Fort McIntosh.
    Corps of Engineers.
        Letters Received.
        Register Book of Letters Received.
    Quartermaster General's Office.
        Letters Received.
        Register Book of Letters Received.
    Department of Texas.
        General Orders.
        Letters Received.
        Register Book of Letters Received.
        Register Book of Letters Sent.
        Special Orders.
        Regimental Returns of the Fifth Infantry.
        Regimental Returns of the First Infantry.
    Western Division.
        Letters Received.
        Register Book of Letters Received.
        Register Book of Letters Sent.
    Secretary of War.
        Letters Received.
        Register Book of Letters Received.

Seb S. Wilcox Papers. St. Mary's University Library, San Antonio, Texas.

Webb County Land Records. County Clerk's Office, Laredo, Texas.

Webb County Jail Records. Webb County Sheriff's Office, Laredo Texas.

Webb County Probate Records. County Clerk's Office, Laredo, Texas.

Zapata County Land Records. County Clerk's Office, Zapata, Texas.

NEWSPAPERS

Austin
  Daily Austin Republican.
  Southern Intelligencer.
  Texas State Gazette.
  Tri-Weekly State Gazette.
Brownsville
  American Flag.
  La Bandera.
  Rio Grande Sentinel.
Cincinnati
  Cincinnati Daily Commercial.
Corpus Christi
  Corpus Christi Caller.
  Ranchero.
Fort Worth
  Fort Worth Press.
Galveston
  Galveston News.
Houston
  Telegraph and Texas Register.
  Daily Telegraph.
Indianola
  Indianola Courier.
Laredo
  Borderland.
  Chaparral.
  El Chinaco.
  La Colonia de Mexicana.
  El Correo de Laredo.
  La Cronica.
  El Democrata Fronterizo.
  El Diputado.
  El Esmeril.
  Evolucion.
  El Figuro.
  Gate City.
  La Guadalupana.
  El Horizonte.
  La Juventud Laredense.
  La Mosca.
  El Mutualista.
  Laredo Morning Record.
  Laredo News.
  La Revista.
  Laredo Times.
  South Texas Citizen.
  Two Republics
  La Union.
Matamoros
  El Ancia.
McAllen
  Monitor.
Monterrey
  Monterey Daily Globe.
New Orleans
  Picayune.
New York
  Evening Post.
  New York Herald.
  New York Times.
Paris
  Paris Press.
Rio Grande City
  Rio Grande Herald.
San Antonio
  San Antonio Daily Express.
  San Antonio News.

UNPUBLISHED MATERIAL

Aleman, Efrain. "A Study of Obituaries in the *Laredo Times:* 1893-1895, 1908-1912," Laredo State University, 1986.

Aristotelidis, Jorge. "The Life of J. C. Martin." Laredo Junior College, 1986.

Benavides, I. M. "Laredo in the Late Spanish and Early American Period," M. A. thesis, University of Texas, 1952.

Bennett, Katherine. "History of Education in Laredo." M. A. thesis, University of Texas.

Brown, Harold Owen. "The Building of the Texas-Mexican Railroad," M. A. thesis, Texas A and I University, 1937.

Brown, Maury Bright, "The Military Defenses of Texas and the Rio Grande Region About 1766." M. A. thesis, University of Texas, 1924.

Compean, Stella, "The Ku Klux Klan in Laredo." Laredo Junior College, 1985.

Crawford, Polly Pearl. "The Beginnings of Spanish Settlement in the Lower Rio Grande Valley." M. A. thesis, University of Texas, 1925.

Da Camara, Kathleen. "The History of the City of Laredo." M. A. thesis, Texas A and I University, 1942.

Garcia, R. O. "A History of the Catholic Church in Laredo." M. A. thesis, Texas A and I University, 1953.

Girard, Mary Offer. "Historical Sketches of Don Andres Martinez and Don Florencio Villarreal." n.d.

Gonzalez, Eddie. "Local Turn of the Century Obituaries, 1895-1905." Laredo Junior College, 1986.

Guajardo, Luciano. "The Republic of the Rio Grande." City Library, Laredo, Texas.

Hagy, Kathy. "A History of the Laredo Fire Department." Laredo Junior College, 1986.

Herrera, Yvonne L. "The Influence of the Mexican Revolution on Laredo." Laredo Junior College, 1986.

Hinojosa, Arnoldo R. "The Development of the Texas Mexican Railway Company." Laredo Junior College, 1975.

Huson, Hobart. "Iron Men: A History of the Republic of the Rio Grande and the Federalist War in Northern Mexico." Archives, Texas State Library, 1940.

Irby, James Arthur. "Line of the Rio Grande: War and Trade on the Confederate Frontier, 1861-1865." Ph.D. dissertation, University of Georgia, 1969.

Lopez, Severita M. "El Pueblo Minero de Dolores, Texas." Laredo State University.

Martin, Karen E. "Crime and the Press: Laredo, Texas, 1910-1912." Laredo Junior College, 1986.

Mayers, George D. "Historical Data and Recorded Events Preceeding the Establishment of Fort McIntosh, Texas." St. Mary's University Library, San Antonio, Texas.

Murillo, Hermelinda Aguirre. "A History of Webb County." M. A. thesis, Southwest Texas State University, 1941.

Pena, Dalia. "A Diabolical Murder." Laredo Junior College, 1985.

Punjabi, Sunita. "A History of The Washington's Birthday Celebration." Laredo Junior College, 1986.

Reyna, Armandina. "Mexican American POW's from Laredo During World War II." Laredo State University, 1986.

Riley, John Denny. "Santos Benavides: His Influence on the Lower Rio Grande, 1823-1891." Ph.D. dissertation, Texas Christian University, 1976.

Salazar, Alex. "The Mining Community of Dolores." Laredo State University, 1985.

Salazar, Maria de Guadalupe. "Preliminary Study of Spanish Land Grants in Webb County." M. A. thesis, Texas A and I University, 1985.

Sandoval, Selina. "The Ku Klux Klan and Laredo." Laredo Junior College, 1986.

Scott, Florence Johnson. "Spanish Land Grants in the Lower Rio Grande Valley." M. A. thesis, University of Texas, 1935.

Sutherland, Thomas S. "Historical Sketch of Webb County." St. Mary's University Library, San Antonio, Texas.

Thompson, Jerry. "A Study of Crime: Frontier Laredo, 1892; Prohibition Laredo, 1922; and Laredo During the Age of Anxiety, 1953." Carnegie-Mellon University, 1979.

Trevino, Alicia. "Antonio Mateo Bruni." Laredo Junior College, 1986.

Trevino, Rosa Nelia. "A Study of the 1860 and 1870 Zapata County Census." Laredo State University, 1986.

Vigness, David Martell. "The Republic of the Rio Grande: An Example of Separatism in Northern Mexico." Ph.D. dissertation, University of Texas, 1951.

_____. "A Survey of the Lower Rio Grande Valley, 1836-1846." M. A. thesis, University of Texas, 1948.

Villarreal, Jr., Felipe. "Dolores, Texas, from 1885-1939." Laredo State University, 1979.

Walsh, Natalie. "The Founding of Laredo and St. Augustine Church." M. A. thesis, University of Texas, 1935.

Wilcox, Seb S. "Laredo Under Spain." Martin High School Library, Laredo, Texas.

_____. "Laredo Through the Years." St. Mary's University Library, San Antonio, Texas.

_____. "Data on Laredo History, 1821 to Date." St. Mary's University Library, San Antonio, Texas.

Worley, Alicia Consuelo. "The Life of John Anthony Valls." M. A. thesis, Texas A and I University, 1954.

Index

Jerry Thompson is Regents Professor of Borderlands History at Texas A&M International University in Laredo. Thompson is the recipient of numerous awards and honors from the Arizona Historical Society, Historical Society of New Mexico, and the Texas State Historical Association. He has twice received the Best Scholarly Book Award from the Texas Institute of Letters, first for his *Civil War to the Bitter End: The Life and Times of Major General Samuel Peter Heintzelman,* and for *Cortina: Defending the Mexican Name in Texas.* Thompson also received the Kate Broocks Bates Award from the Texas State Historical Association for *Civil War and Revolution on the Rio Grande Frontier,* which he co-authored with Larry Jones. He has twice received the Tejano Book Award, first for his biography of Cortina and for editing *Tejanos in Gray: The Civil War Letters of Captains Manuel Yturria and Rafael de la Garza.* Thompson has also received the Senator Judith Zaffarini Medal for his teaching excellence and academic accomplishments, as well as the Texas A&M University System Teaching Excellence Award. Thompson received his BA in history from Western New Mexico University, his MA in history from the University of New Mexico, and his doctorate in history from Carnegie Mellon University. He is a former president of the Texas State Historical Association. Presently, Thompson serves on the Editorial Board of the *Southwestern Historical Quarterly,* and he is a council member of the Texas Institute of Letters. His most recent book, *A Civil War History of the New Mexico Volunteers and Militia* (University of New Mexico Press), won the 2016 Fray Atanasio Francisco Dominguez Award from the New Mexico Historical Association.

Photo by Rolando Santos